Freeway 1

Englisch für FOS/BOS (Klassen 11–12)

Bayern

von
Dr. Thomas Höbel
Herbert Hofbauer
Dagmar Taylor
Jacob Weiß

Ernst Klett Verlag GmbH
Stuttgart • Leipzig • Dortmund

So arbeiten Sie mit Freeway Bayern

Getting started

Anhand eines thematischen Einstiegs werden das Vorwissen aktiviert und erste Themenbezüge hergestellt.

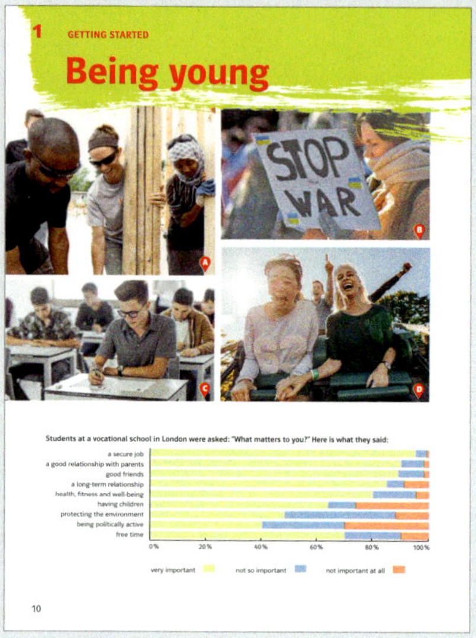

(Exam) Skills

Zentrale (Prüfungs-)Skills werden eingeführt, ausführlich erklärt und direkt angewendet.

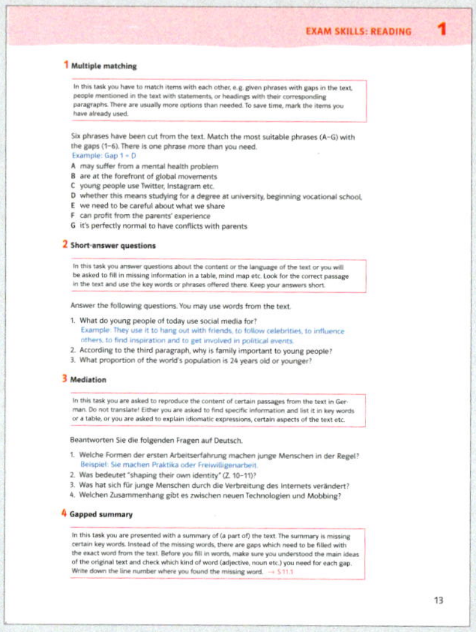

Text

Sachtexte und literarische Texte mit strukturiertem Aufgabenapparat werden erarbeitet.

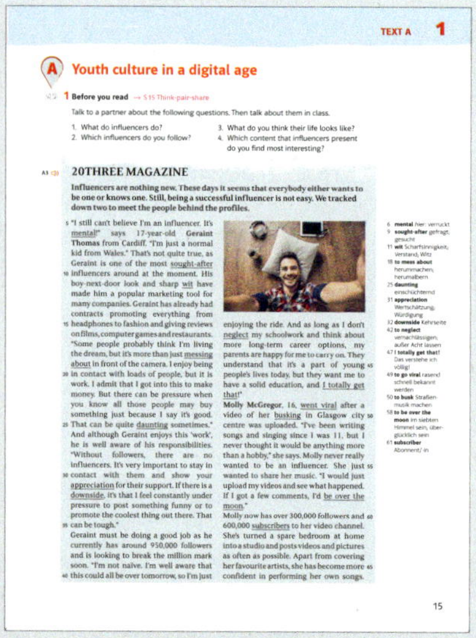

Writing

Zunächst wird anhand relevanter Aufgaben das *material-based writing* vorbereitet und schließlich in einer Schreibaufgabe mit passenden Materialien umgesetzt.

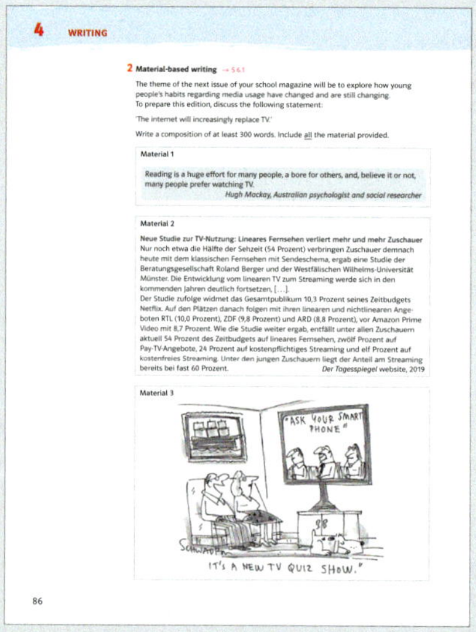

Discussion

Nachdem Sprechübungen die *group discussion* vorbereiten, wird im Anschluss eine Gruppendiskussion entsprechend der Abschlussprüfung durchgeführt.

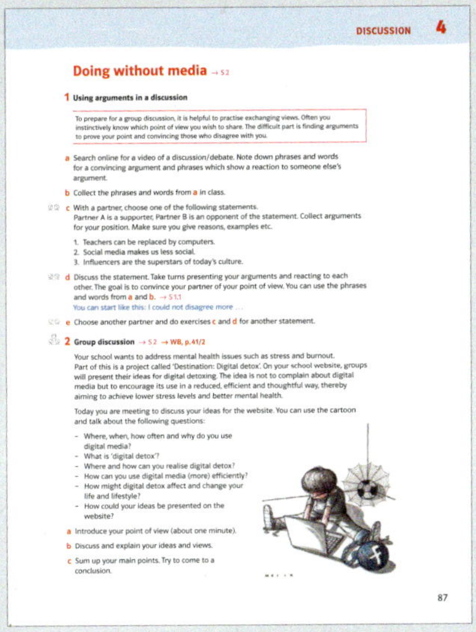
DISCUSSION 4

Doing without media → S 2

1 Using arguments in a discussion

To prepare for a group discussion, it is helpful to practise exchanging views. Often you instinctively know which point of view you wish to share. The difficult part is finding arguments to prove your point and convincing those who disagree with you.

a Search online for a video of a discussion/debate. Note down phrases and words for a convincing argument and phrases which show a reaction to someone else's argument.

b Collect the phrases and words from a in class.

c With a partner, choose one of the following statements. Partner A is a supporter, Partner B is an opponent of the statement. Collect arguments for your position. Make sure you give reasons, examples etc.

1. Teachers can be replaced by computers.
2. Social media makes us less social.
3. Influencers are the superstars of today's culture.

d Discuss the statement. Take turns presenting your arguments and reacting to each other. The goal is to convince your partner of your point of view. You can use the phrases and words from a and b. → S 1.1
You can start like this: I could not disagree more …

e Choose another partner and do exercises c and d for another statement.

2 Group discussion → S 2 → WB, p.41/2

Your school wants to address mental health issues such as stress and burnout. Part of this is a project called 'Destination: Digital detox'. On your school website, groups will present their ideas for digital detoxing. The idea is not to complain about digital media but to encourage its use in a reduced, efficient and thoughtful way, thereby aiming to achieve lower stress levels and better mental health.

Today you are meeting to discuss your ideas for the website. You can use the cartoon and talk about the following questions:

- Where, when, how often and why do you use digital media?
- What is 'digital detox'?
- Where and how can you realise digital detox?
- How can you use digital media (more) efficiently?
- How might digital detox affect and change your life and lifestyle?
- How could your ideas be presented on the website?

a Introduce your point of view (about one minute).

b Discuss and explain your ideas and views.

c Sum up your main points. Try to come to a conclusion.

87

Exam practice

Musterprüfungen dienen dem Training zentraler Prüfungsformate.

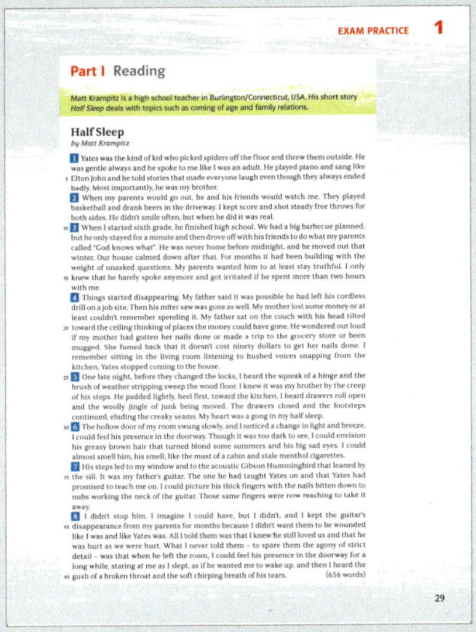
EXAM PRACTICE 1

Part I Reading

Matt Krampitz is a high school teacher in Burlington/Connecticut, USA. His short story *Half Sleep* deals with topics such as coming of age and family relations.

Half Sleep
by Matt Krampitz

1 Yates was the kind of kid who picked spiders off the floor and threw them outside. He was gentle always and he spoke to me like I was an adult. He played piano and sang like Elton John and he told stories that made everyone laugh even though they always ended badly. Most importantly, he was my brother.

2 When my parents would go out, he and his friends would watch me. They played basketball and drank beers in the driveway. I kept score and shot steady free throws for both sides. He didn't smile often, but when he did it was real.

3 When I started sixth grade, he finished high school. We had a big barbecue planned, but he only stayed for a minute and then drove off with his friends to do what my parents called "God knows what". He was never home before midnight, and he moved out that winter. Our house calmed down after that. For months it had been building with the weight of unasked questions. My parents wanted him to at least stay truthful. I only knew that he barely spoke anymore and got irritated if he spent more than two hours with me.

4 Things started disappearing. My father said it was possible he had left his cordless drill on a job site. Then his miter saw was gone as well. My mother lost some money or at least couldn't remember spending it. My father sat on the couch with his head tilted toward the ceiling thinking of places the money could have gone. He wondered out loud if my mother had gotten her nails done or made a trip to the grocery store or been mugged. She fumed back that it doesn't cost ninety dollars to get her nails done. I remember sitting in the living room listening to hushed voices snapping from the kitchen. Yates stopped coming to the house.

5 One late night, before they changed the locks, I heard the squeak of a hinge and the brush of weather stripping sweep the wood floor. I knew it was my brother by the creep of his steps. He padded lightly, heel first, toward the kitchen. I heard drawers roll open and the woolly jingle of junk being moved. The drawers closed and the footsteps continued, eluding the creaky seams. My heart was a gong in my half sleep.

6 The hollow door of my room swung slowly, and I noticed a change in light and breeze. I could feel his presence in the doorway. Though it was too dark to see, I could envision his greasy brown hair that turned blond some summers and his big sad eyes. I could almost smell him, his smell, like the must of a cabin and stale menthol cigarettes.

7 His steps led to my window and to the acoustic Gibson Hummingbird that leaned by the sill. It was my father's guitar. The one he had taught Yates on and that Yates had promised to teach me on. I could picture his thick fingers with the nails bitten down to nubs working the neck of the guitar. Those same fingers were now reaching to take it away.

8 I didn't stop him. I imagine I could have, but I didn't, and I kept the guitar's disappearance from my parents for months because I didn't want them to be wounded like I was and like Yates was. All I told them was that I knew he still loved us and that he was hurt as we were hurt. What I never told them – to spare them the agony of strict detail – was that when he left the room, I could feel his presence in the doorway for a long while, staring at me as I slept, as if he wanted me to wake up, and then I heard the gush of a broken throat and the soft chirping breath of his tears. (656 words)

29

Anhang

Helping hand:
Hilfestellungen zu Aufgaben in den Topics

Skills files:
Alle wichtigen Kompetenzen im Überblick

Grammar files:
Kompaktgrammatik zum Nachschlagen und Lernen

Vocabulary:
Chronologische Vokabellisten zu den Topics

Symbole

(Symbol)	Partnerarbeit
(Symbol)	Gruppenarbeit
→ S 3	Verweis auf die *Skills files*
→ G 4	Verweis auf die *Grammar files*
→ WB	Verweis auf Workbook-Aufgaben
→ H 1	Verweis auf die *Helping hand*

A Audio

V Video

I interaktiv

Alle Audios, Videos, interaktive Übungen und Dokumente zum Schulbuch finden Sie in den Medien zum Schulbuch und im eBook.

INHALTSVERZEICHNIS

INHALTSVERZEICHNIS

Ihr Weg zum Fachabitur

Die Prüfung für das Bestehen des Fachabiturs umfasst folgende Kompetenzen:

1. Leseverstehen

In der Prüfung zum Fachabitur bearbeiten Sie auf Grundlage dreier Texte die folgenden Aufgaben:

- Multiple matching
- Multiple choice
- Short-answer questions
- Gapped summary
- Mediation

In *Freeway Bayern* finden Sie in Topic 1 einen *Exam skills*-Step sowie im Anhang des Schulbuchs die entsprechenden *Skills files* (→ S 4.1), in welchen Ihnen die wichtigsten Grundlagen für diese Aufgaben vermittelt werden. Entsprechende Aufgaben finden Sie im Schulbuch in den Steps *Text A*, *Text B*, *Text C* sowie in *Exam practice*.

2. Schreiben

Unter Berücksichtigung der Aufgabenstellung und dreier Materialien schreiben Sie eine *Composition* (*Material-based writing*), in welcher Sie das jeweilige Thema entsprechend diskutieren.

In *Freeway Bayern* finden Sie in Topic 1 einen *Exam Skills*-Step sowie im Anhang des Schulbuchs die entsprechenden *Skills files* (→ S 6.1), in welchen Ihnen die wichtigsten Grundlagen für das Schreiben der *Material-based writing*-Aufgabe vermittelt werden.
Im Schulbuch finden Sie passende Aufgaben im Step *Writing* sowie in *Exam practice*.

3. Gruppendiskussion

Der letzte Prüfungsteil umfasst die Teilnahme an einer Kommunikationsprüfung in Form einer Gruppendiskussion (*Group discussion*).

In *Freeway Bayern* finden Sie in Topic 2 einen *Exam skills*-Step sowie im Anhang des Schulbuchs die entsprechenden *Skills files* (→ S 2), in welchen Ihnen die wichtigsten Grundlagen für die Gruppenaufgabe vermittelt werden.
Im Schulbuch finden Sie passende Aufgaben im Step *Discussion* sowie in *Exam practice*.

So gehen Sie vor

Ab nun heißt es üben, üben, üben – vor allem die Aufgaben, die Ihnen schwer fallen.
Lesen Sie zunächst den *Exam skills*-Step zum entsprechenden Prüfungsabschnitt, die *Skills files* im Anhang des Schulbuchs sowie die Aufgaben im Schulbuch. Versuchen Sie dann, die Aufgaben im Schulbuch zu lösen. Wie schätzen Sie sich dabei ein?
Es ist zudem hilfreich, Listen mit thematischem Vokabular zu den verschiedenen Themen sowie mit nützlichen Wörtern und Sätzen für die Schreibaufgabe und die Gruppendiskussion zu führen.

Grammatik

„Ich kenne nur zwei Grammatikregeln: ‚klingt richtig' und ‚klingt falsch'". Falls Sie allerdings das Gefühl haben, für das Fachabitur das ein oder andere Thema nachschlagen zu wollen, finden Sie im Anhang des Schulbuchs alle wichtigen Grammatikphänomene in den *Grammar files*. Zudem finden Sie in den *Medien zum Schulbuch* Erklärvideos und interaktive Übungen, auf welche auch im Schulbuch (→ G1) verwiesen werden.

Vokabular

Ihren Wortschatz können Sie mithilfe des *Vocabulary* im Anhang des Schulbuchs erweitern.

Being young

Students at a vocational school in London were asked: "What matters to you?" Here is what they said:

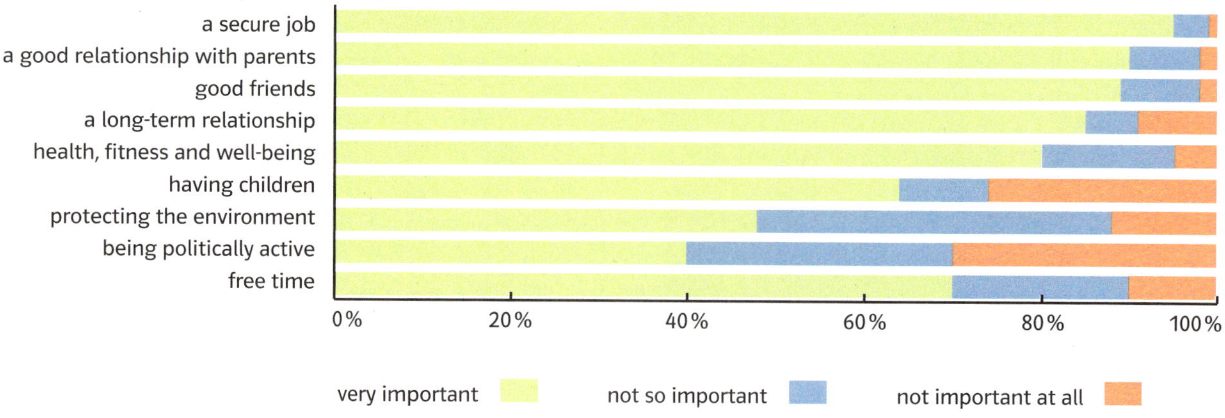

1 Talking about coming of age → WB, p.4–5/1–4; p.6/1

a Match the words from the word bank with the pictures.

to hang out with friends | to be politically active | to enjoy one's free time | to take an exam | to gain work experience | to feel stressed | to demonstrate for a cause | to volunteer | to ride a rollercoaster

b Use the words from **a** to create a mind map about being young. Add more words. You can use the following categories.

free time | education | work | community life | culture | problems | benefits

c What does 'coming of age' mean to you? Write a short statement of about 100 words.

GOOD TO KNOW

Coming of age means the phase of life when teenagers become adults.

2 Working with a diagram → S 10.3

Study the survey and talk about the following questions.

1. Which aspects/issues are most important to young people today?
2. Do you agree with the results? Which result do you find the most surprising?
3. What would be your top five aspects/issues?

A1 3 Listening → S 3 → H 1 → WB, p.6/2

a Listen to the interview about what matters to young people. Answer the following questions. Take notes.

1. Who is conducting the interview and who is being interviewed (name and job)?
2. Which clichés exist about young people between the ages of 16 and 19?
3. What topics matter to young people? (8 topics)
4. What are they not interested in and why?
5. Which topics does the survey expert expect to find in a survey in five years?

b With a partner, discuss how the issues talked about in the interview relate to your own life.

4 Writing a letter → S 6.4 → G 1.9–G 1.13

Where do you see yourself in ten years' time? Think about the following aspects and write a letter to yourself.

family/private life | living situation | job/career | achievements/experiences

5 Creating a vision board about coming of age

a Research pictures online which represent coming of age and your hopes for the future. Give reasons for your choices.

b Create a vision board with the pictures from **a**.

c Present your vision board to the class. The others should say which vision board was most similar to their own and which one impressed them the most.
→ S 15 Gallery walk

GOOD TO KNOW

A **vision board** is a collage of pictures and words representing one's ideas/goals. It can help finding inspiration or motivation.

Doing mixed reading tasks → S 11.2, S 11.3

During the exam you will read 2–3 texts of a factual (e.g. newspaper articles) or literary nature (e. g. extracts from novels) and do tasks on each text. Let's have a look at the five different types of tasks. → S 4.1, S 4.2

Read the tasks first and then the (relevant parts of the) text carefully. Look up any words you do not know that might be important for understanding the text. You can highlight passages in different colours. If you're not sure, make a guess. You will not be marked down for a wrong answer.

A2

Issues facing young people today

As the standard of living has increased over the years, some people believe that life is easier for young people nowadays than it was in the past. While this may not always be the case, it is certainly true that many young people today have almost endless opportunities at their fingertips. When they finish school, young men and women often have the choice of many different careers, or to study, live and work all over the world. Some choose to take time off and travel, learning more about themselves and shaping their own identity. And for those who continue their education, there are various options to get on the path to a future career, **1** starting an apprenticeship or gaining work experience by doing an internship or volunteering.

In addition, we have never had so much access to entertainment, news and stories from around the world. The spread of the internet has changed the way young people learn and communicate. Today's young people may use social media to hang out with friends and follow celebrities, but in contrast to their parents' generation, **2** frequently to influence others, find inspiration and to get involved in political events.

Nevertheless, young people today are still faced with many issues that their parents faced, and one could even argue that today's world is a far more complex and confusing place to grow up in. Young people's relationships with their families can have a huge influence on their lives and the characters they develop. All families have ups and downs, and **3**, siblings and other family members. Despite any disagreements at home, young people need to be able to rely on their families for support and advice as they grow up.

Aside from their families young people also have to deal with their own personal issues. Although school can be the pathway to the future and many opportunities, it can also be a challenging time for young people as they try both to fit in and to find their own identity. Mental health has become an important issue across society. In fact, 10 % of young people (aged 5–16) have a clinically diagnosable mental health problem, and around 20 % **4** in any given year.

Bullying is arguably an even larger issue than it used to be due to advances in technology and the rise of social media. With pictures and comments being sent to thousands or even millions of people within seconds, **5**, and with whom.

Young people aged 24 and under make up over 40 % of the world's population, so it is no surprise that they are visible in many aspects of today's society. As well as commanding large audiences, and sometimes wages, on various social networks, young people today **6** concerning climate change, racism, gender and identity, and freedom of speech.

(521 words)

1 **to face** konfrontiert werden mit
10 **to take time off** eine Auszeit nehmen
10 **to shape** formen
13 **internship** Praktikum
17 **frequently** häufig
29 **mental health** psychische Gesundheit
32 **advance** Fortschritt
38 **concerning** bezüglich; hinsichtlich

1 Multiple matching

In this task you have to match items with each other, e.g. given phrases with gaps in the text, people mentioned in the text with statements, or headings with their corresponding paragraphs. There are usually more options than needed. To save time, mark the items you have already used.

Six phrases have been cut from the text. Match the most suitable phrases (A–G) with the gaps (1–6). There is one phrase more than you need.

Example: Gap 1 = D

A may suffer from a mental health problem
B are at the forefront of global movements
C young people use Twitter, Instagram etc.
D whether this means studying for a degree at university, beginning vocational school,
E we need to be careful about what we share
F can profit from the parents' experience
G it's perfectly normal to have conflicts with parents

2 Short-answer questions

In this task you answer questions about the content or the language of the text or you will be asked to fill in missing information in a table, mind map etc. Look for the correct passage in the text and use the key words or phrases offered there. Keep your answers short.

Answer the following questions. You may use words from the text.

1. What do young people of today use social media for?
   Example: They use it to hang out with friends, to follow celebrities, to influence others, to find inspiration and to get involved in political events.
2. According to the third paragraph, why is family important to young people?
3. What proportion of the world's population is 24 years old or younger?

3 Mediation

In this task you are asked to reproduce the content of certain passages from the text in German. Do not translate! Either you are asked to find specific information and list it in key words or a table, or you are asked to explain idiomatic expressions, certain aspects of the text etc.

Beantworten Sie die folgenden Fragen auf Deutsch.

1. Welche Formen der ersten Arbeitserfahrung machen junge Menschen in der Regel?
   Beispiel: Sie machen Praktika oder Freiwilligenarbeit.
2. Was bedeutet "shaping their own identity" (Z. 10–11)?
3. Was hat sich für junge Menschen durch die Verbreitung des Internets verändert?
4. Welchen Zusammenhang gibt es zwischen neuen Technologien und Mobbing?

4 Gapped summary

In this task you are presented with a summary of (a part of) the text. The summary is missing certain key words. Instead of the missing words, there are gaps which need to be filled with the exact word from the text. Before you fill in words, make sure you understand the main ideas of the original text and check which kind of word (adjective, noun etc.) you need for each gap. Write down the line number where you found the missing word. → S 11.1

Complete the summary with the most suitable words from the text on page 12. Give the line numbers of the words that you used.

The text discusses the various opportunities (l. 6) available to young people – especially those up to the age of 24 – in relation to issues they face. As this group of people makes up almost half of the world's population they are ■ **2** in society. Next to traditional options like continuing their ■ **3** or taking on work in their home country, young people today have the option to experience life anywhere in the ■ **4**, thanks to travelling. However, their families still have a lot of ■ **5** on them as they grow and develop. The internet has brought people closer too; most people use social media at least for keeping in touch with friends. However, young people also use it to take on a more active role, particularly on a ■ **6** level. On the other hand, the internet has given ■ **7** a digital side where people can receive hurtful messages or images everywhere all the time. So external issues like family problems can have serious consequences for the individual, but young people face internal challenges too, for example the pressure to fit in. Consequently, the number of young people with mental health problems is rising. Overall, one thing is for sure: young people will be forming their ■ **8** under these circumstances.

5 Multiple choice

This task can focus on content, the meaning of a word/phrase, the author's intention, the text structure or elimination ('not'-questions). For each question/statement there are four options, but only one is correct. Often the options look quite similar, which is why you need to read them very carefully and make sure you really understand the difference between them.

Choose the most suitable option.

1. According to the first paragraph, what can young people do after school?
   A start their own business
   B get a degree at university
   C travel their own country
   D start a savings plan
2. The world of today's young people …
   A doesn't differ much from their parents' world.
   B is not nice to grow up in.
   C has a strong impact on families.
   D is more complicated than their parents' world.
3. What is an antonym for 'despite' (l. 23)?
   A however
   B because of
   C although
   D in spite of
4. How many young people have a clinically diagnosable mental health problem?
   A 20 out of 100
   B 10 out of 100
   C 0.15
   D a fourth
5. Which movement young people are involved in today is <u>not</u> mentioned in the text?
   A fighting censorship
   B promoting racial equality
   C fighting global warming
   D promoting financial stability

A Youth culture in a digital age

1 Before you read → S 15 Think-pair-share

Talk to a partner about the following questions. Then talk about them in class.

1. What do influencers do?
2. Which influencers do you follow?
3. What do you think their life looks like?
4. Which content that influencers present do you find most interesting?

A3

20THREE MAGAZINE

Influencers are nothing new. These days it seems that everybody either wants to be one or knows one. Still, being a successful influencer is not easy. We tracked down two to meet the people behind the profiles.

"I still can't believe I'm an influencer. It's mental!" says 17-year-old **Geraint Thomas** from Cardiff. "I'm just a normal kid from Wales." That's not quite true, as Geraint is one of the most sought-after influencers around at the moment. His boy-next-door look and sharp wit have made him a popular marketing tool for many companies. Geraint has already had contracts promoting everything from headphones to fashion and giving reviews on films, computer games and restaurants. "Some people probably think I'm living the dream, but it's more than just messing about in front of the camera. I enjoy being in contact with loads of people, but it is work. I admit that I got into this to make money. But there can be pressure when you know all those people may buy something just because I say it's good. That can be quite daunting sometimes." And although Geraint enjoys this 'work', he is well aware of his responsibilities. "Without followers, there are no influencers. It's very important to stay in contact with them and show your appreciation for their support. If there is a downside, it's that I feel constantly under pressure to post something funny or to promote the coolest thing out there. That can be tough."

Geraint must be doing a good job as he currently has around 950,000 followers and is looking to break the million mark soon. "I'm not naïve. I'm well aware that this could all be over tomorrow, so I'm just

enjoying the ride. And as long as I don't neglect my schoolwork and think about more long-term career options, my parents are happy for me to carry on. They understand that it's a part of young people's lives today, but they want me to have a solid education, and I totally get that!"

Molly McGregor, 16, went viral after a video of her busking in Glasgow city centre was uploaded. "I've been writing songs and singing since I was 11, but I never thought it would be anything more than a hobby," she says. Molly never really wanted to be an influencer. She just wanted to share her music. "I would just upload my videos and see what happened. If I got a few comments, I'd be over the moon."

Molly now has over 300,000 followers and 600,000 subscribers to her video channel. She's turned a spare bedroom at home into a studio and posts videos and pictures as often as possible. Apart from covering her favourite artists, she has become more confident in performing her own songs.

6 **mental** *hier:* verrückt
9 **sought-after** gefragt; gesucht
11 **wit** Scharfsinnigkeit; Verstand; Witz
18 **to mess about** herummachen; herumalbern
25 **daunting** einschüchternd
31 **appreciation** Wertschätzung; Würdigung
32 **downside** Kehrseite
42 **to neglect** vernachlässigen; außer Acht lassen
47 **I totally get that!** Das verstehe ich völlig!
49 **to go viral** rasend schnell bekannt werden
50 **to busk** Straßenmusik machen
58 **to be over the moon** im siebten Himmel sein; überglücklich sein
61 **subscriber** Abonnent/-in

71 **it gives me a real buzz** *(ugs.)* es gibt mir einen tollen Kick
74 **to roll with the punches** *(fig.)* die Dinge nehmen, wie sie kommen
79 **appearance** Aussehen; Erscheinung; Auftritt
83 **confidence** Vertrauen; Zuversicht
84 **to showcase one's talent** sein Talent unter Beweis stellen

"I write songs about what I feel, what I worry about, and what I love. I think that's the best way to describe it. It can be pretty scary putting yourself out there for everyone to judge, but it gives me a real buzz when people like my songs."
Of course, the comments aren't always positive, but Molly says she's learnt to roll with the punches. "I'm not a supermodel, I'm a singer. If someone doesn't like my songs, fair enough. But I think it's wrong to be negative towards someone because of their appearance. The comments used to really hurt me, but I don't take any notice anymore. If anything, I'm lucky to be in this position as I can be a role model for others and give them the confidence to showcase their talents and just be themselves." And although the number of her fans has gone through the roof, she says it's not the most important thing. "It's more than chasing followers," she says. "For me it's about having a voice and a platform to express myself. And if my music or anything I post can raise awareness, help somebody in some way, then I'm happy." (662 words)

2 Short-answer questions → WB, p.7/1–2

Copy the table and complete it with information from the text. You may use words from the text.

Name	Main focus of social media activity	Number of followers and subscribers	Motivation for becoming or being an influencer
Geraint	...	...	...
Molly	...	...	...

3 Gapped summary

Complete the summary with the most suitable words from the text. Give the line numbers of the words that you used.

This text provides a look into the lives of two influencers by giving them a ■ **1.** For Geraint it's a dream to live an influencer lifestyle, and his work is centred around ■ **2**, particularly for consumer products. Much of his image is built on appearance and charisma, which can result in ■ **3** to maintain interest and influence people in the right ways. Although he has built up a solid number of followers, he is conscious of the need to finish his education and think of future ■ ■ **4.** The second influencer, Molly, represents a different side of things: she uses her ■ **5** as a creative outlet to inspire her followers. Uploading her music started off as a ■ **6**, so money or fame has never been a driving factor. Her interaction with her followers is emotional since her songs are based on her own personal experiences.

4 Mediation → H1

Beantworten Sie die folgenden Fragen auf Deutsch.

1. Wie stehen Geraints Eltern zu seiner Influencer-Karriere?
2. Wie hat sich Mollys Einstellung zu negativen Kommentaren verändert?

5 Writing a personal email → S 6.4 → H 1

Write an email to either Geraint or Molly. Briefly introduce yourself, then say what you think about the article and what they said about being an influencer. Ask them 2–3 questions.

A4 6 Listening → S 3 → WB, p. 7/3

a Listen to an interview with Molly McGregor. Choose the most suitable option.

1. Molly did not perform her own music at the beginning because …
   A she wanted her own music to remain private.
   B she thought that songs by famous artists would attract more followers.
   C she had not finished any of her own songs.

2. In many of her songs, Molly addresses topics such as …
   A transitioning into adulthood.
   B love and relationships.
   C bullying and mental well-being.

3. By revealing more about herself, Molly wants to show people that …
   A it is OK to have faults.
   B anyone can reach their goals if they are prepared to take risks.
   C she has the potential to be a big star.

b Listen again. What does Molly say about her character? Take notes.

c Would you like to become famous on social media? Give reasons. What would your content be? Talk to a partner.

7 A step further → S 10.3, S 1.1

a What social media do you use on a regular basis? What do you use it for? And how often? Take notes.

b Research online how often people use the social media you have listed in **a**. Compare it to your own use. Talk to a partner.

c Do we use social media too much? Note down pros and cons and prepare for a discussion in class.

d Discuss the use of social media in class.
Get into two groups. One group collects and presents the arguments in favour of social media and the other one against it. The group in favour starts. Take turns exchanging your arguments. React to what has been said by the other group.

USEFUL PHRASES

Agreeing and disagreeing
We'd like to mention that … | We are convinced / certain that … | We couldn't agree more. | That's a good point. | I see where you're coming from, but … | Maybe, but don't you think that …? | I reject the idea that … | It is completely wrong to say that … | On the one hand …, on the other hand … | Although …

e Reflect on the discussion. How did you feel? What went well? What needs more attention/preparation next time? → S 15 Tip-top

B Wish we could turn back time

1 Before you read → H1

a What is your favourite childhood memory? Talk to a partner.
→ G1.3–G1.8

b Think about your daily life. What stresses you out? What do you think are typical stress factors at your age? Create a mind map.
→ S15 Think-pair-share

6 **chord** Akkord
11 **to shrink** schrumpfen
12 **insecure** unsicher; verunsichert
37 **creek** Bach; kleiner Fluss
38 **to roam** umherstreifen
41 **loan** Darlehen; Kredit
42 **the latter** Letztere/-r/-s
55 **to play pretend** so tun als ob
57 **rocket** Rakete

GOOD TO KNOW

You can listen to the song online.

Twenty One Pilots – Stressed Out

1 I wish I found some better sounds
No one's ever heard
I wish I had a better voice
That sang some better words

2 I wish I found some chords
In an order that is new
I wish I didn't have to rhyme
Every time I sang
I was told when I get older
All my fears would shrink

3 But now I'm insecure
And I care what people think
My name's Blurryface and I care
what you think
My name's Blurryface and I care
what you think

4 Wish we could turn back time
To the good old days
When our momma sang us to sleep
But now we're stressed out
Wish we could turn back time
To the good old days
When our momma sang us to sleep
But now we're stressed out

5 Sometimes a certain smell will
Take me back to when I was young
How come I'm never able to identify
Where it's coming from?
I'd make a candle out of it
If I ever found it

6 Try to sell it, never sell out of it
I'd probably only sell one
It'd be to my brother, cause we have the
same nose
Same clothes, home grown
A stone's throw from a creek we used to
roam

7 But it would remind us of when
Nothing really mattered
Out of student loans and tree house homes
We all would take the latter
My name's Blurryface and I care
what you think
My name's Blurryface and I care
what you think

8 Wish we could turn back time
To the good old days
When our momma sang us to sleep
But now we're stressed out
Wish we could turn back time
To the good old days
When our momma sang us to sleep
But now we're stressed out

9 Used to play pretend
Give each other different names
We would build a rocket ship and then
we'd fly it far away
Used to dream of outer space
But now they're laughing at our face singing
"Wake up, you need to make money", yeah

(344 words)

2 Multiple matching → WB, p. 8/1–3

Match the words and phrases (A–F) with the corresponding verses of the lyrics (1–9). There are two verses more than you need.

A chorus (2x)
B wanting to go into cosmic space
C first verse
D nostalgic smell
E musical creativity
F student problems

3 Short-answer questions

Answer the following questions. You may use words from the text.

1. What does the singer complain about in the second verse?
2. Which games did the singer play when he was young?
3. Which stress factors does the singer have to face nowadays (seven items)?

4 Multiple choice

Choose the most suitable option.

1. What does the singer do as soon as he sings?
   A He regrets his voice.
   B He finds new words.
   C He plays the guitar.
   D He has to rhyme.
2. What did the singer's mother do when he was younger?
   A She woke him up early in the morning.
   B She made candles.
   C She put him to bed every night.
   D She encouraged his career.
3. Sometimes the singer …, which reminds him of his childhood.
   A has a strong smell of candles in his nose
   B has an unidentifiable smell in his nose
   C smells his youth
   D smells his mother
4. What would the singer prefer to have?
   A a tree house
   B student loans
   C fame
   D a rocket ship

5 A step further

a In small groups, think of a story for a music video for the song.

b Create a storyboard of 4–6 frames for the video. Pay attention to the action, the characters, the colours and the focus of each frame.

c Present the story and your storyboard to the other groups. → S15 Gallery walk

d Research the actual video clip and compare it to your ideas.

GOOD TO KNOW

A **storyboard** helps to visually organise a story. It consists of a sequence of illustrations or pictures to show what is going on in a scene and how the story evolves. Think of it as sort of a comic book.

Improving your vocabulary

To improve your vocabulary in English, you should work with word families and know how to build different forms of a word correctly. This will not only improve your command of English vocabulary, but it will also help you to speak and write more fluently and understand written texts better.
In general, it's helpful to collect vocabulary from the same topic or theme in a cluster (e.g. in a mind map) and to learn words in chunks (e.g. a verb with its corresponding preposition).

Step A Word families: Let's talk about friends → S 11.1

a Look at the mind map. Make sure you know the meaning of the words included. Then copy the table and use the underlined words to complete it.

What's important to me and my friends
- trust one another
- contact one another regularly
- support one another
- have fun
- enjoy the same things
- share things
- same plans for the future

Noun	Verb	Adjective	Synonym	Antonym
trust	to trust	trustworthy	to have confidence in someone	to mistrust
...	...	...	...	

b Look at the mind map again and add more words concerning friendship to the table.

c Get together in small groups. Write the words from the word bank below down on cards and turn them face down.
One person draws a card and shows it to everyone. Now you have three minutes to write as many sentences as you can using the word or a word from the same word family.
Who has the most sentences? Who was most creative?
Take turns drawing a card.

active | companion | loving | happy | trustworthy | mutual | luck | to care | generosity | loyal | support | honesty | respect

GOOD TO KNOW

noun
= a person, a place, a thing or an idea
verb
= a word that describes an action
adjective
= a word that describes a noun
synonyms
= words with the same meaning
antonyms
= words with the opposite meaning

d Complete the sentences. Decide whether the word you need is an adverb, adjective or noun. Then use the correct form of the word in brackets.

1. My history (*know*) is quite limited, but my best friend always helps me out.
2. My best character traits are (*loyal*), kindness and being fun.
3. I find I can adapt to new situations (*easy*) as long as people are nice.
4. I am confident that I am (*ability*) to make friends wherever I go.
5. Did you know that (*Australia*) call their friends 'mate'?
6. I am convinced that (*trustful*) is one of the most important cornerstones of a friendship.
7. My best buddy always (*helpful*) when I need a dogsitter.
8. The (*major*) of young people considers friends to be as important as family.
9. There are a lot of (*use*) social media apps for finding new friends in another city.
10. If you want to be (*success*) in life, you need good friends to support you.
11. In slang, the word 'homeboy' means a friend from your hometown or (*children*).
12. I (*laughing*) a lot whenever I am with my mates.

Step B **Word formation: Let's talk about jobs** → S11.1

a Use the appropriate suffix to change the words below into professions. Be careful! It is not always enough to just add the suffix to the end of the existing word. Sometimes you need to change the ending / the word completely for it to make sense.

-er | -ian | -ist | -or

1. electricity
2. acting
3. politics
4. art
5. report
6. music
7. flower

Example: drive → driver

b Find five more examples of your own.

c Choose a prefix or a suffix to make a new word out of the word in brackets. You don't need all of them.

Prefixes	Suffixes
dis- | il- | im- | re- | un-	-able | -ance | -ful | -ous

1. We won't finish the project on time. It's ■ (*possible*).
2. I would like to work in the military, but it can be quite ■ (*danger*).
3. In some jobs, your ■ (*appear*) is very important.
4. If you are sometimes an ■ (*patient*) person, then you should not become a teacher.
5. In order to be successful in many professions, you have to speak up when you ■ (*agree*) with someone, even if it may feel uncomfortable.
6. Your letter of application is too long. If I were you, I would ■ (*write*) it.
7. Having good qualifications does not guarantee you a job. There are many university graduates that are ■ (*employed*).
8. I would like to work in the police force to help stop ■ (*legal*) activities.
9. Your ■ (*perform*) in the job interview may determine whether you get the job or not.
10. I think a job involving some travel would be ■ (*enjoy*).

GOOD TO KNOW

prefix
= added to the **beginning of a word** to create a new word with a different meaning

suffix
= added to the **end of a word**, changing the word class and the meaning of the word

C Going your own way

1 Before you read

a With a partner, discuss the options for school leavers mentioned on page 12 (ll.2–13). Write down some pros and cons for each option.

b Compare your results with another pair. Discuss which option you would choose and why. → G1.14, G1.15

CULTURE BOX

The UK education system
After completing GCSE exams in year 11, pupils can take their A levels at school or at a college. A levels are the equivalent of the *Abitur* in Germany and they are necessary if you want to go on to higher education and study at a university. If pupils do not take A levels, they can do NVQ (National Vocational Qualification) courses in a wide range of subjects which tend to be more practical. Another option is to do an apprenticeship, where you work for an employer and study for a qualification (often an NVQ).

A5

Should you go to university or start a business?

Hundreds of thousands of young people in the UK are currently applying for university. But should you still go if you have a great business idea?

Tom Honey never went to university. One summer holiday when he was 16, he started selling ice cream from a local farmer to tourists by the beach in his home town of Braunton, Devon. He started out making around £30 a day, but by the end of the summer, he was taking home £300 a day. Soon he had enough money to buy a pizza oven. When the next summer came around, he started *Stoned*, a stone-baked, wood-fired pizza pop-up, and never looked back.

Hundreds of thousands of young people in the UK are currently applying for university. Many go because their friends do, or because they are not sure what else to do with their lives at such a young age. But the number applying is falling for the first time since 2012 [...] because of the rising cost of student debt. While most of these young people will take up work or apprenticeships, a handful will follow their dream of starting a business.

Cameron Woodford, now 23, started his first business two years ago after spending a year working on super yachts to save. *Now Dating* is an online dating app that encourages people to move into offline dating as soon as possible, setting it apart from other dating apps, Woodford says. [...]

Now Dating attracted £100,000 from angel investors in January. "Starting a business is a full-time commitment," says Woodford, who works from the WeWork office in Paddington. "Every day of the week you'll find yourself thinking about it. It's not an easy thing, and if you're looking for a 9–5 this isn't it, but if you're willing to give up and commit everything, you'll learn more and grow more than you will in any university course."

Woodford, who hails from Australia, says he always struggled at school. "I never felt like university was the right option for me as I didn't really know what I wanted to do

14 **pizza pop-up** Pop-up Pizzarestaurant
32 **to set apart** sich abheben
36 **angel investor** wohlhabende Privatperson, die Startup-Unternehmen finanziert
42 **9–5** 8-Stunden-Job
42 **to be willing to do sth** bereit sein, etw. zu tun
43 **to commit sth** etw. einsetzen
46 **to hail from** stammen von/aus

yet," he says. "I think if you're leaving school and going directly into university, there's a high chance you are following your friends, which will have an adverse effect on what you really want to do and your learning abilities. Distractions will follow."

Honey, meanwhile, says he always got on really well at school. He speaks proudly of his older brother, who studied engineering at Oxford and now works in Cambridge, and his younger sister, who has her sights set on English at Oxford and a career in publishing. "I've always done well in school because I've been surrounded by smart people," he says. "But it was never something I was motivated to do."

By the time he was doing his A-levels, Honey was employing around 20 people and paying salaries. He started looking for business loans to open a restaurant to keep the business going through the winter, when it was too cold for pop-ups. Natwest offered him a £49,000 business loan. [...]

Honey also secured £25,000 in loans from *Virgin Start-Up*, which distributes Government-backed startup loans ranging from £500 to £25,000 to entrepreneurs looking to grow a business under two years old in England or Scotland. The programme was launched in 2013 with a mission to promote entrepreneurship in the UK by another famous school-leaver, Richard Branson.

Branson, who never went to college, likens himself to other successful entrepreneurs, including Steve Jobs, Michael Dell, Bill Gates and Mark Zuckerberg, who learned their skills on the job. "Nobody would question whether any of those entrepreneurs could run a business," Branson told a Malaysian newspaper last year. "They didn't develop their unique and compelling approaches to disruptive innovation and leadership by reading a textbook, but by living through the thrill, dread and sleepless nights that come with being an entrepreneur." [...]

Woodford says it has taken over a year for *Now Dating* to refine its work process and recruit a team ready for expansion. He says aspiring entrepreneurs should take some time away from their routine to think about whether starting a business is right for them.

"My advice is to discover who you are and what problem you want to solve," he says. "Once your mind is away from distractions you'll be able to think clearly about what you want to do and whether you should start your own business." (745 words)

Hazel Scheffield,
The Independent website, 2017

53 **adverse** nachteilig
55 **distraction** Ablenkung
59 **engineering** Maschinenbau
64 **surrounded by** umgeben von
70 **business loan** Geschäftskredit
76 **to distribute** verteilen; ausschütten
77 **government-backed** staatlich gefördert
79 **entrepreneur** Unternehmer/-in
81 **to launch** starten; ins Leben rufen
85 **to liken oneself to sb/sth** sich mit jdm./etw. vergleichen
94 **compelling** überzeugend
94 **disruptive innovation** Innovation, die etablierte Marktregeln aufmischt
96 **thrill** Erregung
97 **dread** Furcht
100 **to refine** verfeinern
101 **expansion** Erweiterung
102 **aspiring** aufstrebend

2 Multiple matching → WB, p. 9/1–2

Match these statements (A–H) with the people from the text (1–3).
You need to use some of the people's names more than once.
There are two statements more than you need.

1 Tom Honey **2** Cameron Woodford **3** Richard Branson

A While my classmates were studying A level Maths, I was already dealing with tens of thousands of pounds in loans.
B You won't learn as much in the classroom as you will in the real world.
C I didn't want to just follow the crowd and go to university.
D I regret not going to university first before starting my business.
E School was never a problem for me, but I just wasn't the academic type.
F Those that have made it big didn't do so because of books, but because they took risks and went for it.
G I'm the boss of over 100 employees.
H You need to completely focus on what you want to do and block out all distractions.

3 Mediation → H1

Ergänzen Sie die folgende Tabelle mit den entsprechenden Informationen über die beiden Jungunternehmer auf Deutsch.

Name	Alter (zur Firmengründung)	Geschäftsidee	Investition(en)
Tom …	…	…	…
Cameron …	…	…	…

4 Multiple choice

Choose the most suitable option.

1. Tom …
   - **A** finished school at 16.
   - **B** didn't attend university.
   - **C** did a bachelor's degree.
   - **D** went to vocational school.
2. Which information about the two entrepreneurs is not mentioned in the article?
   - **A** successes
   - **B** advice to others
   - **C** work challenges
   - **D** family background
3. The number of students applying for university …
   - **A** rose due to better student loans.
   - **B** decreased because of high student loans.
   - **C** rose because they wanted to join their friends.
   - **D** dropped because work seemed more attractive.
4. Cameron has …
   - **A** a 9–5 job.
   - **B** a part-time job.
   - **C** to work extra hours.
   - **D** to work fewer than 3 hours per day.
5. According to Richard Branson, an entrepreneur learns …
   - **A** through textbooks.
   - **B** to struggle regularly.
   - **C** through fear and excitement.
   - **D** from the experience of others.

5 Gapped summary

Complete the summary with the most suitable words from the text sections (ll. 4–26 and 57–84) on pages 22–23. Give the line numbers of the words that you used.

By the time Tom finished high school, he was already paying ■ **1** to 20 employees. Although he did well at school, he decided against ■ **2** because he wasn't motivated enough for higher education. His brother and sister, however, both wanted a ■ **3** after studying. Tom was looking for loans and got one for his start-up from an organisation which is committed to ■ **4** entrepreneurship. Before Tom had a restaurant, he sold local ice cream to ■ **5**. He quickly made a lot of money and was able to buy an ■ **6**. However, he now runs a ■ **7** pizza place and a restaurant for the ■ **8** months.

6 Words matter → S 11.1

a Change these verbs from the text into nouns. → H 1

1. to apply (l. 2)
2. to encourage (l. 31)
3. to commit (l. 43)
4. to employ (l. 68)
5. to secure (l. 75)
6. to distribute (l. 76)
7. to promote (l. 82)
8. to develop (l. 93)
9. to recruit (l. 101)
10. to discover (l. 106)

b Use a prefix to give the following words the opposite meaning.

1. possible (l. 32)
2. directly (l. 51)
3. abilities (l. 55)
4. motivated (l. 66)
5. successful (l. 86)
6. able (l. 109)

c Write down eight other nouns or adjectives. Let your partner write down the opposite meaning for them if there is one.

d Use ten words from **a–c** to describe your idea for a start-up or your dream job.

7 A step further → S 6.2

a What is important to you in a job? What do you want to achieve? Write down your job goals.

b Compare your results with a partner. Write a hit list with your five most important goals in a job.

USEFUL PHRASES

My biggest goal is to become popular / independent / rich / free / …
I dream about going to another country / city / …
I want to have independence / a family / success / a career / fun / challenges / action / …
I'd like to be respected / inspire others / learn from …
Being successful / rich / creative … is the most/least important because …
… should/shouldn't be more important than …
… and … are equally important.

c Discuss the following statement:
'Giving everything for a big career should be the most important goal for young employees.' Write a comment of about 120 words.

Material-based writing

During the exam, you will write a composition about a given topic with the help of materials (e.g. statistics, pictures, quotes, cartoons, poems, short messages or headlines). In your composition you combine the information from provided material with your own thoughts and previous knowledge. The content of the material should be used, but it must not be described or quoted. → S 6.1

Step A Structuring your composition

Your composition should always have the same structure:
Introduction: The first part of the composition introduces the topic and says what makes it interesting/relevant. Give a brief outline of the problem at present and in the past. This part ends with the thesis which contains the central idea of the composition.
Main part: The middle part deals with the topic from different points of view. Either you want to persuade the readers that your point of view is correct or you present arguments for both sides (pro/contra) and leave the readers to decide for themselves. Start a new paragraph for each new argument and use a topic sentence to introduce the argument.
Conclusion: Make a brief statement summarising what you have written in your composition. You may give an outlook on further consequences / possible solutions, state your own opinion, give a recommendation or appeal to the readers. Do not present new arguments.

GOOD TO KNOW

A **thesis** is a sentence at the end of the introduction which states the position a composition will be taking and informs the reader what to expect. This statement should be both specific and arguable.

A **topic sentence** introduces a new paragraph by presenting the argument / main idea this paragraph will be based upon. The rest of the paragraph then supports this idea.

a The following composition deals with the question whether young people should be allowed to vote in elections at 16 and is also based upon the picture on the right. However, the composition is not separated into introduction, main part and conclusion. Divide the composition into the three paragraphs. Give line numbers.

Material

Most modern democracies allow people to vote from the age of 18. In some countries, however, the age has been lowered to 16, for example in Austria and Brazil. This leads to the question whether young people should already be allowed to vote at age 16 or not. First of all, what speaks against lowering the voting age is the fact that voter turnout among young people has been very low in past elections. If the group of 18- to 29-year-olds make so little use of their right to vote, it can hardly be expected that 16- and 17-year-olds would act much differently. Secondly, opponents doubt that young people are mature enough to vote. In order to vote, you need to understand the system of government, and you need to be well-informed about the candidates and parties. Some argue that people under 18 are not really interested in politics. However, there are also strong arguments that speak for lowering the voting age. For one, young people can learn about the principles of the democracies they live in. At school, they can have discussions about political issues, which can help them form their own opinions. Furthermore, if young people are allowed to vote, there is a chance that more of them will develop an active interest in the political process. And most importantly, many of them take part in protests and demonstrations, demanding to be included in important decisions about their future. To conclude, while there may be justified doubts as to how seriously some young people take politics, there is a great chance in giving them the right to vote at 16. The hope is that, if given the opportunity at a young age, they will grow into responsible citizens who take an active part in the democratic process.

b Note down phrases which you think are typical of the three composition parts from exercise **a**.

Step B Preparing your composition → WB, p.10/1–2

Prepare your composition like this:
- Look at the material. Make sure you understand its content and know how to include it in your composition.
- Collect arguments for your composition. Make sure you understand the topic/task.
- Form your own opinion about the topic.
- Make an outline.

Today, young people show a lot of political engagement, for example with regard to climate change or racism. However, they do not often vote in elections.
Discuss the following question:
'If young people don't vote, does it harm society?'

Material

GOOD TO KNOW

In the US, the elephant represents the Republican party while the donkey is the symbol of the Democrats.

a Look at the cartoon above and answer the questions. Take notes.
1. What can you see?
2. What is the connection to the topic question above?
3. Is there a message? If so, what is the message?

You can ask yourself and answer these three questions whenever the material you are offered consists of a cartoon or picture.

b Make a list of arguments, facts and other information that support or contradict the topic question. You can also make a mind map or a table to organise your ideas.

Pros	Cons
– People who don't vote don't support the system they live in – …	– It is hard for young people to decide which party they should vote for because …

c What is your own opinion concerning this topic? Take notes.

d Make an outline: Take notes of what to include in the introduction, main part and conclusion. Look back at the box in **Step A**. Only use five items from **b** and think of supporting arguments, examples, explanations and personal experiences. Then put your arguments in a logical order.

Introduction	base of democracy = participation of everyone topic of great interest for: politicians, … because …
Main part	On the one hand, … on the other hand, …
Conclusion	I strongly believe that …

Step C Writing a first draft → WB, p. 10/3

Pay attention to the question or statement you have to write about and to the number of words you must write.

Write a first draft of your composition. Write about 120 words.
Take into account the question from page 27 and include the material provided.

a Write an introduction. Answer these questions:
1. Which topic is being discussed?
2. What makes the topic interesting/relevant?

b First choose two arguments (one pro, one con) from your list in **Step B**, exercise **b**.
Then write the main part. Use linking words and paragraphs to structure your composition.

c Write a conclusion.
1. Sum up and paraphrase your arguments.
2. State your own opinion.
3. Provide a solution or an outlook.

You can start like this:
In democratic countries, people can take part in politics by voting their representatives in to parliament. …

USEFUL PHRASES

Introduction:
The topic of … is of great interest to … It is an important topic because … The question is: …?

Main part:
Firstly/secondly …
Moreover, … | Either …, or … | not only …, but also …
Another way to look at this is … | On the other hand, …

Conclusion:
In conclusion, … | To sum up, … | All in all, …
In my opinion … | I (dis-)agree with …
Why don't they …? | I think/believe we should … | It would be a good idea to … because …

Step D Checking your composition

Keep an eye on the clock. Make sure there is enough time left to check your composition at the end.

a Check your composition with the help of the following questions.
1. Is the structure clear? Did you use paragraphs, useful phrases and linking words to structure your composition?
2. Is your composition understandable? Do your arguments become clear?
3. Are there any spelling/grammar/punctuation mistakes?

b Keep a list of common mistakes you make. You can use it to check all your writing. Continue to add more aspects to the list.

Punctuation	Grammar
– Start a sentence with a capital letter. – Don't forget full stops, question marks etc. – …	– he/she/it → verb needs an -s – …

Step E Rewriting your composition

Use your results from **Step D** to write the final version of your composition.

Part I Reading

Matt Krampitz is a high school teacher in Burlington/Connecticut, USA. His short story *Half Sleep* deals with topics such as coming of age and family relations.

Half Sleep

by Matt Krampitz

1 Yates was the kind of kid who picked spiders off the floor and threw them outside. He was gentle always and he spoke to me like I was an adult. He played piano and sang like Elton John and he told stories that made everyone laugh even though they always ended badly. Most importantly, he was my brother.

2 When my parents would go out, he and his friends would watch me. They played basketball and drank beers in the driveway. I kept score and shot steady free throws for both sides. He didn't smile often, but when he did it was real.

3 When I started sixth grade, he finished high school. We had a big barbecue planned, but he only stayed for a minute and then drove off with his friends to do what my parents called "God knows what". He was never home before midnight, and he moved out that winter. Our house calmed down after that. For months it had been building with the weight of unasked questions. My parents wanted him to at least stay truthful. I only knew that he barely spoke anymore and got irritated if he spent more than two hours with me.

4 Things started disappearing. My father said it was possible he had left his cordless drill on a job site. Then his miter saw was gone as well. My mother lost some money or at least couldn't remember spending it. My father sat on the couch with his head tilted toward the ceiling thinking of places the money could have gone. He wondered out loud if my mother had gotten her nails done or made a trip to the grocery store or been mugged. She fumed back that it doesn't cost ninety dollars to get her nails done. I remember sitting in the living room listening to hushed voices snapping from the kitchen. Yates stopped coming to the house.

5 One late night, before they changed the locks, I heard the squeak of a hinge and the brush of weather stripping sweep the wood floor. I knew it was my brother by the creep of his steps. He padded lightly, heel first, toward the kitchen. I heard drawers roll open and the woolly jingle of junk being moved. The drawers closed and the footsteps continued, eluding the creaky seams. My heart was a gong in my half sleep.

6 The hollow door of my room swung slowly, and I noticed a change in light and breeze. I could feel his presence in the doorway. Though it was too dark to see, I could envision his greasy brown hair that turned blond some summers and his big sad eyes. I could almost smell him, his smell, like the must of a cabin and stale menthol cigarettes.

7 His steps led to my window and to the acoustic Gibson Hummingbird that leaned by the sill. It was my father's guitar. The one he had taught Yates on and that Yates had promised to teach me on. I could picture his thick fingers with the nails bitten down to nubs working the neck of the guitar. Those same fingers were now reaching to take it away.

8 I didn't stop him. I imagine I could have, but I didn't, and I kept the guitar's disappearance from my parents for months because I didn't want them to be wounded like I was and like Yates was. All I told them was that I knew he still loved us and that he was hurt as we were hurt. What I never told them – to spare them the agony of strict detail – was that when he left the room, I could feel his presence in the doorway for a long while, staring at me as I slept, as if he wanted me to wake up, and then I heard the gush of a broken throat and the soft chirping breath of his tears. (656 words)

1 Multiple matching → WB, p.11/1–2

Match the events (A–H) with the paragraphs (1–8) in the story. There are two events more than you need and two paragraphs without a matching event.

A Yates doesn't communicate any more
B The presence of a ghost
C A throbbing heart
D Where have the items gone?
E There goes the guitar
F Yates asking for forgiveness
G Happy times with the family
H A great storyteller

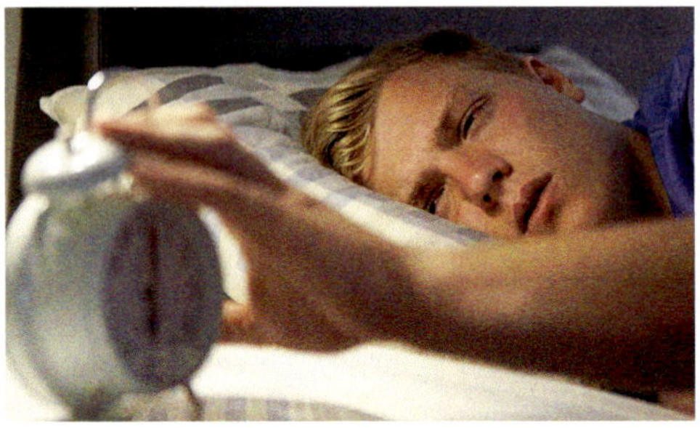

2 Short-answer questions

Answer the following questions. You may use words from the text.

1. Who are the main characters in the story?
2. Where does the story take place?
3. What are the narrator's feelings towards his brother?

3 Multiple choice

Choose the most suitable option.

1. Who is the father's main suspect after the theft?
   A Yates
   B his wife
   C the narrator
   D his own mind

2. What conflict occurs in the story?
   A Yates becomes criminal.
   B Yates becomes very provocative.
   C Yates leaves the family after a fight.
   D Yates' parents don't want him to live at their house any more.

3. According to the narrator, what does Yates smell like?
   A bad breath
   B menthol smoke
   C a cabin in the woods
   D tobacco and an old shack

4. What did Yates promise the narrator?
   A to come back
   B to take him along
   C to teach him the guitar
   D to fight against the parents

5. Why does the narrator know Yates feels remorse?
   A He hears him cry.
   B He leaves a letter.
   C He leaves the guitar.
   D He wakes him up to talk.

6. Which main theme is presented in the story?
   A hatred
   B racism
   C jealousy
   D coming of age

4 Gapped summary

Complete the summary with the most suitable words from the text on page 29.
Give the line numbers of the words that you used.

The narrator describes his memories of his older brother, Yates. Overall, Yates was a kind, gentle and respectful person and when he smiled, it was a ■ **1** smile. He talked to his younger brother like to an ■ **2**. Yates and his friends looked after his younger brother while their parents were out. However, Yates was increasingly absent and soon ■ ■ **3**. After that a ■ **4** seemed to be lifted from the house. Afterwards, things went missing; at first there were lots of ■ **5** explanations. But once money disappeared, their parents knew something was wrong and wanted to change the ■ **6**. One time, the narrator witnessed someone steal his father's ■ **7** guitar, and from the ■ **8** on the wood floor he recognised his brother.

Part II Material-based writing → WB, p. 11–12/3–6

Alcohol is part of almost every social get-together. However, in recent years numbers have shown a change in the consumption of alcoholic drinks.
Write a composition of at least 150 words with regard to the following statement:
'You cannot have a good party without alcohol.'
Include the material provided.

Material

Attitude to life

Let food be thy medicine, thy medicine shall be thy food.
Hippocrates, Greek philosopher (~460BC–370BC)

Health is a state of complete mental, social and physical well-being, not merely the absence of disease. *World Health Organisation*

No road is long with good company.
Turkish proverb

Win if you can, lose if you must, but never quit.
Cameron Trammell, American football player

Jobs fill your pockets, but adventures fill your soul.
Jaime Lyn Beatty, American actress

1 Working with pictures and quotes → S 10.1 → WB, p. 14–15/1–3; p. 16/1

a Choose a picture and match it with a quote. Explain the meaning of the quote in relation to the chosen picture.

b In small groups, present and discuss your results.

2 Working with a diagram → S 10.3 → WB, p.16/2

a Discuss the following questions with a partner:

1. How much do the statistics reflect your own experiences?
2. How often do you do something for your well-being?
3. How much money do you think you spend on your well-being per week?

b Research information about negative effects of the wellness industry online. Compare your results with a partner. Then discuss them in class.

The revenue of the most important sectors of the health and wellness industry in 2020:

Overall revenue: $4.4 trillion
the amount is shown in billions of US dollars

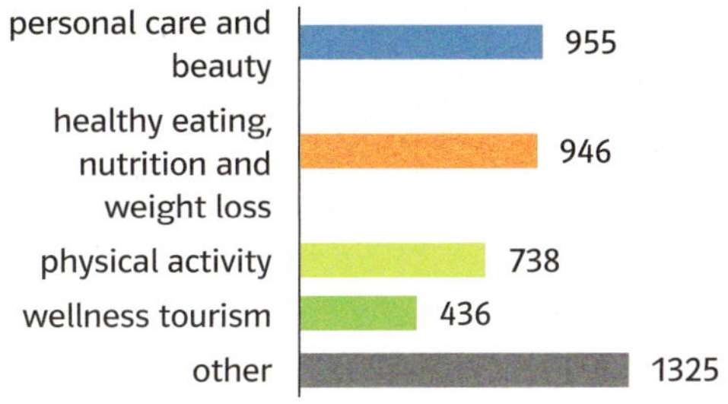

Note: Only the four sectors generating the most revenue are illustrated.
Source: Global Wellness Institute, 2020

A6 3 Listening → S 3

a Listen to Kimberly, a young woman from London, and her story about travelling and well-being. Which of these topics does Kimberly not mention during her story?

A her mental health issues
B activities at her destination
C finding her creative side during the trip
D rebuilding inner strength

b Answer the following questions. Take notes. → H 2

1. Where did Kimberly travel to? Why did she need to get away?
2. How did Kimberly feel at the airport?
3. At which moment did she experience a point of change during her trip? Where was she? What changed?
4. What recommendation does Kimberly give her listeners at the end of her story?

c What makes you or would make you want to get away? Think of a situation or different scenarios. Where do you go / would you like to go? What do you / would you do there? Talk to a partner.

solitude Einsamkeit
petrified gelähmt; versteinert
to take the plunge den Sprung wagen

4 Talking about well-being

a Prepare a 1-minute talk about activities, objects and people that make you feel good.
→ S 15 1-minute presentation

b Walk around the class and present your talk to one of your classmates. Then listen to his/hers. Which aspects do you have in common? Talk to at least three classmates.
→ S 15 Market place

USEFUL PHRASES

Giving reasons
because (of) | since | therefore | consequently | accordingly | as a result of | due to
Giving examples
for example | for instance | take the case of | as shown/illustrated by

A Diet and nutrition

1 Before you read → S10 → WB, p.17/1–2

a Describe which types of food you eat during a day are healthy and which aren't. Discuss your results with a partner. Do you agree on everything? Give reasons.

b Do a survey on diet in class.
- How many classmates are vegetarians/vegan/flexitarians?
- What are the reasons for their choice?
- How many are considering becoming vegetarian or vegan, and why?

USEFUL PHRASES

The diagram/graph/chart shows that …
Out of … people, more than … have (never) …
Over/Under/About 20 % stated/claimed …
Although not many people are …, many …
The reasons for becoming vegetarian/vegan/flexitarian were …
We found out that a lot/few people are … because …

GOOD TO KNOW

The word **Veganuary** is a combination of vegan + January. Veganuary encourages people to try a vegan diet and leave out meat. This is not only healthy but also good for the environment.

c In small groups, create a visual. Decide on how you could visualise the results by using charts, graphs and/or diagrams.

d Present the visual in class. Which one shows the results best?

A7

Veganuary ends on record high with 250,000 participants

Pledges for 2019 plant-based campaign exceeded those in previous four years combined

A record 250,000 people worldwide signed up to the Veganuary movement this year by embracing plant-based diets this month, the campaign has revealed.

As more consumers drop all meat and dairy products from their diet for health or ethical reasons, the charity behind the annual event said the record figures and strong global support had made 2019's Veganuary the most popular since its launch in 2014. Many more people are thought to have taken part in the event without signing the official pledge.

At the same time, Britain's supermarkets are reporting a surge in sales of vegan food and drink, which they expect to continue throughout the year. They are tapping into not only the burgeoning vegan market but also the UK's estimated 22 million "flexitarians", who enjoy meat but want to reduce their meat consumption.

The number of Veganuary pledges for 2019 exceeded those in the previous four years combined, suggesting that veganism is becoming a mainstream movement. The organisers of Veganuary say six in 10 who take the "Veganuary pledge" say they plan to stay vegan.

Thirteen new overseas partnerships increased Veganuary's presence elsewhere in the world – in India, Sweden, Brazil, Argentina, Chile, Peru, Singapore, Malaysia, Australia, South Africa, Japan, Iceland and Russia.

"With a quarter of a million participants this year, Veganuary is finishing on an all-time high," said Rich Hardy, head of campaigns at Veganuary. "I think

3 **pledge** Versprechen
3 **to exceed** übertreffen
7 **to embrace** *hier:* übernehmen
8 **to reveal** preisgeben
15 **launch** Einführung
19 **surge** plötzlicher Anstieg
21 **to tap into sth** etw. erschließen
22 **to burgeon** florieren

Veganuary has reached critical mass now – vegan living is growing; it's here to stay, it's part of the national conversation and it has credibility. That's great news for people, animals and the planet."

Support for the campaign has also led to a vegan boost among food producers, with supermarkets, manufacturers and high street restaurant and pub chains also bolstering their plant-based ranges to meet demand. […]

On supermarket wine aisles, sales of Co-op's own-label vegan varieties have doubled since it rolled out front-of-pack labelling last year. A new organic and vegan white wine has also had a fivefold increase in sales. […]

Sainsbury's has recently started selling fake meat next to the real thing, after a successful trial last year when it launched a new range of plant-based burgers and mince.

Rather than being displayed in a dedicated vegan section, meat and fish alternatives such as jackfruit burgers and mushroom "shroomdogs" are being stocked alongside their meat counterparts in 20 branches of Sainsbury's. (412 words)

Rebecca Smithers,
The Guardian website, 2019

44 **critical mass** *hier:* Eigendynamik
47 **credibility** Glaubwürdigkeit
53 **to bolster** stützen
53 **range** Sortiment
57 **to roll out** herausbringen
57 **front-of-pack** auf der Vorderseite von Verpackungen
66 **dedicated** ausgewiesen
70 **counterpart** Gegenstück

2 Multiple matching → WB, p.17/3

Match the figures (1–5) from the text with their corresponding references (A–G). There are two references more than you need.

1 250,000
2 2014
3 22 million
4 60 %
5 13

A foreign collaborations with Veganuary
B Veganuary participants in 2019
C people who want to remain vegan after Veganuary
D vegan food producers
E when Veganuary began
F when veganism became mainstream
G people who eat meat, but want to eat less of it

3 Short-answer questions → H 2

Answer the following questions. You may use words from the text.

1. According to the charity, what made Veganuary more successful in 2019 than in 2014?
2. Why does Rich Hardy believe that vegan lifestyles will continue to grow?
3. What have supermarkets done in reaction to an increase in veganism? (two things)

4 Mediation

Beantworten Sie die folgenden Fragen auf Deutsch.

1. Warum war 2019 für die vegane Bewegung wahrscheinlich noch erfolgreicher als gedacht?
2. Warum ist die Zahl der Veganismus-Anhänger von 2019 so besonders?
3. Was hat die Supermarktkette Sainsbury's 2018 gemacht?

5 A step further → S 1.1 → G 1.14

Discuss the following questions in small groups. Then share your results in class.

1. Should a vegan diet be the means of achieving a healthy lifestyle? Have you ever tried such a diet or would you like to?
2. Is Veganuary a good way to promote a vegan lifestyle?

B Being mindful

1 Before you read

a What do you do if you feel sad or exhausted? Talk to a partner.

b What could a subject with the name 'mindfulness' be about? You can use the words from the word cloud. → S15 Round robin

A8

Schools of thought: can mindfulness lessons boost mental health?

1 Children are taking 10 minutes out from the hurly burly school day to reflect on their thoughts and their feelings. Some ground themselves by thinking about their feet on the floor, while others concentrate on their breathing.
This is mindfulness, the lessons quickly growing in popularity as an antidote to the stress of being a young person in the 21st century, be it pressure to perform in exams, social media, or the obsession with body image that is reported to even affect primary age children. [...] Stress is a known barrier to learning and a growing number of schools are targeting the emotional health of pupils through schemes such as meditation, mindfulness and the provision of mental health first aiders. [...]

2 The Mental Health Foundation charity wants emotional well-being to be at the heart of the school curriculum. [...] Dr Antonis Kousoulis, its assistant director, said its survey last year found 47% of people aged 18–24 had experienced stress over their body image to the extent of being overwhelmed or unable to cope. "Social media has certainly played a part," he says. "Historically, it was the mirror that was the main driver of perception of our image and how we thought others perceived us. Nowadays, young people are exposed almost on a 24/7 basis to manipulated and heavily edited images, whether that's in advertising or photos of their friends." [...]

3 Secondary school teacher Richard Burnett, who founded the Mindfulness in Schools Project 10 years ago, warns against "quick fix" approaches. "We are a charity started by teachers who wanted to teach children how best to manage their

1 **to boost** steigern
4 **hurly burly** turbulent
6 **to ground oneself** sich erden
10 **antidote** Gegenmittel
13 **obsession** Besessenheit
18 **emotional health** psychische Gesundheit
19 **scheme** Programm; Maßnahme
20 **provision** Bereitstellung
20 **mental health first aider** Ersthelfer/-in für psychische Probleme
24 **curriculum** Lehrplan
29 **overwhelmed** *hier:* überfordert
34 **to perceive** wahrnehmen
34 **to be exposed to sth/sb** jdm./etw. ausgesetzt sein

thoughts and feelings and deal with the rollercoaster of being a young person," he says. It has two training courses for teachers – one aimed at secondary students and another for younger classes. "It's about training your attention to notice what is going on. If you are aware of that, you can choose how to respond [...]," he says. [...]

Teachers at Cherry Tree primary school in Basildon, Essex, say mindfulness lessons are already making a difference. "Children aged eight to 10 in four classes do different exercises for 10 minutes after lunch each day," says school pastoral leader Kim Milsom. "Children have told us that mindfulness helps to calm them down and that they use it at home as well."

4 Tracey Ward, assistant head teacher at Stanley Grove primary academy, reviews her work as a trained mental health first aider:

Being a mental health first aider means you have been trained to spot signs and symptoms and can "intervene early". If you have done the Mental Health First Aid England training you are more aware of depression and anxiety. [...] 97 % of pupils in our school have English as an additional language and 57 % of the population of our area are living in poverty, according to a report last year. Well-being is a priority for us and we want to make sure that if our children are in a crisis in their lives, that we have equipped them with the right coping strategies – ones that are sustainable and that they will be able to use in the future.

5 We have converted our first aid stations into mental and physical health stations and we have trained mental health first aiders to be there at break and lunch times. On their trays the children all have a "first aid kit" – which is a picture of an open case with a red cross on it. They write on it what they need when they are feeling distressed, overwhelmed or anxious. The children love this approach. This week I was at one of the first aid stations when a child had an outburst and came to me saying they were "overwhelmed". I told him to collect his mental first aid kit from the tray and we discussed what he could do. Another child came to us because they had "a busy mind" and we carried out the stress bucket activity. We discussed what was making the stress container full and what could be put in place to empty out some of the water. [...]
Part of our approach is to embrace physical activity to support mental health. One of our well-being activities is the daily mile, marked out on the playground. Every child from nursery to year 6 walks, jogs or runs it every day and they can do it with a friend or a member of staff. We find children are more likely to open up about their feelings outside of the classroom. Our ethos and culture is warm and happy and I think that's a lot to do with the importance we place on mental health and well-being. (785 words)

Liz Lightfoot, *The Guardian*, 2019

59 **pastoral leader** Seelsorger
68 **to spot** erkennen; wahrnehmen
79 **to equip sb with sth** jdn. mit etw. ausstatten; jdn. mit etw. versehen
88 **first aid kit** Erste-hilfekasten
91 **distressed** erschüttert; bekümmert
94 **outburst** Gefühlsausbruch
104 **to embrace** einschließen; aufgreifen

2 Multiple matching → WB, p.18/1–3

Match the headings (A–F) with the corresponding sections (1–5) of the text. There is one heading more than you need.

A Causes of stress
B Recognising and dealing with health and well-being issues
C New methods for combatting stress in schools
D Physical strategies and activities for mental health
E Refocusing stress and relationships
F Refocusing thoughts and feelings

3 Multiple choice

Choose the most suitable option.

1. What causes 47% of young people stress these days?
   A self-perception
   B school pressure
   C parents' expectations
   D romantic relationships
2. What are the tasks and responsibilities of a "trained mental health first aider" according to Tracey Ward?
   A spot indicators
   B inform authorities
   C build first aid stations
   D develop coping strategies
3. How many students at Stanley Grove primary academy aren't native speakers?
   A only 3%
   B under a third
   C almost all of them
   D over half of them
4. How did one child feel at the first aid station?
   A energetic
   B very joyful
   C unconcerned
   D deeply moved
5. How is physical activity part of Stanley Grove primary academy's approach?
   A The daily mile takes away their anxiety.
   B The more they jog, the happier they seem.
   C It's more likely for the students to open up.
   D Running around the playground releases stress.

4 Gapped summary → H 2

Complete the summary with the most suitable words from the text.
Give the line numbers of the words that you used.

Many schools have begun to implement short mindfulness sessions in order to counteract ■ **1**. One charity highlights how important it is to make people more ■ **2** of things happening in their mind, especially because of the effect of modern social media. The founder of a project for mindfulness in schools therefore wants things to go further, and recommends a secure position for emotional well-being at the centre of the ■ **3**. And it certainly works: teachers at one school in Essex have already been able to perceive the ■ **4** since mindfulness sessions were offered. At another school in a poor area, mindfulness has become an essential ■ **5** mechanism for the pupils. The students can turn to specially ■ **6** staff members to help them; and when they do, they are now very good at articulating their feelings following an ■ **7**. The approach also places great emphasis on the ■ **8** side of health, which supports their efforts to improve well-being.

5 Working with an infographic → S10.3

a Describe and analyse the infographic. Relate it to the text on pages 36–37.

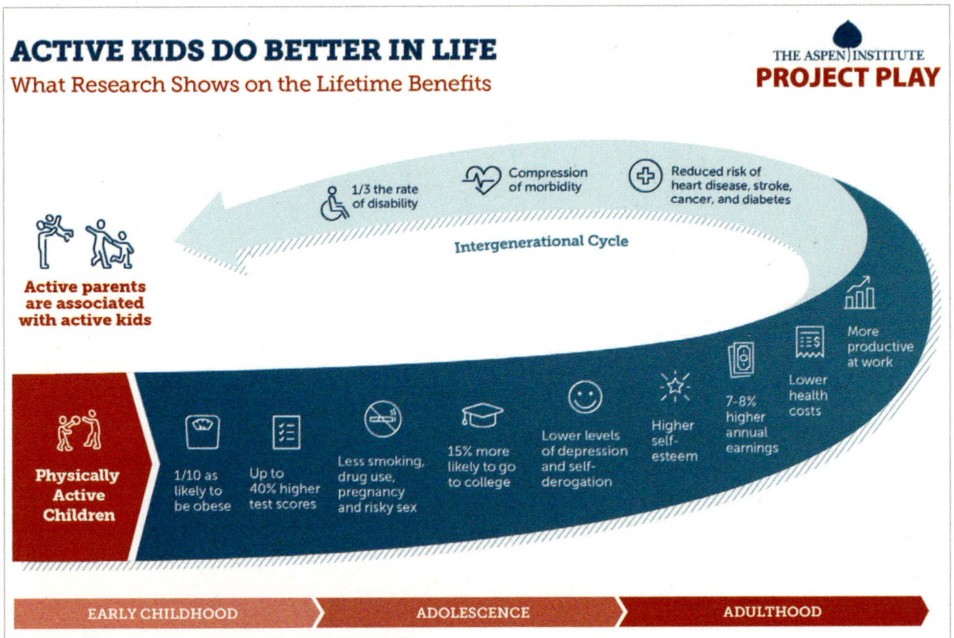

Source: The Aspen Institute – Project Play, 2020

USEFUL PHRASES

Talking about an infographic
The infographic / icon shows / illustrates / is used to visualise … | The infographic states that …% | According to the infographic, the reasons why … is due / thanks to … | The life performance of children depends on … | The benefits of an active lifestyle are … | We found out that … because …

b Write a short text for the school website about why being active is so important in life. Include the information from the infographic in **a**.

6 A step further → S6.4 → G8

a With a partner, think of actions your school already takes to care for students' mental health and further actions your school could take. Take notes.

b Write a formal email to the Mental Health Foundation charity. Explain what you wish would be done to support mental health at your school. Ask for feedback on your ideas.

USEFUL PHRASES

Writing a formal email
Dear …, | Good morning/afternoon, I'm writing to you because … | We would like to … | Could you let me know … | What about …? | I look forward to hearing from you soon. | Yours sincerely/faithfully

c Exchange your email with a partner. Give feedback taking into account the language, register and the content of the email. Would you send your partner's email out? Give reasons. → S15 Peer correction

Working with listening texts → S3

There are different types of exercises to test your listening skills, for example multiple-choice tasks and completion tasks. Even if you are not sure, note something down while listening – this is still better than not writing anything at all.

Step A Before you listen

You are going to hear an interview about 'Students' health'. Guess what the listening text could be about. Think about factors that can have a positive or a negative effect on young people's health. → S15 Round robin

Step B Listening for gist

A9 Listen for the first time and choose the statement that represents the main idea of the listening text.

1. Parents blame teachers for their children's health problems.
2. Being unable to afford good food is one reason why students have adopted an unhealthy lifestyle.
3. Schools are trying to tackle the issue of students' physical and mental health.

GOOD TO KNOW

listening for gist = identifying the general message of a listening text and recognising related statements

listening for detail = extracting relevant information and details from a listening text as well as relating them to each other and understanding them in their cultural context

Step C Listening for detail

A9 Read the assignment carefully and identify keywords. Use a dictionary if necessary. Then listen again and give short answers to the questions.

1. Who belongs to Generation Z?
   Example: people born between 1996 and 2010
2. Which symptoms of stress do students display? Name three.
3. Which possible solutions does Angela mention? Name three.
4. Which two new measures did the school implement a few years ago to support students' health?

Step D Multiple choice and completion tasks

A10 Listen twice to a podcast about a study on students' mental health and complete the tasks below.

1. Which facts about Samuel Bennet are true? Choose the correct answer(s).
   A Samuel is a child psychiatrist.
   B He agrees with Benjamin, a PE teacher, on the importance of sport.
   C Samuel works at the University of Sussex.

2. What were the findings of the study? Choose the correct answer(s).
   A The majority of children became less physically active as they got older.
   B Time spent being sedentary increased by 80–90 % between the ages of 12 and 18.
   C The less active young people are, the more likely they are to suffer from depression.

3. Samuel presents ideas to increase a child's activity levels at school and at home. Copy the list and add further suggestions.

At school	stretching breaks	…	…
At home	emptying the dishwasher	…	…

C The teachings of dark places

1 Before you read

a Make a list of five places you have already visited as a tourist which have touched you emotionally. Compare your list with a partner.

b Look at the picture. What do you know about the place? Would you like to go there? What kind of feelings do you associate with this place?
→ S 15 Think-pair-share

Concentration camp Auschwitz-Birkenau, Poland

A11

Why dark tourism is more important than ever in grim political times

Dark tourism – essentially visiting sites with a dark past, be that genocide, murder or nuclear disaster – is more important than ever in a particularly divisive political climate, according to one dark tourism specialist.

"As is often said: those who do not learn from history are bound to repeat it," says Peter Hohenhaus, who dedicates much of his spare time to visiting sites of mass murders, natural disasters and museums that commemorate such incidents. The Vienna-based 53-year-old [...] says he has visited 90 countries, over 100 cities, and between 600 and 700 dark tourism sites. [...]

The Murambi Genocide Memorial in Rwanda, which commemorates the murder of an estimated 2 million people in the early 1990s, is one of the most affecting dark tourism spots Hohenhaus has ever visited.
"It moved me emotionally to the extreme," he says. "It stands out among all the others because here they've put on display corpses of the victims of the massacres [...]. The guide leads you through room after room. It was at times pretty unbearable: heartbreaking and gut-wrenching in equal measures.

"But rather than opting out after the first room, which would have been an instinctive reaction, you feel a duty to do the circuit to the end and pay your respects to all the victims." [...]

Hohenhaus admits, however, that not all memorials are created equal. He argues: "Sometimes the very fact that a memorial site is not fairly balanced but ludicrously one-sided can actually be part of the attraction from a dark tourism perspective. [...]

In North Korea, tourists are always accompanied by two official tour guides, Hohenhaus says. "They give you the official state-sanctioned version of their history. For instance, with regard to the Korean War they'll always portray it as a great victory against the 'imperialist Yankee aggressors'. They really used such language when I was there in 2005. Or myths that Kim Jong-il had written hundreds of academic books and was the best golf player in history."

[Hohenhaus] insists dark tourism is the most educational form of travelling possible. "I feel like I've learned more about the world in these past few years of intensively pursuing dark tourism than I have throughout my entire formal education or academic career," he says.

Among the best sites, in Hohenhaus's opinion, is the National 9/11 Memorial & Museum in New York. He was impressed

1 **grim** düster; trostlos
3 **essentially** im Wesentlichen
3 **genocide** Völkermord
5 **divisive** kontrovers
7 **to be bound to do sth** zwangsläufig etw. tun
8 **to dedicate** widmen
11 **to commemorate** gedenken
25 **corpse** Leiche
28 **unbearable** unerträglich
28 **gut-wrenching** herzzerreißend
30 **to opt out** aussteigen
38 **ludicrous** lächerlich; absurd; grotesk
54 **to insist** bestehen auf; beharren auf
58 **to pursue** verwirklichen; verfolgen

GOOD TO KNOW

After World War II, Korea was divided into two zones (North and South). Later attempts to reunite failed. Today, **North Korea** is classified as a dictatorship around the Kim dynasty.

The **9/11 Memorial & Museum** commemorates the 11 September 2001 attacks, which destroyed the World Trade Center towers and killed about 3,000 people.

64 **conspiracy theory** Verschwörungstheorie
68 **stunning** überwältigend
72 **to devise** entwickeln; erfinden
74 **to restrain** zurückhalten
74 **genuine** echt; ehrlich
81 **to deem** halten für
81 **exploitative** ausbeuterisch; ausnutzend
88 **misery** Armseligkeit
89 **ultimately** letztendlich
93 **escapism** Realitätsflucht

with how it confronted conspiracy theories surrounding the attack and showed respect to the victims. And the German Military History Museum in Dresden was "nothing short of stunning", according to Hohenhaus. [...] But, he adds, "dark tourists" should pay attention to doing dark tourism right. He has devised his own set of rules to guide him. "Quite simply: be respectful, be restrained, show a genuine interest," he says. "Dark tourism does not go with selfie sticks or the kind of boisterous behaviour you may get away with at more mainstream tourist sites."

He strikes off spots where he is in direct danger of death, like war zones. And sites that he deems "obviously exploitative or voyeuristic" are struck off his list until the situation changes, as are places where the tragedy occurred too recently or is ongoing. For this reason, he sees a separation between dark tourism and so-called "slum tourism", which he argues is about viewing ongoing misery. [...]

Ultimately, however, Hohenhaus firmly believes that dark tourism is a much better way of travelling the world than more traditional holidays. "Why should complete escapism be morally better than confronting actual reality?" he asks. "Nobody has ever been able to explain that to me." (602 words)

Kashmira Gander,
Independent website, 2017

2 Multiple choice → WB, p.19/1–3

Choose the most suitable option.

1. Dark tourism means ...
   A visiting places no one ever visited.
   B visiting historical places of tragedy.
   C visiting emotionally extreme places.
   D learning about the history of a dark place.

2. In North Korea, tourists ...
   A can buy books of Kim Jong-il.
   B cannot visit the country on their own.
   C cannot enter the country without invitation.
   D are impressed by the greatness of the country.

3. In Hohenhaus' opinion, which is a top dark tourism site?
   A 9/11 Memorial
   B Korean War Memorial
   C Murambi Genocide Memorial
   D German Military History Museum

4. What piece of advice does Hohenhaus give concerning dark tourism?
   A Control your emotions.
   B Always go with a guide.
   C Always behave in a respectful way.
   D Learn about the places before you go there.

5. According to Hohenhaus, what is the most important reason for dark tourism?
   A escaping daily life
   B viewing ongoing misery
   C dealing with the real world
   D having an alternative to traditional holidays

3 Gapped summary → H 2

Complete the summary with the most suitable words from the text.
Give the line numbers of the words that you used.

In this article, we are introduced to the topic of dark tourism. The dark tourist Peter Hohenhaus stresses the ■ **1** side of this way of travelling as it has taught him many things. He talks about his experiences at a number of locations. The most emotionally moving one was a genocide memorial with ■ **2** laid out for viewing. As uncomfortable as it was, he describes a sense of ■ **3** to do the whole tour. However, it's not always about the events themselves. Part of the attraction is how the event is portrayed. Visiting the memorials often means being confronted with conspiracy theories or with stories that are built upon ■ **4**. This can be well seen in the particularly ■ **5** accounts given at North Korean sites. Peter Hohenhaus warns that there are certain rules which apply when visiting dark places in contrast to ■ **6** tourist attractions. In addition, he argues against visiting locations attached to ■ **7** tragic events or places where not enough time has passed since the tragedy occurred. One major question that we are left with is why people shy away from dark tourism in favour of trips resulting in ■ **8**.

4 Short-answer questions

Answer the following questions. You may use words from the text.

1. Why is dark tourism important, according to Peter Hohenhaus?
2. What is different at the Murambi Genocide Memorial compared to other memorials?
3. What is essential to a dark tourism site for it to be a good one?

A12 5 Listening → S 3

a Listen to four people talking about their experiences at dark places around the world. Answer the following questions. → H 2

1. Which places have they visited?
2. How did they feel during their visit? Note down as many adjectives as possible.
3. What did they learn at each place? Name one aspect for each speaker.

b Which of the place(s) mentioned in the audio would you like to visit yourself? Give reasons.

Day of the Dead parade in Mexico City

skull Schädel
to be under siege belagert werden
casualty Todesopfer
noose Schlinge

6 A step further → S 6.5

a In small groups, create a poster about the dark places / events of one country. Research its dark places / events online. Then decide on the five most important ones. Consider the following aspects for each place / event:
- What is the historical / political / social background?
- Why do you think this place is of such great interest?
- What can we learn from this place?
- Which pictures illustrate the place well?

b Present your poster to the class. Give each other feedback on the layout and the content of the posters. → S 15 Gallery walk → S 15 Tip-top

Benefits of volunteering → S 6.1

1 Writing an introduction → WB, p. 20/1–2

The introduction should grab the reader's attention. Then state the topic of your composition. Gaining the reader's attention can be achieved in various ways:

- Fact/Figure: By providing an interesting fact
  Example: Only 11.5 percent of school leavers do volunteer work.
- Personal story: By telling a story/anecdote from the writer's own experience
  Example: Before I started volunteer work in Ghana, I had not been interested in Africa.
- Rhetorical question: By asking a (provocative) question in order to make the reader think
  Example: Wouldn't the world be a better place if we all did volunteer work at least once?
- Quote: By using a quote of a famous person referring to the topic
  Example: Helen Keller said: "Alone we can do so little; together we can do so much."

State the topic of your composition. You may use a question to do so.
Example: This leads to the question whether …

a Look at the following introduction and check whether all the relevant aspects from the tip box are mentioned.

We all know someone who did volunteer work. However, the question is 'Should volunteering be obligatory?' For example, in the past, it was normal to care for elderly people at home. Parents lived with one of their children until they died. Nowadays most people neither have room nor time to care for their family members. The number of people living in retirement homes keeps growing and we need increasingly more staff to look after them. This is exactly the issue which the short text "…" published in … on … deals with.

b Write an introduction for the following topic question:
'Should we only eat fruit and vegetables from now on?'

2 Material-based writing

Many students do volunteer work for a short or long period after school.
Comment on the following question:
How does volunteer work benefit young volunteers and the places where they help?
Write a composition of at least 180 words. Include <u>all</u> the material provided.

Material 1

I love places that make you realise how tiny you and your problems are.
Unknown

Material 2

Having a group discussion → S2

A group discussion always has the same structure:

1. **Preparation (by yourself):**
- Understanding the task
- Choosing one's point of view
- Finding one's arguments

2. **Group discussion:**
- Introducing one's topic in about one minute
- Discussing an issue or a question with your group
- Coming to a conclusion

Step A Preparing the discussion

- Read the situation for the discussion and the tasks very carefully.
- Look at the given material and make sure you understand it and are able to present and use it for your arguments.
- Prepare arguments and aspects you would like to include in the discussion.
- Take notes about important aspects, arguments, and helpful words and phrases.
- Look up all the words you do not know. You can use a bilingual dictionary.
- Sometimes you are asked to rank the provided material.

Your school newspaper wants to publish an article about the benefits of travelling, but also the consequences of tourism. You have found different quotes to base your article upon. Decide what your article should talk about, which quote you want to use and how you could structure your article.

In small groups, each group member notes down arguments for why his or her quote should be chosen. Make sure you can explain your quote.

Man cannot discover new oceans unless he has the courage to lose sight of the shore. *Andre Gide, French writer (1869–1951)*

Take only memories, leave only footprints. *Chief Seattle, Suquamish and Duwamish chief (1786–1866)*

Find out how other people live and eat and cook. Learn from them – wherever you go. *Anthony Bourdain, American chef, author and travel documentarian (1956–2018)*

Step B Introducing your topic

Present your most important ideas for the article. State your opinion and the relevance of your chosen quote.

- Use clear language.
- Don't give away everything yet.

USEFUL PHRASES

Introducing a topic

Today I am going to talk about … | I would like to take this opportunity to present my ideas / thoughts about …
The topic of … interests me a lot/is of great interest to me, especially since …
I'm absolutely convinced that … | I firmly believe in … | I've always been in favour of …
I'm for/against the use of …

Step C Main part: Discussion

- Defend your opinion, but stay polite and respectful towards the other participants.
- Refer to the others' arguments when introducing a new argument.
- Turn towards the others when referring to their argument or while they are talking.
- Show that you are confident, but also interested in the others' arguments and their opinion.

Discuss the issue in your group. Also refer to the quotes on page 45.

USEFUL PHRASES

Persuading/objecting
That's a good idea, but … | That might be OK, but … | I really don't think so because … | Why don't you …? | I see what you mean, but … | That's true, but …

Giving reasons
because | since | therefore | consequently | accordingly | As there are … | As a result of … | Due to … | Because of …

Giving examples
for example | for instance | in another case | take the case of | to illustrate | as an illustration | to take another example | as shown by … | as illustrated by … | as expressed by …

Getting more information
Could you tell me some more about …? | Would you mind telling me more about …? | I'd like to know more about … | Something else I was wondering about was …

Agreeing and disagreeing
Exactly. | I couldn't agree more. | That's just what I was thinking. | That's a good point. | I see where you're coming from, but … | I'm not sure if I agree … | Maybe, but don't you think that …?

Comparing and contrasting
Comparing: also | as well as | both | comparatively | in the same way | just as | like | similarly
Contrasting: although | besides | but | compared with | even though | however | in contrast to | instead | nevertheless | on the other hand | rather than | yet

Balancing pros and cons
On the one hand …, on the other hand … | although | however | We shouldn't forget that … | In contrast to … | On the contrary … | Weighing up the pros and cons …

Interrupting politely
If I could just come in here … | Sorry to interrupt, but … | The way I see it … | Um … (repeat until the speaker lets you speak)

Step D Coming to a conclusion

Sum up your most important ideas for the article and try to come to a conclusion.

- Try to find a compromise or solution everyone is happy with.
- It is also OK not to agree with each other at the end.
- You can sum up your most important argument(s)/idea(s) again.
- You can state which arguments/ideas of the others impressed/convinced you the most.

USEFUL PHRASES

Summarising and drawing a conclusion
All things considered … | Taking everything into account … | Briefly … | On the whole … | In short … | Finally … | That's why … | For this reason/these reasons … | Therefore … | As a result … | Consequently …

Part I Reading

Mount Everest traffic jam: 'Wished there was policing'

Mariam Ktiri reached the summit of Mount Everest on May 22, only to get stuck in a traffic jam in the mountain's "death zone" on her descent. The German-Moroccan mountaineer talked to DW about the experience.

It was a picture that went around the world: Congestion on the Mount Everest summit ridge captured by Nirmal Purja. German-Moroccan Mariam Ktiri was one of those stuck in it after reaching the summit of the highest mountain on earth at 2:35 a.m. local time.

"Shortly below the summit, the masses ascended towards us. Many of the people were extremely slow. You could see that they were completely exhausted. It took us about an hour and a half to get below the Hillary Step," she told DW.

For an hour and a half, Ktiri was stuck in the so-called "death zone" where humans can't survive long due to how thin the air is. "Thank God I still had enough oxygen. My Sherpa was constantly checking. At that moment I wished there was policing to stop the people and say: 'Wait until those on their descent have climbed down! Everything else makes no sense.'"

Her sense of accomplishment soon gave way to feelings of disillusionment and frustration as she got caught up in the congestion, despite setting off four hours earlier than planned. "I thought: We set off so early, we didn't even make real breaks," said Ktiri.

"We simply climbed up the mountain in a concentrated manner to avoid this situation. And now on the way back, we were confronted with it. I was angry that people don't think rationally. I tried to signal to those who were coming towards me: Please wait! But they didn't react."

According to Ktiri, the main problem on Everest is those with a lack of climbing experience: "There were some who didn't have a clue. I saw people being dragged by their Sherpas on a short rope as far back as the Khumbu Icefall. If someone can't walk by himself at this point, he is entirely out of place and should turn back."

She hopes that the operators will introduce performance tests to check their clients' mountaineering skills. "The people without a clue are a risk for everyone: for themselves – okay, that's their problem – but also for the others."

According to official estimates, 300 people reached Everest's summit on May 22, a record for a single day. It was a record-breaking spring season in 2019 with around 900 successful summits, though 11 lost their lives in the attempt.

One day after reaching Everest's summit, Ktiri scaled Lhotse with her Sherpa. "I'm so glad I climbed Lhotse too," says Ktiri: "It was like a reward after the frustration at the traffic jam on Everest. On Lhotse on May 23, there were maybe a dozen mountaineers on the route. That was simply beautiful – apart from the corpse, which sits a few meters below the summit."

Climbers are regularly confronted with deaths on these peaks and, on the Lhotse flank, Ktiri had passed the body of Bulgarian Ivan Tomov, who had passed away during his descent a few days earlier due to a high-altitude cerebral edema.

"It looked as if he was looking at the landscape. I was shocked." The feeling intensified later when she passed a group of Sherpas carrying a corpse down. "After that I became quite slow." Despite the psychological upset, she didn't think about turning back, says Ktiri. She was focused on her big goal.

By reaching the summit at Everest, which sits 8,850 meters (29,029 feet) above sea level, Ktiri completed her collection of the "Seven Summits" – the highest mountains each continent has to offer – and all within a year.

Before Everest, Asia's tallest peak, she had scaled Denali (North America, 6,194 meters, 28 May 2018), Elbrus (Europe, 5,642 meters, 13 August 2018), Kilimanjaro (Africa, 5,895 meters, 24 September 2018), Mount Vinson (Antarctica, 4,897 meters, 16 December 2018), Aconcagua (South America, 6,962 meters, 12 January 2019) and the Carstensz Pyramid (Oceania, 4,884 meters, 23 February 2019). [...]

The Seven Summits were "the project of my life until now", says Ktiri. "Mentally, it made me very, very strong. I proved: If you have a goal in mind and you concentrate on it, and above all follow it with discipline, you will always find a way to achieve it. [...]

(728 words)

Stefan Nestler,
Deutsche Welle website, 2019

1 Multiple choice → WB, p. 21/1–2

Choose the most suitable option.

1. What did Mariam notice about the climbers coming up the mountain towards her?
   A They were experienced climbers.
   B None of them had sherpas with them.
   C They were buzzing after reaching the top.
   D They were worn out and taking quite a long time.
2. Which of the following measures did Mariam not take as part of her climb?
   A setting off early
   B taking regular extended breaks
   C fully concentrating while climbing
   D being accompanied by a local Nepalese sherpa
3. What set Mariam's experience of climbing Lhotse apart from that of climbing Everest?
   A It was less crowded.
   B She did it many times over.
   C She did it with a bigger group.
   D She had studied the mountain in greater detail.
4. Which of the following mountains mentioned is not part of the 'Seven Summits'?
   A Everest
   B Aconcagua
   C Lhotse
   D Denali

2 Short-answer questions

Answer the following questions. You may use words from the text.

1. Why was Mariam Ktiri lucky when she got stuck in the death zone?
2. How did Mariam feel when she reached the summit of Mount Everest?
3. What does Mariam suggest to make climbing high mountains a safer experience?

3 Mediation

Beantworten Sie die folgenden Fragen auf Deutsch.

1. Welche riskanten Erfahrungen machte Mariam Ktiri während ihrer Besteigung des Mount Everest? Nennen Sie zwei Erfahrungen.
2. Was war die tragische Begegnung während der Besteigung des Lhotse? Und kommt dies oft vor?
3. Was sagt Mariam über die Erfahrungen rund um das Projekt "Seven Summits"?

Running is a short story by R. S. Thomas, published online in 2011. The story deals with topics such as sport, hope, sense of community, racism and a tragedy.

Running
by R. S. Thomas

1 My uncle was a high school track star. Around here that makes him a reservation legend. I go to the same high school as my uncle did, as my mother did, and all my cousins do, but I'm no track star and I don't fool myself into thinking I'll ever be one. [...]
People still talk about my uncle. They say things like, "Remember Bobby Riley? Man[,] he could run!" They talk about him like he is dead [...]. Maybe it's easier that way, easier for everyone including my uncle. Better to pretend that the boy who ran track is gone.
The first time I remember seeing my uncle run the whole tribe was there, bleachers over-flowing. There were so many of us we formed a solid wall.
Then the race began[,] and everyone had his or her eyes on my uncle or on the idea of my uncle, because he ran so fast he was just a blur. [...]

2 All that year we prayed; little prayers sent up to the sky when everyday tragedies occurred. When Nellie Crow went brain dead at the age of 17 after huffing gasoline, we prayed my uncle would make it to the Olympics. When Edgar Timmons got arrested in the next town over for robbing the mini mart [,...] we prayed that my uncle would make it to the Olympics. When the salmon ran that year and there was less than the year before, with hungry stomachs we prayed that Bobby Riley would make it to the Olympics. And when the lumber company continued to log our land illegally and we were so angry we could hardly speak we sent up silent prayers that Bobby Riley would make it to the Olympics.

3 One late summer day Uncle took me to the city, about an hour's drive from our reservation. When we got there, we went to the movies and got ice cream. He also bought me a pair of running shoes: dark blue with a yellow stripe. I wore my new running shoes on the way home. I curled my feet inside them and felt my legs tingling.
I asked my uncle, "How come you can run so fast?"
He was silent for a minute. I thought maybe he wasn't going to answer. Then he shrugged his shoulders and said, "Maybe if I run fast enough, run long enough maybe none of us will ever have to run again."
I didn't say anything after that. I didn't really understand what he had told me.
As we got about halfway home[,] we caught up to a car ahead of us swerving in and out of its lane. My Uncle nudged his head at the car. "Drunk."
He pulled back a little, keeping a safe distance between us and the car until we could pass, but as we rounded a curve the car went off the side of the road. My uncle pulled over and told me to wait, then got out and ran off toward the car.
Later the police would come with looks and questions for my uncle that sounded more like accusations. Later the drunk man would say he thought the Indian was trying to rob him and he had a permit for his gun. Later the doctors would save my uncle's life, but not his knee. Later, I would get home, take off my new running shoes, with some of my uncle's blood still on them, put them back in the box and put the box onto [a]shelf deep in my closet.

4 I never tried out for track. I haven't given anyone hope I ever will, but sometimes late at night my legs wake me up. They talk to me. They tell me they want to run. They tell me they talk to the muscles of my ancestors and they are jealous. They tell me my ancestors' muscles are warriors and they want to be warriors too. I tell them to be quiet. I roll over and try to go back to sleep, but they say they will never be quiet, never shut-up until I am running.

One night they will wake me and I will listen to them. I will get out of bed, put on my shoes and walk outside. [...] I will run so fast I'll make the earth reverse, go back in time to before my uncle was shot, to before my tribe gave up hope, to before the salmon stopped running. I will run back into the arms of my ancestors, taking my whole tribe with me, and then maybe we will never have to run again. (772 words)

4 Multiple matching → WB, p. 22/3–5

Match the themes (A–G) of the short story with the corresponding text sections (1–4). There are three themes more than you need.

- **A** Hope
- **B** Putting on my uncle's shoes
- **C** The cause of hate
- **D** Communal sacrifice
- **E** Becoming warriors again
- **F** A talented athlete
- **G** Racist accusations

5 Gapped summary

Complete the summary with the most suitable words from the text.
Give the line numbers of the words that you used.

The protagonist discusses his uncle Bobby's reputation as a ■ **1** in his community. He thinks back to how the community put their faith in ■ **2** following local misfortunes, hoping Bobby would compete in the Olympics. At this point of the story the reader doesn't know that Bobby is still alive, but had been shot in the ■ **3.** On the way back from a trip to a nearby town, they had witnessed a ■ **4** driver crashing his car and then shooting at Bobby. A few moments before, the protagonist had ■ **5** Bobby about his talent, but got a cryptic response. Now, after this event, the young protagonist is still resisting the impulse in his ■ **6** to run and live up to his heritage. Eventually, he might do so, revealing the metaphor hidden in Bobby's answer: If only people could outrun time, running fast enough to turn ■ **7** the clock.

Part II Material-based writing

Students Away, a travel agency, has announced an essay competition. The first prize is a class trip to Hamburg for four days.
Write a composition of at least 300 words. Comment on the following question:
'If we consider all the problems of mass tourism, should people just stay at home?'
Include all the material provided.

Material 1

Proteste in Spanien: "Tourist go home!"
Die Besucherzahlen erreichen in Spanien immer neue Rekorde – zum Unmut vieler Einheimischer. Jugend- und Bürgergruppen protestieren mit immer spektakuläreren Aktionen gegen die unerwünschten Massen an Touristen.

Emilio Rappold, *Spiegel* website, 2017

Material 2

Material 3

The very basic core of a man's living spirit is his passion for adventure. The joy of life comes from our encounters with new experiences, and hence there is no greater joy than to have an endlessly changing horizon, for each day to have a new and different sun.

From: *Into the Wild* by Jon Krakauer

Part III Group discussion

After your final exams you would like to go on holiday with some of your classmates. Today you are meeting to plan your trip. You can talk about the following aspects:

- possible destinations
- various activities (party, sports etc.) and fun things to do
- how to make it a great trip for all of you
- how to travel economically and sustainably
- sights
- food and drinks

a Introduce the topic and make some suggestions for the programme (about one minute).

b Discuss your ideas and the offers you found.

c Decide where you want to go and what you want to do there. At the end, sum up your position.

The world of work

Aspects of future occupation's importance to 16–21-year-olds

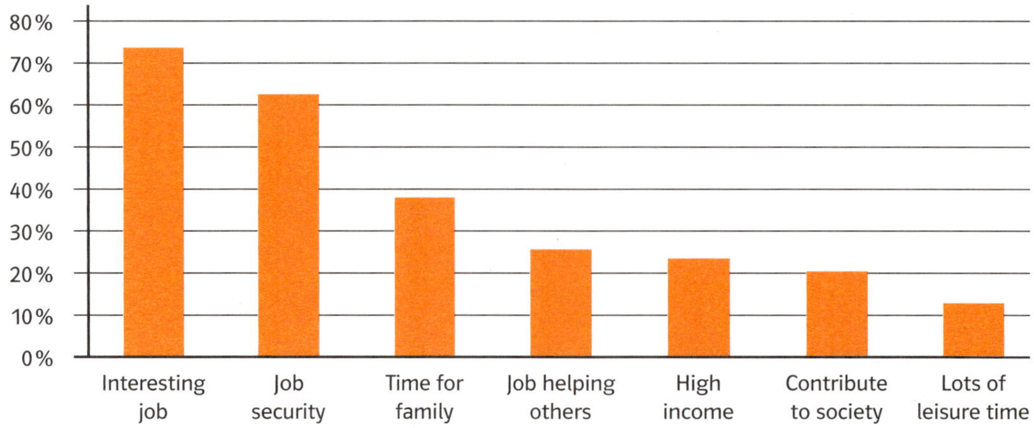

Source: Understanding Society, 2016

1 Talking about pictures → S10.1 → WB, p.24–25/1–3; p.26/1

Look at the pictures on page 52 and do the tasks.

1. Match the words from the word bank with the pictures. You can use a dictionary.

   to brainstorm | automation | gender pay gap | gig economy | glass ceiling | fairness | to earn one's living | equality | wages | to strike | skilled worker | replacement | work-life balance | teamwork | creativity | to work overtime

2. Talk to a partner about why you chose the words and how they are reflected in the pictures.
3. Do the pictures show a more positive or negative aspect of the world of work? Give reasons. → S15 Round robin

GOOD TO KNOW

Gender pay gap
= difference between earnings of men and women

Glass ceiling
= the invisible barrier that prevents a certain group of people (usually applied to women) from rising beyond a certain level in a hierarchy

A13 2 Listening → S3 → G3 → WB, p.26/2

a Listen to the first part of the podcast about today's world of work and complete the following sentences. → H3

1. The online lecture Melanie Bishop gave was named ....
2. ... participants from ... countries were involved in Melanie's lecture.
3. According to Melanie, the gender pay gap refers to ...
4. Germany was the ... country with a pay gap of 19.2%. Only ... and ... had a higher gender pay gap.
5. Some of the reasons for the gender pay gap are ...
6. The wealthiest ... people in the UK have as much money as the poorest ... million.

gross Brutto-
retail Einzelhandel
trade union Gewerkschaft
works council Betriebsrat

A14 **b** Listen to the second part of the podcast. Are the statements true or false? Correct the false statements.

1. The rise of automation will start to cause major unemployment in around 20 years.
2. Melanie argues that new technologies could have a positive effect on employment.
3. The human cloud refers to networks of workers who work on different projects rather than for one company.
4. Many graduates are motivated by financial gains when choosing a company.
5. Trade unions have lost their influence in the modern working world.
6. More online communication means employees need to gain new skills.

3 Talking about a survey → S10.3

Study the diagram on page 52 and answer the following questions.

1. Which aspects of a future job are most/least important to young people today?
2. The diagram is from 2016. Do you think those aspects are still applicable today?

4 Conducting a survey about important job aspects

a Collect your top three aspects from exercise 3 in class and visualise your results in a diagram.

b Discuss your results. What other aspects would you find important?

A Important job skills

1 Before you read → S15 Think-pair-share

What kind of job is your dream job? What are the necessary qualifications and skills for it? Which of these skills and qualifications are important for other jobs as well?

A15

What are the top skills that'll get you a job when you graduate?

Have you got the key skills graduate employers look for? You'll need to give examples of these essential competencies in your job applications and interviews to impress recruiters and get hired.

Graduate employers place a lot of emphasis on finding candidates with the right skills and competencies for their organisations. Depending on the career sector and profession you choose to work in, there could be very specific skills, abilities and knowledge needed to do the job. However, complementing these are general competencies and behaviours that are essential for successful working. These are the key employability skills – the core skills that will make you effective at work, whatever job you do. They are sometimes known as transferable skills because you develop them over time and take them with you as your career develops; think of them as your passport to career success. You'll need to draw on your work experience to give evidence of these skills. [...]

1 ______

This is about knowing how a business or industry works and what makes a company tick. Showing that you have an understanding of what the organisation wants to achieve through its products and services, and how it competes in its marketplace.

2 Communication

This covers verbal and written communication, and listening. It's about being clear, concise and focused; being able to tailor your message for the audience and listening to the views of others.

3 Teamwork

You'll need to prove that you're a team player but also have the ability to manage and delegate to others and take on responsibility. It's about building positive working relationships that help everyone to achieve goals and business objectives. [...]

4 Problem solving

You need to display an ability to take a logical and analytical approach to solving problems and resolving issues. It's also good to show that you can approach problems from different angles.

5 ______

You may not be a manager straight away, but graduates need to show potential to motivate teams and other colleagues that may work for them. It's about assigning and delegating tasks well, setting deadlines and leading by good example.

6 ______

This is about showing that you can prioritise, work efficiently and productively, and manage your time well. It's also good to be able to show employers how you decide what is important to focus on and get done, and how you go about meeting deadlines.

7 ______

Employers want people to have a bit of get-up-and-go. Working life presents many challenges and you need to show

2 **to graduate** einen Abschluss erlangen
4 **competency** Fähigkeit
5 **recruiter** Personalvermittler/-in
13 **to complement** ergänzen
17 **core skills** Kernkompetenz
32 **to compete** *hier:* sich schlagen
37 **concise** präzise
38 **to tailor** zuschneiden
47 **business objective** Geschäftsziel
52 **to resolve issues** Probleme lösen
54 **angle** (Blick-)Winkel
59 **to assign** zuweisen
60 **to set a deadline** eine Frist setzen
64 **to prioritise** Prioritäten setzen

employers that you're the kind of person who will find a way through, even when the going gets tough … and stay cheerfulish. [...]

8 Resilience

Graduate employers look for resilience in their recruits because it enables employees to cope with change, problems and stress. Find out how to develop your resilience and how employers assess it during the recruitment process.

9 Analytical skills

Analytical skills enable you to work with different kinds of information, see patterns and trends and draw meaningful conclusions. Analytical skills are often assessed using aptitude or psychometric tests.

10

Spotting gaps in the market, suggesting ways to improve processes, or coming up with new ideas are all signs of an entrepreneurial approach. You don't have to set up your own business to make use of your enterprise skills; many employers will be looking out for graduate recruits with these qualities. [...] (568 words)

Target Jobs website, 2019

77 **cheerfulish** *(ugs.)* einigermaßen gut gelaunt
78 **resilience** Widerstandsfähigkeit
80 **recruit** neu eingestellte Arbeitskraft
80 **to enable** ermöglichen; befähigen
83 **to assess** beurteilen
90 **aptitude** Begabung
90 **psychometric** *hier:* psychologisch
93 **gap in the market** Marktlücke
98 **enterprise** unternehmerisch

2 Multiple choice → WB, p. 27/1–3

Choose the most suitable option. The tasks refer to lines 1–18.

1. You can best prove your general skills …
   - **A** by describing them in your application.
   - **B** by listing them in your CV.
   - **C** in a job interview.
   - **D** in practical training.
2. Graduate employers look closely at possible candidates to find out …
   - **A** how much they know about a given topic.
   - **B** whether they have the qualifications for the job.
   - **C** how specific their skills are.
   - **D** whether they are easily stressed.
3. Which of the following examples does not fit the definition of "employability skills" given in the text?
   - **A** self-management
   - **B** collaboration
   - **C** educability
   - **D** programming
4. Essential skills for a job …
   - **A** add to your specific skills.
   - **B** are also called specific skills.
   - **C** show your knowledge about a job.
   - **D** show your knowledge about a company.

3 Multiple matching → H 3

Match the headings (A–H) with the paragraphs of the text that do not have one (1, 5, 6, 7, 10). There are three headings more than you need.

- **A** Intercultural competence
- **B** Entrepreneurial skills
- **C** Business acumen
- **D** Leadership
- **E** Willingness to learn
- **F** Organisation
- **G** Perseverance and motivation
- **H** Creativity

4 Mediation

Beantworten Sie die folgenden Fragen auf Deutsch.
Die Fragen beziehen sich auf die Zeilen 19–33.

1. Warum werden die „employability skills“ auch als „transferable skills“ bezeichnet?
2. Weshalb ist es wichtig, in einem Bewerbungsgespräch auf Arbeitserfahrung zurückgreifen zu können?
3. Warum ist es wichtig zu wissen, wie eine Firma „tickt“?

5 Short-answer questions

a Copy the table and add the headings from exercise 4.

b Complete the sentences with the information from the given paragraphs (2–4, 8–9). You may use words from the text.

	Employability skills	
1	…	…
2	Communication	You need to be …
3	Teamwork	Be a team player but also be able to …
4	Problem solving	Look at problems …
5	…	…
6	…	…
7	…	…
8	Resilience	It helps to …
9	Analytical skills	With these skills you can …
10	…	…

c Take notes on paragraphs 1, 5, 6, 7 and 10 and complete the column on the right side of the table.

6 Words matter → S11.1

a Find the matching words for the following definitions given in the text on pages 54–55. Give the line numbers.

A to make/adapt sth to suit a specific need or purpose or to make clothes
B to list or rate sth in order of importance
C a specific time before which sth must be done
D an ability to recover from or adjust to change and misfortunate situations

b Explain the following phrases from the text in your own words.

1. essential competences (l. 4)
2. to make sth tick (ll. 28–29)
3. to delegate (l. 44)
4. get-up-and-go (l. 72)
5. when the going gets tough (ll. 75–76)
6. to draw conclusions (ll. 88–89)
7. to spot gaps in the market (l. 93)

7 A step further → S 10.1

a Get together in small groups. Each of you chooses a picture which best describes how you feel about your skills and qualifications, your strengths and weaknesses. Take notes. Describe the picture to the other members of your group and explain why you chose it.

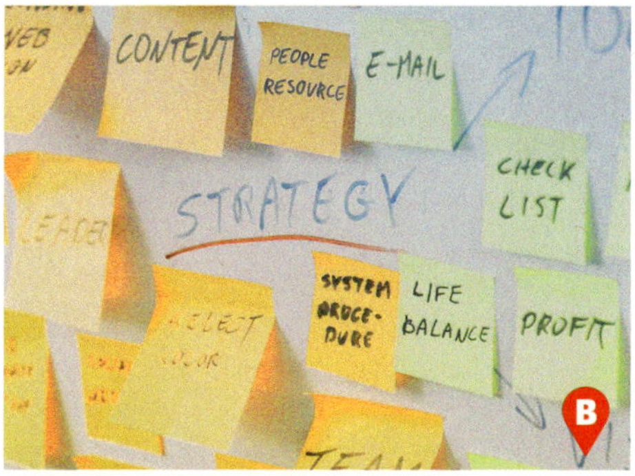

b You have an appointment with a career advisor. In preparation for it they have sent you the following email. Read it and write a reply. Use the information from the text on pages 54–55 and your notes from **a**. Then exchange your email with a partner.
→ S 15 Peer correction

To: student@school…com
From: advisor@careersoffice.support…uk
Subject: Preparation for our meeting next week
Attachment: Article "What are the top skills …"

Dear …,
In order for me to prepare fully for our meeting, I would like you to do a few things for me. First of all, please read the article attached to this email about the skills employers are looking for.
Following this, I would like you to reflect on your own skills and submit a short composition outlining your strengths and weaknesses. This will help us identify what kind of job would be most suitable for you.
Please send me your text in the next couple of days.
I'm looking forward to our meeting next week.
Sincerely,
…

B Modern slavery

1 Before you read

a Choose one item of your outfit (e.g. T-shirt, jacket, shoes) and find out where it was made. Discuss with a partner what you know about the working conditions there.

b Search online to find out about the industry and the working conditions in that country. Share your findings in class.
→ S15 1-minute presentation

Corban Addison studied law at the University of Virginia (USA) and worked as a lawyer for several years. He is active in different human rights initiatives. His novel *A Harvest of Thorns* is about the garment industry and the people who serve it. It describes modern slavery in the developing world and those who want to change the system.

A16

A Harvest of Thorns

by Corban Addison

Jashel looked out the window as the train glided toward Kuala Lumpur, saw the sun peek out from behind the clouds, brightening the city skyline. He thought back to the day he welcomed Mr Amin into his mother's home and took a new path into the future. Mr Amin was from Dhaka, but he was well known in the village. He was a recruiter for an outsourcing agency that placed able-bodied Bangladeshis from the rural areas in employment overseas – construction and housekeeping in the Middle East, electronics in Southeast Asia, and apparel in a dozen countries between Jordan and Vietnam. [...]

'Assalamu alaykum,' said a gray-haired man with glasses. Jashel shook the man's hand. 'Wa alaykum assalam.' 'I am Foysol,' the man said in Bengali, surveying the group. 'My agency works with Mr Amin. Good. All of you are here. Come along. [...]'

His destination had arrived. Before the van stood a metal gate with a large printed sign – Rightaway Garments. The guards waved the van through, and Foysol found a parking spot alongside a handful of other vehicles. He turned off the ignition and swiveled around in his seat.

'Now that we are here, I will take your passports for safekeeping. I will do the same with your work permits. I will return them to you when the time is right.'

Jashel clutched his backpack, feeling a vague sense of foreboding. Mr Amin had said nothing about relinquishing his passport and work permit. In fact, the agent had advised him to keep the documents with him at all times in case a police officer or immigration official ever questioned his legal status. He watched the others reach into their bags and hand over their passports. [...]

Jashel shook his head forcefully. 'The documents are mine. I will keep them safe.'

As soon as he spoke the words, Foysol's expression hardened. 'You are a guest of Malaysia. And you are my guest. You will follow my rules or your stay will be difficult.' He extended his hand, palm open. 'Now, give me your passport.'

Jashel's heart began to race, but still he refused. Foysol glowered at him. 'Let me tell you what will happen if you do not obey. I will report to immigration that you arrived with

7 **outsourcing** *Ausgliederung von Produktion oder Dienstleistungen an Externe*
7 **able-bodied** körperlich gesund
9 **apparel** Bekleidung
11 **to survey** anschauen
15 **alongside** neben
15 **ignition** Zündung
15 **to swivel around** sich umdrehen
18 **permit** Erlaubnis
19 **to clutch** festhalten; umklammern
19 **foreboding** Vorahnung
20 **to relinquish** abgeben
22 **legal status** Aufenthaltstitel
27 **palm** Handfläche
28 **to glower** zornig anschauen
29 **to obey** gehorchen

HIV. They will revoke your work permit. The factory will disown you, and your contract will be void. I will then hand you over to the immigration police, and they will take you to a detention facility where you will rot until you are deported, either because your family bought an airline ticket, or because the government finally decided to get rid of you.' Again, Foysol put out his hand. 'Your passport, please.'

The blood drained from Jashel's face. If Rightaway Garments voided his contract, not only would he forfeit the chance to send money home to his family [...] but the lender from whom he had borrowed two hundred thousand taka would call the note and foreclose on his family's property, leaving them destitute [...].

At that moment, Jashel realized that Foysol held his fate like a parrot in a cage. If he sang the agent's tune, Foysol would watch over him. If he disobeyed, Foysol would ruin him. He slipped a trembling hand into his backpack and withdrew his passport, handing it over to the agent.

Foysol opened it and examined Jashel's picture. He grinned malevolently. 'You're smarter than you look, Jashel Sayed Parveen. Let's hope you stay that way.'

(582 words)

30 **to revoke** widerrufen
30 **to disown sb/sth** sich von jdm./etw. distanzieren
31 **void** ungültig
32 **detention facility** Internierungslager
32 **to rot** verrotten
36 **to forfeit** einbüßen
38 **to foreclose** zwangsvollstrecken
38 **destitute** verarmt; mittellos
43 **malevolent** bösartig

2 Multiple choice → WB, p. 28/1–3

Choose the most suitable option.

1. Which adjective best describes the atmosphere at the beginning of the text (ll. 3–9)?
   A tense
   B romantic
   C optimistic
   D desperate
2. What does Mr Armin's company do?
   A recruiting people from Jordan and Vietnam
   B finding workers for various industries overseas
   C outsourcing the apparel industry to Bangladesh
   D constructing and maintaining houses in the Middle East
3. Where exactly does Jashel arrive in Malaysia?
   A mosque
   B textile factory
   C amusement park
   D immigration detention
4. When first asked to give up his passport, Jashel felt as if ...
   A somebody was threatening him.
   B something was holding him back.
   C something bad was about to happen.
   D there was additional weight in his backpack.

3 Mediation → H 3

Beantworten Sie die folgenden Fragen auf Deutsch.

1. Bevor er ihm unverhohlen droht, wie versucht Foysol Jashel zunächst zu überzeugen, ihm seinen Ausweis auszuhändigen?
2. Welche Konsequenzen spielt Jashel in seinem Kopf durch, falls sein Vertrag aufgelöst würde (zwei Aspekte)?
3. Was ist mit dem Ausdruck „If he sang the agent's tune" (Z. 39–40) gemeint und welche Bedeutung hat er im Zusammenhang mit dem Text?

4 Gapped summary

Complete the summary with the most suitable words from the text. Give the line numbers of the words that you used.

Jashel travels by train to take up a position abroad organised for him by an ■ 1 company – more specifically, by a well-known local man named Mr Amin, who recruits people from ■ 2 parts of Bangladesh. When Jashel arrives at the facility, he and the other recruits meet Foysol, who wishes to take their travel ■ 3, pretending to keep them safe. As Foysol reaches out for them, Jashel hestitates to hand his passport over. Jashel is stuck since he had borrowed a considerable sum from a lender, and his family's property would be at risk if he cannot pay it back. It is clear the agency will cancel his contract, and he will end up in a ■ 4 centre for illegal immigrants if he doesn't obey Foysol's ■ 5. Because of this, he feels powerless and compares himself to a ■ 6 at Foysol's mercy. The text ends by indicating the danger ahead as Foysol ■ 7 smiles and subtly makes fun of Jashel about his difficult position.

5 Working with literature → S 8.5

Discuss the following aspects of the extract of the novel.

1. Explain why Jashel has come to work at Rightaway Garments.
2. Characterise Foysol. Use examples from the text to back up your answer.
3. Comment on Jashel's behaviour. Could he have acted differently?

USEFUL PHRASES

Personal data
... is a 20-year-old young man / middle-aged woman in her forties of ... origin.

Appearance
He/She is described as being attractive | pretty | plain | ugly | elegant | dirty | tall | small | ...
He/She has brown hair | dark | fair skin | ...

Character traits
He/She seems evil | kind | charismatic | (dis-)honest | hard-working | lazy | selfish | brave | cowardly | arrogant | shy | confident | weird | wise | foolish | ...
... is portrayed as ...
... his/her behavior indicates that he/she is ...

6 A step further → S 1.1 → G 1.15

Look at your research in exercise 1 again. Now that you know more about the exploitation going on in many industries, you want to organise a discussion at school to raise awareness about the issue.

a In small groups, think of a catchy name for the event.

b Create an invitation in the form of a social media post, a flyer, an announcement on your school homepage etc.
Make sure to include:
- what you want to raise awareness about
- why it is important to do that
- what we can do to solve the issue

c Present your product to the class. Your classmates give feedback.
→ S 15 Tip-top

C Automating healthcare

1 Before you read

a Describe the situation in the picture. In which job fields can robots be helpful? Exchange your ideas with a partner.

b Think about the advantages and disadvantages of robots as a workforce.
→ S15 Think-pair-share

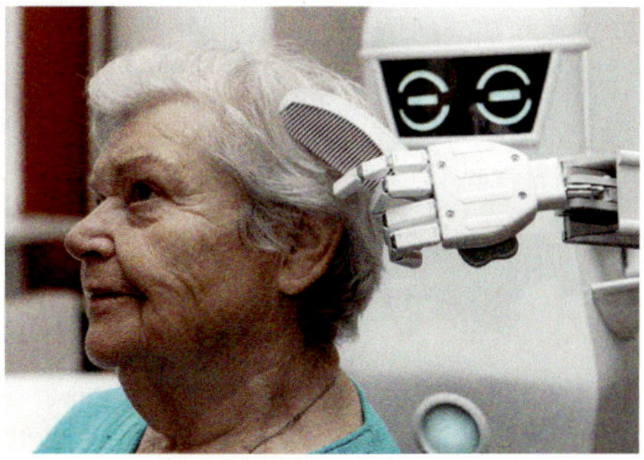

A17

What the world can learn from Japan's robots

Japan is rolling out robots in nursing homes, offices and schools as its population ages and workforce shrinks. What can it teach other countries facing the same problems?

Japan is changing: a rapidly ageing society, a record-breaking influx of visitors from overseas, and more robots than ever. That's where the country's young people come in. *Gen J*, a new series by *BBC Worklife*, keeps you up to speed on how the nation's next generation is shaping the Japan of tomorrow.

At a sleek office building in Shinagawa, Tokyo, workers are strolling in and out for lunch. As they walk through the glass doors, they pass two security guards, each dutifully flanking the passage in stern silence. It all seems pretty unremarkable, until you realise one of those security guards is a robot. Standing up to five feet tall with wheels and a blue police cap, "his" name is Ugo. His battery lasts up to half a workday, and every two hours he'll do a routine patrol around the building – even summoning lifts by pushing the call button himself. His digital "face" – which usually displays two big blue cartoony eyes – is replaced with the Japanese text for "on duty".

"It's important for the robot to feel cute, so you're not intimidated," says Ken Matsui, CEO of Mira Robotics, the start-up behind Ugo. Right now, the police bot – whose built-in camera allows guards downstairs to see things from the robot's point of view – is one of only two prototypes in the country. But Matsui says companies in China and South Korea are interested in his company's work, which also includes cleaning robots for use in houses and schools.

In recent years, headlines, pundits and politicians have often warned that we're in the midst of a job-stealing robot revolution; but roboticists argue that their creations will complement, rather than replace, us. In Japan, the robots are already here – what's more, many are actively embracing the robot age, from suburban nursing homes to the highest levels of government, which announced an investment of 100bn yen ($100m) in robot development a few years ago. Some entities are even highlighting robotic colleagues as a selling point to young, new recruits. [...]

In Tokyo's Silver Wing nursing home, about two dozen seniors are sitting in the common area as pudding cups are distributed. In the middle of the room is a staff member and a humanoid robot named Pepper, who is leading the room in group games and exercises. [...] But it's not only in the common room that robotics is being employed. Upstairs, staff have access to robotic exoskeletons that fit around the waist and lower back: these apparatuses ease the severe body strain as

2 **to roll sth out** etw. auf den Markt bringen
3 **to shrink** schrumpfen
6 **influx** Zustrom
10 **to keep sb up to speed** jdn. auf dem Laufenden halten
17 **to flank** flankieren
24 **routine patrol** Routinerundgang
25 **to summon a lift** einen Aufzug rufen
42 **pundit** Experte/Expertin
43 **to be in the midst of** mittendrin sein
54 **entity** Einheit; Einrichtung
66 **exoskeleton** Außenskelett; tragbares Exoskelett
68 **body strain** körperliche Belastung

75 **fertility rate** Geburtenrate
88 **advisory firm** Beratungsfirma
89 **deployment** Verwendung
99 **top vendor** Spitzenlieferant/-in
105 **favour** Vorteil
109 **to itch to do sth** begierig sein/ darauf brennen, etw. zu tun

they help their elderly clients get in and out of bed. (Some studies have shown that over 80% of nurses in Japan experience lower back problems.)

"Japan is facing major demographic challenges due to the elderly wave, low fertility rates and a shrinking population. This leads to a number of issues facing Japanese society which the West can learn from," says Roger A Søraa, robotics researcher at Centre for Technology and Society in Norway. "Elderly care facilities and hospitals see a severe lack of healthcare workers; there are not enough humans to do the tasks the way they used to be done." [...]

Still, whether Japan will lead a 'robots in the workforce' revolution remains unclear. Rian Whitton, senior robotics analyst at global tech market advisory firm ABI Research, says that robot deployment in places like nursing homes is low in practice and that Japan's recently eased rules for low-wage migrant workers show that the government knows widespread automation isn't yet possible. He also points out that China and the US, for example, are quickly catching up to Japan in areas like homecare robotics. "Ultimately, Japan is going to go from the top vendor for robotics globally, as it used to be, to being a relatively strong player alongside Germany, South Korea, Singapore and Taiwan," he says. "[Japan] will lose influence relative to the Chinese and American robotics ecosystems." [...]

Yet in Japan's favour is its very long history of embracing robots, not fearing them. In the West, pop culture and media often frame robots as job-stealing Terminators itching to start a revolution. [...]

(718 words)

Bryan Lufkin, *BBC* website, 2020

2 Short-answer questions → H 3 → WB, p. 29/1–2

Answer the following questions. You may use words from the text (ll. 1–72).

1. What is the series *Generation J* about?
2. What is special about the security guard named Ugo?
3. What are Ugo's duties?
4. Do a lot of companies have someone like Ugo? Is there a reason?
5. Which two forms of robots are used in Tokyo's Silver Wing nursing home?
6. Which tasks do they perform there?

3 Gapped summary

Complete the summary with the most suitable words from the text (ll. 73–109). Give the line numbers of the words that you used.

Japan is still leading the way in robotics but other major players are ■ ■ **1**. Whereas in the West people are rather reluctant about robotics, Japan has a way of ■ **2** robots. They have to use robots in hospitals for example because there are just not enough ■ ■ **3**. Moreover, the population in Japan is getting older on average, leading to ■ ■ **4**. The Japanese government realises that ■ **5** will not be the ultimate solution just yet. Thus, they have made it easier for ■ **6** workers from abroad to come to Japan. It remains to be seen whether there will actually be a robotics ■ **7** led by Japan.

4 Mediation

Beantworten Sie die folgenden Fragen auf Deutsch.

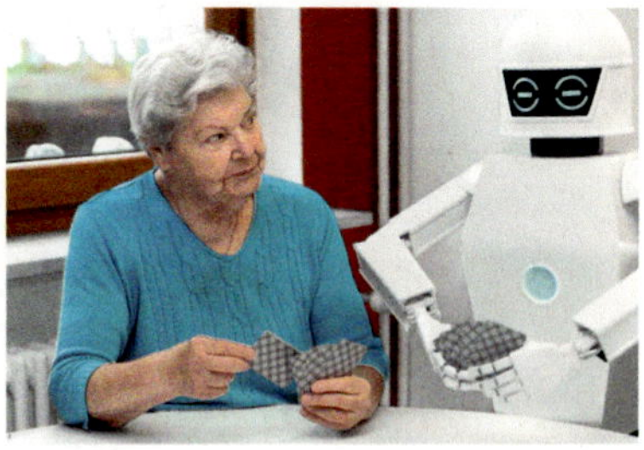

1. Wie verändert sich Japan derzeit noch neben rekordverdächtigem Tourismus und immer mehr Robotik?
2. Was ist laut Ken Matsui wichtig, damit Roboter nicht bedrohlich wirken?
3. Für welche Arbeitsbereiche entwickelt Mira Robotics Roboter?
4. Erläutern Sie knapp, welche zwei Seiten es bei der Diskussion um Robotik gibt.

5 Words matter → S 11.1

a Make a list of ten important words from the text referring to robots in social life.

b Compare your words with a partner and agree on 15 words. Give reasons.

c Compare your list with that of another pair. Agree on the 20 most important words and write them on cards. Put the cards in a pile and take turns to pick a card. Talk for 30 seconds about the word in the context of our changing world.

6 Working with texts

a Analyse the structure of the text.
1. When does the author use narrative elements in his article?
2. What effect does this have on the reader?

b Why does the author quote Ken Matsui and Roger A Søraa?

A18 7 Listening → S 3 → WB, p. 29/3

Listen to the podcast 'Social change'. Copy the table. For each topic, take notes on the type of change discussed. Write down the pros and cons.

	Topics	Type of change	Pros	Cons
1	Cars and the automobile industry	…	…	…
2	Equality and gender roles	…	…	…
3	The world of work	…	…	…
4	Social lives	…	…	…

to hamper (be)hindern
obsolete überflüssig
abusive beleidigend

8 A step further → S 1.1

a Organise a discussion on the following question:
'Should robots take care of elderly people?'

Get together in groups of four: two students are in favour of robots as caregivers and two are against it.
Make a list with arguments to support your point of view. To better prepare for the discussion, you can note down counterarguments the others might come up with.

b Discuss the question in your group presenting your pro and con arguments.
Then make a list of the three strongest pros and cons. Share your findings in class.

Working from home → S 6.1

1 Collecting and analysing arguments → H 3 → WB, p. 30/1–2

In order to plan your composition efficiently, you can follow these steps:
1. Read the task carefully and mark important information (e.g. the topic question, word count etc.). Then scan the material. Is there anything that strikes you right away?
2. Brainstorm on the topic. What do I know about the topic? What do I find interesting about it?
3. Organise your brainstorming. You can use mind maps, a pro/con table or you simply outline ideas using bullet points.
4. Structure your ideas. What is your thesis? What can you use for your arguments?

A good structure for an argument is: topic sentence – supporting fact(s) – example(s)
This will take some time, but it will save you time and energy later when you actually put your thoughts on paper.

a The world of work is rapidly changing. More and more people are working remotely – in their 'home offices'. Plan your composition as presented in the box above on the following question:
'What are the advantages and disadvantages of the new approaches in the world of work?'

Material 1

Das Ziel der Neuen Arbeit besteht nicht darin, die Menschen von der Arbeit zu befreien, sondern die Arbeit so zu transformieren, dass sie freie, selbstbestimmte, menschliche Wesen hervorbringt.

Frithjof Bergmann, founder of the 'new work'-movement

Material 2

b Compare your writing plan with a partner. How do your approaches differ? What would you do differently? → S 15 Tip-top

c Analyse the following argument with the help of these tasks:

1. Identify the different elements (thesis, topic sentence, supporting fact, example).
2. How has the material been used in the argument?
3. Choose three expressions that you would like to use in your own composition.

Remote working is another positive aspect of the new world of work. In some jobs, people can work from anywhere in the world. These people are often called 'digital nomads' because they can travel and work at the same time, for example in a café or on the train, and regularly change places. All they need is the right equipment: A laptop and a solid internet connection. Of course, this new way of working is especially suitable for people whose main tasks are done at their laptop. Most digital nomads come from the US, with 15 million people working remotely. The huge advantage of remote working is that it provides a flexible and self-determined approach to work.

d Write a composition of at least 180 words on the topic question from **a**.
Use <u>all</u> the material provided.

Planning your career → S 2

1 Talking about preferences and giving advice

a What is important in your future job? Give reasons.
Take notes on the following aspects:

- inside vs. outside
- people/material vs. computers
- change vs. routine
- team work vs. work alone
- analysing vs. creating
- responsibility vs. strong boss
- work vs. free time

USEFUL PHRASES

I like/don't like … | I'd like to … | I would rather … | I'd prefer … | I (really/quite/don't) love/enjoy/don't mind … | … is important/not important to me.

b Prepare a 1-minute talk: What are your plans after graduating?
Consider your notes from **a**. → S 15 1-minute presentation

c Get together with a partner. Listen to each other's 1-minute talk and take notes.
Give feedback. Was it well-presented? → S 15 Tip-top

d The pictures show different jobs. Give your partner advice on a suitable job.
Give reasons. Feel free to include a job other than the ones given. → H 3

gardener

researcher

web developer

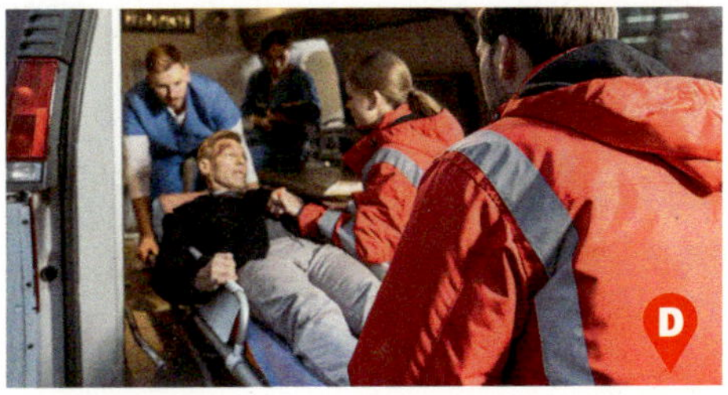

paramedic

construction engineer

craftsman/-woman

2 Group discussion

Your school is planning a 'Careers day' to inform students about their options after graduating. Your group has been asked to present ideas for that day. Today you are meeting to discuss your ideas and plan your next steps.
You can talk about the following points:
- Who should be invited (e.g. guest speakers)?
- How could you make this event special?
- What could attract many visitors?
- What activities could you offer?
- What do students need to plan their future?
- Where can students find advice and information?
- When is advice (un-)useful?

GOOD TO KNOW

A **careers day** is a great chance for students to learn about different jobs. Professionals share their experiences and advice and talk about educational requirements, job possibilities and career potential.

Material

Sectoral job aspirations of students aged 14/15 and 17/18 in the UK

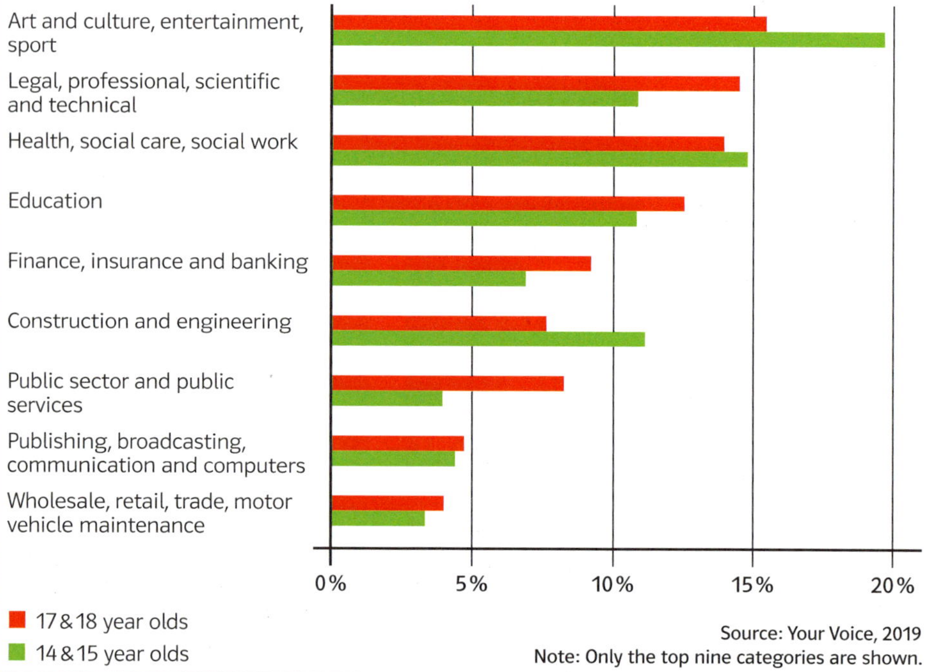

Source: Your Voice, 2019
Note: Only the top nine categories are shown.

a Introduce the topic and say what could help you to plan your future. What important aspects do you need to consider for the event? (about one minute)

b Discuss and explain your ideas. What would you like to offer on the careers day? You can include the given material.

c Sum up your ideas and positions. Try to agree on a list of ideas for your careers day.

Part I Reading

Dave Eggers is an American writer, editor and publisher. The following text is the introductory chapter of *The Circle*, a novel set in the near future. It was published in 2013 and tells the story of Mae Holland's career in a global tech company.

The Circle

by Dave Eggers

MY GOD, MAE thought. It's heaven.

The campus was vast and rambling, wild with Pacific color, **1**, shaped by the most eloquent hands. On land that had once been a shipyard, then a drive-in movie theater, then a flea market, then blight, there were now soft green hills and a Calatrava fountain. And a picnic area, with tables arranged in concentric circles. And tennis courts, clay and grass. And a volleyball court, where tiny children from the company's daycare center were running, squealing, weaving like water. Amid all this was a workplace, too, four hundred acres of brushed steel and glass on the headquarters **2**. The sky above was spotless and blue.

Mae was making her way through all of this, walking from the parking lot to the main hall, **3**. The walkway wound around lemon and orange trees and its quiet red cobblestones were replaced, occasionally, by tiles with imploring messages of inspiration. "Dream," one said, the word laser-cut into the red stone. "Participate," said another. There were dozens: "Find Community." "Innovate." "Imagine." She just missed stepping on the hand of a young man in a grey jumpsuit; he was installing a new stone that said "Breathe."

On a sunny Monday in June, Mae stopped in front of the main door, standing below the logo etched into the glass above. Though the company was less than six years old, its name and logo – a circle surrounding a knitted grid, with a small 'c' in the center – **4**. There were over ten thousand employees on this, the main campus, but the Circle had offices all over the globe, and was hiring hundreds of gifted young minds every week. It had been voted **5** four years running. [...]

A million people, a billion, wanted to be where Mae was at this moment, entering this atrium, thirty feet high and shot through with California light, on her first day working for **6**.

She pushed open the heavy door. The front hall was as long as a parade, as tall as a cathedral. There were offices everywhere above, four floors high on either side, every wall made of glass. Briefly dizzy, she looked downward, and in the immaculate glossy floor, she saw her own face reflected, looking worried. She shaped her mouth into a smile, **7**.

"You must be Mae."

Mae turned to find a beautiful young head floating atop a scarlet scarf and white silk blouse.

"I'm Renata," she said.

"Hi Renata. I'm looking for –"

"Annie. I know. She's on her way." A sound, a digital droplet, came from Renata's ear. "She's actually ..." Renata was looking at Mae **8**. Retinal interface, Mae assumed. Another innovation born here.

"She's in the Old West," Renata said, focusing on Mae again, "but she'll be here soon." [...]

"So you've seen the pool, the sports area." Renata waved her hand off toward a blue parallelogram and an angular building, the gym, rising behind it. "Over there there's the yoga studio, crossfit, Pilates, massages, spinning. I heard you spin? Behind that there's the bocce courts, and the new tetherball setup. The cafeteria's just across the grass ..." Renata pointed to the lush rolling green, with a handful of young people, dressed professionally and splayed about like sunbathers. "And here we are."
They stood before the Renaissance, another building with a forty-foot atrium, a Calder mobile turning slowly above.
"Oh, I love Calder," Mae said.
Renata smiled. "I know you do." They looked up at it together. "This one used to hang in the French parliament. Something like that."
The wind that had followed them in now turned the mobile such that an arm pointed to Mae, as if welcoming her personally. Renata took her elbow. "Ready? Up this way."
They entered an elevator of glass, tinted faintly orange. Lights flickered on and Mae saw her name appear on the walls, along with her high school yearbook photo. WELCOME MAE HOLLAND. A sound, something like a gasp, left Mae's throat. [...] Just when she couldn't stand it anymore, the photo disappeared. "Yeah, everything's on sensors," Renata said. "The elevator reads your ID, and then says hello. Annie gave us that photo. You guys must be tight if she's got high school pictures of you. Anyway, hope you don't mind. We do that for visitors, mostly. They're usually impressed." (772 words)

1 Multiple matching → WB, p. 31/1–2

Eight phrases have been cut from the text. Match the most suitable phrases (A–J) with the gaps (1–8). There are two phrases more than you need.

A the world's most admired company
B but was seeing something else
C could be found everywhere around the campus
D were already among the best-known in the world
E of the most influential company in the world
F and yet the smallest detail had been carefully considered
G feeling a presence behind her
H the only company that really mattered at all
I trying to look as if she belonged
J but did not realize that somebody was there

2 Meditation

Beantworten Sie die folgenden Fragen auf Deutsch.

1. Wie sieht die Umgebung des Firmengebäudes aus (3–4 Aspekte)?
2. Warum ist es erstaunlich, dass die Firma weltbekannt ist?
3. Warum fühlt sich Mae an ihrem ersten Arbeitstag privilegiert?
4. Wie kann Renata wissen, wo Annie in dem Moment ist?
5. Wie reagiert Mae auf die Willkommensnachricht im Aufzug?
6. Warum erscheint die Willkommensnachricht?

Not simply overtime work

Jack Ma

One of China's richest men has been criticized for endorsing the controversial culture of 12-hour workdays in the country's red-hot tech industry, saying employees who worked longer hours will get the "rewards of hard work." Jack Ma, founder of e-commerce giant Alibaba, has spoken out on social media [...] in support of the Chinese work practice known as "996". The number refers to working from 9 am to 9 pm six days a week and is said to be common among the country's big technology companies and start-ups. "If we find things we like, 996 is not a problem," Ma said in a blog post [...] on Chinese social media site Weibo. "If you don't like [your work], every minute is torture," he added.

Ma's comments prompted criticism from Chinese social media users. "Did you ever think about the elderly at home who need care, (or) the children who need company?" wrote a Weibo user with the online moniker stupidcan123, in response to Ma's post. "If all enterprises enforce a 996 schedule, no one will have children because of a lack of time", they added.

Chinese state media also slammed those companies that make staff put in long hours at the office, without referencing Ma's post directly. "Advocating hard work and commitment does not mean forcing overtime," wrote state-run newspaper *People's Daily* in a commentary published Sunday. "The mandatory enforcement of 996 overtime culture not only reflects the arrogance of business managers, but also is unfair and impractical."

Ma said that he did not intend to defend the practice of working long hours, but wanted to "pay tribute" to employees who did. "The real 996 is not simply overtime work," he said, adding that everyone has the right to choose their own lifestyle but those who work shorter hours "won't taste the happiness and rewards of hard work." [...] Ma said he had never regretted working 12-hour days. "I personally think that 996 is a huge blessing," he said. "How do you achieve the success you want without paying extra effort and time?" Ma added that any prospective employees of Alibaba, one of the world's biggest tech companies, should be prepared to work 12 hours a day if they want to succeed. "Or why bother joining? We don't lack those who work eight hours comfortably," he said.

Other high-profile figures in China's tech industry have reportedly defended long working hours in the technology industry. Richard Liu, founder of Alibaba rival JD.com, reportedly criticized employees at the company who did not work hard enough as "slackers." [...]

Long workdays in the high tech sector are not unique to China. Tesla co-founder Elon Musk has previously said he worked up to 120 hours per week when the electric vehicle maker struggled with production delays. "There are way easier places to work, but nobody ever changed the world on 40 hours a week," he posted on social media site Twitter in November last year. (491 words)

Serenitie Wang and Daniel Shane, *CNN* website, 2019

3 Short-answer questions → WB, p. 31/3; p. 32/4

Answer the following questions. You may use words from the text.

1. Which metaphorical expression is used to illustrate that China's technology industry is very successful?
2. What does '996' stand for?
3. What parts of the population suffer from 996 although they don't work?
4. Why does Alibaba still expect 996 from its employees?

4 Multiple choice

Choose the most suitable option.

1. What criticism has been voiced in social media regarding 996?
   A The birth rate will decline.
   B The elderly will not be able to keep up.
   C Enterprises are forced to implement 996.
   D There are companies that employ children.

2. What's the Chinese state media's attitude towards 996?
   A They strongly criticise the idea of 996.
   B They call for hard work and commitment.
   C They think that Jack Ma might have a point.
   D They recommend the mandatory enforcement of 996.

3. What does 996 mean to Jack Ma personally?
   A It is a source of regret.
   B He feels blessed because of it.
   C It is a requirement for success.
   D He has to put in more effort than needed.

4. Who did Richard Liu call "slackers"?
   A critical employees
   B defensive employees
   C over-motivated employees
   D underperforming employees

5. Which statement best sums up Elon Musk's attitude to long working hours?
   A Working 120 hours is easy.
   B Social media is my favourite tool.
   C Tesla requires you to work harder.
   D There is no progress without long hours.

Young people's opinion about work and skills

[...] Conducted through UNICEF's U-report platform – a messaging tool that empowers young people to speak out on issues that matter to them – the poll found that 63 % of the almost 11,000 youth across 136 countries who took the survey believe it is likely they will have the career they want in the future.

So why are many young people so positive? And what would the almost two in five young people who are pessimistic like to see to help them achieve their potential? [...]

Building resilience and adaptability through the pandemic

I wish life was a game which came with instructions, but unfortunately we don't have that roadmap that can tell us exactly what we should do to get to where we want to be.
– Praise Majwafi, 22, South Africa

A topic we talked about was the impact of the pandemic on young people. Participants agreed that because the past year has been so challenging, it has taught them to manage through uncertainty. [...]

"Being flexible and adaptable is something we've all had to get used to," added 22-year old Praise Majwafi, a social entrepreneur from South Africa.

Having been forced to manage through a very challenging year may have given many young people the confidence that if they can overcome this, they can overcome anything. [...]

Today's education system isn't fully meeting the needs of young people
I feel like I am learning all the theory and the content which is really important, but not the practical skills I will need later in the field, which is a huge miss.
– Ulises Brengi, 21, Argentina

When asked what would make the biggest difference for them to achieve their career goals, 32 % of the young people who took the U-report poll selected job-ready skills programmes in school, ahead of things like access to on-the-job training (28 %), access to relevant online resources (20 %), and a good mentor (19 %). [...]

Soft skills are just as important as technical abilities
We are feeling disconnected, and what does it come down to? It's about communication. And more than anything for me, it's about active listening.
– Andrea De Remes, 25, Mexico

Learning job-ready skills isn't just about acquiring the technical abilities to do the job; soft skills are just as important. We all agreed that to be successful, young people will need to become lifelong learners and build strong soft skills such as leadership, creativity and communication. [...]
The only way to create sustainable skills programmes is by involving young people themselves. By continuing to listen to them, businesses, governments, international organizations and other stakeholders can better understand the challenges young people are facing and engage them in the development of solutions.

Young people are the key to a better future
Praise shared a powerful vision for the future, one in which youth are at the centre of global progress. "In the hands of the largest generation of young people in history, the potential for global progress is unlimited," she said. "And through purposeful engagement and collaboration, nothing can stand in our way." [...]
Let's all work together to make Praise's vision a reality. (518 words)

Nadi Albino and Robert E. Moritz, *We Forum* website, 2021

5 Gapped summary → WB, p. 32/5–6

Complete the summary with the most suitable words from the text (ll. 8–27).
Give the line numbers of the words that you used.

22-year-old Praise said that she wished for better ■ **1** to know what she was supposed to do and thereby introduces the text section about ■ **2** and adaptability. Being ■ **3** and able to adapt to new circumstances, especially during the challenging years of the pandemic, is something young people had to learn for themselves. But they got used to managing ■ **4** and eventually believed in their ability to ■ **5** every possible obstacle in life. The next section described how today's ■ ■ **6** does not provide all the necessary knowledge and skills for the world of work which students will encounter after graduation. Ulises complained about having learnt all of the ■ **7** and content but not having had any practice. So it does not come as a surprise that a third of the students asked in the poll said they would wish for a better ■ **8** skills curriculum. Many also hoped to get better on-the-job ■ **9**.

6 Mediation

Beantworten Sie die folgenden Fragen auf Deutsch.

1. Weshalb spricht der Artikel zu Beginn von einer positiven Einstellung der jungen Menschen gegenüber ihren zukünftigen Berufschancen?
2. Welche wichtigen Fähigkeiten nennt Andrea De Remes?
3. Laut Zeilen 36–39, wie kann man mit den Herausfordungen, denen junge Menschen heute begegnen, am besten umgehen?
4. Welche Vision teilt Praise gegen Ende des Artikels mit?

Part II Material-based writing

In recent years, many steps have been taken to ensure men and women receive equal chances at work. Nevertheless, there is still a lot to be done.

Write a composition of at least 300 words. Comment on the following question: 'What are reasons for gender inequality in the world of work and what can be done to reach equality?'
Include all the material provided.

Material 1

Until we get equality in education, we won't have an equal society.
Sonia Sotomayor, associate justice of the Supreme Court of the United States

Material 2

Quotenregelung

Regelung, die vorsieht, dass in bestimmten Funktionen oder Positionen bestimmte gesellschaftliche Gruppen, besonders Frauen, in einer bestimmten Zahl vertreten sein sollen.

Quelle: Duden

Material 3

Part III Group discussion

University scientists approached your school to get an insight into what the young generation thinks about the future of work. They are interested in what you think this future will look like. You are asked to come up with a ranking of the most influential issues.

Work in small groups. Each of you chooses one of the following subjects (A–D). Discuss the issues and create the ranking. The quotes below might help you to come up with ideas.

A automation/robotics in the workplace
B fair wages/basic income
C gender in the workplace
D work-life balance

> The skills needed to succeed in today's world and the future are curiosity, creativity, taking initiative, multi-disciplinary thinking and empathy.
> *Tiffany Shlain, American filmmaker and author*

> As basic automation and machine learning move toward becoming commodities, uniquely human skills will become more valuable.
> *Devin Fidler, American entrepreneur*

> Demand quality, not just in the product you buy, but in the life of the person who made it.
> *Orsola de Castro, Italian fashion designer*

> We need to do a better job of putting ourselves higher on our own 'to do' list.
> *Michelle Obama, former First Lady*

a Introduce the topic and present the issue you think is most influential. Make sure to include the most important reason (about one minute).

b Discuss the issues and quotes in your group.

c Sum up the discussion and your position in a statement. Try to agree on a ranking of the issues.

The digital age

The media's the most powerful [thing] on earth. They have the power to make the innocent guilty and to make the guilty innocent, and that's power.
Malcolm X, African-American minister and human rights activist

We don't need politicians, we've all got iPhones and computers, right? So any decision that has to be made, any policy, we just put it online. Let the people vote – thumbs up, thumbs down, the majority wins. That's a democracy.
Jack, character in the series 'Black Mirror'

The great thing about social media was how it gave a voice to voiceless people.
Jon Ronson, British journalist, author and filmmaker

You are what you share.
Charles Leadbeater, authority on innovation and creativity

GOOD TO KNOW

Black Mirror is a British science-fiction series dealing with contemporary social issues and technological innovations.

1 Working with pictures and quotes → S10.1 → WB, p. 34/1–3; p. 35/1

a Look at the pictures and the devices the people are using. Explain how these devices are used and their significance for the individual and society.

b Read the quotes on page 74 and think about their message. Take notes. Then compare your ideas with a partner and discuss them. → H4

c In class, collect the positive and negative effects of digitalisation. → S15 Round robin

2 Listening → S3 → WB, p. 35/2

a Listen to the first part of the podcast 'The growing role of media in our lives'. Answer the questions. Take notes.

1. What is the earliest form of media mentioned by Nina Khan?
2. How does Nina Khan define the term 'media'?

clay tablet Tontafel
to acquit freisprechen

A19 b Make a list of the milestones in the history of media from clay tablets to the internet. What makes each of the milestones special?

A20 c Listen to the second part. Take notes on what the following numbers refer to.

7.8 billion | 4.8 billion | 95 % | 87 % | 39 % | 54 % | 2013 | 2018 | 6.42 | 5.46

d Fill in the table with the missing information.

1. effects of social media on public life in different countries (3 examples)	– Africa: … – …
2. types of media used daily before the internet existed	– radio – …
3. use of media today (5 examples)	– sending text messages – …

3 Creating a timeline → S10.2

a Look at the picture and explain what point it is trying to make. Do you agree with it? Give reasons and discuss in class.

b In small groups, use your results from exercise 2 and the picture and make a timeline for media.

c Present your timeline to the class. Discuss the different results. → S15 Tip-top

A A different way of life

1 Before you read → G1.5 → H4

Imagine someone has lived in the wilderness for the last 15 years and has now moved to a big city. What has changed in his or her absence? Talk about it to a partner. You can use the pictures below for ideas.

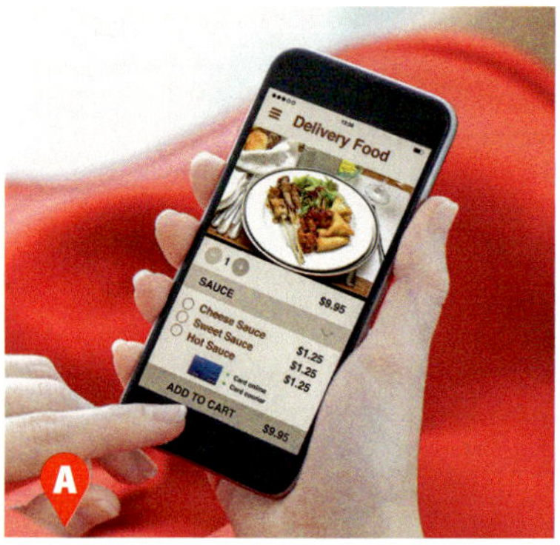

The narrator in the novel *Eleanor Oliphant is Completely Fine* by Gail Honeyman is a young woman who some people regard as out of the ordinary; others call her weird. At the age of 30, Eleanor is slowly changing her life. Carefully and step by step, she begins to get to know people around her after having spent long years of her childhood and adolescence kept away from the company of others.

A21

Eleanor Oliphant is Completely Fine

by Gail Honeyman

A young man with a grey shirt and a shiny tie was staring at the banks of giant TV screens. I approached, and informed him that I wished to purchase a computer. He looked scared.

'Desktop laptop tablet,' he intoned. I had no idea what he was talking about.

'I haven't bought a computer before, Liam,' I explained, reading his name badge. 'I'm a very inexperienced technology consumer.'

He pulled at the collar of his shirt, as though trying to free his enormous Adam's apple from its constraints. He had the look of a gazelle or an impala, one of those boring beige

6 **to intone** anstimmen; intonieren
7 **name badge** Namensschild
10 **constraint** Beschränkung
10 **impala** Impala *(afrikanische Antilopenart)*

animals with large, round eyes on the sides of its face. The kind of animal that always gets eaten by a leopard in the end.
This was a rocky start.
'What will you be using it for?' he asked, not making eye contact.
'That's absolutely none of your business,' I said, most offended.
He looked like he might cry, and I felt bad. He was only young. I touched his arm, even though I hate touching.
'I'm afraid I'm a bit anxious because it is absolutely imperative that I am able to go online this weekend,' I explained. His nervous expression remained in place.
'Liam,' I said slowly, 'I simply need to purchase some sort of computer equipment that I can use in the comfort of my own home in order to conduct some internet-based research. I may in time send electronic messages from it. That is all. Do you have something suitable in stock?'
The boy stared heavenwards and thought deeply. 'A laptop and mobile internet access?' he said. Why was he asking me, for goodness' sakes? I nodded and handed over my debit card.
When I got home, slightly giddy at how much money I'd spent, I realized that there was nothing to eat. Friday was margherita pizza day, of course, but my routine was, for the first time ever, somewhat out of kilter. I recalled that I had a flyer in the tea towel drawer, something that was put through my letterbox a while ago. I found it easily and smoothed it out. There were money-off coupons along the bottom, which had expired. I guessed the prices would have gone up, but assumed that the phone number had stayed the same, and they presumably still sold pizzas. Even these old prices were ridiculous, though, and I actually laughed out loud at them. In Tesco Metro, the pizzas cost a quarter of that price.
I decided that I'd go for it. Yes, it was extravagant and indulgent, but why not? Life should be about trying new things, exploring boundaries, I reminded myself. The man on the other end of the line told me that the pizza would arrive in fifteen minutes. I brushed my hair, took off my slippers and put my work shoes back on. I wondered how they managed with the black pepper. Would the man bring a pepper mill with him?
Surely he wouldn't grind it over the pizza while he stood on the doorstep? I put the kettle on in case he wanted a cup of tea. They had told me on the phone how much it would cost and I took out the money, put it in an envelope and wrote Pizza Pronto on the front. I didn't bother with the address. I wondered whether it was the done thing to tip, and wished I had someone to ask. [...]
In the end, the pizza experience was extremely disappointing. The man simply thrust a big box into my hand and took the envelope, which he then rudely ripped open right in front of me. I heard him mutter fuck's sake under his breath as he counted the coins.
I had been collecting fifty-pence pieces in a little ceramic dish, and this had seemed the perfect opportunity to use them up. I'd popped an extra one in for him, but received no thanks for it. Rude. (672 words)

13 **rocky** holprig
18 **imperative** zwingend erforderlich
21 **to conduct research** eine Recherche durchführen
27 **giddy** schwindelig
29 **out of kilter** aus dem Gleichgewicht
36 **indulgent** *hier:* maßlos
41 **to grind** mahlen
41 **to put the kettle on** Teewasser aufsetzen
44 **it is the done thing to** es gehört sich, zu …
44 **to tip** Trinkgeld geben

2 Short-answer questions → WB, p. 36–37/1–3

Answer the following questions. You may use words from the text.

1. What does Eleanor need a computer for?
2. Why is Eleanor offended at the question of the shop assistant?
3. Why is it important for Eleanor to have a pizza that day?
4. What does Eleanor do in the 15 minutes before the pizza is delivered?
5. Why is the pizza delivery man angry while counting the money?

3 Multiple matching

Match the statements and questions (A–I) with the person who could have thought or spoken them (1–3). There are two statements/questions more than you need.

1 Eleanor 2 Shop assistant 3 Pizza delivery man

A Would you like to come in?
B I'm about to lose control.
C Don't look at me that way!
D I don't have the time for this bullshit.
E Is that all?
F Are you lazy or incompetent?
G Are you crazy or stupid?
H It's a special offer.
I Are you sure you can handle it?

4 Words matter

a Read the text again focusing on Eleanor's perspective. Collect phrases from the text which show that the incidents are described from Eleanor's point of view. Explain why.

Example: "He looked scared." (l. 4) – personal impression, he does not tell her that he is scared, it is her interpretation

b Fill in the table with the phrases you have found.

The way Eleanor sees the world around her	...
The comparisons Eleanor makes	...
The words Eleanor uses to describe people and situations	...
The words Eleanor uses to describe her emotions	...

5 Writing a personal email → S 6.4

Write an email to Eleanor giving her some advice on how to deal with people she meets in the world around her.

USEFUL PHRASES

Making suggestions and giving advice
I was wondering if you have ever thought of ... | Have you ever thought of ...? | I think it might be a good idea to ... | Don't you think it might be a good idea to ...? | If I were you, I'd perhaps ... | Why don't you ...? | I'd suggest ...

6 A step further → S 15 Placemat

a Work in groups of four. Copy the placemat onto a sheet of paper. Each member chooses a corner and an aspect or a device of modern life from pages 74 and 76.

b Write down pros and cons about this aspect / device on your side of the placemat.

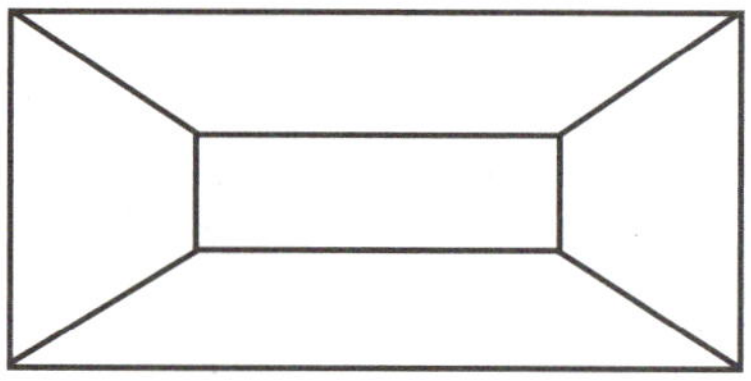

c Turn the placemat to the next side and add more pros and cons to your classmate's notes. Repeat this until you have completed all sides. Then agree on the most important pro and con of each aspect or device.

d In class, discuss if you were able to find more pros or more cons in your placemat and what this means for modern life.

B The power of images

1 Before you read

Look at the picture and talk to a partner.

1. What do you know about this event? When did it happen and where?
2. How does the picture make you feel?

A22

The power of images in global politics

1 We live in a visual age. Images shape international events and our understandings of them. Photographs, cinema and television influence how we view and approach phenomena as diverse as war, humanitarian disasters, protest movements, financial crises and election campaigns. The dynamics of visual politics go well beyond traditional media outlets. Digital media, from Twitter to Instagram, play an increasingly important role across the political spectrum, from terrorist recruitment drives to social justice campaigns. Fashion and video games are frequently derived from and enact the militarised world we live in. Drones, satellites, and surveillance cameras profile terrorist suspects and identify military targets. Images surround everything we do. This omnipresence of images is political and has changed fundamentally how we live and interact in today's world. [...]

2 It has become common to speak of a visual turn in the study of global politics: the recognition that images and visual artefacts play an increasingly crucial role in depicting and shaping the world we live in.

Our understanding of terrorism, for instance, is inevitably intertwined with how images dramatically represent the events in question, how these images circulate world-wide, and how politicians and the public respond to these visual impressions. Take the terrorist attacks of 11 September 2001. There is no way to understand the origin, nature and impact of the event without understanding the role of images. The attack was designed for visual impact. Images circulated instantly around the globe, giving audiences a sense of how shocking and terrible the event was. Many of these emotional images not only shaped subsequent public debates and policy responses, including the war on terror, but also remain engrained in our collective consciousness.

3 Images are, of course, not new, nor have they replaced words as the main means of communication. Images and visual artefacts have been around from the beginning of time. The visual has always been part of life. Images were produced not only to capture key aspects of human existence, but also to communicate these aspects to others. Examples range from prehistoric cave paintings that document hunting practices to Renaissance works of art. Some of these images and cultural artefacts we still see today and they continue to influence our perception and understanding of the world.

4 But, there are two ways in which the politics of images has changed fundamentally.

6 **to approach** (sich) nähern; annähern
10 **media outlet** Medienkanal
12 **increasingly** zunehmend
14 **recruitment** Anwerbung
17 **to enact** *hier:* darstellen; inszenieren
18 **surveillance** Überwachung
19 **suspect** Verdächtige/-r
20 **target** Ziel
21 **omnipresence** Allgegenwärtigkeit
27 **visual artefact** visueller Gegenstand
28 **crucial** entscheidend; äußerst wichtig
32 **inevitable** unvermeidlich
32 **intertwined** verflochten; verknüpft
35 **to circulate** kursieren; in Umlauf sein
42 **visual impact** bildliche Wirkung
47 **subsequent** anschließend; folgend
49 **engrained** fest verankert
49 **collective consciousness** kollektives Bewusstsein
57 **key aspect** Kernpunkt

70 **reach** Reichweite
79 **instantaneously** sofort; unverzüglich
93 **political intent** politische Absicht
97 **unprecedented** beispiellos; noch nie dagewesen
100 **foundation** Grundlage
102 **dismantling** Abbau
102 **division** Teilung; Aufteilung
106 **at stake** *hier:* um die es geht
108 **to deceive sb** jdn. täuschen
109 **glimpse** (flüchtiger) Blick
110 **seductive** verführerisch
112 **to reveal** enthüllen; aufzeigen
116 **to embody** verkörpern; darstellen
118 **evidential** nachweisbar; beweiskräftig
119 **to reinforce** bekräftigen; verstärken
124 **spectator** Zuschauer/-in
127 **graspable** begreifbar
131 **politically partial** politisch einseitig

First is the speed at which images circulate and the reach they have. Not that long ago, during the time of the Vietnam War, it would have taken days if not weeks for a photograph taken in the war zone to reach the front-page of, say, the *New York Times*. In today's digital world, a photograph or a video can reach audiences world-wide immediately after it has been taken. Media networks can now make a local event almost instantaneously global, whether it is a terrorist attack, a protest march, an election campaign rally or any other political phenomena.
Second is what one could call the democratisation of visual politics. It used to be that very few actors – states or global media networks – had access to images and the power to distribute them to a global audience. Today, everyone can take a photograph with a smartphone, upload it on social media and circulate it immediately with a potential world-wide reach. Any individual or small group, no matter what their location or political intent, can potentially produce and circulate images that, in today's new media language, go viral. The result is an unprecedented visualisation of both our private lives and our political landscape: a visual communication revolution that has shaken the foundations and hierarchies of established media networks. We see a dismantling of the division between broadcaster and viewer, producer and consumer. [...]

5 Photographs offer a good illustration of the issues at stake. They appear to communicate clearly and truthfully, yet they deceive us. They seem to give us a glimpse of the real. They provide us with the seductive belief that what we see in a photograph is an authentic representation of the world: a slice of life that reveals exactly what was happening at a particular moment. The illusion of authenticity also masks the political values that such photographic representations embody. The assumption that photographs are neutral, value free and evidential, is reinforced because photography captures faces and events in memorable ways.
It is precisely the illusion of authenticity that makes photographs such powerful tools to convey the meaning of political events to distant audiences. Spectators view and re-view crises through various media sources until the enormity of the event seems graspable. In doing so, photographs not only shape an individual's perception but also larger, collective forms of consciousness.
Photographs are thus politically partial and not just because they can be manipulated and faked. All images – still and moving ones – always express a particular perspective. [...] (805 words)

Roland Bleiker,
E-International Relations website, 2018

GOOD TO KNOW

The **Vietnam War** was a conflict between South and North Vietnam between 1955 and 1975. The North was supported by the Soviet Union and the South by the US.

The **9/11 attacks** were a series of terrorist attacks by Islamic extremists against the US. The terrorists crashed two planes into the World Trade Center towers in New York City and one into the Pentagon in Arlington/Virginia. Almost 3,000 people died and about 25,000 were injured.

2 Multiple choice → WB, p. 38/1–3

Choose the most suitable option.

1. Paragraph 1 states that the presence of media in every part of our lives …
   A is a sign of military influence.
   B makes every piece of information a political one.
   C shows how strong traditional forms of media still are.
   D changes reality more and more into a video-game reality.

2. Which of the following statements is not true according to section 2?
   A Images of terrorist attacks form our understanding of such events.
   B The shocking images influenced the subsequent miltary campaign after 9/11.
   C It is not widely recognised that images play such an important role in our lives.
   D The terrorist attacks of 11 September 2001 were intended to have a visual effect.

3. What would be the most suitable heading for section 3?
   - **A** Images for life
   - **B** The importance of art
   - **C** The visual aspect of communication
   - **D** Creative visions for global understanding

4. Section 4 states that …
   - **A** barriers between viewers and broadcasters are still high.
   - **B** the visualisation of our lives has a certain democratising dimension.
   - **C** photographs of war zones still need time to reach the established media.
   - **D** the unexpected visualisation of our lives is positive for established media networks.

5. Photographs …
   - **A** can cause crises.
   - **B** are usually neutral.
   - **C** express a general perspective.
   - **D** represent the world in a formative way.

3 Gapped summary

Complete the summary with the most suitable words from the text (ll. 51–104). Give the line numbers of the words that you used.

Throughout history, images provided a snapshot of different ■ **1** of our existence. Even now many of these images deeply ■ **2** our understanding of the world around us. While words are – of course – still our most used ■ **3** of communication, images have become more and more powerful over time. To start with, images can be distributed with a much greater ■ **4** over a greater distance. Local events can get ■ **5** attention within minutes. Moreover, nowadays, anyone has the chance to share visual media with ■ **6** around the world. This is no longer just limited to official media ■ **7**. The power is truly in the hands of each ■ **8**.

4 Mediation → H 4

Beantworten Sie die folgenden Fragen auf Deutsch.

1. Was bewirken Bilder zu bestimmten Ereignissen?
2. Was bedeutet „visual turn in the study of global politics“ (Z. 26)?
3. Warum ging zum Beispiel der Anschlag auf das World Trade Center ins kollektive Bewusstsein über?
4. Wie war die Situation der Berichterstattung während des Vietnamkrieges?
5. Was ist mit der „Demokratisierung“ der Bildverbreitung gemeint?

5 Words matter → H 4

a Create a mind map for 'media' with words from the text on pages 79–80. Then compare your results with those of a partner and add more words. → S 11.1

b Write a definition for the following words. → S 11.3

1. election campaign (ll. 8–9)
2. social justice (ll. 14–15)
3. politician (l. 35)
4. policy response (ll. 47–48)
5. revolution (l. 99)

c Write a short text about a situation when the media made an impact on politics. If necessary, search online for an example. You can use the words from your mind map from a.

d Exchange your text with a partner. Do you think he or she chose a good example?
→ S15 Tip-top

6 A step further

a The photos below are all iconic.
Choose one picture and note down your first reaction (e.g. associations, emotions).

Albert Einstein, 1951

Tiananmen Square, Beijing/China, 1989

Moon landing, 1969

Eli Harold, Colin Kaepernick, Eric Reid (from left to right), 2016

The fall of the Berlin wall, 1989

Dolly the cloned sheep

b In small groups, do some online research on the historical and /or political background of the picture. Then analyse the picture, paying attention to the message it conveys. In your opinion, what makes it special?

c Create a poster about the picture and its background information.

d Present your poster in class. → S15 Gallery walk

e In class, discuss whether the pictures represent the historical or political event in an accurate way.

GOOD TO KNOW

iconic picture
= a picture that is widely known and evokes emotions or memories of a certain event which it has come to represent

GOOD TO KNOW

Online research
Make sure you use reliable sources which …
- are written by respectable people or institutions;
- are up to date;
- are neutral and objective;
- cover different perspectives;
- include expert proof or personal experience;
- have correct grammar and spelling.

C Welcome to a smarter world

1 Before you read → WB, p. 39/1

a Think about a typical day and brainstorm situations in which your personal data is recorded by someone else. Consider the kind of information you make available and what data you would consider private. → S15 Think-pair-share

b In class, discuss who might be interested in accessing your data and for what purpose.

Andreas Weigend's work focuses on social mobile technology, big data and consumer behaviour. In the introduction to his book, he uses a first-person narrator although it is a non-fictional text.

A23

Data for the people: How to make our post-privacy economy work for you

by Andreas Weigend

How can we ensure that data are for the people?

At 6:45 a.m., the alarm on my mobile phone wakes me up. Eager to start the day, I carry my phone to the kitchen while I scan through my email and Facebook notifications. My phone's GPS receiver and wifi register the changes in location, logging my shift a few meters north and east. As I <u>pour</u> myself a cup of coffee [1], the phone's <u>accelerometer</u> tracks how quickly I walk and the <u>barometer</u> registers when I'm going up the stairs. Because I have Google apps installed on my phone, Google has a record of all these data.

After breakfast, [2] to Stanford University. The electricity company has put in a "smart" <u>meter</u>, which registers the decrease in electricity use as I turn off my lights and unplug my mobile devices. When I open the garage door, the meter <u>detects</u> the usage signature specific to it. Thus, as I pull my car out onto the street, my electricity provider has [3]. When my phone's signal gets picked up by different <u>cellular signal towers</u>, so does my mobile phone carrier.

On the road, a camera installed on a street corner takes a photo of my <u>license plate</u> in case I speed through a red light. Thankfully, [4] today so I won't be greeted with a ticket in the mail. But as I go on my way, my license plate is photographed again and again. Some of those cameras belong to the local government, while some belong to private companies that are analyzing the data to identify patterns of mobility – which they sell to police departments, <u>land developers</u>, and other interested parties.

When I get to Stanford, I use the EasyPark app on my phone to pay the parking fee. The money is [5], and the university parking team is notified that I'm paid up, so both the school and my bank can see that I'm on campus starting at 9:03 a.m. When my phone stops moving at a car's pace, Google infers this is where I have parked and logs the location, so that I can look it up in case I forget later. It's also time to check my Metromile <u>insurance</u> app, [6] from the car's <u>on-board</u> diagnostic system. I can see in an instant that my fuel efficiency was lower today – nineteen miles per gallon – and that I spent $2.05 on gas for my <u>commute</u>.

After my day at Stanford, I'm planning to meet up with a new friend back in San Francisco. We "virtually" met each other when we both commented on a post by a

8 **to pour** gießen; einschenken
8 **accelerometer** Beschleunigungsmesser
9 **barometer** Luftdruckmesser
12 **meter** (Verbrauchs-) Zähler
13 **to detect** feststellen; entdecken
15 **cellular signal tower** Sendemast (*Mobilfunknetz)*
17 **license plate** Nummernschild
22 **land developer** Bauunternehmen; Bodenerschließer
28 **insurance** Versicherung
28 **on-board** fahrzeugeigen
30 **commute** Pendelstrecke

33 **mutual** gemeinsam
37 **paraphernalia** Zubehör
39 **head shop** *Geschäft für Tabak, Cannabis etc.*

mutual friend on Facebook, and liked **7**. It turned out we had more than thirty Facebook friends in common, more than enough reason to meet up. Google Maps predicts that I'll get to my new friend's place at 7:12 p.m., and as usual the prediction is correct within a few minutes. As it happens, my friend lives above a store that sells tobacco products as well as various paraphernalia used for smoking marijuana. The GPS receiver on my smartphone doesn't differentiate between the apartment and the store, however. As far as my carrier and Google are concerned, I've ended my day with a visit to the head shop – **8** Google shows when I check the weather forecast before going to bed.
Welcome to the social data revolution. (626 words)

2 Multiple matching → WB, p. 39/2; p. 40/3

Eight phrases have been cut from the text. Match the most suitable phrases (A–J) with the gaps (1–8). There are two phrases more than you need.

A automatically debited from my bank account
B enough data to know I'm no longer at home
C a fact revealed to me by the ads
D which shows how many miles I made
E which has been recording data about my drive
F and really start to get going
G each other's take on the topic
H and start the coffee machine
I I'm on my best behaviour
J I'm ready to make my way

3 Gapped summary → H 4

Complete the summary with the most suitable words from the text.
Give the line numbers of the words that you used.

The text follows a person's journey through their daily routine. From the minute he is woken by his ■ **1**, an installed device ■ **2** his location as he moves. The first thing he does is look at his social media ■ **3**. Throughout the day, various devices collect data about where he goes, what he does, and even how he does it. His phone, for example, uses various apps to trace the ■ **4** of his movements, while data from his energy provider ■ **5** his absence based on the decrease in usage. On his way to the university, his car's ■ ■ **6** is photographed by a camera, which once again reveals his location and the exact time. All of these apps, including his parking app and and his car insurance app, can collect ■ **7** and sell the information to advertising companies. As the narrator begins to drive to a friend's place, his navigation software offers a ■ **8** of the duration of the journey, which is particularly accurate. Based on his location at the friend's house, the GPS on his phone assumes that he was at the ■ ■ **9** below the apartment.

4 Mediation

Erklären Sie die Verwendung des Begriffs „post-privacy economy" (Z. 1) im Textzusammenhang.

5 A step further → S 6.4 → WB, p. 40/4

a Write a formal email to the author of the article to discuss the following question: 'Why should we bother about data security?'

b In small groups, give feedback to each other. → S 15 Peer correction

Is TV necessary? → S 6.1

1 Using connectives → S 5.2 → WB, p. 41/1

Connectives are words that are essential for turning individual sentences into a coherent and logical text. We use connectives to show how two sentences relate to each other (result, condition, consequence etc.).
Furthermore, these words also structure and organise your paragraphs and, in fact, the whole text.

a The sentences (A–E) show five combinations of the two statements "I have got a TV" and "I watch the film" using five different connectives. Match the correct person/ meaning (1–5) with the sentences. Then try to think of more combinations.

A If I have a TV, I will watch the film.
B Although I have a TV, I won't watch the film.
C As I had a TV, I could have watched the film.
D Because I don't have a TV, I won't watch the film.
E I don't have a TV; nevertheless, I watched the film.

1 sb who can't watch
2 sb who missed the film
3 a magician
4 sb who does not plan to watch
5 sb who hopes to watch TV

b Read the composition on the benefits and dangers of watching TV. Find a suitable connective for each gap (1–15). Try to use a different expression every time. → H 4

Television is one of the most popular forms of entertainment all over the world. **1**, it was called the 'idiot box' **2**, back then, it was all about entertainment. It did not have as many informative channels as it does now. **3**, television has since changed. More and more channels now offer us knowledge and information along with entertainment. **4**, this essay will look at the benefits and dangers of watching TV.

5, the invention of television has given us various benefits. TV gives us access to a cheap mode of entertainment. As they are very affordable, we can now all own one. **6**, it keeps us updated on the latest international events. It is now possible to get news from all corners of the world. **7**, television offers educational programmes improving our knowledge of science and wildlife, to name just a few. **8**, TV also motivates individuals to develop skills such as cooking, gardening or DIY. This pushes people to do better and try out new things.

9, TV also has a negative side that can even be harmful for children and young people. **10**, we have to admit that there is a lot of inappropriate content on TV such as violence, drugs and crime, and certainly too much explicit sex bordering on pornography. **11**, it is also harmful to our health. Don't forget, when watching TV we do not move much, while, at the same time, we tend to have lots of snacks, washed down with lots of sugary drinks. Certainly not a healthy lifestyle.
12, the most dangerous aspect of all is the great amount of fake information that we see on TV. Many media channels now only promote the propaganda of governments and powerful organisations, thus misinforming citizens. This is a danger we must not ignore.

13, there is nothing wrong with being entertained by TV. **14**, it is extremely important not to be naïve. We must be critical about how much we watch and what we watch. Parents should keep an eye on the viewing habits of their children. **15**, we should not believe everything we see and hear on TV. We must be the better judge and make wise choices in the channels and programmes we view.

2 Material-based writing → S 6.1

The theme of the next issue of your school magazine will be to explore how young people's habits regarding media usage have changed and are still changing.
To prepare this edition, discuss the following statement:

'The internet will increasingly replace TV.'

Write a composition of at least 300 words. Include all the material provided.

Material 1

Reading is a huge effort for many people, a bore for others, and, believe it or not, many people prefer watching TV.

Hugh Mackay, Australian psychologist and social researcher

Material 2

Neue Studie zur TV-Nutzung: Lineares Fernsehen verliert mehr und mehr Zuschauer
Nur noch etwa die Hälfte der Sehzeit (54 Prozent) verbringen Zuschauer demnach heute mit dem klassischen Fernsehen mit Sendeschema, ergab eine Studie der Beratungsgesellschaft Roland Berger und der Westfälischen Wilhelms-Universität Münster. Die Entwicklung vom linearen TV zum Streaming werde sich in den kommenden Jahren deutlich fortsetzen, […].
Der Studie zufolge widmet das Gesamtpublikum 10,3 Prozent seines Zeitbudgets Netflix. Auf den Plätzen danach folgen mit ihren linearen und nichtlinearen Angeboten RTL (10,0 Prozent), ZDF (9,8 Prozent) und ARD (8,8 Prozent), vor Amazon Prime Video mit 8,7 Prozent. Wie die Studie weiter ergab, entfällt unter allen Zuschauern aktuell 54 Prozent des Zeitbudgets auf lineares Fernsehen, zwölf Prozent auf Pay-TV-Angebote, 24 Prozent auf kostenpflichtiges Streaming und elf Prozent auf kostenfreies Streaming. Unter den jungen Zuschauern liegt der Anteil am Streaming bereits bei fast 60 Prozent.

Der Tagesspiegel website, 2019

Material 3

Doing without media → S2

1 Using arguments in a discussion

To prepare for a group discussion, it is helpful to practise exchanging views. Often you instinctively know which point of view you wish to share. The difficult part is finding arguments to prove your point and convincing those who disagree with you.

a Search online for a video of a discussion/debate. Note down phrases and words for a convincing argument and phrases which show a reaction to someone else's argument.

b Collect the phrases and words from **a** in class.

c With a partner, choose one of the following statements.
Partner A is a supporter, Partner B is an opponent of the statement. Collect arguments for your position. Make sure you give reasons, examples etc.

1. Teachers can be replaced by computers.
2. Social media makes us less social.
3. Influencers are the superstars of today's culture.

d Discuss the statement. Take turns presenting your arguments and reacting to each other. The goal is to convince your partner of your point of view. You can use the phrases and words from **a** and **b**. → S1.1
You can start like this: I could not disagree more …

e Choose another partner and do exercises **c** and **d** for another statement.

2 Group discussion → S2 → WB, p. 41/2

Your school wants to address mental health issues such as stress and burnout. Part of this is a project called 'Destination: Digital detox'. On your school website, groups will present their ideas for digital detoxing. The idea is not to complain about digital media but to encourage its use in a reduced, efficient and thoughtful way, thereby aiming to achieve lower stress levels and better mental health.

Today you are meeting to discuss your ideas for the website. You can use the cartoon and talk about the following questions:

- Where, when, how often and why do you use digital media?
- What is 'digital detox'?
- Where and how can you realise digital detox?
- How can you use digital media (more) efficiently?
- How might digital detox affect and change your life and lifestyle?
- How could your ideas be presented on the website?

a Introduce your point of view (about one minute).

b Discuss and explain your ideas and views.

c Sum up your main points. Try to come to a conclusion.

Part I Reading

9 Positive Effects Of Social Media You Might Not Know About

[...] There's a lotta research out there about the negative effects of social media on everything from our mental health to the quality of our relationships and even our ability to concentrate at school or work. But, what isn't often spoken about is the positive side effects of social media. [...]

Benefit 1: It empowers through education
Think about all the accounts you follow on social media. Whether it's fashion brands or fitness bloggers, each of these accounts has probably helped you learn something new. That might be by running a virtual workshop, sharing how-to-style tutorials [...] or even just writing oh-so-brilliant captions that reveal practical tips and tricks about a particular topic.
Social media is a fantastic tool to empower audiences with educational content. [...]

Benefit 2: It boosts global connectivity
Who are the accounts you interact with most on social media? Where are they based? Chances are that you're connected with users located in different cities, states and countries around the globe. [...]
With the world at our fingertips, we can share ideas, collaborate and communicate with people from a range of backgrounds on social media. [...]

Benefit 3: It builds engaged communities
[...] Whether you're a member of a [...] group about your favorite TV series or have joined a virtual book club [...], social media gives us the power to find and connect with like-minded users from across the world. [...] And for those of us living in remote or regional areas? Social media communities make it possible to feel a sense of connectedness, even while we're physically distant from each other. [...]

Benefit 4: It provides support and solidarity on social media
[...] One of the most powerful positive effects of social media is its ability to provide support and solidarity. Groups and accounts on social media can help us navigate common stumbling blocks like getting fit, navigating heartbreak and even more poignant struggles like overcoming addiction, dealing with a chronic illness or processing grief.
In times of loneliness, stress and anxiety, social media can act as a powerful tool to bring people together to support and lift each other up when they need it most. [...]

Benefit 5: You can learn new skills
Want to master a new instrument? Even considered giving yoga a try? What about learning how to cook delicious pasta from scratch? Thanks to social media, you can learn how to do all of the above online (and for FREE!).
[...] Unlike traditional educational experiences that require signing up to a course or institution (usually with a hefty fee attached), you can learn a range of fun, practical skills from the comfort of your couch using social media. [...]

Benefit 6: It brings people together in moments that matter
[...] From civil rights protests to a global health crisis, these [...] events have irrevocably changed the way we live our daily lives and see the world around us. [...]
Using social media, these important causes have been able to call for donations, share important information and find innovative ways to unite users in meaningful and powerful ways. From lobbying the government to organizing demonstrations and even

the coordination of relief efforts, social media has the ability to connect and unite groups to make a positive impact on the world during times of crisis. [...]

Benefit 7: It raises awareness for brands working for good
[...] not-for-profit organizations, charities, community groups and socially-conscious brands are all leveraging the power of social media to connect with new people and audiences around the globe.
With 88 % of shoppers looking to support brands that help them live sustainably, the demand for ethical and socially-conscious businesses has never been greater. [...]
And for consumers? Social media enables them to discover new organisations and brands working for good, giving them greater choice to shop and support brands aligned with their values. [...]

Benefit 8: It gives customers the chance to shape meaningful change
Ever wished you could help design the next products your favorite brand creates? Want to have a say in the type of content businesses share with you? Have you got a brilliant idea for a new event, podcast or blog post? [...] Social media enables an open dialogue to connect brands and customers to ask for feedback, advice or constructive criticism. [...]

Benefit 9: It gives people the chance to laugh
And our favourite positive effect of social media? The LOLs of course! Social media enables brands to show their funny side with GIFs, memes and oh-so-relatable quotes that give us all a reason to giggle. Not only does this forge strong connections between brands and customers, but also brightens our days in a time when we could all use a reason to laugh. [...] (778 words)

Plann that website

1 Multiple choice → WB, p. 42/1–2

Choose the most suitable option.

1. Educational content ...
   A gives audiences writing skills.
   B makes audiences good bloggers.
   C can be found everywhere on the Internet.
   D is shared nearly everwhere on social media.

2. Social media users who are connected often ...
   A feel powerful.
   B share the same ideas.
   C share the same background.
   D work in the same work sector.

3. Social media users can find support for questions on ...
   A health, emotions and solidarity.
   B fitness, relationships and navigation.
   C relationships, health and work processes.
   D health, relationships and mental problems.

4. Groups on social media ...
   A have changed our everyday lives.
   B organise digital protest movements.
   C can unite users for powerful actions.
   D bring people and governments together.

5. On social media, brands and other organisations can ...
   - **A** achieve global power.
   - **B** increase the demand for their products.
   - **C** connect with audiences with the same values.
   - **D** change most shoppers' attitudes towards sustainability.

6. Customers ...
   - **A** can take part in business processes.
   - **B** are asked to share their ideas with businesses.
   - **C** need to give their feedback on brands more often.
   - **D** should be more positive when contacting companies.

Separating fact from fiction is tougher than ever

News media have long challenged the honesty of politicians and held them to account, but things have been turned on their head. We're living in a world where politicians in democratic nations now accuse media of being "an enemy of the people" and purveyors of "fake news."

That's just one of the many challenges preventing traditional news media from effectively combating fake news – the perception they are part of the problem, not the solution. Eroding trust in media [...] is the heart of the problem. Before mainstream media can do anything to combat fake news, it has to make sure their own houses are in order, both with editorial content and advertising and especially with sponsored content and native advertising from third-party providers.

In the past, you needed a lot of resources to start a rumour or propaganda campaign. It took media power and resources to start a rumour and spread it widely. But those days are gone, thanks to social media. The reach is massive; anyone can start a rumour and, if they feed it to the right channel, it spreads within minutes. In today's world, we are drowning in fake news – either propaganda that masquerades as editorial content, or false content designed to generate advertising revenues through increased web traffic.

To make matters worse, what we still think of as "mass media" – television, radio and newspapers – are minuscule compared to social platforms, the new mass media, where it is easy to share false and misleading posts, either by design or inadvertently. Just look at the numbers: Facebook has 1.4 billion daily users, while its sister platform Instagram counts 500 million. Twitter has 157 million. Snapchat, the current preference of the young, boasts 61 million. The New York Times, by contrast, claims about four million, the Wall Street Journal and USA Today 6 million, and the Times of London 1 million – a mere drop in the bucket comparatively.

Thanks to that dynamic, a big part of the population now consumes and shares its news via social media, often without realizing what they share is false. More than two million people shared, commented and reacted to the false story that President Obama banned the Pledge of Allegiance in US schools. Nearly a million did the same with a story that falsely claimed, "The Pope endorsed Donald Trump". And more than 3,000 Facebook advertisements and links that targeted US voters were created and paid for by Russian entities.

Even news media professionals, who should know better, have been taken in – we've all seen stories spread by mainstream media that came from spurious sources. And that's just the tip of the iceberg – it's hard to tell what's true or not on social platforms because it's hard to determine the source of the content beyond the friend who shared it. It's no wonder that two-thirds of Americans in a recent poll said they are greatly confused by media, or that nearly half think news media makes up stories. In this environment, trusted media are needed more than ever. Consumers are overloaded; we are exposed to media for 12 hours each day and are hit by more than 3,000 advertising messages a day. News media can't compete with social media in terms of reach, but it can compete and win in terms of accuracy, and in terms of once again becoming a reliable source of credible news that cuts through all the noise. But to do so – and the only chance they have – is to build up trust again with good quality journalism and quality advertising. The industry is not yet doing so. In many countries, trust in media is at all-time lows. [...]

(616 words)

Dietmar Schantin, *Institute for media studies* website, 2018

2 Mediation → WB, p. 43/3

Beantworten Sie die folgenden Fragen auf Deutsch.

1. Was müssen die Medien tun, bevor sie Fake News bekämpfen?
2. Warum haben es die „alten" Massenmedien schwer?
3. Warum glaubt die Hälfte der Amerikaner, dass Medien Nachrichten erfinden?
4. In welchen Bereichen können traditionelle Medien die sozialen Medien übertreffen?

3 Gapped summary

Complete the summary with the most suitable words from the text. Give the line numbers of the words that you used.

Even in ■ **1** countries, elected politicians are expressing their distrust in the media. Over time, ■ **2** has become more frequent on news websites, causing the line between neutral and one-sided content to blur. Another issue is the increased efficiency which came with ■ **3** media. Nowadays, our news feeds are full of ■ ■ **4** which aim to either influence our perceptions or make money. The media landscape has tipped in favour of these ■ **5** as opposed to traditional media. Account ownership on social media outlets is hundreds if not thousands of times bigger than subscriptions to traditional newspapers, which are now just a ■ **6** in a vast ocean of clickbait articles and videos. It's no wonder that people are ■ **7** by all these developments, especially given the number of stories with unknown sources. The only chance traditional news outlets have is to regain their reputation as ■ **8** sources. Only then can they recover the ■ **9** they have lost.

Cory Doctorow is a Canadian writer of science fiction. The novel *Little Brother* is about four teenagers in San Francisco, which – after a terrorist attack – is about to be controlled by police. The four characters defend themselves against the Department of Homeland Security's attacks on the Bill of Rights.

Little Brother

by Cory Doctorow

They took me outside and around the corner, to a waiting unmarked police car. It wasn't like anyone in that neighborhood would have had a hard time figuring out that it was a cop car, though. Only police drive big Crown Victorias now that gas had hit seven bucks a gallon. What's more, only cops could double-park in the middle of Van Ness Street without getting towed by the schools of predatory tow-operators that circled endlessly, ready to enforce San Francisco's incomprehensible parking regulations and collect a bounty for kidnapping your car.

Booger blew his nose. I was sitting in the back seat, and so was he. His partner was sitting in the front, typing with one finger on an ancient, ruggedized laptop that looked like Fred Flintstone had been its original owner.

Booger looked closely at my ID again. "We just want to ask you a few routine questions."

"Can I see your badges?" I said. These guys were clearly cops, but it couldn't hurt to let them know I knew my rights.

Booger flashed his badge at me too fast for me to get a good look at it, but Zit in the front seat gave me a long look at his. I got their division number and memorized the four-digit badge number. It was easy: 1337 is also the way hackers write "leet," or "elite."

They were both being very polite and neither of them was trying to intimidate me the way that the DHS had done when I was in their custody.

"Am I under arrest?"

"You've been momentarily detained so that we can ensure your safety and the general public safety," Booger said.

He passed my driver's license up to Zit, who pecked it slowly into his computer. I saw him make a typo and almost corrected him, but figured it was better to just keep my mouth shut.

"Is there anything you want to tell me, Marcus? Do they call you Marc?"

"Marcus is fine," I said. Booger looked like he might be a nice guy. Except for the part about kidnapping me into his car, of course.

"Marcus. Anything you want to tell me?"

"Like what? Am I under arrest?"

"You're not under arrest right now," Booger said. "Would you like to be?"

"No," I said.

"Good. We've been watching you since you left the BART. Your Fast Pass says that you've been riding to a lot of strange places at a lot of funny hours."

I felt something let go inside my chest. This wasn't about the Xnet at all, then, not really. They'd been watching my subway use and wanted to know why it had been so freaky lately. How totally stupid.

"So you guys follow everyone who comes out of the BART Station with a funny ride-history? You must be busy."

"Not everyone, Marcus. We get an alert when anyone with an uncommon ride profile comes out and that helps us assess whether we want to investigate. In your case, we came along because we wanted to know why a smart-looking kid like you had such a funny ride profile?"

Now that I knew I wasn't about to go to jail, I was getting pissed. These guys had no business spying on me – Christ, the BART had no business helping them to spy on me. Where the hell did my subway pass get off on finking me out for having a "nonstandard ride pattern?"

"I think I'd like to be arrested now," I said.

Booger sat back and raised his eyebrow at me.

"Really? On what charge?"

"Oh, you mean riding public transit in a nonstandard way isn't a crime?"

Zit closed his eyes and scrubbed them with his thumbs.

Booger sighed a put-upon sigh. "Look, Marcus, we're on your side here. We use this system to catch bad guys. To catch terrorists and drug dealers. Maybe you're a drug dealer yourself. Pretty good way to get around the city, a Fast Pass. Anonymous."

"What's wrong with anonymous? It was good enough for Thomas Jefferson. And by the way, am I under arrest?"

"Let's take him home," Zit said. "We can talk to his parents."

"I think that's a great idea," I said. "I'm sure my parents will be anxious to hear how their tax dollars are being spent – "

I'd pushed it too far. Booger had been reaching for the door handle but now he whirled on me, all hulked out and throbbing veins. "Why don't you shut up right now, while it's still an option? After everything that's happened in the past two weeks, it wouldn't kill you to cooperate with us. You know what, maybe we should arrest you. You can spend a day or two in jail while your lawyer looks for you. A lot can happen in that time. A lot. How'd you like that?"

I didn't say anything. I'd been giddy and angry. Now I was scared witless.

(829 words)

4 Multiple matching → WB, p. 43/4; p. 44/5

Match the statements (A–H) with the character who could have thought or spoken them (1–3).

1 Marcus **2** Booger **3** Zit

A I will never understand the parking rules in San Francisco.
B My cold just isn't getting any better.
C When are they going to give us new equipment?
D Spelling is not one of my best skills.
E I need to keep my distance.
F He doesn't realise the seriousness of the situation he's in.
G I think we should put him into prison for his behaviour after all.
H The way I felt changed once again.

5 Short-answer questions

Answer the following questions. You may use words from the text.

1. Why wasn't it hard to realise that the waiting unmarked car was a police car? (two reasons)
2. Why has Marcus been detained by the police?
3. Why does Marcus feel relieved?
4. Why does the police officer tell Marcus to shut up?

Part II Material-based writing

World Press Freedom Day on 3 May reminds governments of the need to respect press freedom and freedom of speech. Furthermore, everyone who uses modern media is reminded of their responsibilty when sharing and spreading content and information. To honour this day, all the students from your school have been invited to write an essay for the school website discussing the following issue:

'Freedom of speech is important but has to coexist with responsibility and limits.'

Write a composition of at least 300 words. Include all the material provided.

→ WB, p. 44/6

Material 1

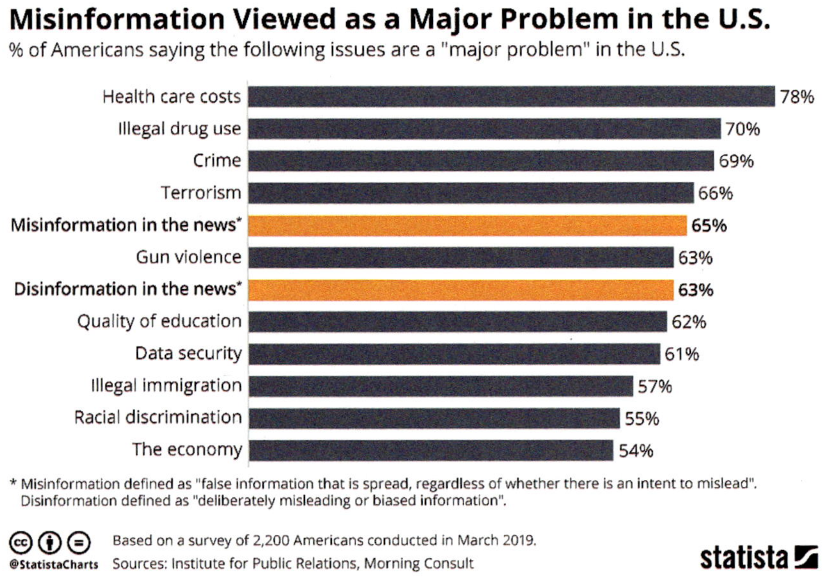

Material 2

Material 3

CHARTA DER MEINUNGSFREIHEIT

1. Meinungsfreiheit ist ein universelles Menschenrecht und als solches nicht verhandelbar. [...]
2. Die Meinungsfreiheit beinhaltet das Recht auf Information, die Pressefreiheit sowie die Freiheit des Publizierens und der Berichterstattung. [...]
4. Meinungsfreiheit verpflichtet zu einem Umgang, der von gegenseitigem Respekt, Zuhören, Ausredenlassen, Reflexion und argumentativem Abwägen geprägt ist.
5. Hetze und Hass werden nicht von der Meinungsfreiheit gedeckt, sondern beschädigen sie. Die Meinungsfreiheit endet da, wo die Würde eines Menschen angegriffen wird.
6. Meinungsfreiheit bedeutet nicht, frei von Kritik zu sein. Kritik ist der Beginn einer inhaltlichen Auseinandersetzung und somit wichtiger Bestandteil des Meinungsbildungsprozesses. [...]

Quelle: Börsenverein des Deutschen Buchhandels e.V.

Part III Group discussion

Media and technology play an important part in our lives. Thus, in the context of teaching media literacy, your school is organising a discussion with the title 'We are living in a media world'.

You can include the perspectives of the following people:

students | young people | conservatives | liberals | business people | senior citizens | teachers | parents | technology addicts | people with disabilities | ...

During the discussion you can talk about the following questions: → WB, p. 44–45/7

- Where, when, how and why do we use media and technology?
- Where is the border between intensive use and addiction?
- What is an acceptable, appropriate or a desirable use of media and technology? What is not?
- Where do media and technology make life easier and where more complicated?
- Where are media and technology indispensable?

a Introduce your main argument (about one minute).

b Discuss and explain your ideas and views. Be precise regarding which media / technological device you are talking about.

c Sum up your points of view. Try to come to a conclusion.

Diversity in society

Sexual orientation in Germany, 2020

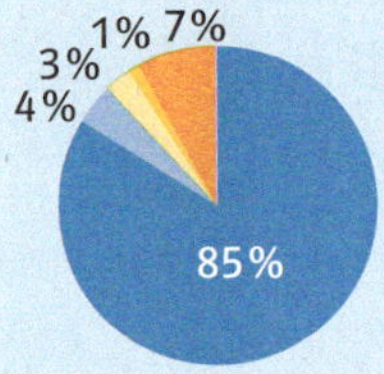

- heterosexual
- homosexual
- bisexual
- other
- not specified

Source: Statista, 2022

German population by age, 2021

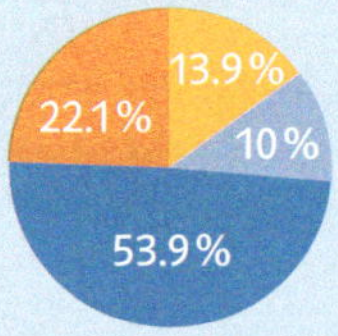

- 1–14
- 15–24
- 25–64
- 65 and older

Note: The different ages are represented in 4 instead of 10 groups.

Source: Statista, 2023

German population by background, 2021

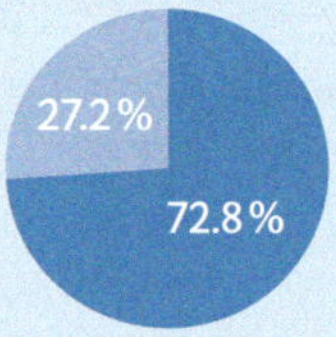

- without a migrant background
- with a migrant background: 52.6% German nationality / 47.4% foreign nationality

Source: Statistisches Bundesamt Mikrozensus, 2023

GOOD TO KNOW

Identity
= who you consider yourself to be (the character and personality of an individual)

1 What is 'diversity'?

a In small groups, make a mind map about diversity and the issues linked to it. Share your results in class.

b Write a definition of the term 'diversity'.

c Find other definitions of 'diversity' online. Compare them with your own definition. What differences did you find? Discuss your results.

2 Working with pictures → S 10.1 → WB, p. 46–47/1–3; p. 48/1

a With a partner, find a caption for each picture on page 96. Point out which aspect of diversity each picture shows.

b Choose one of the pictures. Which positive and negative situations might the person/people in your picture encounter in their everyday life? → S 15 Round robin

3 Working with diagrams → S 10.3

a Look at the diagrams on page 96. Research online and compare the numbers given with your region/your city/Bavaria. → S 15 Think-pair-share

b In small groups, choose one diagram and find more information about this group of people. Then present your findings in class.

4 Listening → S 3 → WB, p. 48/2

A24 **a** Listen to the first part of the podcast 'Diversity in society.' Answer the questions. Take notes.

1. According to Virginia McDowell, why is the United States a diverse country?
2. Which cultural background does McDowell have herself?
3. Which example does she give for parallel societies in many American cities?
4. Since when has it been possible for a 'Black' and a 'White' person to get married in Alabama?
5. What is the percentage of hate crimes committed based on ethnicity?
6. What can the individual citizen do to contribute to 'healthy diversity'?

A25 **b** Listen to the second part of the podcast. Are the statements true or false? Correct the false statements.

1. Duane Gilford represents the 2SLGBTQ+ community.
2. The + in the abbreviation stands for love, acceptance and pride.
3. In the 1970s, people who weren't straight were all called 'gay'.
4. AIDS started in the 1980s.
5. Homophobia means 'prejudices against people's sexual orientation'.
6. The *Vancouver Pride Parade* started over 30 years ago.
7. The members of the 2SLGBTQ+ community hope that in the future they can just be themselves without being confronted with prejudice.

mutual gegenseitig
to embrace annehmen
prejudice Vorurteil
outreach group Kontaktgruppe
straight heterosexuell

GOOD TO KNOW

AIDS (Acquired Immune Deficiency Syndrome) is the final stage of HIV. While numbers of HIV-affected people are higher in the LGBTQ+ community, it is important to know that everyone can get HIV.

'Black' and **'White'** are purely sociocultural labels given to people. They do not represent actual skin colours.

5 Discussing diversity → H 5

a Take notes on how to embrace diversity in today's society. Consider these questions.

1. What are the consequences of diversity for everyday life?
2. Which positive effects does a diverse society bring about?
3. Which conflicts do we encounter in a diverse society?
4. What does diversity mean for each individual within a community?

b Get together in small groups and discuss the questions from exercise **a**.

c Present your findings in class. Are your results similar or do they differ greatly?

A Gender: Changing perspective

1 Before you read

a Work with a partner. Partner A makes a list of gender stereotypes for men, partner B for women. Act out one of these stereotypes in class.

b Discuss the following questions in class. → S 15 Think-pair-share → H 5

1. What are the reasons for such stereotypes?
2. What are the consequences? What happens to people who do not conform to these stereotypes?

c With a partner, search online to find detailed information about the term 'LGBTQ+'. Then answer the following questions.

1. What does the abbreviation 'LGBTQ+' stand for?
2. Which aspects does the term cover?
3. What is the history of the term? How has it changed over time?

CULTURE BOX

Traditionally, people took it for granted that there were two genders – male and female. This is what is known as a binary perception of gender. However, there are people who do not see themselves as being one or the other and therefore use the term non-binary.

A26

Changing more than pronouns: a non-binary teen fights education laws

Santi Ceballos worked to change Arizona's curriculum laws that focused sex education on heterosexuality and left them out

1 non-binary nicht-binär *(Geschlecht, das weder ganz weiblich, noch ganz männlich ist)*
19 **hormone** Hormon
19 **to stave off** abwenden; hinausschieben
22 **condominium** Eigentumswohnung

1 Sometimes, other kids call Santi "it". "It's sort of like treating me as a different species," said Santi Ceballos, who goes by they/them pronouns, looking straight into the camera for a video [...] last year. The video was made in an effort to educate others about what it means to be gender nonconforming. "There's not only two genders!" Santi continues. "Just let us be who we want to beeee ..."

Santi Ceballos, right, stands with mom Carol Brochin and brother Joaquin Ceballos outside their home in Tucson, Arizona.

2 Today, at 13, they have let their wavy, golden-brown hair grow past their shoulders, with thick bangs over eyelashes long enough to graze oversized aviator glasses. Hormone blockers have staved off puberty, leaving Santi's face round and their skin clear and hairless. Outside of their small condominium in central Tucson, near the University of Arizona campus, Santi wears the classic teenager outfit: an oversized windbreaker and black skinny jeans with ripped knees.

3 Santi has had a long and sometimes painful journey, says their mother, Carol Brochin, an education professor. She teaches future public school teachers and has seen what she calls a real lack of empathy and understanding of the issues facing non-binary and transgender kids. "I tell my pre-service teachers, 'You have to be prepared. The kids are going to transition,'" Brochin says. Although there's no official data for Arizona, Brochin estimates there are about 140 families in the Tucson area with kids who identify as non-binary or trans. In 2017, a study by the Williams Institute at the UCLA School of Law estimated that 0.7 % of kids in the US between ages 13 and 17 – about 150,000 teens – identify as transgender.

4 When Brochin realized her own kid was struggling with identity, she looked for support. In 2017, she enrolled Santi in a popular program outside of Tucson for kids who identify all over the gender spectrum called *Camp Born This Way*, [...] funded by the *Southern Arizona Aids Foundation*. As campers were assigned name badges with preferred pronouns at orientation, Santi asked for a name badge with he/him. They had never met a non-binary person until that day at camp, and the impact was almost immediate. The next day, Santi asked to switch their pronouns to they/them. "That's when I came out, kind of," they said, smiling shyly. Brochin says it's not uncommon for kids to transition at *Camp Born This Way*. (She's now a member of the camp's steering committee.) "People often talk about it as, like, you come down the mountain and there's lots of tears and then you have to re-enter society," she says.

5 Re-entry was not easy for Santi. They came home feeling empowered – and, at the same time, more vulnerable than ever. A few weeks later, Santi transferred from a traditional public school with uniforms and kids who teased them for playing with the girls but using the boy's bathroom, to a charter school with a gender neutral restroom and overall more progressive views, such as a focus on social justice and environmental sustainability. Joaquin, their brother who is 20 months older, changed schools, too. He didn't like the "busy work" at his old school. But he also wanted to protect Santi. "Because of this," he says, gesturing up and down dramatically at his sibling sitting next to him. Everyone at the table laughs, including Santi.

6 Seventh grade was going so much better than sixth, for both kids. But then it came time for sex education. The boys and girls were separated. Santi was told to pick, which was very upsetting to them, and the curriculum included nothing beyond heterosexual basics, thanks to a 1991 Arizona law called *No Promo Homo*. Arizona was one of seven states in the US with such laws.

7 Santi's backslide after that was evident. "It caused a lot of dysmorphia and suicidal ideation," Brochin recalls. She got Santi counseling and they got better, she says. But she wanted to make a change. So did Santi. In March, a group called *Equality Arizona*, backed by the *National Center for Lesbian Rights and Lambda Legal*, filed a lawsuit against the state, claiming that by focusing sex education only on heterosexuality, Arizona was violating the Equal Protection Clause of the 14th amendment of the US constitution. The plaintiff, along with the *National Center for Lesbian Rights and Lambda Legal*, was Santi. Within days, the state legislature had voted to repeal the law. Governor Doug Ducey immediately signed the repeal – and *No Promo Homo* was gone. [...] (783 words)

Amy Silverman,
The Guardian website, 2019

33 **transgender** transsexuell
34 **pre-service teacher** Lehrer/-in in Ausbildung
47 **to enrol** (sich) einschreiben; anmelden
49 **gender spectrum** Bandbreite der Geschlechter
52 **to assign** zuweisen; zuordnen
54 **orientation** Einführung
57 **immediate** direkt; unmittelbar; spontan
63 **steering committee** Führungskomitee; Leitungsgruppe
69 **to feel empowered** sich bestärkt fühlen
75 **charter school** *(AE)* *Schule, die mit öffentlichen Mitteln finanziert wird, aber nicht den Schulbehörden untersteht*
97 **backslide** Rückfall
98 **dysmorphia** Dysmorphophobie *(krankhaft eingebildete Hässlichkeit)*
99 **suicidal ideation** Selbstmordgedanken
105 **to file a lawsuit** eine Klage einreichen
109 **amendment** (Verfassungs-)Zusatz
110 **plaintiff** Kläger/-in
113 **state legislature** gesetzgebende Versammlung auf Bundesstaatsebene

GOOD TO KNOW

UCLA
= University of California, Los Angeles

2 Multiple choice → WB, p. 49/1–3

Choose the most suitable option.

1. According to the first paragraph, Santi …
   A seems rather shy on video.
   B enjoys being referred to as "it".
   C is quite open about their views.
   D asks others to come out of their shells, too.

2. Which statement is not true according to paragraph 2?
   A Santi is on constant medication.
   B Santi already attends university.
   C Santi has rather childlike features.
   D Santi wears rather typical clothes.

3. Which statement is true according to paragraphs 3 and 4?
   A Mrs Brochin is a former school teacher herself.
   B Santi was deeply troubled after the first day at *Camp Born This Way*.
   C Mrs Brochin wishes there were more families facing similar issues in her region.
   D Carol Brochin tries to raise awareness regarding the issue among future teachers.

4. The general tone of the text can best be described as …
   A critical.
   B sombre.
   C factual.
   D enthusiastic.

3 Mediation

Beantworten Sie die folgenden Fragen zu den Abschnitten 5 und 6 auf Deutsch.

1. Welche schlechte Erfahrung machte Santi an der alten Schule nach der Rückkehr aus dem Camp?
2. Welche Beispiele werden für die fortschrittlicheren Ansichten an Santis neuer Schule angeführt?
3. Was waren die Motive von Santis Bruder, ebenfalls die Schule zu wechseln?
4. Warum war der Sexualkundeunterricht für Santi eine schlimme Erfahrung?

4 Short-answer questions

Answer the following questions using information from paragraph 7.
You may use words from the text.

1. What mental issues did Santi have after the school's sex education programme?
2. According to *Equality Arizona*, the way sex education was conducted at schools in Arizona was in conflict with which document?
3. What was Santi's role during the legal proceedings?
4. What was the outcome of the lawsuit?

5 Writing a blog post → S 6.3 → G 1.3, G 1.5

Pick one of the people mentioned in the text (Santi, Carol, Joaquin …). Write a blog post which this person might have written a week after Santi transferred to a new school. Write about 150 words. You can use the phrases from the box on page 101.

USEFUL PHRASES

This post is about …
I recently …
Did you know that …? | Have you heard of …? | I couldn´t believe that … | I was surprised by …
Considering the fact that …
As you can imagine …
What is … like in your country/school?
Shouldn't we …?

6 Listening → S 3 → H 5

A27 **a** Listen to an episode of the radio show 'Identity 101'. The person being interviewed is Noah Brooks, a professional athlete who just recently came out. While listening, answer the questions below.

shoutout to (infml) ein großes Dankeschön an
release Erleichterung

1. Which professional sports league does Noah Brooks play in?
2. How does Noah describe his childhood?
3. When did Noah realise that he was not heterosexual?
4. What was Noah's main concern about coming out?
5. Why did Noah not simply start going out with men?
6. How did Noah's bosses react to his decision to come out?
7. What is Noah's hope for the future regarding others' coming out?
8. How does Noah feel about his coming out now?

b Do you know of other examples of professional athletes or celebrities who have come out? Talk about these examples in class. You can also use the pictures on the right. Which reactions might there have been? Think of fans, colleagues, the press, …

Kristen Stewart

Jake Daniels

7 A step further

Gender stereotypes are still prevalent in our society. This causes many people among the LGBTQ+ community a lot of anguish. Your class wants to try and change the situation for the better at your school.

a With a partner, make a list of ideas on how to tackle the issue of gender stereotypes at your school. You can use examples from the text on pages 98–99.

b Get together in small groups. Discuss your ideas from **a**. Then put together a list of five aspects which you consider to be the most important.

c Now leave your group and pair up with a member of a different group. Exchange your ideas. → S15 Milling around

USEFUL PHRASES

Discussing stereotypes
to tackle an issue | to change attitudes | to work against prejudice | to take legal action | to introduce a new law | anti-discrimination legislation | equal opportunities | glass ceiling

B Celebrating diversity

1 Before you read → WB, p. 50/1

a Do some research online about a famous person with a different ethnic background than yours who inspires you or is a role model for you. Give reasons for your choice. Then prepare a short presentation about this person. You can consider the following aspects:

cultural background | education | values | traditions | obstacles | success | influence(s)

b Present your person to the class. Your classmates should think about the famous person they found most impressive. What new knowledge did you gain while listening to the presentations? Talk about it in class. → S 15 1-minute presentation → G 5, G 6

A28

Ethnic diversity makes Britain's culture great. It would be a disaster if we lost it

8 **squad** Mannschaft
14 **artwork** *hier:* Kunstobjekt
15 **to imprint** bedrucken
19 **prospect** *hier:* aussichtsreiche/-r Künstler/-in
28 **output** Leistung
32 **to remould** umgestalten
54 **outsized** übergroß

A couple of weeks ago, a young black man from south London stood up in front of tens of thousands of people and delivered one of the most celebrated performances in the history of Glastonbury. A few days later, an England cricket squad – almost half of whom were born abroad or are from an ethnic minority background – made it into the semifinals of the World Cup. Meanwhile over at Tate Modern, a British artist of Nigerian origin is displaying an artwork made up of thousands of books imprinted with the names of migrants who have made significant contributions to British culture.

Today, some of our most brilliant prospects in art and culture are from minority ethnic or migrant backgrounds. We present a gloriously multicultural face to the world. And that is important not just for the story we tell to others, but for the stories we tell ourselves. Think of the cultural power of the first Asian families on EastEnders, the breakthrough of Soul II Soul in the 1980s, or the nation-defining literary output of Zadie Smith.

The British actor Riz Ahmed refers to this as "stretching the flag, so it's big enough to embrace all of us". He is talking about how art can remould how we see ourselves and the country that we live in. The Pakistani-British heritage of his youth is just as much a part of our modern national story as the playing fields of Eton, remote Shetland communities or the multi-ethnic melting pots of Leicester, Birmingham and London. But it is only through the representation of that experience in our national culture that those truths are cemented across the whole country.

We should be confident and proud about this story – yet it is too rarely told.

Now a report from Global Future does exactly that, demonstrating not only the increasing diversity of our cultural industries, but how popular that diversity is. According to the report, nearly 40% of our leading cultural figures are from migrant or minority ethnic backgrounds. In other words, diversity is making an outsized contribution to British culture. And the size of the contribution is going up all the time: five years ago it was less than a third.

Global Future's survey of 2,000 UK adults suggests nearly seven in 10 of us agree that diversity has improved our culture, against 15% who disagree. Food, music and sport are the cultural industries where people believe diversity has had the greatest impact.

GOOD TO KNOW

Akram Khan is a British dancer and choreographer.

Soul II Soul is a British dance and R&B band formed in 1988.

Zadie Smith is a British novelist, essayist and short-story writer.

Riz Ahmed is a British-Pakistani actor and rapper.

Eton College is a well-known public school for boys founded in 1440.

This is music to my ears, of course. Britain is my home. I was born here, I have lived my whole life here, and I have pursued my life's passion here. As a dancer, Britain has been my stage.

It is our culture that makes me most proud to be British. That same culture has been a welcoming home for my own work: where a British dancer of Bangladeshi origin can pursue a career blending the Indian kathak style with contemporary forms. This openness to diversity is visible in many arenas: just look at the Notting Hill carnival every year. Or take the Turner [P]rize, where the artists shortlisted in the last two years have been of German, Fijian, Israeli, Zanzibari, Palestinian, Jamaican and Bengali heritage.

Diversity is what makes Britain's culture great. But recently it has felt as though we have lost sight of this self-evident truth. Brexit, polarisation and the poisonous debate about immigration threaten to turn our diversity into division. That would be a historic disaster for the country.

And yet when it comes to our culture, we are not really divided at all. We are united in our admiration for the acting of Idris Elba, the athleticism of Jessica Ennis-Hill and the artistry of Anish Kapoor and many more. It is essential that we remind ourselves of that fact, at a time when our politics seems geared towards making us forget it.

We can – and should – always do more. There are still serious barriers to entry for people of a minority ethnic background into our major cultural industries. In some cases, exclusivity in the arts is increasing rather than decreasing. Our culture should be ours collectively, not reserved for a few – and we have to work tirelessly to make sure that is the case.

But let's never lose sight of what makes Britain so special. Our differences fuel our creativity. And our exposure to all the cultures of the world does nothing but improve our own. (754 words)

Akram Khan,
The Guardian website, 2019

74 **to blend** mischen; vermischen
75 **contemporary** zeitgenössisch
85 **self-evident** selbstverständlich
98 **to be geared towards** abzielen auf
111 **exposure** Kontakt; Konfrontation; Ausgesetztsein

GOOD TO KNOW

Idris Elba is a British actor, producer and musician.

Dame Jessica Ennis-Hill is a British track and field athlete.

Anish Kapoor is a British-Indian sculptor.

2 Gapped summary → H 5 → WB, p. 50/2

Complete the summary with the most suitable words from the text (ll. 70–99). Give the line number of the words that you used.

Akram Khan states that the interest in ■ **1** is visible in many art forms, cultural events and dance performances. It can also be seen in ■ **2** careers, for example those of Idris Elba, athletes such as Jessica Ennis-Hill and artists like Anish Kapoor. The author of the article himself is ■ **3** to be British because the culture allows him to mix the Indian style of dancing with a ■ **4** form of expression. While Khan acknowledges the huge advantages dancers from around the world have in Great Britain, he criticises the fact that in recent years Brexit, ■ **5** and dangerous disputes about immigrants are leading to a loss of acceptance of British diversity. Khan claims that if people do not see the value of diversity, the country will suffer a ■ ■ **6**. People should remind themselves of their ■ **7** for the talents of artists from such diverse backgrounds because the British are ■ **8** in their appreciation, even though their ■ **9** may cause them to forget this.

3 Mediation

Beantworten Sie die folgenden Fragen zu Zeilen 29–69 auf Deutsch.

1. Was ist mit „stretching the flag“ (Z. 30) gemeint?
2. Womit setzt Khan das pakistanisch-britische Erbe des Schauspielers Riz Ahmed gleich?
3. Khan bezeichnet die britische Diversität als Geschichte, auf die man stolz sein kann. Was aber sieht er als Problem?
4. Welche Personengruppe umfasst 40 Prozent in Großbritannien?
5. Was bezeichnet Khan als „music to my ears“ (Z. 65)?

4 Short-answer questions

Answer the following questions referring to lines 58–113.
You may use words from the text.

1. What did a recent survey show?
2. Which two nationalities does Khan represent?
3. What is the opposite of 'diversity', according to Khan?
4. Although there are so many talented people among ethnic minorities, what problem does Khan still see?

Akram Khan

5 Words matter → S 11.1

a Find the synonyms of the words below in the text. Give the line numbers.

1. a sports team
2. to show
3. important
4. far away
5. influence
6. to go after

b Find the words in the text that match the definitions. Give the line numbers.

1. a person who is probably going to become famous through their art
2. to take someone in your arms
3. to stick things together with the help of a material which gets very hard
4. to be bigger than the norm
5. a kind of fence or wall that stops people from going somewhere

6 A step further

a In small groups, search online to find more information about the *Turner Prize*, *EastEnders* and the *Notting Hill Carnival*. Give reasons why Akram Khan mentions them in his text. → H 5

b In your group, find similar events or series in Germany. What is their main focus? What makes them special? → S 15 Round robin
Examples: Karneval der Kulturen – an intercultural event in Berlin / Türkisch für Anfänger – a series about a German-Turkish patchwork family / Deutscher Filmpreis – German prize dedicated to films

c Do you think a German artist would write a similar article about Germany? Discuss in class.

C Inclusive workplaces

1 Before you read

a With a partner, research online information about the issue of 'disabilities'. Consider the following aspects:

kinds of disabilities | issues of political correctness when talking about the topic | problems disabled people are often confronted with in everyday life

b Present your results in class.

A29

Forget stereotypes ... how to recruit talented, neurodiverse employees

By improving workplaces and recruitment, firms can attract neurodiverse talent. Entrepreneurs and workers with autism and dyspraxia offer advice

James Neely used to work in an open-plan office. His journey to work included busy, stressful train journeys. "I tended to isolate myself from people, so I had my headphones on and turned up all day and I wore a cap to limit my peripheral vision and reduce the light," he says. However, the 33-year-old data analyst struggled to find the quiet he needed at work. Eventually he had a breakdown. During subsequent treatment for anxiety and depression he was diagnosed with an autistic spectrum condition.

Neely now works for Auticon, a company that employs 15 full time IT consultants who have autism. They work on projects at major companies in the UK, including Experian and GlaxoSmithKline. Neely's found comfort in his new role. "We have back-office support from project managers and job coaches," he says. This takes off some of the pressure if a difficult situation arises. The job coaches encourage Auticon's consultants to take regular time off, which, Neely says, helps to "avoid the build up of anxiety or sensory overload". They also assist them with prioritising tasks and ensure the workplace environment is comfortable.

In the UK, just 16 % of autistic adults are in full time employment, according to the National Autistic Society. And yet research has shown autistic traits can be associated with high numbers of unusual responses on divergent thinking tasks; a mark of creativity, which is sought after by ambitious startups. Meanwhile, research from University of Montreal suggests that people with autism are up to 40 % better at problem solving.

Ray Coyle, Auticon's CEO, says there's a strong business case for employing neurodiverse people. One of Auticon's clients, Siemens, say the two Auticon consultants who were working for them increased the team's product testing efficiency by 50 % within their first week. Coyle adds: "The fact that Auticon is profitable [revenues have grown by around 50 % each year since 2014] shows that our business model is sound and reflects the quality of our workforce."

Dr Linda Buchan is director of Cheshire-based Axia-ASD Ltd, which offers assessment services, including for autism spectrum disorders. She says while running a small business with neurodiverse staff can bring particular challenges, the benefits are clear. Buchan has dyspraxia. She says many people assume dyspraxia just affects coordination, but it goes much further. "Dyspraxia can affect any muscle groupings in the body, it can affect your sense of time, distance and visual tracking too."

2 **neurodiverse** neurodivers *(umfasst neurobiologische Unterschiede u.a. Autismus, AD(H)S, Dyskalkulie, Legasthenie und Dyspraxie)*
4 **autism** Autismus *(eine neurologisch-genetisch bedingte Wesensart)*
4 **dyspraxia** Dyspraxie; Koordinationsstörung
5 **open-plan office** Großraumbüro
10 **peripheral vision** Umgebungswahrnehmung
15 **anxiety** Angst; Unruhe
24 **back-office support** Hintergrundunterstützung
37 **trait** Eigenschaft; Merkmal
39 **divergent** abweichend
53 **revenue** Ertrag; Einnahmen
55 **sound** tragfähig; sicher
60 **disorder** Störung
67 **muscle grouping** Muskelgruppe
69 **visual tracking** visuelle Erfassung

72 **to do admin** Verwaltungsarbeit erledigen
76 **to go off on tangents** (immer wieder) abschweifen
80 **off-the-wall** unkonventionell
91 **in plenty of time** frühzeitig
97 **dyslexic** legasthenisch
101 **niche** Nische

For Buchan, who employs 11 people, dyspraxia affects her ability to do admin; she struggles with dates and finds writing difficult. To stay organised, she relies on lists. But she also notes the positive sides. "Dyspraxic people can go off on tangents and that can take you to a really interesting place. We're good at noticing detail and we can be good at innovating and coming up with off-the-wall ideas." [...]

Sarah Hendrickx, an autism consultant and trainer, suggests that simple changes can make a huge difference to neurodiverse people's experience of work. "[For example, neurodiverse] people can find it difficult to take in a lot of information from multiple sources at once." This can make group meetings a challenge, and so Hendrickx recommends providing an agenda in plenty of time, that minutes are taken and that clear action points are emailed to attendees afterwards.

The recruitment process could be better streamlined too, adds Hendrickx. She is autistic, dyslexic and has Tourette syndrome, and was diagnosed as an adult: "Some highly talented, unusual thinkers may have struggled for many years to find their niche, and [might] not look great on paper." [...] (620 words)

Hazel Davis, *The Guardian* website, 2017

2 Multiple matching → WB, p. 51/1–2

Match the statements (A–F) with the people (1–4) from the text.
There are two statements more than you need.

1 James Neely **2** Ray Coyle **3** Dr Linda Buchan **4** Sarah Hendrickx

A I sometimes surprise my colleagues with my eccentric and unconventional suggestions.
B Many people find me not easy to work with, but that is largely due to their lack of knowledge regarding my condition.
C It is hard for me to cope with too much sensory input.
D It is really beneficial to work with neurodiverse employees.
E If your business is rather small, hiring neurodiverse staff might bring big challenges.
F Don't just look at grades and diplomas. If given the chance, neurodiverse people have a lot to offer.

3 Gapped summary → H 5

Complete the summary with the most suitable words from the text (ll. 1–44). Give the line numbers of the words that you used.

Before he went to work for Auticon, James Neely suffered a lot, for example on his way to work, which was always a rather ■ **1** undertaking for him. At work, the surroundings were too much for him to bear and thus he experienced a complete ■ **2**. Only then did doctors diagnose him as being ■ **3**. His new job is better suited to his needs. Neely now gets a lot of ■ **4** from his superiors. This at least reduces the ■ **5** that often cannot be fully avoided in the world of work. Neely and others also get help when it comes to ■ **6** the items on their to-do list. Up to now, only a minority of people with autism are integrated into the workforce. However, attitudes are changing. Especially ■ **7** are keen on making use of these individuals' creativity.

4 Mediation

Beantworten Sie die folgenden Fragen auf Deutsch.

1. Mit welchen Einschränkungen muss Dr. Linda Buchan im Berufsalltag zurechtkommen?
2. Was hilft ihr bei der Organisation ihres Alltags?
3. Warum sind laut Sarah Hendrickx Teambesprechungen für neurodiverse Mitarbeiter oft ein Problem?
4. Welche Tipps führt Hendrickx an, um dieses Problem zu lösen?

5 Words matter → S 11.1

a Copy the table and put the linking expressions from the word bank in the right columns.

moreover | therefore | furthermore | consequently | however | in spite of | whereas | since | as a result | only if | although | unless | nevertheless | additionally | despite

addition	cause/effect	condition	contrast
and	due to	…	…
…	…	…	…

b Find further examples of such phrases in the text and add them to your list.

c Write a short statement about your idea of inclusion of all people in the workplace. Use as many linking words from **a** as possible to structure your text.

6 A step further → G 4 → S 6.5

a In small groups, discuss the following questions and take notes.

1. Which other disabilities do you know of?
2. Where do people with such disabilities encounter problems at school, in town (shops, traffic), at work etc.? What kind of problems are they?
3. What can be done to help them / to make their life easier / to allow full participation in everyday life?
4. What can we learn from them? How can society profit from them?

b Based on your results from **a**, create a poster for your community in which you inform people about the issue.

c Present your posters to the class. Give each other feedback.
→ S 15 Gallery walk → S 15 Tip-top

Disability and sports → S 6.1

1 Improving your arguments → WB, p. 52/1

a To make your arguments more varied, you can use different phrases and expressions. Match the following phrases and expressions (1–6) with their German equivalents (A–F).

1 The urgency of this particular matter can hardly be overestimated.
2 Considering the aforementioned points, it is quite obvious that …
3 It should also be mentioned that …
4 There is only one conclusion we can draw from all of this.
5 Certainly a good compromise can be found.
6 This is cause for a lot of concern.

A Das ist Grund zur Besorgnis.
B Man kann sicher einen Kompromiss finden.
C All das lässt nur einen Schluss zu.
D Die Dringlichkeit dieses speziellen Aspekts kann man kaum genug betonen.
E Wenn man diese Dinge betrachtet, wird einem klar, dass …
F Man sollte auch erwähnen, dass …

b With a partner, make a list of further useful phrases and words in German and their English equivalents.

2 Material-based writing

Doing sports plays a major role in many people's lives; this is also true for people with disabilities. In your composition, point out why it is important that people with disabilities get the opportunity to take part in the world of sports, and ways of achieving this goal.

Write at least 300 words. Include all the materials provided.

Material 1

Wir wollen die ganze Welt verändern. Eine neue Initiative soll zu einer neuen Wahrnehmung für Menschen mit Behinderung sorgen. Ihr seid Helden! Ihr seid das Beste, was die Menschheit zu bieten hat.

Andrew Parsons, president of the International Paralympic Committee

Material 2

Percentage of adults (age 18–64) who get no physical activity, by disability type

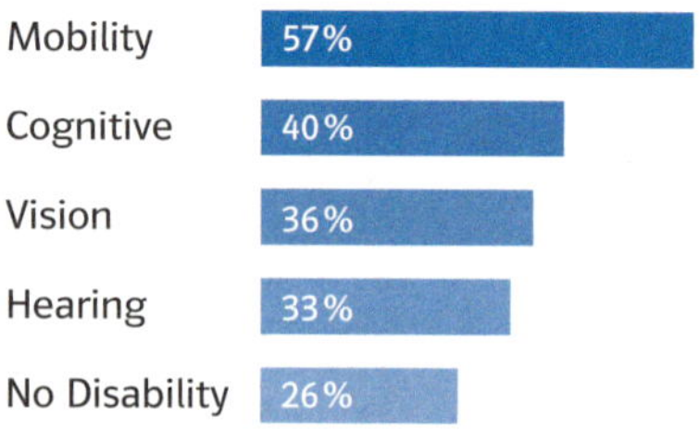

Source: CDC National Center for Statistics, National Health Interview Survey, 2009–2012

Material 3

Anti-bullying theme day → S2

1 Reacting to the statements of others

When you take part in a group discussion, you should try to make your conversation sound as natural as possible. An important element is how you react to the statements of others. There are different ways of how you can express agreement or disagreement with the other participants' statements.

a Look at the useful phrases. Find more examples for the different categories.

USEFUL PHRASES

Agreeing	Disagreeing	Nuancing	Clarifying
Absolutely!	Well, I wouldn't say that.	That's a good point. However, …	I was wondering if you could explain …
I couldn't agree more because …	I'm not sure about …	I see where you're coming from, but …	I'd like to know more about …
You're absolutely right. Consequently, we …	Well, it depends on …	We shouldn't forget that …	Do you see what I mean?
	I seriously doubt that …		
	I strongly disagree.		

b With a partner, make a list of controversial statements. Then take turns making a statement and reacting to it. Give reasons for your reaction.

Example:
Partner A: I think every company needs someone who represents the needs of disabled people.
Partner B: You're absolutely right. Without these representatives, people with disabilities could easily be overlooked.

2 Group discussion

As a member of your school's student council, it has been brought to your attention that there are more and more victims of bullying. It is your intention to change the situation for the better. In today's meeting you develop a plan for an 'anti-bullying theme day'. Include the following aspects:

1. Agree on a slogan for the theme day.
2. Discuss what the main reasons for bullying are and how you can address them.
3. How can your school embrace and celebrate diversity and being different?
4. Plan three main events for the theme day. Work out as many details as possible.

a Present your main idea (about one minute).

b Discuss and explain your ideas and the different aspects you wish to include on the theme day.

c Sum up your points of view. Try to come to a conclusion.

Part I Reading

Day of the Girl is critical, but support is needed year-round, say campaigners

1 The International Day of the Girl is critical in highlighting girls' rights globally, but action is urgently needed to reverse the damage of the pandemic, campaigners have said. "Girls who were once hopeful about their futures say to us: 'We're not sure if we're going to achieve our dreams now, if we're ever going to go back to school'," said Emily Wilson, chief executive of UK and Uganda-based organisation Irise International, which works to combat period poverty.

2 The Day of the Girl, celebrated each year on 11 October, is core to the charity's funding drives, with donations on the day contributing up to 10% of its yearly income. "There is always a risk that girls' rights becomes an add-on," said Wilson. "So these mainstream peaks in engagement on days like today have really helped change attitudes. The Day of the Girl gives us the opportunity to share our reports with policymakers, and push the issues we work on all year more centre-stage."

3 Mwangala Mukelabai, Zambian representative for the Campaign for Female Education (Camfed), who is taking over the NGO's Twitter account to share her journey of activism for girls' education, agreed. "Girl child day is important to me because it is on this day that we make sure the voices of girls are heard and highlight the challenges that they face to the world," she said.

4 This year's International Day of the Girl, which was adopted by the UN in 2011, makes closing the digital gender gap its focus. Maliha Abidi, a 25-year-old Pakistan-born artist and neuroscience student, is launching Women Rise, a collection of 10,000 non-fungible tokens (NFTs) [...]. Abidi said she hoped her project would drive more girls into the tech and blockchain industries. But in a world where men are up to 50% more likely to access the internet than women, more work needed to be done to ensure girls don't miss out on the technology boom. Abidi said governments and institutions must prioritise girls at risk of dropping out of education early, if the gender digital divide is to be closed. "When we talk about the digital world in connection to girls' education, or girls in general, it's not just about connecting girls to the internet." Leaders must ensure girls interested in Stem (science, technology, engineering and maths) subjects can stay in those fields, all the way from school to university to a job, she said. "It's about helping them reach that finishing point."

5 [...] Many countries have made great strides in girls' rights over the past 10 years. In 2015, the UN made gender equality one of its 17 sustainable development goals for 2030. In 2014, the African Union launched a continent-wide campaign to end child marriage, encouraging its 55 member states to pass laws, make action plans and support communities.

6 In the run-up to Day of the Girl last October, girls' equality charity *Plan International* kickstarted its #FreeToBeOnline campaign. It led to more than 66,000 people signing an open letter urging social media companies to protect girls from abuse and harassment. Instagram, Facebook and WhatsApp agreed to team up with young people to discuss solutions for girls' online safety. In 2017, 24 girls in Ecuador, supported by Plan International, drafted a resolution addressing violence against girls to the national assembly. [...]

7 Wilson said in Uganda, Irise has had to cancel its menstruation education programmes in schools, which remain closed. The organisation has instead diverted resources to tackling the rise in child marriage and teenage pregnancies among the estimated 10 million Ugandan girls who have missed out on an education since last March.

8 Olutope Olatilewa, the Nigeria-based founder of mentoring programme African ChangeMakers Women Network, said: "Society is confused about where to place the girl child; she is caught in between the categories of women's rights and children's rights. But little visibility is given to girls' rights specifically." Her mentoring scheme across 54 African countries aims to build leadership skills. "But even that is not enough – we are just scratching the surface of what we must do."

9 The global network Girls Not Brides said the spike in donations and support for girls received on 11 October needs to continue throughout the rest of the year for there to be long-term change. While rates of child marriage have gone down over the past decade, the decline is not fast enough to end the practice by 2030, said Nerida Nthamburi, a Kenya-based partnership officer for Girls Not Brides. The group estimates that progress must become six times faster to meet the UN target. The Day of the Girl is critical to the movement, said Nthamburi, because "it creates a deliberate platform that focuses attention on the seldom-heard voices of girls who know best – girls who have felt the pain and live through the risk [of child marriage] every day". "Unless we accelerate progress as a global community – governments, leaders, parents and religious leaders – we are likely to see a rollback," said Nthamburi. (835 words)

Georgina Quach,
The Guardian website, 2021

1 Gapped summary → WB, p. 53/1

Complete the summary with the most suitable words from the text (paragraphs 1–4). Give the line number of the words that you used.

During the pandemic, many girls started to doubt whether they can ■ **1** their aspirations, given the uncertainties of the times. According to Emily Wilson, it is essential to make sure that the International Day of the Girl is not only used to collect ■ **2**, which is also important, but to put the important ■ **3** charities like *Irise International* deal with into the spotlight.
An aspect that is supposed to get special attention is the ■■ **4** regarding information technology. Maliha Abidi, for example, tries to ensure that girls are not left too far behind during the current ■■ **5**. She emphasises the fact that it is not sufficient to help get girls into the STEM area, but to support them so they can persevere until they arrive at the ■■ **6**.

2 Mediation

Beantworten Sie die folgenden Fragen auf Deutsch.

1. Inwiefern ist die #FreeToBeOnline-Kampagne relevant, um Geschlechtergerechtigkeit voranzubringen?
2. Welches Ziel verfolgt die Organisation von Olutope Olatilewa im Hinblick auf eine geschlechtliche Gleichstellung?
3. Wie beschreibt Nerida Nthamburi die Entwicklung im Bereich Kinderehen? Welche Gefahr droht?

Abdi Nor Iftin was born in Mogadishu, Somalia, to nomadic parents. He survived war and famine. In 2009, he and his brother fled to Kenya and then in 2014, won a visa to the USA in a lottery. Today, he lives in the state of Maine and is an advocate for refugee and immigrant rights. In 2018, his autobiography *Call Me American* was published, telling his story of his journey to America.

Call Me American

by Abdi Nor Iftin

Every day we batted different houses and buildings in different towns. Ten miles, twenty miles, and sometimes as far as eighty miles. We had to finish batting a whole house within the same day, **1**. Lunch break was only thirty minutes. Milton and Sean ate doughnuts, sometimes burgers they brought with them. I always sought a clean place and prayed. They both would come look at me **2**.

"What are you doing?" Milton asked me. During the prayer I am not supposed to speak, so I was quiet and answered when I finished. "I was praying." Milton picked up his phone and called everyone else who worked at the company and even his old lady.

He made fun of the whole thing. "This dude bows and says he's praying," he said with a laugh.

I had to tell them that I am Muslim, **3**. "They got Muslims in Africa?" Sean asked. Of course they thought all Muslims look like Osama bin Laden.

After work, Milton and Sean would stop at a convenience store to buy beer and cigarettes. Often they would ask to borrow money from me until the next payday. I always gave them a few dollars when they asked, but they never paid me back. I wasn't sure if it would be polite to remind them on payday.

One day on the job my hard hat disappeared. Another day my staple gun, then my winter coat. When I asked what could have happened, Milton laughed and said, "That's what happens when you're new here." The boss said he couldn't do anything. I had to buy a new hard hat and a new staple gun from the shop. I had no idea who was stealing my stuff until one day I found my hard hat in the back of Milton's pickup truck. The same guys I'd been working with for months, and when I asked, they said nothing! It was humiliating, and **4**.

I asked Joey to put me on a different batting squad, and I was told to work with a guy named Tom. He was respectful to me, rolling down his window when smoking weed. He had been to prison several times, due to drugs, and he said he wanted to stop. But he explained that he needed the weed to do his job. [...]

Tom and I got along well. I felt it was safe to leave my things in his truck. He wanted to see the world outside the United States; he wanted to explore. He told me he liked watching *National Geographic TV* shows. He watched shows about the Maasai Mara and Serengeti national parks in Kenya and Tanzania. We talked about lions, hyenas, and wildebeests. I told him stories about my mom and dad facing lions in real life. I liked Tom, but I noticed the drugs he took to cope with work also seemed to cause his troubles. [...]

Many of the guys on the batting squad had lost their licenses from drunk driving, so they all gave each other rides home. Milton gave Sean a ride, and Tom picked up two other people. I asked if someone could give me a ride home, and Milton said **5** gas money. None of the other guys gave him gas money, but he wanted twenty dollars a week from me. I told him I was happy to walk home, even though I was so tired and dirty after work.

I don't know if the guys on the batting squad were racist; 6. But it did feel like something I understood very well: the tribalism of Somalia. I have heard Americans complain that Africans bring on their own problems with their tribal feuds, and there is some truth to that. But these Maine guys had a tribe too. Maybe they didn't call themselves Darod or Hawiye, but it was a tribe, and I definitely was not a member. So I had to walk home, up Main Street, looking like some homeless guy in my filthy work clothes and covered in pink fiberglass threads. Fortunately, the people of Yarmouth got to know me and realized 7. When I got home, I took off my rough clothes, took a warm shower, dressed up nice, and walked back toward Main Street to relax at the Dunkin' Donuts. People waved and smiled. I started to feel like part of the community and not just an outsider like I felt at work. (791 words)

3 Multiple matching → WB, p. 53/2

Seven phrases have been cut from the text. Match the most suitable phrases (A–J) with the gaps (1–7). There are three phrases more than you need.

A it felt as if my American dream was shrinking
B the resentment was mutual
C I would have to pay him
D I hadn't been in America long enough to know about that
E so we moved fast
F I felt my anger swelling
G bowing my head and reciting the Koran
H it felt impossible to continue like this
I I was just a hard-working guy
J I have to pray five times a day

4 Short-answer questions

Answer the following questions. You may use words from the text.

1. According to the narrator, what do Americans consider to be a major cause of the bad situation in Africa?
2. Who does the narrator resemble on his way home due to his stained work clothes?
3. The narrator is not able to really integrate at work. How is the situation in his free time?
4. How does the narrator realise that the people of Yarmouth have started to accept him?

Age discrimination: older Australian workers viewed as slow to learn

Despite an increasingly mature workforce, Australian companies aren't addressing the challenges or countering the stereotypes faced by older workers

1 The trope of the older worker thrust back into the hurly-burly of working life made for great comedy in the 2015 film The Intern. But in reality, this scenario isn't always such a laughing matter. Older workers face unique hardships. Hampered by unfair stereotypes about their abilities, their role in society and their responsibilities, they are regularly overlooked for interviews, jobs, promotions and recognition. The Australian Human Rights Commission's 2016 report Willing to Work found 27% of people over the age of 50 reported experiencing age discrimination at work, a third of the most recent episodes occurring when applying for a job. One-third of those gave up looking for work.

2 Age discrimination was particularly acute among older women, who were more likely to be viewed as having outdated skills, being slow to learn, or as being likely to do an unsatisfactory job. Seniors with disabilities face an even steeper uphill battle for jobs and recognition. The bias against age can be overt; four in 10 companies surveyed by the Australian Human Rights Commission said they avoided employing anyone over the age of 55. In some cases, older individuals applying for jobs are leaving their age off their CVs and editing their work history to make their age less obvious.

3 But age discrimination can also be more subtle: inadvertent exclusion from work-related social activities and circles, repeatedly being passed over for promotion or training opportunities in favour of younger workers, or being parodied by younger workers, says Prof Peter Gahan, director of the University of Melbourne's Centre for Workplace Leadership. "Certain ways of expressing things, or throwaway lines, are ageist, and they have the effect of excluding people from the social context of work and we need to be conscious of those things," Gahan says.

4 Yet the reality is our population is ageing; one quarter of Australians are over the age of 55, with that predicted to increase to one-third in the next decade. As a result, industry is taking a second look at older workers, and not a moment too soon, according to Dr Ruth Williams, research fellow at the Centre for Workplace Leadership. "We hear all about the challenges and the doom and gloom, and the tsunami of [older] people but the mindset needs to be completely flipped," Williams says. "They are a huge untapped resource and they're an untapped market as well for businesses."

5 Older workers bring a lifetime of experience, networks and tacit knowledge that can't simply be written down and left for their successors. They also have a lot to offer customers. Williams points to companies such as hardware retailer Bunnings, which is recognising the value of employees' past experience. "You're actually talking to an ex-plumber or an ex-electrician who could know exactly – or better – what you might need to do your home renovation," Williams says. Another reason to employ older workers is to better reflect the demographics of your customer base, she says. The banking, retail and hospitality sectors particularly stand to benefit from taking on older workers for face-to-face roles, as the customers most likely to use these services (rather than going online) are themselves older individuals.

6 How can companies overcome the barriers that are making it harder for older workers to find and keep rewarding jobs? One important step is to counter the perception among younger workers that the older generation are competition for increasingly scarce employment and

advancement opportunities. "It tends to intensify these negative attitudes, and particularly attitudes that suggest that perhaps by staying in the workforce longer, older people might be taking opportunities from younger people in society," Gahan says. But when this mindset is challenged, research has shown it has a positive impact on the attitudes of younger workers towards their older colleagues. Younger workers also stand to benefit significantly from the experience, wisdom and insights of older colleagues, whose own professional focus might shift as they reach peak points in career development. "They turn their attention to things [which] they perceive as legacy issues; how can they help others in the workplace, how might they be a mentor and help develop younger people in the workplace," Gahan says.

7 There are lessons to be learned from efforts used to counter sex discrimination in the workplace. Williams says using quotas could be one way to at least kickstart better recruitment of older workers, as could having older staff involved in recruitment and hiring. Williams argues we still have a long way to go to address the many challenges facing older Australians who want to stay in the workforce, and efforts to counter ageism in the workplace are still very much in their infancy. "There's a growing demand but at the moment it is kind of like lip service really; there's not a great deal being done at this point in time," she says. "However, there's more of a groundswell for things to happen, so we're at a tipping point."

(848 words)

Bianca Nogrady,
The Guardian website, 2017

5 Multiple choice → WB, p. 53/3

Choose the most suitable option.

1. Which statement is true about older people and the world of work?
   - **A** Older people are often not keen on finding a new job.
   - **B** Older people often have to do internships to prove their value.
   - **C** The process of applying for a new job is particularly discouraging for the older generation.
   - **D** More than a third of older workers have been discriminated against at the workplace due to their age.
2. According to the second paragraph …
   - **A** some older people lie about their age when they apply for a job.
   - **B** some firms try to hide the fact that they do not want to hire older staff.
   - **C** women have fewer work skills and therefore even less of a chance on the labour market.
   - **D** the situation is worst for those older citizens who also have some sort of bodily impairment.
3. Which form of discrimination against older employees is <u>not</u> mentioned in paragraph 3?
   - **A** Older employees are given humiliating tasks.
   - **B** Younger colleagues often ridicule older co-workers.
   - **C** Although they deserve it, older employees are denied promotion.
   - **D** Older employees are not invited to Christmas parties or similar occasions.

4. Dr Ruth Williams puts forward the claim that …
   A there are ways to stop society from ageing too rapidly.
   B the rising number of older citizens will be society's downfall.
   C companies can make a fortune if they win over older people as customers.
   D companies are still completely unaware of the potential older workers have to offer.

5. Which of the following aspects is not mentioned in paragraph 5?
   A Salespeople who used to have other jobs can be a huge benefit.
   B Work experience cannot simply be passed on to the next generation.
   C Older people might prefer to deal with a peer when it comes to finances.
   D Older employees could teach the younger colleagues when it would be better to be silent.

6 Mediation

Beantworten Sie die folgenden Fragen auf Deutsch.

1. Wie nehmen die jüngeren Leute die älteren oft wahr?
2. Was meint der Autor mit „legacy issues" in Abschnitt 6 (Z.114)?
3. Inwieweit könnte man Lehren aus dem Kampf gegen Geschlechterdiskriminierung ziehen?
4. Wie schätzt Williams die aktuelle Lage im Kampf gegen Altersdiskriminierung in der australischen Arbeitswelt ein?

Part II Material-based writing

Our society is becoming more and more diverse. Reflect on the following question:

'Which role does the media play in the development towards more diversity in our society?'

Write a composition of at least 300 words. Include all the material provided.
→ WB, p. 54/4

Material 1

Unsere Gesellschaft ist vielfältig. Unsere Arbeitswelt auch. Vielfalt geht uns alle an: Denn Diversity ist wichtig für den Zusammenhalt in unserer Gesellschaft. Über 900 Organisationen zeigten am #DDT21 #FlaggefürVielfalt!
Über 900 Organisationen setzten mit mehr als 2.700 Aktionen am 9. Deutschen Diversity-Tag ein Zeichen für Vielfalt in der Arbeitswelt. Unsere Kernthemen platzierten wir in TV-Beiträgen, im Radio und in Podcasts, in Artikeln in Tages- und Wochenzeitungen.

Auf Twitter belegten die Hashtags #DDT21 und #FlaggefürVielfalt die vorderen Ränge der deutschen Twitter-Trends. Lassen Sie sich von den digitalen Beiträgen auf Twitter, Facebook und Co. auf unserer Social Media Wall inspirieren.

Charta der Vielfalt website, 2022

Material 2

Diversity is the one true thing we all have in common. Celebrate it every day.
Winston Churchill, former Prime Minister of the UK (1874–1965)

Material 3

Models from the series *Germany's Next Topmodel*, 2022

Part III Group discussion

You are members of your school's student council. At your school, there are students with a lot of different backgrounds, religions, and ethnicities. In order to celebrate this, in today's meeting you work out a preliminary plan for a 'Diversity appreciation day'. Talk about the following aspects and include as many details as possible:

1. Develop a slogan for this theme day.
2. Decide which of the pictures below should be used for the advertising posters for the theme day.
3. Come up with at least three events which should take place during the theme day.

a Introduce the ideas you think would be most important for the theme day (about one minute).

b Discuss and explain your ideas for the slogan, the picture and the three events.

c Sum up your points of view. Try to come to a conclusion.

Ecological issues

Source: UNO

1 Working with pictures → S 10.1 → WB, p. 56–57/1–6

a Look at the pictures on page 118. Answer the questions. You can use the words from the word bank.

1. What is the message in picture A?
2. What solutions do pictures B–D present to ecological problems?

pollution | climate | nature | change | wasteland | destruction | technology | resources | to reduce | to protect | to strengthen | to take action

b The pictures represent different areas of ecological action: political activism, technology, agriculture, urban planning. How can each area contribute in adapting to the consequences of climate change? Which other areas can you think of?
→ S 15 Think-pair-share

2 Talking about the Sustainable Development Goals (SDGs) → H 6 → WB, p. 58/1

a Look at the SDGs. Which of the goals are about the environment? Try to explain these goals to a partner. Take turns.

b Collect words you need to talk about all the SDGs and organise them in a mind map.

3 Researching information online → S 13.1 → WB, p. 58/2

a Search online to find detailed information about one of the SDGs concerning the environment. What has already been achieved in this area? What needs to be done? Prepare a short presentation.
Example: Sustainable economy – Just 100 companies responsible for 71 % of global emissions

b Present your results to the class. → S 15 1-minute presentation

4 Creating a vision board → G 1.9, G 1.10

a Look at the issues presented on pages 118–119 again. In small groups, create a vision board with your vision of a desirable future. Use key words and pictures.

b Present and explain your vision to the other groups. → S 15 Gallery walk

c Discuss in class what your views of the future of the planet and its inhabitants regarding the SDGs are. Are you pessimistic or optimistic? Explain.

USEFUL PHRASES

Expressing probability/predicting
Definitely: Of course, it'll … | It's going to … | There's no question that … | It's safe to say …
Probably: It'll probably … | We expect it to … | We wouldn't be surprised if …
Perhaps: We guess it might … | There's a chance it'll …
Probably not: We doubt (if) it'll … | We don't think it'll …
Definitely not: Of course it won't … | There's no chance of it …-ing. | We're absolutely sure it won't …

GOOD TO KNOW

Attaining peace and prosperity for people and the planet is a complex but inevitable challenge as United Nations officials recognised at the Sustainable Development Summit in 2015. All UN member states adopted the 2030 Agenda for Sustainable Development. At its core are 17 **Sustainable Development Goals (SDGs)**, an urgent call for action for all countries in a global partnership.

A Ecology and economy

1 Before you read

a Do a survey about your classmates' shopping habits: How often do you shop, where and what do you buy? If online, how much do you send back? Take notes.

b In small groups, discuss the results of the survey. How environmentally friendly are your shopping habits?

c Read the headline of the text. What does it refer to? → S15 Round robin

A30

6 **fleeting** flüchtig
9 **solid waste** Festmüll
20 **Energy Saving Trust** *Brit. Organisation für Energieeffizienz und Nachhaltigkeit*
23 **raw material** Rohstoff
33 **consumerism** Konsumdenken
34 **rampant** grassierend
35 **retailer** Einzelhändler/-in
52 **carriage** Transportkosten
53 **to penalise** bestrafen
62 **viable** machbar

The hidden environmental cost of your online shopping

There's still something magical about the idea of browsing a world of goods online, choosing what you want and having it delivered to your door, sometimes within hours. You may give a fleeting thought to the environmental impact when you are drowning in excess packaging (nearly a third of solid waste in the US comes from e-commerce packaging) but it's easy to ignore the rest of it. Such as the fact that Amazon, in figures released last year, emits nearly as much carbon dioxide as a small country. We are buying more online than ever – and younger age groups are less likely to shop locally than people over 55, according to a new survey.

Our rapidly growing delivery culture is a challenge, says Tim Anderson, head of transport at the Energy Saving Trust. "It's easy to go online and buy things cheaply. They might have been shipped from far off countries, manufactured from raw materials and they arrive at our homes at little or no cost."

In an ideal world, online shopping could be a better option than making individual trips to the store (large weekly grocery deliveries can be the better choice – as long as we don't make additional supermarket trips ourselves). We do not live in an ideal world, however, but one in which profit and consumerism are rampant. We don't behave – and online retailers don't encourage us to behave – in a sensible way, says Julian Allen, researcher at the transport studies department at the University of Westminster.

Once, we were prepared to wait, but now we want same-day delivery.

That, says Allen, "tends to mean stuff gets moved in smaller and smaller quantities. We have vehicles shooting all over the place making single deliveries. We have the concept of 'free' delivery, which is a selling point for retailers, but it's not really free in the sense of what it costs them and what it costs in environmental terms."

People also buy things, particularly clothes, with the intention of returning much of the order, resulting in more carriage and mileage. "They are not being penalised financially for doing that," says Allen.

The growth in hot-food delivery services, such as Deliveroo and Uber Eats, has been enormous. "It's sheer inefficiency to move a single meal in a car or motorbike," says Allen. "Bicycles would help in terms of pollution, but the trend has been to move away from bikes as these firms expand their networks, and it's not viable."

So what should we do? "Shop locally, [especially] if you can use sustainable transport," is Anderson's advice.

And Allen thinks we should be more patient and consolidate orders into one delivery at a time. "Rather than having them delivered to your home, choose to pick them up at a nearby collection point. [Couriers] can bring a lot of stuff to one place."

Don't then make a special trip by car to collect it, says Allen: "Work it into your daily commute."

Perhaps best of all would be to think before you click. (510 words)

Emine Saner, *The Guardian* website, 2020

75 **commute** Pendelstrecke

2 Multiple matching → H 6 → WB, p. 59/1–2

Match the statements (A–H) with the correct people or services (1–4) from the text. You can use a person or service up to three times.

1 Tim Anderson **2** Julian Allen **3** hot-food delivery service **4** Amazon

A Unfortunately the intelligent and environmentally conscious customer does not really exist.
B The user-friendly systems make us forget the environmental price we pay for our purchases.
C Sorry, but the customers want it now – they want it hot. We cannot go really green.
D Why not combine shopping with supporting retailers next door?
E The "I don't want to wait" culture is to be blamed for that.
F Don't blame us for the emissions. If the clients didn't want it, we wouldn't be that big.
G It is not as if there were no ways to shop green.
H With those distances, we need cars.

3 Gapped summary

Complete the summary with the most suitable words from the corresponding sections (ll. 1–25 and ll. 63–77) of the text. Give the line numbers of the words that you used.

Our world is changing and so are our shopping habits, resulting in a quickly increasing ■ ■ **1**. Online shopping is particularly popular among younger ■ ■ **2**, but not only there. Admittedly it is almost ■ **3** just to click somewhere on a website and the next day the article arrives at your door. Yet, convenient as this may be we must not forget the ■ **4** this has on our environment. A delivery includes not only our purchases but also huge amounts of ■ **5** which is simply thrown away. In addition we must not forget the ■ ■ **6** that is produced by having the goods ■ **7** to us, sometimes from the other end of the world, as well as the resources from which the goods are ■ **8**. To go green, we need not give up online shopping completely but instead of having many small deliveries it would help to ■ **9** our orders into bigger ones. Most importantly to become more ■ **10** we must rethink what we purchase as well as how we shop.

4 Mediation

Beantworten Sie die folgenden Fragen auf Deutsch.

1. Unter welchen Umständen könnte Online-Shopping nachhaltiger sein als herkömmliches Einkaufen?
2. Wie sieht Julian Allen das Konzept von „free delivery" (Z. 45)?
3. Welchen konkreten Vorschlag macht Tim Anderson?
4. Wie könnte für Julian Allen Online-Shopping ökologischer werden?

5 Listening → S 3

CULTURE BOX

In the late 1980s, governments in several democratic countries wanted to ban certain kinds of plastics to reduce pollution. However, environmentalists popularised the slogan "Reduce. Reuse. Recycle". Yet the plastics industry largely ignored the first two suggestions and promoted recycling as the perfect solution to the waste crisis. In turn, governments agreed to fund recycling schemes which included exporting waste, apparently to recycle it abroad.

landfill Mülldeponie

A31 **a** Listen to the first part of the podcast and answer the questions.

1. Where is Nick Martin reporting from? Why is he there?
2. What is Tony Wong's job?
3. What is Tony Wong's problem?
4. What is Tony Wong's connection with the UK? Why is the British material at Wong's business?

A32 **b** Listen to the second part of the podcast. What do the following numbers refer to? Take notes.

44 % | 50 % | 20 | 60 % | 25

6 A step further

Look at the graph showing the Country Overshoot Days 2022 of different countries in the world and read the text. Answer the following questions. Take notes.

1. Which order of countries did you expect? Which date or dates do you find surprising?
2. What might the reasons be for the differences in the dates?

Country Overshoot Days 2022
When would Earth Overshoot Day land if the world's population lived like …

Data: National Footprint and Biocapacity Accounts 2023

GOOD TO KNOW

Earth Overshoot Day marks the date when the amount of resources used in a year exceed what Earth can regenerate in that year.
We use up stocks of ecological resources and at the same time accumulate waste, especially in the form of carbon dioxide, which we release into the atmosphere.
In 2022, Earth Overshoot Day was reached on 28 July.

B Facing climate change

1 Before you read → S 10.1

a With a partner, explain the message on the sign in the picture.

b Discuss what forms of change the sign may want to encourage. → S 15 Round robin

Jacinda Ardern (born in 1980) was Prime Minister of New Zealand from 2017 to 2023. In 2017 she had also been elected head of the Labour Party. In her politics, she focuses on social equality. She was widely recognised for introducing strict gun laws after the deadly shooting in a mosque in Christchurch in March 2019.

New Zealand national statement to United Nations General Assembly 2019

[...] Mr. President, Mr. Secretary-General, Friends,

1 I greet you in *te reo Māori*, language of the *tangata whenua*, or first people, of Aotearoa New Zealand. I do so not just because it is the same way I would begin an address if I were at home, but because there are challenges we face as a world that I know no better way to express. Māori concepts like *kaitiakitanga*. The idea that each of us here today are guardians. Guardians of the land, of our environment and of our people. There is a simplicity to the notion of sovereign guardianship. [...] We, the political leaders of the world, have been the authors of our own domestic politics and policies. Decisions have been our own, and we have lived with the consequences. But the world has changed. Over time we have become increasingly interdependent. We see more and more often domestic decisions that have global ramifications. [...]

2 There is perhaps no better example of our absolute interdependence than climate change. When the United Nations Secretary-General visited the Pacific region this year, he saw first-hand how countries that have produced the fewest greenhouse gas emissions are now facing the most catastrophic effects. In his words: "To save the Pacific, is to save the whole planet." In fact seven out of the 15 most climate affected nations in the world sit within the Pacific region. Places like Tuvalu, with a population of just over 11,000 people, barely contributes to global emissions but is paying the price for our collective inaction. Atolls so low lying that in weather events the water on either side of it can flow together and join at the narrowest points. Engulfed by the sea. [...]

3 In New Zealand, we have plenty of work to do. We may only make up 0.17% of global emissions, but like so many others, our gross emissions have been rising steadily since the 1990s. That's why we have coupled ambition with action. Over the past two years since we took office New Zealand has produced our own Zero Carbon legislation, which puts our domestic economic transformation in line with the objective of a 1.5°C limit in global temperature increase. We've continued with our goal of planting 1 billion trees. We have created a $100 million green investment fund. We've stopped issuing new offshore oil and gas exploration permits. We're creating a plan to achieve 100% renewable electricity generation, and to incentivise low emission transport options. And we're supporting our Pacific neighbours with projects to increase solar power,

GOOD TO KNOW

You can watch the speech online.

8 **guardian** Hüter/-in; Wächter/-in
10 **domestic** Inlands-; inländisch
12 **interdependent** voneinander abhängig
13 **ramification** Auswirkung
21 **collective inaction** kollektive Untätigkeit
22 **engulfed** umschlungen; überflutet
27 **objective** Ziel
30 **oil and gas exploration** Erkundung von Gewinnungsstätten für Erdöl und -gas
30 **permit** Erlaubnis; Genehmigung
31 **to incentivise** einen Anreiz schaffen für

33 **water supplies *(pl)*** Wasserversorgung
35 **vast bulk** Großteil
46 **to tackle sth** etw. angehen; etw. anpacken
47 **fossil fuel** fossiler Brennstoff
47 **subsidies *(pl)*** Subventionen
49 **APEC** Asiatisch-Pazifische Wirtschaftsgemeinschaft
52 **tariff** Zoll
52 **to reap the benefits** Vorteile einstreichen
54 **to compete on an even footing** auf dem gleichen Niveau konkurrieren
61 **fierce** heftig; kämpferisch
64 **innate** angeboren
66 **inherently** grundsätzlich; von Natur aus

reduce the use of diesel generators, protect coastlines and stop sea water entering water supplies.

4 But some answers to the climate challenge are easier than others. The vast bulk of our greenhouse gas emissions for instance, don't come from transport, energy generation or waste – but from one of the things that we pride ourselves on. Our food production for the world. We know this requires us to adapt. In fact our farming leaders have made their own commitment to cutting emissions from food production. Over the next five years we will collaborate with farmers to build systems in New Zealand which every farmer will be able to use to measure, manage and reduce their own farm's emissions. [...] New Zealand will never produce all the food the world needs, no matter how many sheep you may think we have. But we can produce the ideas and technology the world needs for everyone to farm and grow in the most sustainable way possible.

5 New Zealand is determined to do good, and be good for the world. And that is why we are also focused on tackling the billions of dollars that countries spend annually on fossil fuel subsidies – billions that could instead be spent on transitioning to new forms of clean energy generation. Despite commitments to phase out such subsidies by groups like the G20 and APEC, we are still struggling to see concrete action. It's time to do things differently. [...] It's time for trade deals to become a force for good on climate action. They need to stop allowing perverse subsidies that incentivise pollution, and finally remove tariffs on green technology. Fossil fuel companies should no longer reap the benefits of subsidies that our farmers and many others have been asked to give up. Without the billions in subsidies that go to the fossil fuel industry, green energy can compete on an even footing. It's both the most fair and economically consistent thing to do.

6 My question is will you join us? And this is where we return to the concept again that challenges our modern political environment. We are being asked to make decisions that are local, but with consequences that are global. And yet, it is what climate change requires us to do. [...] Our globalised, borderless world asks us to be guardians not just for our people, but for all people. [...]

If instead of fierce nationalism or self-interest, we seek to form our tribes based on concepts that can and should be universal. What if we no longer see ourselves based on what we look like, what religion we practice, or where we live. But by what we value. Humanity. Kindness. An innate sense of our connection to each other. And a belief that we are guardians, not just of our home and our planet, but of each other.

We are borderless, but we can be connected. We are inherently different, but we have more that we share. We may feel afraid, but as leaders we have the keys to create a sense of security, and a sense of hope. We just need to choose. (944 words)

Jacinda Ardern, former Prime Minister of New Zealand, *Newshub* website, 2019

2 Multiple matching → WB, p. 60/1–2

Match the headlines (A–H) with the paragraphs (1–6) of the text.
There are two headlines more than you need.

- **A** Traffic is not always the main problem
- **B** Global Guardians call for acting globally
- **C** We must start changing and acting now
- **D** It concerns all, but some are more threatened than others
- **E** Let's act where we are for the common good
- **F** Think green and act locally
- **G** We are called to protect
- **H** We are not just talking, we are taking action

3 Multiple choice

Choose the most suitable option.

1. The word 'us' in line 7 refers to the …
   A Maori.
   B people of the world.
   C people of New Zealand.
   D United Nations General Assembly.

2. According to paragraph 2, it is true that …
   A collective inaction increases global emissions.
   B global interdependence does not only concern climate change.
   C the biggest polluters are also the countries most affected by climate change.
   D greenhouse gas emissions of the Pacific region have the most catastrophic effects.

3. What is not explicitly mentioned in paragraph 3 is that …
   A Zero Carbon legislation has made New Zealand climate-neutral.
   B New Zealand is responsible for less than 1% of global emissions.
   C New Zealand's environmental projects include collaboration with other countries.
   D New Zealand is on the way to only using renewable sources for generating electricity.

4. According to paragraph 4, …
   A New Zealand's farms mainly breed sheep.
   B New Zealand exports most of the food produced there.
   C farming is New Zealand's key problem in the fight against greenhouse gas emissions.
   D technology from around the world has made farming in New Zealand as sustainable as possible.

5. In paragraph 5 Jacinda Ardern …
   A demands subsidies for green technology.
   B complains about the continued subsidies for fossil fuels.
   C demands subsidies in order to make green energy competitive.
   D wants more promises from the G20 to phase out subsidies for fossil fuels.

6. Jacinda Ardern's main intention is to …
   A accuse the leaders of the world of collective inaction.
   B show that due to fierce nationalism, we can only act locally.
   C make the leaders of the world act together against climate change.
   D highlight the success of New Zealand's environment policies and actions.

4 Short-answer questions → H 6

Answer the following questions. They only refer to paragraphs 1–3 and 6.
You may use words from the text.

1. What is the politically correct term for New Zealand's 'native peoples'?
2. What is a key reason for the need to take action together?
3. Which phrase tells you that New Zealand is not only talking but actually doing something for the environment?
4. What is New Zealand's goal concerning vehicles?
5. Which two obstacles must be overcome for there to be global environmental action?
6. Which two things can the politicians achieve if they make the right choice?

5 Working with texts → S7

a Match the rhetorical devices (1–5) with the quotations (A–E).

1 contrast (antithesis)	A To save the Pacific, is to save the whole planet. (ll. 17–18)
2 enumeration	B We've continued … We have created … We've stopped … We're creating … (ll. 28–33)
3 repetition	C New Zealand will never produce … But we can produce … (ll. 41–43)
4 anaphora	D Humanity. Kindness. An innate sense of our connection to each other. And a belief that we are … (ll. 63–64)
5 parallelism	E … each of us here today are guardians. Guardians of the land … (ll. 7–8)

b Find further examples of these devices in Jacinda Ardern's speech.

c Analyse how Jacinda Ardern uses facts, numbers and statistics in her speech.

d Describe the effect that the devices from **a** have on the audience.

6 Words matter → S11.1 → H6

a Look again at Jacinda Ardern's speech. Find as many words as possible from the world of politics. Put them into a table or make a list.

Politics			
nouns	verbs	adjectives	…
people	to face challenges	sovereign	
…	…		

b In groups, add more words to your list. Use a dictionary. Present your results to the class.

7 A step further → S7 → WB, p. 60/3

a Jacinda Ardern tells us how New Zealand is trying to protect the environment. In small groups, search online to find information and projects from other countries, regions or cities. Collect facts, numbers and statistics.

Low water level of the Rhine in Cologne

b With a partner, use the results of your research to write 2–3 paragraphs of such a speech for your country/region/city. When writing, use what you learned about style in exercise **5**. You can also copy Jacinda Ardern's style to make your speech as convincing and effective as possible.

c Present your speech to the class. Vote for the most convincing speech.

C Green cities

1 Before you read

How do you imagine a 'green city'? Note down your thoughts. → S 15 Think-pair-share

Ecotopia: The Notebooks and Reports of William Weston is a utopian novel by Ernest Callenbach, published in 1975. In the book, the reporter William Weston describes one of the first ecological utopias.

GOOD TO KNOW

A **utopia** is an imaginary, ideal society where everybody lives in peace and harmony. In a **dystopia**, society sometimes seems like a utopia at first, but turns out to be the opposite. The action is often set in a sad, frightening future.

A33

Ecotopia

by Ernest Callenbach

The streets of Ecotopia's capital

San Francisco, May 5. As I emerged from the train terminal into the streets, I had little idea what to expect from this city – which had once proudly boasted of rising from its own ashes after a terrible earthquake and fire. San Francisco was once known as "America's favorite city" [1]. Its dramatic hills and bridges, its picturesque cable cars, and its sophisticated yet relaxed people had drawn visitors who returned again and again. Would I find that it still deserves its reputation as an elegant and civilized place?

I checked my bag and set out to explore a bit. The first shock hit me at the moment I stepped onto the street. There was a strange hush over everything. I expected to encounter something at least a little like the exciting bustle of our cities – cars honking, taxis swooping, clots of people pushing about in the hurry of urban life. What I found, when I had gotten over my surprise at the quiet, was that Market Street, [2], has become a mall planted with thousands of trees. The "street" itself, on which electric taxis, minibuses, and delivery carts purr along, has shrunk to a two-lane affair. The remaining space, [3], is occupied by bicycle lanes, fountains, sculptures, kiosks, and absurd little gardens surrounded by benches. [...] There is even the occasional song of a bird, unbelievable as that may seem on a capital city's crowded main street.

Scattered here and there are large conical-roofed pavilions, with a kiosk in the center selling papers, comic books, magazines, fruit juices, and snacks. (Also cigarettes – the Ecotopians have *not* managed to stamp out smoking!) The pavilions turn out to be stops

5 **to boast** prahlen; angeben
7 **picturesque** malerisch
8 **sophisticated** kultiviert; gebildet
10 **to set out to do sth** sich daranmachen, etw. zu tun
11 **hush** Schweigen; Stille
12 **bustle** Gewimmel
13 **clots of people** Menschentrauben
17 **to occupy** füllen; einnehmen
20 **scattered** verstreut
22 **to stamp out** ausrotten

23 **contraption** Vorrichtung; Gerät
24 **to resemble** ähneln
24 **to be fond of** gern haben; mögen
25 **to steer** steuern; lenken
26 **to fail to do sth** versäumen, etw. zu tun; es nicht schaffen, etw. zu tun
28 **to creep** schleichen; kriechen
29 **to charge** berechnen; verlangen
33 **density** Dichte
34 **to displace** verlagern
36 **obstruction** Hindernis
36 **pothole** Schlagloch
39 **medieval** mittelalterlich
40 **stroller** Spaziergänger/-in
40 **gawker** Gaffer/-in
40 **loiterer** Bummler/-in; Herumlungernde/-r
42 **to lack in** mangeln an
43 **precaution** Vorsichtsmaßnahme
48 **nondescript** unauffällig
48 **hideous** hässlich; scheußlich
51 **sturdy** fest; stabil
51 **to disperse** zerstreuen; (sich) verteilen
57 **to spout** von sich geben
57 **abandon** Hingabe
58 **inevitable** unvermeidlich; zwangsläufig
60 **hard-headed** stur
61 **abolition** Abschaffung
68 **residential area** Wohngebiet

on the minibus system, **4**. These buses are comical battery-driven contraptions, resembling the antique cable cars that San Franciscans were once so fond of. They are driverless, and are steered and stopped by an electronic gadget that follows wires buried in the street. (A safety bumper stops them in case someone fails to get out of the way.) To enable people to get on and off quickly, during the 15 seconds the bus stops, the floor is only a few inches above ground level [...]. These buses creep along at about ten miles an hour, **5**. They charge *no* fare. When I took an experimental ride on one, I asked a fellow passenger about this, and he said the minibuses are paid for in the same way as streets – out of general tax funds. Smiling, he added that to have a driver on board to collect fares would cost more than the fares could produce. [...]

Despite the quiet, the streets are full of people, though not in Manhattan densities. (Some foot traffic has been displaced to lacy bridges which connect one skyscraper to another, sometimes 15 or 20 stories up.) Since practically the whole street area is "sidewalk," nobody worries about obstructions – or about the potholes which, **6**, are planted with flowers. I came across a group of street musicians playing Bach, with a harpsichord and a half dozen other instruments. [...] Once I even saw a juggler and magician team, working a crowd of children – it reminded me of some medieval movie. And there are many strollers, gawkers, and loiterers – people without visible business who simply take the street for granted as an extension of their living rooms. Yet, despite so many unoccupied people, the Ecotopian streets seem ridiculously lacking in security gates, doormen, guards, or other precautions against crime. And no one seems to feel our need for automobiles to provide protection in moving from place to place.

I had noticed on the train that Ecotopian clothes tend to be very loose, with bright colors striving to make up for what is lacking in style and cut. This impression is confirmed now that I have observed thousands of San Franciscans. The typical Ecotopian man wears nondescript trousers [...] topped with an often hideous shirt, sweater, poncho, or jacket. Despite the usually chilly weather, sandals are common among both sexes. The women often wear pants also, but loose-flowing gypsy-like skirts are more usual. [...]

Ecotopians setting out to go more than a block or two usually pick up one of the sturdy white-painted bicycles that **7** are available free to all. Dispersed by the movements of citizens during the day and evening, they are returned by night crews to the places where they will be needed the next day. When I remarked to a friendly pedestrian that this system must be a joy to thieves and vandals, he denied it heatedly. He then put a case, **8**, that it is cheaper to lose a few bicycles than to provide more taxis or minibuses. Ecotopians, I am discovering, spout statistics on such questions with reckless abandon. They have a way of introducing "social costs" into their calculations which inevitably involves a certain amount of optimistic guesswork. It would be interesting to confront such informants with one of the hard-headed experts from our auto or highway industries – who would, of course, be horrified by the Ecotopians' abolition of cars.

As I walked about, I noticed that the downtown area was strangely overpopulated with children and their parents, besides people who apparently worked in the offices and shops. My questions to passersby (which were answered with surprising patience) revealed what is perhaps the most astonishing fact I have yet encountered in Ecotopia: the great downtown skyscrapers, **9**, have been turned into apartments! Further inquiries will be needed to get a clear picture of this development, but the story I heard repeatedly on the streets today is that the former outlying residential areas have largely been abandoned. [...] The residents now live downtown, in buildings that contain not only apartments but also nurseries, grocery stores, and restaurants, as well as the shops and offices on the ground floor. (1032 words)

2 Multiple matching → H 6 → WB, p. 61/1

Nine phrases have been cut from the text. Match the most suitable phrases (A–L) with the gaps (1–9). There are three phrases more than you need.

A lie about the streets by the hundreds and
B but they come every five minutes or so
C which is not only technologically creative, but sensitive to nature
D once a mighty boulevard striking through the city down to the waterfront
E which may not be totally farfetched
F and people wait there out of the rain
G where the scars of the earthquake are still most visible
H as they develop in the pavement
I once the headquarters of far-flung corporations
J which is huge
K favouring decentralized and green building construction
L and had an immense appeal to tourists

3 Short-answer questions

Answer the following questions. They refer to lines 1–32.
You may use words from the text.

1. Which phrase tells you that San Francisco used to look with pride at its comeback after a natural disaster?
2. What does the narrator experience right at the beginning of his visit that he didn't expect?
3. What has replaced cars in Ecotopia?
4. What illustrates the return of the natural world to the city centre's main streets?
5. Ecotopia wants to be a green and healthy place. Where have they not been successful?
6. What is the economic reason for there being no charge for public transport?

4 Mediation

Beantworten Sie die folgenden Fragen auf Deutsch.

1. Welche zwei Gegensätze (zu Beginn und am Ende) überraschen den Erzähler (Z. 33–44)?
2. Welche Modegewohnheit erscheint dem Erzähler etwas unlogisch bzw. überraschend?
3. Die öffentlichen Fahrräder für alle sind leicht zu stehlen. Warum ergibt das System für die Bürger trotzdem Sinn?

5 Listening → S 3 → WB, p. 61/2

A34 a Listen to the first part of the podcast 'Cities of the future'. Complete the text.

holistic ganzheitlich

Jordan Whitehouse works as an urban planner and part-time lecturer. He is interested in the connection between ■ 1 and sustainability. Therefore in addition to planning houses, streets, ■ 2 and structures, he also reflects on the people living and working there. For his job he considers most important a ■ ■ 3. In other words, those responsible for planning the cities of the future must look at the architecture as well as the ■ ■ 4. As the number of people increases, ■ 5 is a key issue. In addition, the cities of the future must be able to deal with ■ ■ 6 such as ■ 7. On top of that, these cities must have ■ 8 transport networks that are not only safe but also reduce ■ 9.

urban sprawl Zersiedelung (einer Stadt)
sanitation sanitäre Anlagen

A35 b Listen to the second part of the podcast and choose the most suitable option.

1. Jordan thinks the city of the future …
   A is a utopia.
   B must be planned carefully to be successful.
   C will be a sustainable, safe and forward-thinking city.
2. It is correct that …
   A people living in cities fight for space.
   B good city planning also considers an increase in population.
   C cities should spread out into the undeveloped land around them.
3. The problem of urban sprawl in LA and Rio de Janeiro …
   A is a result of huge traffic problems.
   B is caused by a lack of urban planning.
   C leads to huge areas with homeless people.
4. Planning a city of the future …
   A must primarily consider social services.
   B should always start with the basic facilities.
   C means foremost realising futuristic and utopian ideas.

A36 c Listen to the third part. Answer the questions. Take notes.

1. What is the idea behind smart cities?
2. What percentage of the world's population will live in cities by 2050?
3. What should a smart city provide for its inhabitants? (Name three things.)

GOOD TO KNOW

Anton Brzezinski is an American artist of Polish descent. He painted this picture called 'City of the future' in 1951.

6 A step further → S 6.6, S 10.1 → G 4 → H 6

a Describe and analyse the painting on the right in detail and compare it to Ecotopia's capital city, San Francisco.

b Think about what the world might look like in 50 or 100 years. Write the opening page for a novel set in the future. Write about 250 words in which you …
- set the scene,
- describe the atmosphere and
- introduce the main character or characters.

Decide whether you will depict a utopia or a dystopia and which issues to include (e.g. surveillance, climate change, artificial intelligence, pandemics).

c Exchange your text with a partner and give each other feedback.
→ S15 Peer correction

Rethinking transport → S 6.1

1 Using numbers and statistics → S 10.3 → WB, p. 62/1–2

In the exam, the material for a composition often includes diagrams and statistics. These are very useful for supporting your arguments. Therefore it is important that you understand diagrams and that you can include statistics in your composition.

Look back at your findings in exercise **7a** on page 126. Choose one of the issues or projects you found. Use the information to write a blog post on why young people should support this issue/project. Include numbers and statistical information.

2 Working with pictures and cartoons → S 10.1, 10.2

When writing a composition, you must not describe a picture or cartoon. Instead you should use the message of a picture or a cartoon to support your text, e.g. as an idea for your introduction or to support your argument. A picture could also give you the idea for an argument. Therefore, it is important that you understand pictures and cartoons. The following points can help you:

For pictures:
- What do you see?
- What are the important parts of the picture?
- Is something not the way you would expect it to be?

Further questions for cartoons:
- Is there a caption?
- What is the message?

a Look at the picture and cartoon and then answer the questions above. Come up with ideas on how to use them in a composition about sustainability.

A

B

b In small groups, search online to find pictures and cartoons relating to the environment and sustainability. Show your pictures to each other and explain them. Discuss the message and how you could use them in a composition.

3 Material-based writing

To protect and save the environment, decisive action is needed now.
Therefore, discuss the following proposition:

'Saving the environment does not require more environmentally friendly vehicles but less traffic.'

Write a composition of at least 300 words. Include <u>all</u> the material provided.

Material 1

<u>Zahl der Autos pro Haushalt nimmt zu</u>
Die Zahl der Autos in Deutschland hat im vergangenen Jahr weiter zugenommen. Anfang Januar 2021 waren bundesweit 48,2 Millionen Pkw zugelassen. Das waren 14 Prozent mehr als zehn Jahre zuvor, wie das Statistische Bundesamt mitteilte. In den privaten Haushalten ging der Trend in den vergangenen zehn Jahren offenbar allen Klimasorgen zum Trotz zum Zweit- oder Drittwagen: Im Jahr 2010 kamen auf 100 Haushalte rechnerisch 102 Autos. Zehn Jahre später waren es 108, wie die Statistiker mitteilten.

Tagesschau website, 2021

Material 2

Mode of travel in Scotland in 2018

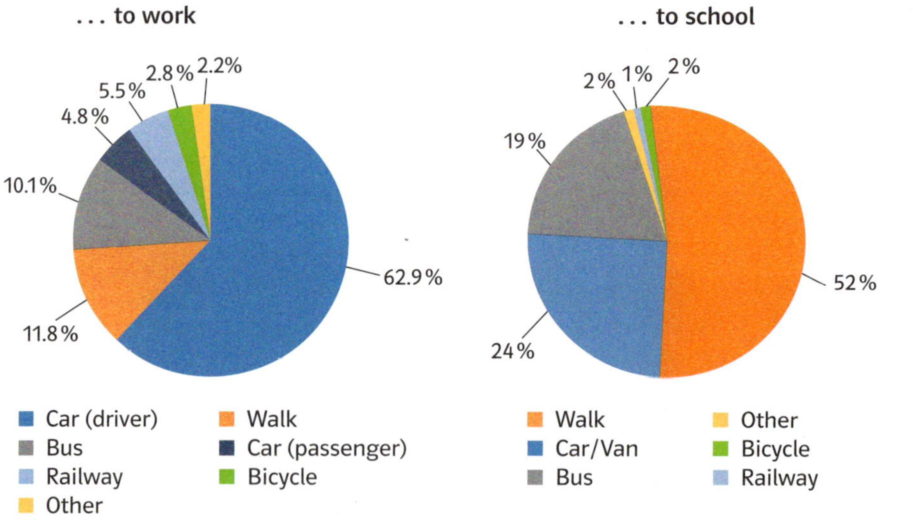

Source: Transport Scotland, 2018

Material 3

Electric cars aren't pollution-free; they have to get their energy from somewhere.
Alexandra Paul, American actress

'Save the planet' exhibition → S2

1 Using examples

In a group discussion use specific examples to explain who could do what, where, when, how and why. This allows you to get more depth into your arguments, to differentiate and to present a more nuanced view.

Get into groups. Your teacher reads out a topic (e.g. saving water at home, using less energy, green transport, sustainable fashion, eco-friendly food …). Within two minutes, come up with as many examples and aspects as possible. You can use the illustration below. The group with the most ideas wins.

2 Group discussion

Many young people demonstrate in the streets for protecting the environment. Yet, demonstrations are one thing, specific actions are another. In order to motivate young people and young families to reflect on their lifestyle and hopefully make it more environmentally friendly, your school has been invited to design an 'Inspiring Green Living – YOU Save the Planet' exhibition in a pavilion (about the size of two classrooms) in the city centre.

You are a member of the SMV team that is planning this pavilion. Today you are meeting to discuss your ideas and plan your next steps. At this meeting, you can talk about the following questions.

- What is not green living?
- How could young people and young families change their lifestyles to protect the environment? Why should they do this?
- How far should these changes go?
- What might be limits to green living? Why? Can they be overcome? How?
- How do you want to present your suggestions? Remember, the point is not to accuse, but motivate and inspire young people and young families to follow a greener lifestyle.

a Present your main idea (about one minute).

b Discuss and explain your ideas and views.

c Sum up your ideas and different positions. Try to come to a conclusion.

Part I Reading

How to feed the world in the next crisis

[...] Farmers are important custodians of much of the world's land. They manage "almost three-quarters of the land in England, producing food for people today and protecting land for the next generation", says Emma Howard Boyd, chair of the UK's Environment Agency. Globally, half of the world's habitable land is currently used in agriculture. "A lot of responsibility for managing these issues falls on their shoulders, they need more support from wider society to make good decisions and keep going."

Howard Boyd identifies extreme weather – being made worse by climate change – as an example of how farmers are pushed to the limit. The UK, for example, experienced its wettest February on record in 2020, followed by the sunniest spring. In California and Australia, wildfires decimated enormous areas of parched land.

"The climate emergency will increasingly shift us from one extreme to the other, and water, whether too much, too little, or its quality, will be a big concern," says Howard Boyd.

While the effects of drought on soil quality and risk of wildfires are more obvious, too much water brings its own problems. [...] The solution, says Howard Boyd, needs to be multidisciplinary, including financially incentivising sustainable farming practices, creating habitats for nature recovery and establishing new woodland. "When we think about innovation, we usually think about new technology, but I'm hoping to see a more integrated approach with the natural resources we already have," says Howard Boyd. [...]

For those farmers working in drier climates than Britain, climate change is resulting in land degradation – the quality of the land being farmed is decreasing. Land degradation affects almost half of the world's population, as soil erodes away and nutrients are depleted. The challenge for farmers is to reverse this trend while feeding a growing population.

[...] "Africa is probably the largest continent in terms of the amount of land that is affected by land degradation," [says Ibrahim Thiaw, of the UN Convention to Combat Desertification]. "But if you go to Asia, because of the size of the population, you have more people in Asia affected by land degradation than anywhere else in the world."

The good news is that there are solutions to land degradation, too, says Thiaw. "We can still restore degraded land into productive land." Thiaw [...] believes land degradation could be solved with the comparatively low-tech "regenerative agriculture".

This style of agriculture encourages the use of cover crops ensuring the land is covered with one crop or other the whole year – and areas of tree cover, both of which help to prevent soil erosion by wind or rain, maintain water and help to sequester carbon in the ground [...].

"We don't think it is enough to sustain the topsoil that we have now – we think we need to regenerate it because the world has lost about a third of its topsoil," says Jeff Harmening, president of food producer General Mills. [...]

General Mills has set a target of transforming one million acres of farmland using regenerative agriculture by 2030. [...]

"It is just a start but it is a good start [...]. If we do not get started now we are not going to like the result. We really can't wait," [says Harmening].

[...] "The intensification of agricultural production has come with unsustainable exploitation of natural resources," says Pierre Ferrand, an agroecologist at the Food and Agriculture Organization of the United Nations (FAO) in the Asia-Pacific region. "This […] exposes communities to more hazards. Large-scale livestock production has been driving natural habitat loss and has pushed the agricultural frontier into wilder and less-arable lands […]." […]

The Asia-Pacific region is home to nearly 75% of the world's small-scale family farmers, fishers and livestock producers, who between them generate 80% of the region's food. […]

Family farmers will continue to play a very important role in the future, [Ferrand] says. "Family farmers are about much more than just production, they are also about stewardship – stewardship of the soil, seeds, biodiversity and human-animal interactions that make up a family farm – which is a fundamental dimension to consider in order to prepare for the next global food crisis."

However, there is a problem looming in the not-too-distant future if we keep putting so much responsibility at the booted feet of farmers: farming is an increasingly unfashionable job.

[…] "I think that farming has a very, very bad image problem," says Kimbal Musk, co-founder of urban farming company Square Roots. […]

But Square Roots is offering an alternative in the form of indoor farms in the centre of Brooklyn and Grand Rapids Michigan. At Square Roots, young farmers are given their own modified shipping container in which they can grow healthy foods, like kale, herbs and salads. Much of the work can be done from home using an app that updates the farmer in real time with information about the climate inside their container. Younger farmers much prefer this lifestyle, says Musk. […]

Whether it is high-tech, app-powered, urban farms, or family businesses handed down through generations, the people who produce the food we eat have an opportunity to arrest climate change, and consumers, in turn, can shape that through the choices they make. If we all make the right choices, we might avert the next global crisis. (869 words)

Willam Park, *BBC* website, 2021

1 Multiple choice → WB, p. 63/1

Choose the most suitable option.

1. Which statement is true?
   A Droughts are as much a problem as floods.
   B Areas usually experience one form of extreme weather.
   C Pushing the limits of farming has made climate change worse.
   D Extreme weather caused by climate change is the only limiting factor for farming.
2. What is <u>not</u> explicitly mentioned in lines 42–50?
   A Land degradation means soil is lost.
   B Land degradation is an international problem.
   C Food is less nutritious because of land degradation.
   D Farmers must help the land while still using it for farming.
3. 'Regenerative agriculture' …
   A is more suitable for areas of tree cover.
   B is an attempt to reduce carbon emissions.
   C encourages farmers to plant mainly cover crops.
   D uses plants to prevent the loss of soil and water.

4. According to Pierre Ferrand, …
   - **A** we use more and more land for agriculture.
   - **B** natural resources must not be exploited at all.
   - **C** large-scale livestock production used less arable lands.
   - **D** small-scale farmers are less important from year to year.

5. Taking care of the land …
   - **A** increases the bad image of farming.
   - **B** gives a lot of responsibility to farmers.
   - **C** makes farming an increasingly unfashionable job.
   - **D** is a problem looming in the not too distant future.

6. The last paragraph emphasises that …
   - **A** we need high-tech urban farms.
   - **B** everyone can contribute to preventing the next global crisis.
   - **C** consumers must change their choices to stop climate change.
   - **D** we need to stop climate change to prevent the next global crisis.

2 Multiple matching

Match the statements (A–J) with the correct people (1–5) from the text. You will have to use some of them twice. There are two statements more than you need.

1 Emma Howard Boyd
2 Ibrahim Thiaw (2x)
3 Jeff Harmening (2x)
4 Pierre Ferrand
5 Kimbal Musk (2x)

A One way might be to move the 'fields' into the cities.
B We need to do more than just protecting what we have got.
C If they are to safeguard the land for us, we must not leave them to do this alone.
D Young people are particularly interested in growing healthy foods like herbs and salads.
E The problem is indeed enormous, but there is hope.
F Doing it somewhere else in a different way might attract people.
G Africa is huge, but there are more people in Asia.
H Asia is most affected by land degradation.
I Focusing on industrial-scale farming alone is not possible.
J Delaying action is not an option.

Costa Rica's answer to range anxiety

1 […] On the road to Monteverde, Costa Rica, […] the restaurant El Sol sits on a cliff's edge […]. It looks like a traditional roadside restaurant […]. Except it also has a silver cylinder with green lettering in the parking lot, the area's first electric vehicle (EV) charging station. […]

The station is part of Monteverde's Ruta Eléctrica, Latin America's only grassroots charging network created to head off "range anxiety" – the worry that a vehicle won't have enough charge to reach its destination – and develop electric-vehicle-friendly communities outside of cities.

Pre-pandemic, Monteverde received over 200,000 visitors annually; most of them in large SUVs […]. To compensate, climate activists and business owners decided to create a charging network to promote electric vehicle tourism, installing its first plug points in 2019.

A lack of infrastructure is one of the primary challenges to electrifying Latin America's transport sector. Most charging networks in the region are established through state-sponsored systems or large charging companies that are generally conglomerated in cities. In contrast, Ruta Eléctrica is jumpstarting this process in remote towns through deceptively low-tech solutions: reserved parking spots, clear signage, online maps, and accessible, well-maintained plug points.

"We're not waiting for the government to install chargers," says Katy Van Dusen […], founder of the Monteverde Commission for Resilience to Climate Change (Corclima), […] of which Ruta Eléctrica is one initiative. "Businesses can offer charging infrastructure anywhere there's electricity. It's a matter of making it available to electric vehicles."

2 Costa Rica has installed close to 200 semi-rapid and rapid charging stations, but the majority of them are in and around San Jose. Another roughly 85 charging points, […] have grown out of Ruta Eléctrica.

While installing fast charging stations is prohibitively expensive for most rural businesses, Van Dusen and her team engage hotel and restaurant owners, coffee shops, tour operators and nature reserves to offer free charging for clients. While waiting for their vehicles to charge, visitors can eat, sleep, shop or hike. Van Dusen calls this "charging with a purpose".

As the pandemic upended tourism, businesses saw an opportunity to attract new clients and double down on sustainability through Ruta Eléctrica. At Hotel Belmar, offering free charging has attracted electric vehicle drivers. "In rural areas like Monteverde, people are actually more environmentally conscious," says Richard Garro, the hotel's sustainability manager. "It's part of why people come here." […]

Since most of Ruta Eléctrica's network is to support travellers, pushing rental car companies to offer electric vehicles is critical. Only a handful of companies currently include electric cars as part of their fleet. While uncertainty around the resale of used electric vehicles is one barrier, lack of charging infrastructure in tourist destinations outside of cities is another. […]

3 […] In addition to its ambitious decarbonisation plan, nearly 100% of its electricity is generated from renewable sources, deforestation was banned in 1996 and a moratorium on oil and gas production could become law later this year.

[…], Monteverde plays a leading role in sustainability in the country. […]

"Monteverde is a trailblazer. Sustainability tourism models for the country came from the work people were doing there," says Monica Araya, […] cofounder of Asomove, Latin America's first electric vehicle association. […]

4 Yet the transport sector is still a major sustainability challenge for Costa Rica, accounting for over half of the country's carbon emissions. Like in many countries,

cars are aspirational in Costa Rica, a symbol of progress. Car ownership is on the rise, and the traffic-logged central valley has the third highest vehicle density in Latin America, [...].
Investment in public transportation is a cornerstone of the country's infrastructure plan, with a focus on an electric train network and high-speed buses. But First Lady Claudia Dobles says that a cultural shift will not happen through policy alone. [...] "Without citizen participation, there is no decarbonisation plan."

5 Corclima is now scaling the model into a national network, Rutas Eléctricas Costa Rica. It has already expanded to La Fortuna, an ecotourism hub to the north, and will launch in Nosara, a beach community on the Pacific. By the end of 2022, it hopes to reach 14 towns. [...]
Information sharing is a key benefit of Rutas Eléctricas. What's been learned in Monteverde is being shared with other communities.
"Most business owners came on board as an opportunity to attract new customers," says Luis Perez, the first Ruta Eléctrica coordinator in Monteverde [...]. "They aren't necessarily interested in networking and connecting. But the other 20 % [...] are spreading the idea." [...]

6 While electric vehicles are a small fraction of the 1.4 million cars on Costa Rican roads, numbers are projected to increase exponentially by 2023. This may lead to challenges ahead, such as how businesses can recoup the cost of electricity. Since electricity is nationalised, only government utilities are authorised to sell it. [...]
But for now, most business owners aren't worried about electricity costs. Johnny Calderon, the owner of [...] a tour company in La Fortuna, had his first visit from an electric vehicle user this month. [...] "I don't care if it takes time to get EV clients. I want to be part of the change. Maybe some day it will have an economic benefit but that's not why I'm doing it."

(855 words)

Reena Shah, *BBC* website, 2021

3 Multiple matching → WB, p. 63/2

Match the headlines (A–I) with the paragraphs (1–6) of the text.
There are three headlines more than you need.

A Interests and benefits
B Promoting ecotourism in rural areas
C A sustainable solution
D Plans for an improved infrastructure
E Environment first, profit later
F By the people, for the tourists (but not only)
G A growing network
H Too many tourists, too little electric vehicle tourism
I Still a long way to go

4 Mediation

Beantworten Sie die folgenden Fragen auf Deutsch.

1. Erklären Sie die Überschrift des Textes unter Bezug auf Abschnitt 1. Was ist ein damit verbundenes Ziel von Ruta Eléctrica?
2. Was meint Van Dusen mit „charging with a purpose“ (Z. 59)?
3. Wie ist der Anteil von E-Autos bei Autovermietungen? Nennen Sie zwei Gründe dafür.
4. Was zeigt Costa Ricas überdurchschnittlichen Einsatz für das Klima? Nennen Sie drei Beispiele.
5. Warum ist der Autoverkehr eine wesentliche Herausforderung für Nachhaltigkeit in Costa Rica? Welche Gründe nennt der Text hierfür?

5 Short-answer questions

Answer the questions for paragraphs 1 and 4–6. You may use words from the text.

1. What is a major obstacle in expanding electric mobility in Latin America?
2. Where do you find most of Costa Rica's e-mobility?
3. What is a key element of the government's strategy for sustainable traffic?
4. What is an important advantage of Rutas Eléctricas for furthering electric mobility?
5. Why did the majority of businesses join Rutas Eléctricas?
6. What is the prediction for electric mobility in Costa Rica in the near future?
7. Why can't shops and cafés ask their customers to pay for charging their e-cars?

6 Gapped summary

Complete the summary with the most suitable words from the text (sections 1–2). Give the line numbers of the words that you used.

If you want to ■ **1** electric mobility for tourists, you must ensure that there is a reliable charging network ■ **2**, not only in big cities but also in remote towns as well as in ■ **3** areas. While some people say that this is the job of the ■ **4**, in Monteverde in Costa Rica, people decided to take matter into their own hands by founding Ruta Eléctrica: a ■ **5** network to develop a charging infrastructure outside the big cities, where at present you still find the ■ **6** of charging stations in Costa Rica. A strength of Ruta Eléctrica is that, instead of relying on very expensive fast-charging stations, they focus on a ■ **7** approach that actually does not require more than ■ **8**.
The people in Monteverde consider electric vehicles not only to be a way of reducing the huge numbers of petrol-powered cars clogging the town's streets. For the people there they are also an ■ **9** to support local businesses. The hope is that while their vehicles are charging, the tourists will become ■ **10** of the shops and restaurants in Monteverde. After all, the tourist sector has been severely upended by the Covid pandemic. Anything that helps is welcomed, especially an ■ **11** like Ruta Eléctrica that is good for tourism and the environment.

The novel *Dry* was written by American author Neal Shusterman and his son Jarrod. The apocalyptic thriller is about the gradual drying up of water in America and the state of emergency that follows.

Dry

by Neal and Jarrod Shusterman

Day one

Saturday, June 4th

The kitchen faucet makes the most bizarre sounds. **1** It gurgles like someone drowning. It spits once, and then goes silent. Our dog, Kingston, raises his ears, but still keeps his distance from the sink, unsure if it might unexpectedly come back to life, but no such luck. Mom just stands there holding Kingston's water bowl beneath the faucet, puzzling. Then she moves the handle to the off position, and says, "Alyssa, go get your father." [...]

"Dad," I shout out into the garage, "kitchen issues." My father's feet stick out from underneath his Camry like the Wicked Witch. **2**

"Can't it wait?" my father says from beneath the car. But I'm already sensing that it can't.

"I think it's major," I tell him.

He slides out, and with a heavy sigh heads for the kitchen. Mom's not there anymore. Instead she's standing in the doorway between the kitchen and the living room. She's just standing there, the dog's empty water bowl still in her left hand. **3**

"What's so important that you gotta drag me out of –"

"Shush!" Mom says. She rarely shushes Dad. She'll shush me and Garrett all day, but my parents never shush each other. **4**

She's watching the TV, where a news anchor is blathering about the "flow crisis." That's what the media's been calling the drought, ever since people got tired of hearing the word "drought." Kind of like the way "global warming" became "climate change," and "war" became "conflict." But now they've got a new catchphrase. **5** They're calling this the "Tap-Out."

Uncle Basil emerges from his vapor cloud long enough to ask, "What's going on?"

"Arizona and Nevada just backed out of the reservoir relief deal," Mom tells him. "They've shut the floodgates on all the dams, saying they need the water themselves." Which means that the Colorado River won't even reach California anymore. [...]

Suddenly the image switches to a live press conference, where the governor addresses a gathering of antsy reporters. "This is unfortunate, but not entirely unexpected," the governor says. "We have people working around the clock attempting to broker a new deal with various agencies."

"What does that even mean?" Uncle Basil says. Both Mom and I shush him.

"As a precautionary measure, all county and municipal water districts in Southern California are temporarily rerouting all resources to critical services. **6** I'd like to personally assure everyone that this is a temporary situation, and that there is nothing to be concerned about." [...]

I go to the kitchen to try the tap myself – as if I might have the magic touch. Nothing. Not even the slightest dribble. Our faucet has coded, and no amount of resuscitation will bring it back. I note the time, like they do in the emergency room: 1:32 p.m., June 4th. *Everyone's going to remember where they were when the taps went dry,* I think. **7**

In the kitchen behind me, Garrett opens the fridge and grabs a bottle of Glacier Freeze Gatorade. He begins to guzzle it, but I stop him on the third gulp. "Put it back," I tell him. "Save some for later."
"But I'm thirsty *now*," he whines, protesting. He's ten – six years younger than me. Ten-year-olds have issues with delayed gratification. It's almost finished anyway, so I let him keep it. I take note of what's in the fridge. A couple of beers. Three more bottles of Gatorade, a gallon of milk that's down to the dregs, and leftovers. You know how sometimes you don't realize how thirsty you are until you take that first sip? Well, suddenly I get that feeling just by looking in the refrigerator. **8**

I can hear neighbors out in the street now. We know our neighbors – run into them occasionally. The only time whole bunches of them come out into the street at the same time is July Fourth, or when there's an earthquake.
My parents, Garrett, and I gravitate outside as well, all of us standing, strangely, looking to one another for some kind of guidance, or at least validation that this is actually happening. Jeannette and Stu Leeson from across the street, the Maleckis and their newborn, and Mr. Burnside, who's been eternally seventy years old for as long as I can remember. [...]

"Okay," my dad finally says, "which one of you pissed off Arizona and Nevada?" Everyone chuckles. Not because it's particularly funny, but it eases some of the tension.
Mr. Burnside raises his eyebrows. "Hate to say I told ya so, but didn't I say they'd hoard what's left of the Colorado River? We let that river become our only lifeline. We should never have let ourselves become so vulnerable."
Used to be no one much knew or cared where our water came from. **9** But when the Central Valley started to dry up and the price of produce skyrocketed, people started to pay attention. [...]
"Las Vegas still has water," someone points out. Our neighbor, Stu, shakes his head. "Yeah – but I just tried to book a hotel in Vegas. A million hotel rooms, and not a single one available."
Mr. Burnside laughs ruefully, as if taking pleasure in Stu's misfortune. "One hundred twenty-four thousand hotel rooms, actually. Sounds like a whole lot of people had the same idea." [...] (957 words)

7 Multiple matching → WB, p. 64/3–5

Nine phrases have been cut from the text. Match the most suitable phrases (A–L) with the gaps (1–9). There are three phrases more than you need.

A Was there bottled water at the supermarket?
B But I cannot stress enough the need to keep calm.
C It was just always there.
D A new stage in our water woes.
E Uncle Basil is hidden behind a storm cell of e-cig vapor.
F Every kid learned about the Central Valley and the Colorado River in school.
G It's an unspoken rule.
H It's the closest thing I've ever had to a premonition.
I We have been in this situation before.
J It coughs and wheezes like it's gone asthmatic.
K Like when a president is assassinated.
L I get a chill, but I don't yet know why.

8 Gapped summary

Complete the summary with the most suitable words from the text on pages 140–141. Give the line numbers of the words that you used.

Alyssa and her family are facing a serious problem when the ■ **1** in the kitchen runs dry. They immediately understand that this is the beginning of a ■ **2** crisis that, though certainly not unexpected, still surprises them. It is the result of an ongoing ■ **3** caused by global warming. In his ■■ **4** the governor tells the people to stay calm. He says that the ■ **5** of water supplies is only a precautionary step until they manage to ■ **6** a new arrangement with several organisations involved. Despite the governor's reassurance, Alyssa suspects the "flow crisis", a ■ **7** she does not trust, is not just a temporary occurrence. That is also why she tells her brother off when he quickly finishes a bottle of Gatorade. When the neighbours meet in the street, there is a lack of ■ **8** among them as well as a growing awareness of how ■ **9** they have become. With no easy escape route ■ **10**, such as going to Las Vegas, they realise, perhaps too late, that they should have paid more attention to the growing threat to their water supply. It has run dry without any hope of ■ **11**.

Part II Material-based writing

Pollution and destruction of the environment concern us all. Comment on the following statement:

'Saving the planet requires more than words.'

Write a composition of at least 300 words.
Include all the material provided.

Material 1

The greatest threat to our planet is the belief that someone else will save it.
Robert Swan, British explorer

Material 2

Trend zum guten Leben – Jugend befürwortet nachhaltigen Konsum

Gefragt nach Themen [...] liegt der Umweltschutz in seiner Wichtigkeit – genannt von jedem fünften – weit vor Tierschutz und Migration. Laut der Studie lassen sich Jugendliche für nachhaltigen Konsum begeistern. Vor allem die Bereiche Mobilität – mit mehr als 800 Ideen und Vorschlägen –, Lebensmittel (700) sowie plastikfreies Einkaufen (250) werden als geeignet für nachhaltigen Konsum betrachtet. Auffällig sind zwei Ausnahmen: Jugendliche verbinden nachhaltiges Handeln „nur selten mit fairem und ökologischem Textilkonsum sowie umweltschonendem Tourismus" [...]. Dabei hätten hoher Kleidungskonsum und Flugreisen einen großen Einfluss auf die Ökologie.
Stuttgarter Zeitung website, 2019

Material 3

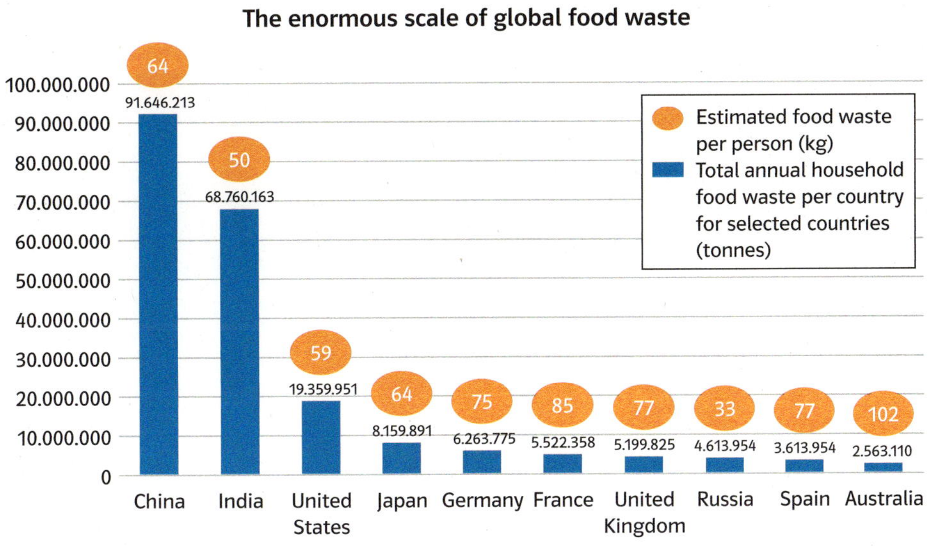

Source: UNEP Food Waste Index Report, 2021

Part III Group discussion

This year your school is doing a globalisation awareness project. As part of this project your group is planning a 'Save water' video for the project website.
The film should be about five minutes long. It shows how and where water is wasted and, more importantly, what we can do to save water. The tone of the film should not be accusing, but should motivate to take action.

Today you are meeting to discuss your ideas and plan your next steps. You can talk about the following questions.

- Where is water wasted?
- What can individuals do to save water?
- How do you wish to present this in your film?

a Present one or two of your ideas (about one minute).

b Discuss the issues.

c Sum up the discussion in one statement per person (this does not mean that you have to agree). Try to come to a conclusion.

Social issues

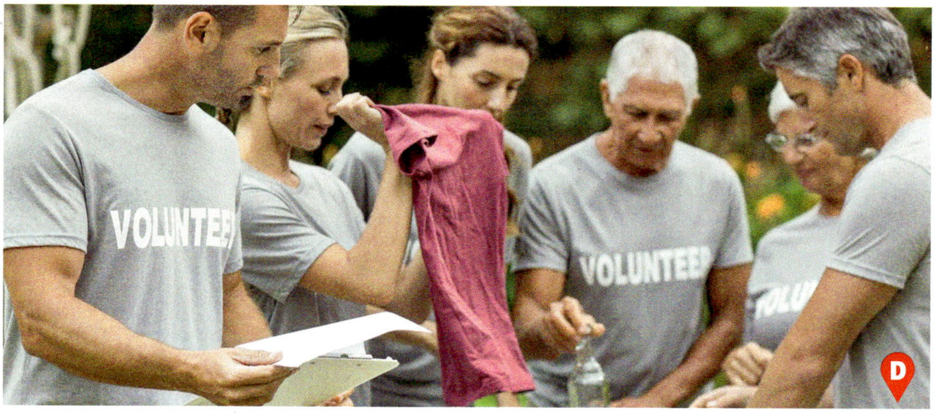

Love is my fortune
Cause all the bucks don't make much sense
They don't bring you happiness
Thirsty Merc – The good life

Imagine there's no countries
It isn't hard to do
Nothing to kill or die for
And no religion, too
John Lennon / Yoko Ono – Imagine

I'm beautiful in my way 'cause God makes no mistakes
I'm on the right track, baby, I was born this way
Lady Gaga – Born this way

1 Working with pictures → S10.1 → WB, p. 66–67/1–3

a Which picture catches your attention first? Describe it to a partner and explain why you chose it.

b Use the words from the word bank to talk about the social issues in the pictures.

drugs and crime | #sobriety | gender roles | #MeToo | to stand up for one's rights | #AffordableHousing | to rent | social conflicts | charity | to donate | wealth and poverty

c Search online to find addtional pictures that show other social issues. Present them to the class. Explain your choices. → S15 Round robin

2 Social issues in music

a Social issues have often been expressed in music. In small groups, choose one of the songs from page 144 and search online to answer the following questions.

1. Which issues and problems does the song talk about?
2. Which genre does the song represent?
3. What is the historical context?
4. Do you agree with the views in the song?

b Find another song which deals with a social issue and which you like. Prepare a short presentation about this song and say why you like it. → S 15 1-minute presentation

c Do you think music has an influence on society and social issues? Discuss in class.

3 Listening → S 3 → H 7 → WB, p. 68/1

A37

Listen to the podcast 'Looking at today – Thinking for tomorrow: Top social issues in the USA'. Take notes on the following aspects.

1. Which social issues are mentioned?
2. Note down one detail about each issue.

to make ends meet über die Runden kommen
incarceration Inhaftierung
mandatory verpflichtend
burden Belastung

4 Creating a video → S 12

Your class is participating in a project on social issues. The aim of the project is to become aware of current social issues in different countries, how they affect people there and what could or should be done to make the situation better.

a Work in small groups. Each group chooses a country (except the USA) and brainstorms different social issues and problems of it. Create a mind map.

b Look again at your results from **a** and exercise **3**. Search online to find out about the situation for your chosen country.

c Create a short podcast or video about the situation in this country. Collect words you need to talk about the most pressing issues and what is being or could be done to deal with them. How do you want to present the issues in your video or podcast?

d Present your videos and podcasts. Then discuss which actions seem the least or most promising. → S 15 Think-pair-share

USEFUL PHRASES

Structuring
I'm going to … | I would like to talk about … | To begin with … | Now I want to describe … | There are three things to consider: Firstly … Secondly … Thirdly … | Finally …

Giving reasons
because | since | therefore | As there are … | As a result of … | Due to … | Because of …

Giving examples
for example | in another case | to illustrate | as shown/illustrated by …

Summarising
All things considered … | Taking everything into account … | As a result … | Consequently …

A Living in a modern world

1 Before you read → G 2

a In small groups, discuss how your living situation would ideally look like as a university student, an apprentice or a young family.

b Choose one country and research online what the living situation looks like in reality for such people. What are the reasons or causes for these situations? Present your results in class.

A38

'Co-living': the end of urban loneliness – or cynical corporate dormitories?

With communal space and amenities all shared in what are sometimes vast complexes, co-living is billed as a solution to the housing crisis – but others say it's simply an attempt to cash in on it.

In the industrial chic lobby of the *Collective*, a huge apartment block in the northwest London neighbourhood of Willesden Junction, a set of posters advertise its events series for residents. [...] The 550 residents who call this building home pay a monthly rent starting at £1,085 to live in rooms that are hotel-sized but which benefit from a number of communal amenities, like the events. There's a cinema room, a co-working space that converts into a music venue, [...] a library that feels like a co-working space, a restaurant and a bar. [...]

Benjamin Webb, 37, has lived at the *Collective* for eight months and likes it enough that he is now a "community ambassador". He says co-living offered him a sense of freedom after two decades renting in London. "I was looking for flexibility rather than being sucked into the cycle of letting agents, paying £2,000 each time you move and being locked in a contract," says Webb, who works as a PA in the finance industry. "The *Collective* gave me that flexibility, but what kept me there – and I've extended my original contract – is the community and all the other things that come with it." Indeed, the *Collective* doesn't market itself as apartments. It calls itself a "global living movement", and is one of a growing number of "co-living" developments that cater to a distinctly millennial market.

In Berlin there is *Quarters*, a co-living developer that now has properties in New York and Chicago and has just announced a $1bn expansion to build many more across the US and Europe. *WeWork*, the co-working behemoth, now runs *WeLive*: fully furnished apartments available for flexible rental in New York and Washington DC. The chic "digital nomad community" *Roam* has set up co-living and co-working hubs in San Francisco, Miami, Tokyo and Bali [...]. It sells a dream lifestyle, that of a modern, flexible, "creative" worker who has bid farewell to the deskbound nine to five and instead jets around the world, dropping in to work remotely from exotic locations.

Each company presents its accommodation as a solution to the urban housing crisis. Here, at last, is a way to provide affordable homes for younger people cut out of the market, while at the same time pooling resources, fostering community and catering for an increasingly mobile generation. With 4.8 million Britons now self-employed, co-living is pitched as a utopian response to a rapidly changing society. But what from one angle looks like a revolutionary proposition can just as easily be seen from another as a cynical

2 **corporate** Firmen-; Unternehmens-
2 **dormitory** Wohnheim; Schlafsaal
3 **communal** Gemeinschafts-
3 **amenities** Ausstattung; Annehmlichkeiten
4 **to be billed** beworben werden; angekündigt werden
5 **attempt** Versuch
5 **to cash in** abkassieren *(ugs.)*
23 **ambassador** Botschafter/-in
26 **to suck into** einsaugen; aufsaugen
27 **letting agent** Immobilienmakler/-in
32 **to extend** verlängern
34 **indeed** in der Tat; tatsächlich; allerdings
38 **to cater to** abzielen auf
41 **developer** Bauunternehmen; Entwickler/-in
45 **behemoth** Ungeheuer; Koloss
46 **furnished** möbliert
50 **hub** Zentrum; Knotenpunkt
53 **to bid farewell** auf Wiedersehen sagen
62 **to foster** fördern; pflegen
65 **to be pitched as** gelten als
67 **angle** (Blick-)Winkel
68 **proposition** Aussage; These

ploy by property developers to cash in on a generation living in the "age of loneliness", locked in a perpetual struggle to find a place they can call home.

Vlad Calus, 23, co-founder of social media startup *Planable*, sees it the second way. He moved into the *Collective* with a business partner two years ago. "People were nice and friendly but we were shocked to see these 'boxes' being called rooms," he says. "Unfortunately, co-living places are trying to squeeze every living space into the same building, which makes it unliveable for the long-term."

Collective living has other downsides. Post-grad student Emma Kay, 32, who was among the first people to move in when the *Collective* opened three years ago, found herself unnerved by some of the ways the building operated, such as when she bought a drink from the bar and took it outside. "The next day I got an email saying they'd seen me on CCTV with a glass in the smoking area and if I did it again there would be consequences," she says. "It felt quite uncomfortable knowing whatever you do is being watched, and if you break the rules for a minor offence you'd get in trouble."

To Matthew Stewart, a researcher and designer at the University of Westminster, co-living led by developers cannot be a radical alternative because it lacks the social intent of collective living. [...] "The *Collective* make similar claims about solving the housing crisis but it doesn't stand up," Stewart says. "Teige [a Czech theorist, 1900–1951] was talking about a mixture of different ages, generations, classes – it wasn't targeted at a specific group. It was more about democratising housing, rather than just having these enclaves of millennials who are being charged a lot of money."

Yet the *Collective* is far from the only vision of what "co-living" might look like. *Marmalade Lane*, a 42-home multigenerational "oasis", was unveiled this May in Cambridge. [...] *Marmalade Lane* was created through a participatory design process that involved its future residents. It has a mix of homes, ranging from four-bedroom houses to one-bedroom apartments, with a central "common house" providing a focal point where the community can eat together and socialise. Everyone can also make use of communal laundry, gym, meeting rooms and garden, and the organisation is managed by its residents using consensus-based decision-making. [...] (857 words)

Will Coldwell, *The Guardian* website, 2019

70 **ploy** Trick; Masche
73 **perpetual** immerwährend
81 **to squeeze** drücken; pressen; quetschen
84 **downside** Kehrseite; Nachteil
97 **offence** Vergehen; Straftat
102 **to lack** mangeln; fehlen
103 **intent** Absicht; Vorsatz
117 **to unveil** öffentlich vorstellen; enthüllen
121 **to range from ... to** reichen von ... bis
127 **laundry** Wäscherei; Waschküche

2 Multiple matching → WB, p. 69/1–2

Match the statements (A–H) with the correct people or organisations (1–6). There are two statements more than you need.

1 Benjamin Webb
2 Roam
3 Vlad Calus
4 Emma Kay
5 Matthew Stewart
6 Marmalade Lane

A It can feel like a mix of a boarding school and Big Brother. Not good!
B This is not about where you live but how you live.
C I would describe it as accommodation for the people by the people.
D This is not my dream place, but I cannot afford to live somewhere else.
E At present I have no intention to move, but it is great to know I easily could if I wanted to.
F I really enjoy the communal amenities like the cinema and the bar.
G It cannot live up to expectations if it targets only one group of people.
H I can put up with it, but it is definitely only a temporary option, nothing permanent.

3 Mediation

Beantworten Sie die folgenden Fragen auf Deutsch.

1. Was bietet *The Collective* außer Zimmer?
2. Was macht für Benjamin Webb „Co-Living" attraktiv?
3. Wie vermarktet sich *Roam*?
4. *The Collective* u.a. verstehen sich als „utopian response" (Z.66). Wie begründen sie diese Sicht?
5. Wie hätte das Ideal für *The Collective* und andere ausgesehen? Wie ist die Realität?
6. Wie unterscheidet sich *Marmalade Lane* von den anderen Modellen, die der Text nennt?

4 Multiple choice

Choose the most suitable option.

1. *The Collective* ...
   A offers 550 units for living.
   B is in the centre of London.
   C mainly does not offer large flats.
   D consists of a number of buildings in Willesden Junction.

2. What is not explicitly mentioned in the text? Benjamin Webb ...
   A has lived in London for 20 years.
   B has been a community ambassador for eight months.
   C originally did not plan to stay in the *Collective* so long.
   D thinks that the Collective gives him a certain amount of freedom and choice.

3. Which is true?
   A *WeLive* started in New York.
   B *Quarters* is a growing company.
   C *Quarters* operates mainly in the USA.
   D *WeWork* began by renting out fully furnished apartments.

4. *Roam* ...
   A has only American and Asian clients.
   B only attracts clients from digital companies.
   C focuses on people who travel a lot to exotic locations.
   D markets itself as a way of life rather than accommodation.

5. According to lines 57–73 ...
   A co-living does indeed offer community in an age of loneliness.
   B these co-living companies are the solution to the urban housing crisis.
   C 4.8 million Britons see co-living as the response to a fast-changing society.
   D it is difficult for the young and mobile generation to find accommodation they can afford.

6. In contrast to the *Collective*, *Marmalade Lane* ...
   A offers fewer events.
   B consists of 42 houses.
   C is not managed by a big company.
   D does not charge millennials so much money.

5 Short-answer questions → H7

Answer the following questions. They refer to lines 6–39 and 67–113.
You may use words from the text.

1. What does the *Collective* call its concept?
2. Which two descriptions underline the fact that the *Collective* does not offer large flats?
3. What are companies that are developing co-living being accused of?
4. Why does Vlad Calus think that these co-living concepts are not a sustainable solution?
5. If co-living was really the answer, what should it be about (but is not)?

6 Words matter → S 11.1

a In small groups, look again at the text on pages 146–147. Collect words and phrases which can be used for making a property attractive for renting. Put the words into a mind map.

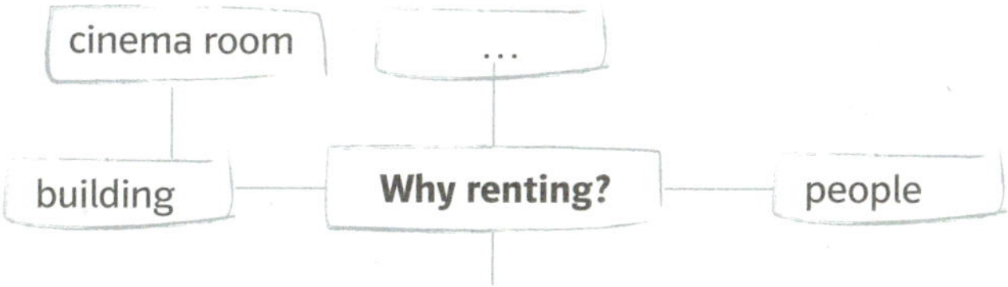

b Research online advertisements for flats and/or house sharing.
Add more words to your mid map from **a**. Present your results to the class.

7 A step further

a You are a group of students sharing a flat or a house. You have one room free. Use the words and phrases from exercise **6a** and write an ad to find a housemate or flatmate.

b Display your ads in class. → S 15 Gallery walk

c Each student chooses one or two ads from other groups and writes a letter to this group explaining why he or she would be the ideal person for the vacant room.

d In your groups, read the applications. Make a shortlist of the best two candidates for your house or flat. Then interview those candidates. Why would they be the most suitable person to share your accommodation with?

e Present your new roommate to the class. Give reasons for your choice.

USEFUL PHRASES

Writing an ad
shared apartment | located near ... | fully furnished | close to shops/school/university | near public transport | rent including heating/... | ...

Writing an application
I saw your ad ... | I think I pefectly match your requirements / I am a suitable candidate for this accommodation because ... | I have experience in ... | During my work placement / gap year with ... | gained further experience in ...

Interviewing
We wanted to ask you ... / to inform you ... | We're happy to tell you that ... | You will be pleased to hear that ... | We regret to inform you that ... | I'm afraid that ... | Unfortunately we are unable to ... | Could you please ... | We would appreciate it if you ...

B Divides and gaps

1 Before you read

a Answer the following questions.
→ S15 Think-pair-share

1. Which cities and regions of Britain do you know?
2. What do you know about them?
3. Which parts of Britain do you know little about?
4. What could be the reason for that?

b With a partner, choose one of the following places. Search online to find information about the population, business, industry, tourism …

Bath | Birmingham | Bristol | Cambridge | Cardiff | Hull | Leeds | Liverpool | Manchester | Newcastle upon Tyne | Oxford | Reading | Sheffield | Sunderland | Winchester | York

c Present your results to the class and compare them. What does the information tell you about Great Britain? Can you relate your findings to the headline of the text?

A39

Why North-South is not England's only divide

1 **divide** Spaltung; Kluft
6 **to evolve** sich entwickeln
12 **long-term driver** *hier:* langfristige Triebkraft
17 **output** Leistung; Ausstoß
21 **average** Durchschnitt
30 **to profess** behaupten; erklären
32 **Northern Powerhouse** *Regierungsprogramm, das den Norden GBs durch Investitionen in Technologie und Infrastruktur stärken soll*
34 **mayor** Bürgermeister/-in

1 The North-South divide is a theme often used by – and against – politicians to highlight inequality in the UK, and election time is no exception. But this gap has evolved over time, and is by no means the only geographical divide in the country.
Productivity – or how efficiently we produce goods and services – is regarded by many economists as the most important long-term driver of living standards. If you want to improve quality of life over time, you need to produce more per person than you did previously. On this measure, there is still a clear North-South divide. Looking at output per worker across the country, London is producing goods and services worth £26,000 more per person than the per-head average of the North West, North East and Yorkshire regions. In absolute terms, this gap has almost doubled since 2001.

2 This isn't about workers in the north being less productive though. It's because the UK's most productive sectors, such as finance and technology, are concentrated in the South of England. Politicians have in the past professed their ambition to rebalance the UK economy away from London by forming the Northern Powerhouse, creating regional metro mayors and a regional transport body. But commentators are divided as to how much these have helped fix the problem.

3 Not all economic gaps are North-South. When it comes to jobs, the divide is more about big cities versus the rest. Employment has traditionally been far lower in cities, but the good news is that this gap has closed - wherever you live in the UK. Since 2009, jobs growth has been concentrated in large urban areas of the country, with almost a million jobs created across 12 of the UK's largest cities such as Cardiff and Liverpool. Metropolitan areas like Sheffield, Merseyside and London have seen the strongest growth, with a 6% rise in the 18 to 60-year-old employment rate since 2012. This urban-led jobs growth has particularly benefitted groups who are more likely to be unemployed such as younger workers and ethnic minorities, who are more likely to live in cities. Despite this welcome growth, there is still a regional divide in our jobs market. For example, employment in the South West is 8%–10% higher than Northern Ireland, the region with the lowest employment.

4 Of course, it's also important to look at how well-paid these jobs are. When it comes to salaries, it's very much a case of London versus the rest. Median hourly pay – the point at which half of workers earn more and half earn less – is £18 an hour in London. That's 27% higher than the South East, the next best-paid region and 48% higher than the East Midlands, which is England's lowest paid region. However, over the past decade, the pay gap between London and the rest of the UK has fallen thanks to big increases in the minimum wage. It currently stands at £8.21 for over-25s, about 59% of median hourly pay, up from 46% in 1999. [...]

5 Of course, some parts of the country also have lower costs of living, including lower house prices. When it comes to housing, the North-South divide is very much present. While pay packets may be smaller in the North, so too are mortgage and rental payments. The average property price in London is £475,000 – three-and-a-half times as much as the cheapest region in England, the North East. A similar picture emerges when it comes to housing affordability. [...]
Once housing costs are factored in, London falls from the UK's highest income region to the middle of the pack.

6 Britain's geographical divides are important because of how they affect which opportunities are available to us, and our standards of living. There are signs we are moving in the right direction. In 1990, household incomes in the South East were over 40% higher than in Scotland, which was then the poorest part of the UK. Today, South East incomes are 20% higher than the current poorest region, the North East.

7 The big challenge for anyone wanting to close the North-South divide is to do more to reduce the big gaps in economic performance. More positively, when it comes to jobs and pay – which is how most people experience the economy – the gap has shrunk over the past decade, with fewer unemployment blackspots than before. So, the North-South divide is still with us, even though it has started to shrink on some important measures. Closing it – and the UK's other divides – once and for all is a challenge that all the political parties say they want to embrace.

(772 words)

Charlie McCurdy, *BBC* website, 2019

65 **median** mittlere/-r/-s; Mittel-
65 **hourly pay** Stundenlohn
75 **minimum wage** Mindestlohn
83 **mortgage** Hypothek
88 **to emerge** sich abzeichnen; entstehen
90 **to factor in sth** etw. berücksichtigen; mit etw. rechnen

2 Multiple matching → WB, p.70/1–3

Match the headlines (A–I) with the sections (1–7). There are two headlines more than you need.

- **A** It is also a question of making ends meet
- **B** Finally, more better-paid jobs in cities
- **C** Despite progress, a lot of work remains to be done to truly unite the UK
- **D** Despite more jobs in urban regions, the divide remains
- **E** Overcoming unemployment is key
- **F** A growing divide
- **G** More jobs but not more money
- **H** Not being skilled enough has got nothing to do with it
- **I** The situation has improved, but where you live still influences how you live

3 Mediation

Beantworten Sie die folgenden Fragen auf Deutsch.

1. Außer dem Nord-Süd-Gefälle, was für ein Gefälle erwähnt der Text noch?
2. Wie hat sich das Stellenangebot seit 2009 verändert?
3. Was bedeuten die Werte £18, 48%, £8.21, 59%, 46%?
4. Warum ist London trotz hoher Löhne nicht die Region mit dem höchsten realen Einkommen?
5. Welche Konsequenzen bringt das wirtschaftliche Nord-Süd-Gefälle für die Menschen mit sich?
6. Welche Verschiebung hat es seit 1990 gegeben?

4 Short-answer questions → H7

Answer the following questions. You may use words from the text.

1. How has the North-South divide developed in the first two decades of this century?
2. How does the text explain the North-South divide concerning productivity?
3. How do people view the government's actions to strengthen the North?
4. Who has profited most from the new jobs in big cities?
5. Which part of the UK has got the worst job situation?
6. Which part of the UK was worst off in the early 1990s?
7. Which phrase does the text use for places with a high rate of people out of work?

A40 5 Listening → H7

heyday Höhepunkt
decline Niedergang
mill Fabrik
alive and kicking gesund und munter

a Listen to different people talking about the North-South divide. What is their main message?

b With a partner, take notes concerning the following aspects.

1. history of the North-South divide
2. stereotypes about London and the North
3. science in the Northwest
4. manufacturing and education
5. northshoring
6. perception of the Northeast outside the UK

c Compare your notes and complete them.

6 A step further → G4

Do similar economic divides exist in other places, e.g. in Germany, in the EU, within continents ...?

a In small groups, choose a region or country and research information and statistics about it online. Consider aspects like education, health care, life expectancy etc.

b Prepare and give a short presentation of your findings.
→ S15 1-minute presentation

C The future of money

1 Before you read → G 2

What would you do if you received a fixed amount of money per month for the rest of your life? How would that affect your career and lifestyle choices?
→ S 15 Think-pair-share

Rosalyn Kelly is a British writer of novels and short stories. She studied English Literature and Language in Oxford and travelled around the world. In her short story *One wage* she writes about an 'ideal' country where everyone gets the same wage.

A41

One wage

by Rosalyn Kelly

There it was, in her hand. Ready to be spent. Ready to do what it was meant to do, be what it was meant to be. But she couldn't do it. She couldn't fight this urge any longer and she stuffed it back in her pocket and left the shop. She was going to save it. Hoard it. Gather it until she had piles hidden in her flat. Illegal, of course, and shameful. But Roo had made up her mind, this money, her money, was not being spent today.

She walked home. Through the happy streets of London, **1**. She smiled back, the money weighing heavily in her jeans. She'd already spent most of her wage that month, as required by Fair State, and this was a tiny amount, **2**. Hardly significant.

Deep down, she knew the state would find out. Every working person in England was paid the same monthly wage, no matter the job, **3**, whether cleaning the streets or engineering the latest robot. And they were each given access to free services including healthcare, education, childcare, cultural activities and gyms. Every able person was expected to work. Those who couldn't, through disability or illness, were still paid their salary. But those who wouldn't, **4**, were sent for reconditioning and, if that failed, were eliminated. Fair State knew who was working and who was not, who was on parental leave, who was starting work at eighteen or taking a one year sabbatical from work to study, who was retiring at sixty-five. They were all paid the same wage until they died, in cash every month, the corrupt banks long ago demolished.

The state analysts would crunch the data and know that someone, somewhere, hadn't spent their full salary that month. The paid-out figure differing from the total spent in shops and on services, as all sales were reported meticulously back to the state. But they couldn't know it was her. Out of fifty-five million people in England, they couldn't know.

She let herself into her flat, **5**, the one universal wage eradicating crime as everyone had the money to buy exactly what they wanted, whenever they wanted it. [...] Every person had a standardised home, a single, like Roo, had a one bedroom flat. A couple or family had corresponding bedrooms to their numbers. Green space was a five minute walk from every home. There were no empty buildings or second homes, or palaces with two people living in them. A fair distribution of wealth and life to all. People were happy, Roo was happy. At least, she thought she was. But, sitting on her luxurious sofa, with all the latest technology and trinkets glimmering around her, she pulled out the unspent coins. [...]

[S]he'd need to replace the sofa soon, **6**. To ensure people kept spending their wages, the law stated that one-year-old items were dropped off at one of the many R&R (Restore & Regenerate) centres to be broken down, recycled and used again to create new products with zero waste [...].

4 **urge** Drang
5 **to hoard** (an)sammeln; horten
6 **to gather** sammeln; zusammentragen
16 **reconditioning** *hier:* Umerziehung
21 **to crunch (the) data** Daten verarbeiten
23 **meticulously** akribisch
25 **to eradicate** auslöschen
32 **trinket** Zeug; Plunder

41 **sprightly** beweglich; lebhaft
43 **to wince** zucken; zusammenzucken
49 **to be worked to the bone** gezwungen werden, hart zu arbeiten
56 **takeover** (Macht-)Übernahme
59 **to seize** beschlagnahmen
60 **barely** kaum
62 **to inherit** erben
65 **to flaunt** offen missachten
66 **smoothly** glatt; reibungslos
66 **shelter** Schutz; Obdach
71 **tatty** zerschlissen

A knock at the door and then the voice of her elderly neighbour, Janice. "Are you home, Roo?"
"Yes, come in!" Roo jumped up and arrived at her lounge door just as Janice did; she was surprisingly sprightly for eighty-one.
"I'm sorry, dear, I've caught you in the middle of dinner."
[...] Janice chuckled and then lowered herself onto Roo's sofa, **7**. Roo winced, praying Janice wouldn't feel it through the cushion. For the first time, she wanted her neighbour out of the flat.
"I won't stay long. Just wanted to say a quick hello. Please, continue." Janice waited for Roo to sit and take a mouthful of food. "Had a good weekend?"
Roo nodded, chewing, and Janice continued. "In my day, the weekend was only two days, not three. Can you imagine! We were worked to the bone, and for what? Terrible wages and a fear of growing old in poverty. But this new government is the best, truly. Don't you think? You're too young to remember how it was. A shocking wealth divide, no time for family or leisure just work, work, work."
This was Janice's favourite topic, about how awful the time before the revolution was, twenty-three years earlier. Before the One Wage party took control of Government and introduced the Fair State. Roo had been two. Her mother was part of the revolution and died during the Takeover of Westminster. Roo's father, Dinesh, was a staunch resister of the One Wage ideology (her parents had divorced when she was six months old, **8**). Dinesh was "filthy rich", according to her official heritage report, and didn't want to share his wealth. [...] Like many others, Dinesh was eliminated, his wealth seized and distributed amongst every person in England. Roo barely remembered him, she'd been six when he died and she'd moved to the children's care home. A flash passed behind her eyes – perhaps I have inherited my father's love of money?
"You know, dear, I saw another inspection yesterday, when I was visiting my daughter. A Money Addict dragged from his house, screaming how the money wasn't his, **9**. I just can't understand why anyone would flaunt the rules! They are in place to keep the fabulous system running smoothly, to give us all the same shelter, food, jobs, quality of life. Why would anyone want to hoard money? It's evil."
Roo choked on a noodle and dropped her fork with a clatter. "Take a sip of water, dear. That's it." Janice shuffled on the cushion and frowned. "I think it's time you got a new sofa ..."
Roo's eyes widened. "Yes, it's coming up to one year. It's terribly uncomfortable and tatty now isn't it. Here, let me help you up."
"No, no, I can make it." Janice heaved herself up. "I should be getting on." [...]

(1009 words)

2 Multiple matching → WB, p.71/1–2

Nine phrases have been cut from the text. Match the most suitable phrases (A–K) with the gaps (1–9). There are two phrases more than you need.

A as all were equal
B to her happy home
C and taken away to be reconditioned
D although it was barely used
E or were too old
F an eighth of the total
G due to their conflicting opinions
H unlocked of course
I right on top of the hoard
J everyone smiling at her
K through laziness

3 Gapped summary → H7

Complete the summary with the most suitable words from the text (ll. 1–33). Give the line numbers of the words that you used.

Roo lives in an England where the One Wage party is in control, which is the result of a revolution that happened 23 years before. The party introduced the so-called Fair State, which is based on the ideology of everybody earning one ■ **1** wage. Rich and poor people don't exist any more; they had achieved a fair ■ **2** of money among all the people in the country. Since then it has become absolutely ■ **3** to hoard money. People offering resistance are taken away and often, like Roo's father, they are ■ **4**. While all this has resulted in ■ **5** crime and ■ **6** to free healthcare, education and so forth, not everybody is totally happy. Thus, Roo wants to save money, even though she knows that the state ■ **7** controls people, forcing them to spend all their money. Roo can't help her love of money. Yet, she also knows that if she is caught during an inspection, she will be sent away for ■ **8**.

4 Words matter → S11

a Read the definitions and search for the corresponding words in the text. Give the line numbers.

1. a strong desire or impulse
2. to accumulate and hide sth
3. relating to everyone
4. to make certain of sth
5. being old
6. sb who refuses to accept sth
7. to take away by an authority
8. to receive as a legacy
9. to be pulled away against your will
10. to disregard or disrespect

b Choose five of the words from **a** and write sentences with them.

A42 5 Listening → S3

a Listen to the podcast 'Universal basic incomes' and answer the following questions. Take notes.

1. What is a universal basic income?
2. What does Meghan say about the distribution of wealth in the world?
3. Which places have experimented with a basic income (name three)?

b With a partner, make a list of the arguments for and against a universal basic income.

6 A step further → S15 Opinion line

a Decide whether you are for or against a universal basic income. If you are for it, stand on the left side of the classroom; if you are against it, stand on the right side.

b In small groups, talk to people from your side about the reasons and arguments for your position. Find further arguments in addition to what you have heard.

c Now form small mixed groups with people from the other side. Discuss your views.

d Has your opinion changed after the discussions? Stay where you are or move to the other side. Discuss your reasons for staying or changing sides in class.

Social and antisocial behaviour → S 6.1

The conclusion is an essential part of a composition. In the conclusion, you can summarise your arguments, state your opinion, or give an outlook. The conclusion makes sure there are no loose ends. However, it does not present new arguments. It offers the logical result of all you have written up to this point.

1 Planning and analysing a conclusion → WB, p.72/1

There is not just one way of writing a good conclusion. The following points can help you to write a convincing conclusion.

1. When planning your composition, the first option is to arrange your arguments and then write a fitting conclusion. Sometimes though, it can be easier to do exactly the opposite. Plan the conclusion first, deciding what your position is. Based on this, look at your thoughts and ideas and then choose and organise your arguments accordingly.
2. When you write your conclusion, ask yourself:
   - Does the conclusion really answer the topic question?
   - Does it offer a clear position or opinion?
   - Does it pick up and connect with the arguments presented in the main body of the text?
   - Is the conclusion really the logical consequence of your order of arguments?
   - Does your conclusion really complete and round off the text?

a Here is an extract from an essay on the topic 'It wasn't like that in my day.' Was your parents' generation really better than today's youth?
Look at the three different conclusions (A–C) and analyse them regarding the questions above. How well do they fulfil the function of a conclusion? How do they pick up and relate to the rest of the text? → S15 Round robin

Well, our parents' generation is right to think of us teenagers as problematic. Every day we can see in the news that teenagers have committed some crimes. [...] On the other hand, our parents' generation was wilder and worse than our teenagers today. In the early 60s, the hippie movement was a time full of drugs, free love, and student protests. This generation was against everything: the government, the war in Vietnam, nuclear weapons and so on. [...] That shows that our parents' generation was also very rebellious.

A In conclusion, I must say that our generation isn't the well-behaved generation. Yet, our parents weren't as innocent as they sometimes want to make us believe. I think both of us have good sides and bad sides. If it wasn't like that, I think our lives would be quite boring.

B In conclusion, it must be said that there are arguments for and against both views. I think everybody should make their own decision about this topic.

C All in all, our parents' generation wasn't better than the youth is today. Consequently, sentences like "It wasn't like that in my day" are really nonsense.

b Now look at the conclusion of Text B (page 151, ll.104–117) and analyse it.

2 Material-based writing

The learning environment in schools improves if antisocial behaviour is reduced.
In order to develop specific actions, the SMV has invited all pupils to share their views on the following questions:

'What is antisocial behaviour in school? What causes it? What can be done in school to prevent it?'

Write a composition of at least 300 words. Include all the material provided.

Material 1

Material 2

Angriff auf Lehrerin: Mehr „asoziales Verhalten" nach Corona
JRuşen Tayfur, *WAZ* website, 2022

Volltrunken auf E-Scooter: Junggesellenabschied endet auf Kölner Polizeiwache
Kölner Stadt-Anzeiger website, 2022

Abhängen, pöbeln, prügeln: Immer mehr Schulschwänzer werden zum Problem
Jens Reichenbach, *NW* website, 2022

Material 3

Preventing anti-social behaviour

Early intervention is crucial because the first symptoms of anti-social behaviour can be seen before the age of 15.
Education, positive engagement in a community, mentoring and sports and recreation programmes help to support these children/teenagers by teaching them important life skills, fostering social inclusion and diverting them from crime.

'Love the world' project → S2

1 Using questions

Questions are a powerful and useful tool to improve your group discussion. They can help you with discourse management as well as with content.

Here are a few tips on how to use questions to your advantage:
- Try to end your contributions with a question. Often it is easier to react to a question than to a statement.
- With a question you control who is to speak next. Either you have a question for everyone (What do you all think?) or you put the question directly to a specific person (Tom, what's your view?).
- You can also use questions to summarise points: Are we all happy with this? Have we got all aspects? Is there anything else, or can we go to the next point? …
- With questions you can differentiate and ask for details:

Yes, but have you considered …? | Should we not also talk about …? | This idea is OK, but what about…? | What is the situation if you look at it from this perspective? | Why do you think so? | How is this to be realised? | …

a Look again at the pictures and issues on page 144. Choose one. With a partner, come up with as many questions as possible in three minutes. Then choose a different picture or issue.
Example: picture A: Living in a city
Questions: How do people live in big cities? Where do the rich people live? …

b In small groups, choose one of the social issues mentioned in this topic. The first person in the group presents one argument. All the others must reply with a question. Then the next person in the group presents another argument and so on.

2 Group discussion

There are good reasons why many people see the world as just one problematic place. At the same time, people from different cultures in every continent continue to use their creative talents to bring joy and inspiration to their communities, preserve local traditions, protect the Earth etc.

To highlight that there are not just problems in the world, but that there are many reasons to be happy and optimistic, your school is planning to launch a '50 Reasons to Love the World' website. Each class will be invited to present their answers to the question 'Why do you love the world?'

Today your group has come together to discuss your ideas and suggestions and to come up with a shortlist of six reasons for the website.

a Present one or two of your ideas (about one minute).

b Present your reasons for loving the world and how they could be introduced on the website. Discuss why they should or should not be on your final list.

c Sum up your ideas and positions. Try to come to a conclusion.

Part I Reading

Mentors stopping youth crime and giving hope in West Midlands

[...] three people tell how they are helping to stop crime in their neighbourhoods.

The fatal stabbing of a young father [...], just outside Birmingham, four weeks into the first UK lockdown was enough for Tanayah Shah to realise Covid-19 could not stop his youth work. [...]

"I [...] could see young people were still [...] getting involved in crime," said Tanayah. "I thought, 'Nah, I cannot stay indoors no more'."

In the 1990s, Tanayah was himself a member of a street gang, but after a stint in prison decided to turn his life around. He [...] decided to concentrate on stopping other young people following in his footsteps.

In 2019 he set up TSA Projects, a not-for-profit organisation working with young people through media and sport, helping them realise their potential, [...] by creating opportunities. Not just in Birmingham, but across the UK.

When lockdown happened, Tanayah got hold of bikes and scooters so he could take his youth work outside within Covid-19 restrictions.

"We tried sitting on Zoom and talking. I don't believe it works," he said. "Those young people who aren't engaging on Zoom, those are the ones who are going to get up to no good. They are the ones I want to reach." [...]

"Unfortunately, one of our young people has been arrested on [suspicion of] attempted murder. There are one or two who we couldn't help, [...]. Some of them come from horrid backgrounds. In a sense, they didn't stand a chance."

Among those helped is Dre, who has discovered a hidden talent for music. "It made me realise that in life I needed a sense of responsibility," [...]"Before, I [...] was only really going out to do bad things. So when I did the music thing, it just came naturally and I thought, 'I should be there'." The 19-year-old is even helping other young people, to "steer them on to the right path and navigate them away from violence". [...]

[...] Most of the day a group of young people gather outside Debi Ramsey's house on the Smith's Wood estate [...], perhaps appearing like they might be up to no good. In reality they are "young marginalised lads" with nowhere else to go, said Debi, [...].

Over the past year she has set up a youth organisation, although unofficially it's been running in her own garden for years. With a caravan operating as a music studio and hangout, it's no wonder everyone flocks to her.

"Nobody else was doing it," she said, when asked what her motivation was. "Smith's Wood is an area where people struggle, young people have been disengaged for the past 15-20 years when youth services started closing – youth clubs and activities," [...]

"I started noticing there really wasn't a lot of [...] support [...]."

Her group is called SASS – Smithswood Access to Services and Support. Debi helps families with education [...] and accessing services, as well as talking and most importantly listening to some of the young people that come to her. [...]

"We don't judge. Rather [...] we try to give them some hope and reason for engaging with us. We have five young people on mentoring courses, [...] and then there are those who are using our media and music studio projects." [...]

[...] Aaron, 24, turns to Debi "to get help with anything to do with life". He said: "The music studio is a place where I can go to express myself. I don't have to talk. I just get it out."

Debi's passion lies in not just supporting these young people but changing people's perceptions – sharing photos on social media of some of the teenagers litter picking, helping elderly people in the local area and creating green spaces.

"Debi has helped me get a job and have a mentor. I wish people could just see how much she does," said Aaron. "She treats everyone […] with the same respect whoever they are. She gives us an opportunity that we don't have."

[…] Women's safety, racism and dealing with grief are some of the discussions that young people have shared online over the past few months on the online platform On Point WM. Jenna Varndell runs the self-funded service for young people in the West Midlands and has based the idea around positive stories, as told by them.

[…] "We've really got to adjust the way we think, in order to really make our communities more cohesive," she said. "If you can start at an early age and educate young people, it's a really, really good start for their future. How do we make them care about their communities in the future?" […]

For Jed, 16, […] [On Point WM has] been a vital part of his life. It's been a place to meet new people and "give him a voice" on subjects he'd not […] thought about before. […] "I feel that now we have more of a voice, because everything is spoken about by adults. We don't really hear anything from young people, these days."

(820 words)

Stephanie Miskin, *BBC* website, 2021

1 Multiple matching → WB, p.73/1–2

Match the statements (A–I) with the correct people (1–6) from the text. You must use some names twice.

1 Tanayah Shah **2** Dre **3** Debi Ramsey **4** Aaron **5** Jenna Varndell **6** Jed

A You needn't complain about young people if you don't give them any opportunities.
B Here I am heard.
C Ignoring the problems was no longer an option for me.
D I try to make more people change direction, just like I have, through this project.
E This place gives me an emotional outlet without the need to talk to other people.
F I discovered a talent unknown to myself.
G Instead of talking about them, we must include them and listen to them.
H A project isn't good if it doesn't reach the target group. You must go where they are.
I We are all equal. It is here that I experienced it to be really true.

2 Short-answer questions

Answer the following questions. You may use words from the text.

1. Since when has Tanayah been active for young people? Where?
2. According to Tanayah, why was it impossible to help some young people?
3. Which phrase tells you that young people are not as bad as they seem?
4. How do you know that problems for and with young people did not start with Covid19?
5. Why do the young people Debi works with like her?
6. What is Jed's central criticism?

100 women on 100 years of voting

In 1918, following years of bitter struggle, (some) women finally gained the right to vote. To mark this centenary, we asked 100 politicians and campaigners, [...] to reflect [...] on this momentous anniversary.

When the first British women gained the right to vote, the celebrations were muted. The Great War was still raging in February 1918, and the suffragette movement itself had splintered over whether to pause its campaign during the hostilities. "The [...] rejoicing... which in prewar days would have greeted the victory, were absent when it came," reflected Sylvia Pankhurst in her 1931 book *The Suffragette Movement*. "The sorrows of the world conflict precluded jubilations."

A century later, though, we should savour the triumph as fully as we can. The Representation of the People Act added 8.5 million women – those over 30 who owned property or were graduates voting in a university constituency – to the electoral roll. It also gave the vote to 5.6 million more men after their voting age was lowered to 21, and the property qualification abolished. The general election in December 1918 consulted an electorate three times the size of the one before it.

One victory led to another. The bar to women running for parliament was quickly removed, and the first female MP was elected that year [...].

Yet progress for women has often felt painfully slow. When a 32-year-old, pregnant Harriet Harman was elected in 1982 there were still only 19 female MPs. The 2017 election was the first time more than 200 women were elected, 208 out of 650 seats. Ask female MPs now, and many worry the climate of vitriol on social media is putting off talented candidates, as is the spectre of sexual harassment. And there is still a "motherhood trap" – childless women are over-represented at the top level because it is still so hard to balance caring responsibilities with a political career.

Set against this are the achievements of the women's movement. Maternity leave rights, equal pay, domestic violence legislation – all of these were hard fights, and they will never be truly won, because laws are not enough. [...] rights are of little use unless they can be enforced.

Still, we should be optimistic. Female MPs now have strength in numbers – they are rarely a lone voice in a room full of men, having to apologise for speaking at all. And true to the spirit of the suffragettes – who came from all kinds of political traditions – there is always quiet, cross-party feminist work happening in the Commons. [...]

So what's next? [...] here are politicians, campaigners and other prominent women on what the vote means to them – and where we should go next.

Shirley Williams, *Leader of the Liberal Democrats in the House of Lords, 2001–2004*

Shirley Williams

[...] Hearing from my parents what people like Mrs Pankhurst had gone through, I saw not voting as a betrayal. I don't feel that as much now, though I think if you're disillusioned with politics, your job is to fight the disillusionment, not just give up. I voted the minute it was legal to do so, when I was 21, and at every opportunity after that. [...] When I first got elected in 1964, there were 29 female MPs.

Being a woman in parliament was pretty odd. I remember being patronised when I first got in – men literally patted me on the head and said: "That's a very good speech dear." That was quite a common attitude.

Catherine Mayer, *Writer and co-founder of the Women's Equality party*

Catherine Mayer

I think voting is an incredibly important exercise in democratic rights and a duty. I will vote in any democratic process that I'm entitled to participate in, [...]. One reason I co-founded the Women's Equality party was hearing women talking about not using their vote because of the lack of options available. The fact that politics is not an easy space for women makes it

Nicola Sturgeon

more important for them to be involved, not less. In 1913, Emmeline Pankhurst said that the vote would create equality for women. Of course, that's not the case. [...] In this centenary, we can celebrate what progress has been made, but we also have to recognise what hasn't been achieved [...] and how much the rights [...] that have been achieved are now under threat.

Nicola Sturgeon, *First Minister of Scotland & leader of the Scottish National Party (since 2014)*

[...] I have always been a voter, but for too many people the simple act of voting remains remote. The reasons for non-participation in elections are many, but all too often it is those who are most marginalised in society – and who ironically stand to gain the most – who choose not to exercise their democratic rights. It is incumbent on all of us who hold public office to try and change that.

(796 words)

Helen Lewis, *The Guardian* website, 2018

3 Gapped summary → WB, p.73/3; p.74/4

Complete the summary with the most suitable words from the text (ll. 1–50). Give the line numbers of the words that you used.

In November 2018 we remembered the 100th ■ **1** of the end of the ■ ■ **2**. In 2018 we could also celebrate the ■ **3** of a victory in the struggle for women's rights. Through the Representation of the People Act women ■ **4** the vote, at least those women who had been to university or had ■ **5**. This law also ■ **6** other restrictions which prevented people from voting. As a result, the number of people on the ■ ■ **7** tripled overnight. Still, the changes did not stop there. In 1918 women were no longer kept from running for office in an ■ **8**. Yet, in those days nobody seriously thought that 100 years later a third of the ■ **9** would be women.

4 Mediation

Beantworten Sie die folgenden Fragen auf Deutsch. Sie beziehen sich auf Zeilen 58–122.

1. Abgesehen von mehr weiblichen Abgeordneten, die auch gehört werden, was gibt noch Grund optimistisch zu sein?
2. Welche Erfahrung mit männlichen Kollegen machte Shirley Wiliams am Anfang ihrer Karriere?
3. Was stellt Catherine Mayer 100 Jahre nach Pankhursts Ziel der Gleichberechtigung fest?
4. Welchen Widerspruch bedauert Nicola Sturgeon? Welche Forderung leitet sie daraus ab?

5 Multiple choice

Choose the most suitable option.

1. When women finally got the right to vote in 1918, there was no loud rejoicing because …
   A the suffragette movement had fallen apart.
   B it had been such a bitter struggle to achieve it.
   C the full victory of women was absent until 1931.
   D the continuing war seemed to forbid celebrations.

2. The Representation of the People Act …
   A gave all women over 30 the right to vote
   B also extended the right to vote to more men.
   C gave the vote to women who owned property.
   D allowed all university graduates over 21 to vote.

3. The slow progress of women's voting rights was caused by …
   A too few talented women.
   B sexual harassment on social media.
   C the lack of people electing female MPs.
   D difficulties in being a mother and a politician.

4. Which is true?
   A The law to ensure equal pay is difficult to enforce.
   B Thanks to the women's movement, there is a law against domestic violence.
   C Maternity leave rights were the first achievement of the women's movement.
   D Despite being a strong group, female MPs remain a lone voice in a room full of men.

5. According to Shirley Williams, …
   A it should be legal to vote when you are 21.
   B in 1964 women MPs were accepted and respected by men.
   C not voting is always a betrayal of the work of Mrs Pankhurst.
   D if you are not happy with politics, you should stand up and do something.

6. What is Catherine Mayer's view?
   A The vote has created equality for women.
   B She votes only if there is not a lack of options available.
   C Politics will never be an easy space for women to be involved.
   D What has been achieved for women, must then also be protected.

The book *Wild* tells the story of how the author Cheryl Strayed walked 1,100 miles on the Pacific Crest Trail. While walking, she reflects on the ups and downs of her life including her marriage, the problematic relationship with her mother, and her heroin addiction.

Wild. A Journey from Lost to Found

By Cheryl Strayed

"Maybe I'm pregnant," I joked [...]. "Are you?" asked Amie. "I could be," I said, **1**. I'd had sex a few weeks before with a man named Joe. I'd met him the previous summer in Portland, when I'd gone there to visit Lisa and escape my trouble. I'd been there only a few days when he'd walked up to me in a bar [...].

He was twenty-four and I was twenty-five. I hadn't slept with anyone since Paul and I had broken up three months ago. That night we had sex on Joe's lumpy futon on the floor and barely slept, **2**. [...]

"Have you ever tried heroin?" he asked in the morning.

I shook my head and laughed idly. "Should I?"

I could've let it drop. Joe had only started using it when he met me. It was something he did separate from me, with a group of friends he'd made **3**. I could've glided right past it, but something compelled me to pause instead. I was intrigued. I was unattached. In my youth and sorrow, I was ready to self-destruct.

So I didn't just say yes to heroin. I pulled it in with both hands.

I was cuddled up with Joe, postsex, on his ratty couch the first time I used it, **4**. We took turns sucking up the smoke from a burning dab of black tar heroin that sat on a sheet of aluminum foil through a pipe that was made of foil too. Within a few days, I wasn't in Portland to visit Lisa and escape my sorrows anymore. I was in Portland falling into a drug-fueled half love with Joe. I moved into his apartment above an abandoned drugstore, where we spent most of the summer having adventuresome sex and doing heroin. In the beginning, it was a few times a week, then it was every couple of days, then it was every day. First we smoked it, then we snorted it. But we would never shoot it! we said. Absolutely not.

Then we shot it. It was good. It was like something beautiful and out of this world. Like I'd found an actual planet that I didn't know had been there all along. Planet Heroin. The place where there was no pain, where it was unfortunate but essentially okay that my mother was dead and my biological father was not in my life and my family had collapsed and I couldn't stay married to the man I loved. At least that's how it felt **5**.

In the mornings, my pain was magnified by about a thousand. In the mornings there weren't only those sad facts about my life. Now there was also the additional fact that I was a pile of shit. I'd wake in Joe's squalid room [...]. In the bathroom, I'd wash my face and sob into my hands for a few fast breaths, getting ready for the waitressing job I'd picked up at a breakfast place. I'd think: This is not me. This not the way I am. Stop it. No more. But in the afternoon I'd return with a wad of cash to buy another bit of heroin and I'd think: Yes. I get to do this. I get to waste my life. I get to be junk.

But this was not to be. Lisa called me one day and said she wanted to see me. I'd stayed in touch with her, hanging out for long afternoons at her place, telling her glimmers of what I was up to. As soon as I walked into her house this time, I knew something was up.

"So tell me about heroin," she demanded.

"Heroin?" I replied lightly. What could I possibly say? It was inexplicable, **6**. "I'm not becoming a junkie, if that's what you're worried about," I offered. I was leaning against her kitchen counter, watching her sweep the floor.

"That's what I'm worried about," she said sternly.

"Well, don't," I said. I explained it to her as rationally and playfully as I could. It had been only a couple of months. We would stop soon. Joe and I were simply messing around, **7**. "It's summertime!" I exclaimed. "Remember how you suggested that I come here to escape? I'm escaping." I laughed, though she didn't laugh along. [...]

She challenged my every statement, questioned my every rationale. She swept and swept the floor as our talk turned into an argument. She eventually became so furious with me that she swatted me with the broom.

I went back to Joe's and we talked about how Lisa didn't understand.

Then, two weeks later, Paul called. He wanted to see me. Right now. Lisa had told him about Joe and about my using heroin, and he'd immediately driven seventeen hundred miles straight through from Minneapolis to talk to me. I met him within the hour at Lisa's apartment. It was a warm, sunny day in late September. [...]

"Just tell me why you're doing this to yourself," he demanded, **8**. He reached across the table and took my hands, and we held on to each other, locked eye to eye, tears streaming down first my face, then down his. He wanted me to go home with him that afternoon, he said evenly. Not for a reunion with him but to get away. Not from Joe, but from heroin.

(928 words)

6 Multiple matching → WB, p.74/5–6

Eight phrases have been cut from the text. Find the most suitable phrase from the list (A–J) for the gaps (1–8). There are two more than you need.

- **A** his eyes gentle, his face so familiar to me
- **B** all alone and far from home in this city
- **C** talking until the sun rose, mostly about him
- **D** doing something fun
- **E** a week after we'd met
- **F** suddenly terrified
- **G** whom I didn't know
- **H** while I was high
- **I** like we had so often in the past
- **J** even to me

7 Gapped summary

Complete the summary with the most suitable words from the text (ll. 17–52). Give the line numbers of the words that you used.

In this extract Cheryl Strayed tells the reader of her time in Portland. Originally Cheryl goes there to get away from her ■ **1**. Instead she starts a ■ **2** love affair with a guy called Joe. When he invites her to try out heroin, she does not reject it, but embraces it with ■ ■ **3**. At first it is just an addition to her summer of ■ **4** love-making. With the drug Cheryl no longer feels the pain caused by all the tragic events in her life. Yet, soon the drug takes its toll. The ■ **5** apartment in which she lives with Joe mirrors how she is turning into a ■ **6** who wastes her life. When Lisa confronts her with this unpleasant truth and demands the reason for Cheryl's behaviour, Cheryl has to admit that the whole situation is ■ **7** to her. Like many addicts Cheryl denies the seriousness of her habit by saying her drug consumption was just for fun. No matter how seemingly logically and, at the same time, ■ **8** Cheryl presents her view, Lisa does not believe her. She calls Paul to get Cheryl out of this situation.

8 Mediation

Beantworten Sie die folgenden Fragen auf Deutsch.

1. Warum lehnt Cheryl Strayed Joes Angebot, Heroin zu nehmen, nicht einfach ab?
2. Welche negativen Ereignisse aus ihrem Leben nennt der Text?
3. Erläutern Sie die widersprüchlichen Gefühle, die Cheryl durch Heroin erfährt (während des Konsums und danach).
4. Was meint Cheryl mit dem Satz „I knew something was up"?
5. Was versucht Cheryl Lisa weiszumachen?

Part II Material-based writing

Your school is organising a discussion about various aspects of social justice in the world around us. In preparation, all pupils are invited to write a composition with the title 'Rethinking social justice'. Write at least 300 words. Include all the material provided.

Material 1

When I give food to the poor, they call me a saint. When I ask why the poor have no food, they call me a communist.

Dom Helder Camara, Archbishop of Olinda and Recife (1964–1985)

Material 2

Material 3

Soziale Ungleichheit
Über die Hälfte der Menschheit lebt in Armut, das heißt von weniger als 5,50 Dollar am Tag. Drei Milliarden Menschen haben keinen Zugang zu grundlegender Gesundheitsversorgung und drei Viertel aller Arbeitnehmer*innen keinen Zugang zu sozialer Sicherung. […]
Um ein gutes Leben für alle zu erreichen, brauchen wir ein gerechtes Wirtschaftssystem […], sodass extreme Ungleichheit erst gar nicht entsteht. Eine sozial und ökologisch gerechte Wirtschaft werden wir also nur erreichen, wenn wir das Wirtschaftssystem umfassend und konsequent demokratisieren. […]
Dafür braucht es:

- Bildung, Gesundheit und soziale Sicherung müssen allen Menschen zugänglich sein […].
- Unternehmen, die demokratisch und gemeinwohlorientiert verfasst sind, damit ihr Handeln allen und nicht nur den Kapitalgebern und Eigentümern dient.
- Vielfältige, inklusive und durchlässige Marktstrukturen statt exzessiver Machtkonzentration bei einzelnen Konzernen.

Source: *Oxfam* website

Part III Group discussion

Your school wants to organise an 'alcohol and drug abuse prevention' project. The format will be an event week with different activities focusing on the following issues:

1. Presenting information about drugs (including alcohol and nicotine).
2. Preventing alcohol and drug abuse.

Particularly the second part should not accuse anybody. It should be positive and motivate young people to say no to drugs.

You are a member of one of the groups planning this event week. In today's meeting, you can talk about the following questions.

- Why, when and where do young people drink alcohol and smoke?
- What other substances are used by young people? Why?
- What are the dangers of alcohol and drugs?
- How could alcohol and drug abuse be prevented?
- How can your points be presented?
- What are your ideas for events or activities for the project?

a Present one or two of your ideas (about one minute).

b Discuss the issues. Be polite and respect the other participants and their opinions.

c Sum up the discussion in one statement. In your group, try to come to a conclusion.

Diese Aufgaben bieten zusätzliche Hilfestellungen zu den Aufgaben in den Topics.

Topic 1

GETTING STARTED

A1 3 Listening → S 3 → SB, S. 11

Listen to the interview about what matters to young people. Complete the sentences with the missing words.

1. The interview is conducted by ■ Ronay and the person who is being interviewed is ■ Ryan, who works at Official ■, a research institution specialising in ■ and ■.
2. Common clichés about young people include that they only care about a ■ ■ ■ and what's going on ■ ■ ■.
3. The topics which matter to young people are: finding a ■ job which also involves doing something they like and find meaningful, health, fitness and ■, personal ■, protecting the ■ and racism and ■ ■.
4. Young people were not interested in specific ■ ■ because they could not ■ with them or they did not ■ them.
5. The person interviewed expects that in a future survey the topics will revolve around health, climate ■ and finding a ■ ■, as well as local issues (e.g. ■ ■).

TEXT A

4 Multiple choice → SB, S. 16

Read the text on pages 15–16. Choose the most suitable option.

1. Why does Geraint constantly feel under pressure?
   A He thinks he needs to present the newest stuff on the market.
   B He thinks he needs to advertise the trendiest products and be hilarious.
   C He feels that people want very exciting and entertaining videos all the time.
   D He thinks he needs to release funny videos and present great products all the time.

2. What expectations do Geraint's parents have with regard to his influencer career?
   A He should focus on his school performance.
   B He should consider different career options.
   C They support his career, but they consider a good education important too.
   D He should invest completely in his career because it is part of young people's lives today.

3. What is Molly's reaction concerning negative comments about her videos?
   A She always ignores them and focuses on the positive ones.
   B They hurt her, but she manages somehow to overcome them.
   C They hurt her although she knows they are part of the business.
   D They used to be very hurtful, but now she's learnt to overlook them.

4. What is the greatest benefit Molly finds in her influencer career?
   A It gives her a voice to help others.
   B She can make money while having fun.
   C She can express her opinions and feelings.
   D She can raise awareness about the music business.

5 Writing a personal email → S 6.4 → SB, S.17

Write an email to either Geraint or Molly. Briefly introduce yourself, then say what you think about the article and what they said about being an influencer. Ask them 2–3 questions. You can use the words and phrases from the box.

USEFUL PHRASES

Writing a personal email
Dear (name), | Good morning/afternoon, | Hello, ...
I am writing to you because .../ ... to inform you ... | I would like to ...
I would like to know about ... | While reading, I asked myself ...
I look forward to hearing from you soon.
Kind regards | All the best | Best wishes

TEXT B

1 Before you read → SB, S.18

b Think about your daily life. What stresses you out? What do you think are typical stress factors at your age? Complete the mind map with the words from the word bank. Add more words.

debt | unemployment | break-up | illness | deadline | moving house | pandemic | racism | task

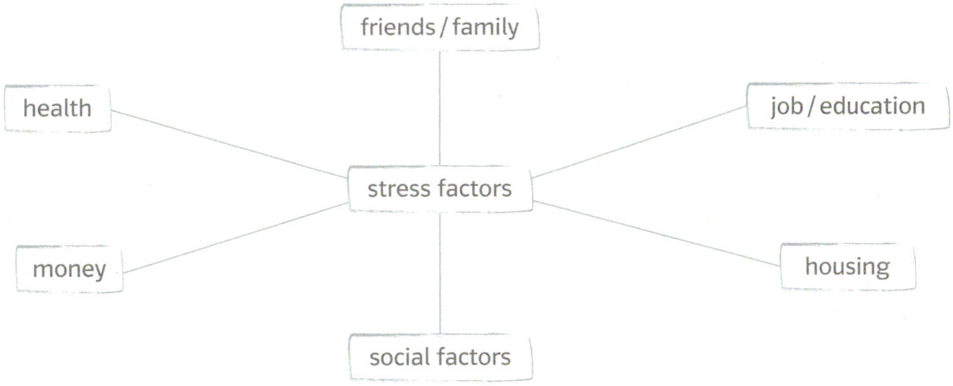

TEXT C

3 Short-answer questions → SB, S. 24

Read the text on pages 22–23. Answer the following questions. You may use words from the text.

1. How old were Tom and Cameron when they launched their company?
2. What was their business idea for their company?
3. What did Tom's brother study and what does his sister want to study?
4. Who invested in them and how much?
5. What advice does Cameron give at the end?

6 Words matter → SB, S. 25

a Match the beginnings of the nouns (1–10) with the right ending (A–F).

1 appli-	A -er (2x)
2 encourage-	B -tion (2x)
3 commit-	C -ment (3x)
4 employ-	D -y
5 secur-	E -ity
6 distribu-	F -cation
7 promo-	
8 develop-	
9 recruit-	
10 discover-	

Topic 2

GETTING STARTED

A6 3 **Listening** → S 3 → SB, S. 33

b Choose the most suitable answer.

1. Where did Kimberly travel to?
   A Spain
   B Madeira
   C the Canary Islands
   D the island of Menorca

2. Why did she need to get away?
   A She suffered from depression and anxiety.
   B She had a bad break-up with her first love.
   C She felt lost in life and wasn't eating any more.
   D She felt pressure to choose a job after finishing high school.

3. How did Kimberly feel at the airport?
   A She felt relaxed.
   B She felt bad for leaving.
   C She felt anxious because everyone was watching her.
   D She was very worried about having forgotten something at home.

4. Where was she when her situation changed?
   A Walking along the beach.
   B Sitting in a café by the beach.
   C Eating out alone in a restaurant.
   D Sitting in the cable car while sightseeing.

5. What recommendation does Kimberly give the audience at the end of her story?
   A To take a risk
   B To find one's boundaries
   C To start a new phase in life
   D To encourage everyone to feel happy

TEXT A

3 Short-answer questions → SB, S. 35

Answer the following questions. The line numbers can help you.
You may use words from the text.

1. According to the charity, what made Veganuary more successful in 2019 than in 2014? (ll. 5–17)
2. Why does Rich Hardy believe that vegan lifestyles will continue to grow? (ll. 40–48)
3. What have supermarkets done in reaction to an increase in veganism? (two things) (ll. 55–71)

TEXT B

4 Mediation → SB, S. 38

Bearbeiten Sie die folgenden Aufgaben zu den Zeilen 83–116 auf Deutsch.

1. Beschreiben Sie, was die Wohltätigkeitsorganisation unter dem „first aid kit" (Z. 88) versteht?
2. Übertragen Sie die Metapher „a busy mind" (Z. 99) ins Deutsche und erklären sie diese im Textzusammenhang.
3. Erklären Sie die Herangehensweise der Organisation, wenn sie von „our approach is to embrace physical activity" (Z. 104–105) spricht.

TEXT C

3 Gapped summary → SB, S. 43

Complete the summary with the most suitable words from the text on pages 41–42. Give the line numbers of the words that you used. The given line numbers, may help you.

In this article, we are introduced to the topic of dark tourism. The dark tourist Peter Hohenhaus stresses the ■ **1** (ll. 54–60) side of this way of travelling as it has taught him many things. He talks about his experiences at a number of locations. The most emotionally moving one was a genocide memorial with ■ **2** (ll. 22–25) laid out for viewing. As uncomfortable as it was, he describes a sense of ■ **3** (ll. 30–34) to do the whole tour. However, it's not always about the events themselves. Part of the attraction is how the event is portrayed. Visiting the memorials often means being confronted with conspiracy theories or with stories that are built upon ■ **4** (ll. 49–53). This can be well seen in the particularly ■ **5** (ll. 35–41) accounts given at North Korean sites. Peter Hohenhaus warns that there are certain rules which apply when visiting dark places in contrast to ■ **6** (ll. 73–78) tourist attractions. In addition, he argues against visiting locations attached to ■ **7** (ll. 80–85) tragic events or places where not enough time has passed since the tragedy occurred. One major question that we are left with is why people shy away from dark tourism in favour of trips resulting in ■ **8** (ll. 89–96).

A12 🔈 **5 Listening** → S 3 → SB, S. 43

a Listen to four people talking about their experiences at dark places around the world. Complete the table with the missing information.

Speaker	Place, he/she visited	Adjectives and nouns to describe the experience	What they have learnt from the experience
1	…	surprise, …	– you'll always be there in spirit. – there's nothing to fear when …
2	Tunnel Museum in Bosnia-Herzegovina	…	there is a lot of … which comes out in times of …
3	…	eerie	…
4	Apartheid Museum in Johannesburg	…	– people were classified by … – there was a violent end of … – although there is … now, there is still work to be done.

Topic 3

GETTING STARTED

A13 🔈 **2 Listening** → S 3 → G 3 → SB, S. 53

a Listen to the first part of the podcast about today's world of work and complete the following sentences with words from the word bank.

Estonia and Latvia | over-represented | become mothers | 2000 | low-paid | 100 | New Work, Old Problems | 9 | part-time | 18 | to have breaks | third-highest | average gross earnings

1. The online lecture Melanie Bishop gave was named '■ ■, ■ ■'.
2. ■ participants from ■ countries were involved in Melanie's lecture.
3. According to Melanie, the gender pay gap refers to a difference in ■ ■ ■.
4. Germany was the ■ country with a gap of 19.2 %. Only ■ and ■ had a larger gender pay gap.
5. Some of the reasons for the gender pay gap are that women are more likely to ■ ■ in their careers as many ■ ■. When they do return to work, it's often ■ and they are ■ in ■ occupations.
6. The wealthiest ■ people in the UK have as much money as the poorest ■ million.

TEXT A

3 Multiple matching → SB, S. 55

Match the headings (A–E) with the sections of the text (1–5).

A Entrepreneurial skills
B Business acumen
C Leadership
D Perseverance and motivation
E Organisation

1 "This is about knowing how a business or industry works and what makes a company tick …" (ll. 26–33)
2 "You may not be a manager straight away, but graduates need to show …" (ll. 55–61)
3 "This is about showing that you can prioritise, work …" (ll. 62–69)
4 "Employers want people to have a bit of get-up-and-go …" (ll. 70–77)
5 "Spotting gaps in the market, suggesting ways to improve processes, …" (ll. 92–100)

TEXT B

3 Mediation → SB, S. 59

Beantworten Sie die folgenden Fragen auf Deutsch. Die Zeilenangaben können Ihnen helfen.

1. Bevor er ihm unverhohlen droht, wie versucht Foysol Jashel zunächst zu überzeugen, ihm seinen Ausweis auszuhändigen? (Z. 19–34)
2. Welche Konsequenzen spielt Jashel in seinem Kopf durch, falls sein Vertrag aufgelöst würde (zwei Aspekte)? (Z. 35–38)
3. Was ist mit dem Ausdruck „If he sang the agent's tune" (Z. 39–40) gemeint und welche Bedeutung hat er im Zusammenhang mit dem Text?

TEXT C

2 Multiple choice → SB, S. 62

Choose the most suitable answer.

1. What is the series Generation J about?
   A It's about today's world of work and its workers.
   B It's about how older Japanese generations influence the next one.
   C It's about how Japan's next generation is shaping the country's future.
   D It's about robots and how they are replacing tomorrow's human workers.

2. What is special about the security guard named Ugo?
   A He is able to work more hours than others.
   B He is a police bot able to do routine patrol.
   C He is very handsome with his big blue eyes.
   D He is the cutest robot among his AI colleagues.

3. What are Ugo's duties?
   A Flanking the passage to greet new guests
   B Patrolling the building and summoning lifts
   C Replacing human guards by doing their tasks
   D Greeting visitors and making sure they don't feel intimidated

4. Do a lot of companies have someone like Ugo?
   A As of yet, only few facilities have robots.
   B No, Japan is still sceptical about their employment.
   C There are already two prototypes and more to come.
   D Over 80 % of companies have already engaged at least one robot.

5. Which two forms of robots are used in Tokyo's Silver Wing nursing home?
   A A personal robot for each elderly person and a robot helping in the kitchen.
   B A robot helping to ease body strain and an animator robot in the common room.
   C A fitness coach leading exercises and a robot who carries people in and out of bed.
   D A staff-organising robot and a robot which engages with the elderly in the common room.

WRITING

1 Collecting and analysing arguments → SB, S. 64

a The world of work is rapidly changing. More and more people are working remotely – in their 'home offices'. Plan your composition as presented in the box on page 64 on the following question:
'What are the advantages and disadvantages of the new approaches in the world of work?'
You can use the words and phrases from the box.

USEFUL PHRASES

We should consider the (dis-) advantage of … which enables …
On the one hand, … on the other hand…
In addition | Furthermore | Besides
On the contrary | By comparison | However |
flexibility | freedom | work-life balance | demanding | workload | potential | remote work | | daily structure | productivity | to participate | responsibility | agile | meaningful | co-working | virtual workplace | anonymous | digital infrastructure | work equipment

DISCUSSION

1 Talking about preferences and giving advice → SB, S. 65

d The pictures on page 65 show different jobs. Give your partner advice on a suitable job. Give reasons. Feel free to include a job other than the ones given.
You can use the phrases from the box.

USEFUL PHRASES

Giving advice
I think you should/could … because …
I (strongly) recommend … since you mentioned …
Since you liked …, my (personal) recommendation would be …
You talked about …, therefore, my advice would be …
Due to …, it would be a good idea to …
Make sure you (don't) …
Why don't you …?
If I were you, I'd …
In my experience … is really interesting/helpful/…

Topic 4

GETTING STARTED

1 Working with pictures and quotes → S 10.1 → SB, S. 75

b Match the quotes (1–4) with their message (A–F). There are two messages more than you need. Then compare your ideas with a partner and discuss them.

1 The media's the most powerful [thing] on earth. They have the power to make the innocent guilty and to make the guilty innocent, and that's power.
Malcolm X, African-American minister and human rights activist

2 We don't need politicians, we've all got iPhones and computers, right? So any decision that has to be made, any policy, we just put it online. Let the people vote – thumbs up, thumbs down, the majority wins. That's a democracy.
Jack, character in the series 'Black Mirror'

3 The great thing about social media was how it gave a voice to voiceless people.
Jon Ronson, British journalist, author and filmmaker

4 You are what you share.
Charles Leadbeater, authority on innovation and creativity

A People no longer define themselves by character, but by how they present themselves on social media.
B One should be aware that information on the internet, which is presented as fact, is being used by individuals or institutions to support their interests, that it has been rendered for their cause.
C If the people themselves create news, it is less influential than news published by big publishing houses.
D Media has the ability to influence our opinions, behaviour and attitudes. It is often through its lens that we see the world.
E If we use social media and other digital devices to vote, decisions would be more democratic than if politicians decided for us.
F Social media enables people to express their opinions, gain increased attention for their cause and find like-minded people around the world to organise a movement together.

TEXT A

1 Before you read → G 1.5 → SB, S. 76

Imagine someone has lived in the wilderness for the last 15 years and has now moved to a big city. What has changed in his or her absence? Talk about it to a partner. You can use the pictures on page 76 and the words and phrases from the box.

USEFUL PHRASES

Comparing past and present aspects/events
Today people use … to communicate | to shop | …
While this person lived in the wilderness, … were invented.
This person might have used a CD player | the radio | … to listen to music, but today people …
Nowadays, people don't …, but instead they …
There are new ways of … in big cities, for example …

TEXT B

4 Short-answer questions → SB, S. 81

Answer the following questions. You may use words from the text.

1. What do pictures about certain events provoke?
2. What does 'visual turn in the study of global politics' (l. 26) mean?
3. What made the World Trade Center attacks in 2001 remain engrained in our collective consciousness?
4. How did the media report news during Vietnam War?
5. What is meant by the 'democratisation' of visual politics (l. 84)?

5 Words matter → SB, S. 81

a Create a mind map for 'media'. Use the words from the word bank. Add more words.

visual | images | photographs | television | traditional media | digital | drone | satellite | surveillance camera | to depict | impression | to circulate world-wide | audience | to shape one's view | debate | representation | collective consciousness | painting | perception | front-page | video | local | global | media network | to distribute | smartphone | to upload | social media | to go viral | broadcaster | authenticity | value-free | powerful | spectator | source | to manipulate | to fake | perspective | means of communication

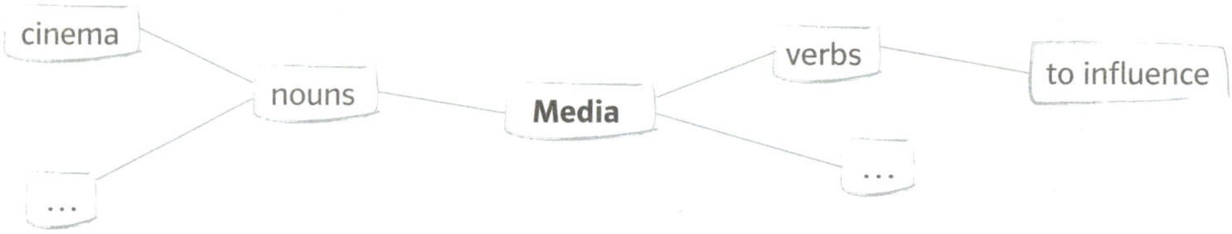

TEXT C

3 Gapped summary → SB, S. 84

Complete the summary with the most suitable words from the text. The first letter of the word is given to help you. Give the line numbers of the words that you used.

The text follows a person's journey through their daily routine. From the minute he is woken by his p-■ **1**, an installed device r-■ **2** his location as he moves. The first thing he does is look at his social media n-■ **3**. Throughout the day, various devices collect data about where he goes, what he does, and even how he does it. His phone, for example, uses various apps to trace the p-■ **4** of his movements, while data from his energy provider d-■ **5** his absence based on the decrease in usage. On his way to the university, his car's l-■ p-■ **6** is photographed by a camera, which once again reveals his location and the exact time. All of these apps, including his parking app and and his car insurance app, can collect d-■ **7** and sell the information to advertising companies. As the narrator begins to drive to a friend's place, his navigation software offers a p-■ **8** of the duration of the journey, which is particularly accurate. Based on his location at the friend's house, the GPS on his phone assumes that he was at the h-■ s-■ **9** below the apartment.

WRITING

1 Using connectives → S 5.2 → SB, S. 85

b Read the composition on the benefits and dangers of watching TV and match the connectives (A–S) with the gaps (1–15) in the text.

A because
B Finally
C Firstly
D However
E In addition
F In conclusion
G Initially
H Last but not least
I Moreover
J Nonetheless
K On the one hand
L Secondly
M Similarly
N Still
O Thus

Television is one of the most popular forms of entertainment all over the world. **1**, it was called the 'idiot box' **2**, back then, it was all about entertainment. It did not have as many informative channels as it does now. **3**, television has since changed. More and more channels now offer us knowledge and information along with entertainment. **4**, this essay will look at the benefits and dangers of watching TV.

5, the invention of television has given us various benefits. TV gives us access to a cheap mode of entertainment. As they are very affordable, we can now all own one. **6**, it keeps us updated on the latest international events. It is now possible to get news from all corners of the world. **7**, television offers educational programmes improving our knowledge of science and wildlife, to name just a few. **8**, TV also motivates individuals to develop skills such as cooking, gardening or DIY. This pushes people to do better and try out new things.

9, TV also has a negative side that can even be harmful for children and young people. **10**, we have to admit that there is a lot of inappropriate content on TV such as violence, drugs and crime, and certainly too much explicit sex bordering on pornography. **11**, it is also harmful to our health. Don't forget, when watching TV we do not move much, while, at the same time, we tend to have lots of snacks, washed down with lots of sugary drinks. Certainly not a healthy lifestyle.
12, the most dangerous aspect of all is the great amount of fake information that we see on TV. Many media channels now only promote the propaganda of governments and powerful organisations, thus misinforming citizens. This is a danger we must not ignore.

13, there is nothing wrong with being entertained by TV. **14**, it is extremely important not to be naïve. We must be critical about how much we watch and what we watch. Parents should keep an eye on the viewing habits of their children. **15**, we should not believe everything we see and hear on TV. We must be the better judge and make wise choices in the channels and programmes we view.

Topic 5

GETTING STARTED

5 Discussing diversity → SB, S. 97

a Take notes on how to embrace diversity in today's society. Consider these questions. You can use the ideas provided for each question.

1. What are the consequences of diversity for everyday life?
   using the toilet / public transport | doing sports | accessing public places | shopping for clothes | participating in one's community
2. Which positive effects does a diverse society bring about?
   different views / abilities / ways of living / life experiences | broaden one's horizon
3. Which conflicts do we encounter in a diverse society?
   different religious beliefs / languages | bullying | denial of racism / discrimination
4. What does diversity mean for each individual within a community?
   finding one's place | understanding | respect | tolerance | acceptance | participation

TEXT A

1 Before you read → SB, S. 98

b Discuss the following questions in class. You can use the words and phrases from the box below.

1. What are the reasons for such stereotypes?
2. What are the consequences? What happens to people who do not conform to these stereotypes?

USEFUL PHRASES

People often use stereotypes for other people / groups because we learnt them from our family / friends / the media / … / don't spend enough time with ….
Stereotypes influence how we think about / behave toward …
People affected by stereotypes feel / experience / begin to believe …
prejudice | discrimination | bullying | inequality | to stigmatise sb | low self-esteem | anxiety | to be biased / intolerant / narrow-minded | authenticity | to prevent | expectation | to act a certain way | assumption | unfair | trauma | lonely | isolated

A27 6 Listening → S 3 → SB, S. 101

a Listen to an episode of the radio show 'Identity 101'. The person being interviewed is Noah Brooks, a professional athlete who just recently came out. While listening, complete the sentences from the text.

1. I'm very pleased to say that I'm joined by our guest, Noah Brooks, a player for the ■.
2. I was lucky to have a ■ childhood. We were an ■ family, so it was all about sports.
3. I only worked it out myself (being gay) about ■ or ■ years ago.
4. I needed to be secure, ■, since I was about to take a big risk in my career.
5. But I live in the ■ ■. It's hard to suddenly start dating a dude without people raising their eyebrows.

6. Though I had a conversation with some of the team's senior management after telling some of the guys on the team, and they were super ■.
7. I hope that in the future coming out doesn't even need to ■ …
8. But honestly, now it just feels like ■, it's a non-issue now.

TEXT B

2 Gapped summary → SB, S.103

Complete the summary with the most suitable words from the text (ll.70–99) on pages 102–103. The given line numbers may help you.

Akram Khan states that the interest in ■ **1** (ll.46–57) is visible in many art forms, cultural events and dance performances. It can also be seen in ■ **2** (ll.91–99) careers, for example those of Idris Elba, athletes such as Jessica Ennis-Hill and artists like Anish Kapoor. The author of the article himself is ■ **3** (ll.39–45) to be British because the culture allows him to mix the Indian style of dancing with a ■ **4** (ll.70–82) form of expression. While Khan acknowledges the huge advantages dancers from around the world have in Great Britain, he criticises the fact that in recent years Brexit, ■ **5** (ll.83–90) and dangerous disputes about immigrants are leading to a loss of acceptance of British diversity. Khan claims that if people do not see the value of diversity, the country will suffer a ■ ■ **6** (ll.83–90). People should remind themselves of their ■ **7** (ll.91–99) for the talents of artists from such diverse backgrounds because the British are ■ **8** (ll.91–99) in their appreciation, even though their ■ **9** (ll.91–99) may cause them to forget this.

6 A step further → SB, S.104

a In small groups, read the information about the *Turner Prize*, *EastEnders* and the *Notting Hill Carnival*. Give reasons why Akram Khan mentions them in his text.

The **Turner Prize** is a prominent event in British culture. It is named after the English painter Joseph M. W. Turner and presented every year to a British visual artist. The prize was first awarded in 1984 and has become the UK's most famous art award representing all media. Since 2004, it has been worth £40,000.
Among the award winners are the controversial art duo Gilbert & George (1986), British-Indian sculptor Sir Anish Kapoor (1991), Damien Hirst (1995), British painter Christopher Ofili (1998), British artist Lubaina Himid (2017).

EastEnders is a British soap opera that has been broadcast on BBC One since 1985. It was created by Julia Smith and Tony Holland and is set in the East End of London in the fictional borough of Walford. The series presents the everyday life of local residents and their families. The main characters are the Beale and Fowler family. Other characters include the Jewish doctor Harold Legg, the Anglo-Cypriot Osman family, a black father and son Tony and Kelvin Carpenter, the single mother Mary Smith and the Bangladeshi couple Saeed and Naima Jeffery.

The **Notting Hill Carnival** is an annual Caribbean festival and has taken place in London since 1966. Each August the streets of the Notting Hill area of Kensington fill with around two and a half million people, making this event one of the world's largest street festivals. It is led by members of the British Afro-Caribbean community.

TEXT C

3 Gapped summary → SB, S. 106

Complete the summary with the most suitable words from the text (ll. 1–44). The given parts of speech may help you (n = noun, v = verb, adj = adjective). Give the line numbers of the words that you used.

Before he went to work for Auticon, James Neely suffered a lot, for example on his way to work, which was always a rather ■ **1** (adj) undertaking for him. At work, the surroundings were too much for him to bear, and thus he experienced a complete ■ **2** (n). Only then did doctors diagnose him as being ■ **3** (adj). His new job is better suited to his needs. Neely now gets a lot of ■ **4** (n) from his superiors. This at least reduces the ■ **5** (n) that often cannot be fully avoided in the world of work. Neely and others also get help when it comes to ■ **6** (v, -ing-form) the items on their to-do list. Up to now, only a minority of people with autism are integrated into the workforce. However, attitudes are changing. Especially ■ **7** (n) are keen on making use of these inividuals' creativity.

Topic 6

GETTING STARTED

2 Talking about the Sustainable Development Goals (SDGs) → SB, S. 119

b Use the following verbs with the words from the infographic to explain the SDGs (e. g. to reduce poverty, to end hunger, to improve access to clean water).

to strengthen | to establish | to ensure | to achieve | to encourage | to promote | to empower | to take action on/against | to restore | to create | to provide for | to render sth (+ adj) | to reduce | to fight | to combat | to tackle | to protect

TEXT A

2 Multiple matching → SB, S. 121

Match the statements (A–H) with the correct people or services (1–4) from the text. Use a person or service as often as indicated.

1 Tim Anderson (2x) **2** Julian Allen (3x) **3** hot-food delivery service (2x) **4** Amazon (1x)

A Unfortunately the intelligent and environmentally conscious customer does not really exist.
B The user-friendly systems make us forget the environmental price we pay for our purchases.
C Sorry, but the customers want it now – they want it hot. We cannot go really green.
D Why not combine shopping with supporting retailers next door?
E The "I don't want to wait" culture is to be blamed for that.
F Don't blame us for the emissions. If the clients didn't want it, we wouldn't be that big.
G It is not as if there were no ways to shop green.
H With those distances, we need cars.

TEXT B

4 Gapped summary → SB, S. 125

Complete the summary with the most suitable words from the text (ll. 1–34). Give the line numbers of the words that you used. The given parts of speech may help you (n = noun, v = verb, adj = adjective, pl = plural).

In her speech Jacinda Ardern calls for urgent action to protect the environment. At the beginning she stresses that all people are called upon to be ■ **1** (n, pl) of this planet. ■ **2** (n, pl) such as climate change must be faced by all the people of the world together. Politicians can no longer focus just on their ■ **3** (adj) policies. They must understand that in our ■ **4** (adv) globalised world decisions we make in one country have ■ **5** (n, pl) for the whole world. To illustrate her point she uses the example of Tuvalu, one of the places that have ■ **6** (v, simple past) the fewest ■ **7** (n, pl) of CO_2. Still Tuvalu is in danger of becoming the victim of the most ■ 8 (adj) results of global pollution. In other words, these ■ 9 (n, pl) might soon be flooded if no action is taken. Thus, we need investment in green projects that lead to a ■ 10 (n, sg) in our transport systems, in the way we generate electricity (e.g. with an ■ 11 (n) in the use of renewable sources of energy) and so on.

6 Words matter → SB, S. 126

a Look at the words referring to politics from Jacinda Ardern's speech on pages 123–124. Put them in the right column.

to achieve | to adapt | APEC | to be determined to do | to become interdependent | borderless | to collaborate | collective inaction | commitment | concept | concrete action | to contribute | to couple ambition with action | to create | domestic | to focus on | force | G20 | global | globalised | to incentivise | interdependence | land | leader | legislation | local | to make decisions | nation | nationalism | objective | to pay the price for | policy | political | population | president | to protect | ramification | to reduce | security | to stop | subsidies | to support | to tackle | to take office | transformation | tribe | universal | to value

Politics			
nouns	verbs	adjectives	names
people	to face challenges	sovereign	…
…	…	…	

TEXT C

2 Multiple matching → SB, S. 129

Nine phrases (A–I) have been cut from the text. Find the most suitable gap (1–9) for each.

A lie about the streets by the hundreds and
B but they come every five minutes or so
C once a mighty boulevard striking through the city down to the waterfront
D which may not be totally farfetched
E and people wait there out of the rain
F as they develop in the pavement
G once the headquarters of far-flung corporations
H which is huge
I and had an immense appeal to tourists

6 A step further → S 6.6, S 10.1 → G 4 → SB, S. 130

b Think about what the world might look like in 50 or 100 years. Write the opening page for a novel set in the future. Write about 250 words in which you …
- set the scene,
- describe the atmosphere and
- introduce the main character or characters.

You can use the phrases below. Decide whether you will depict a utopia or a dystopia and which issues to include (e.g. surveillance, climate change, artificial intelligence, pandemics).

USEFUL PHRASES

Describing scenery
beautiful | dramatic | impressive | natural | picturesque | strange | ugly | unique | unnatural | …

Describing atmosphere
calm | clean | idyllic | lonely | noisy | peaceful | polluted | sacred | suspenseful | threatening | …

Describing characters
aggressive | confident | determined | honest | nasty | open-minded | passionate | relaxed | reliable | selfish | smart | unsure | violent | …

Topic 7

GETTING STARTED

3 Listening → S3 → SB, S.145

A37

Listen to the podcast 'Looking at today – Thinking for tomorrow: Top social issues in the USA'. What is said about these issues? Match the words and phrases from the word bank (A–Z) with the right social issue (1–7).

A 13–17% of Americans below poverty line
B Americans save less than people in other developed nations
C based on how income relates to the cost of living
D children in underfunded schools are more likely to drop out
E crime is linked to racism
F depends on where children are born
G difficult to afford the basic necessities
H a disproportionately high number of prisoners are from poor communities and communities of colour
I funding comes from local taxes
J harsh drug laws
K is much better in rich communities than in poor communities
L mandatory minimum sentences
M many people have little money left over to save
N more people are incarcerated than in any other country
O most employers offer health insurance to their full-time employees
P no universal healthcare
Q not created equal
R number of people living in poverty is rising
S often high extra expenses
T part-time employees, the self-employed and unemployed must pay more
U social safety nets for the poor are removed
V system is privatized
W tax breaks for the rich
X the most vulnerable people are affected
Y wages do not keep up with costs of living
Z wealth is in the hands of the top 1%

1. unequal distribution of wealth	...
2. poverty	...
3. unequal education funding	...
4. crime and incarceration	...
5. health issues	...
6. increased cost of living	...

TEXT A

5 Short-answer questions → SB, S.149

Answer the following questions. You may use words from the text. The given line numbers may help you.

1. What does the *Collective* call its concept? (ll.30–39)
2. Which two descriptions underline the fact that the *Collective* does not offer large flats? (ll.11–19 and ll.74–83)
3. What are companies that are developing co-living being accused of? (ll.64–73)
4. Why does Vlad Calus think that these co-living concepts are not a sustainable solution? (ll.74–83)
5. If co-living was really the answer, what should it be about (but is not)? (ll.103–113)

TEXT B

4 Multiple choice → SB, S.152

Choose the most suitable option.

1. The North-South divide … (ll. 2–8)
   A has a long history.
   B highlights political inequality.
   C is only a geographical divide in the country.
   D is a theme politicians only address during election time.

2. Productivity … (ll. 9–24)
   A in London has doubled since 2001.
   B has a crucial influence on living standards.
   C is a concept used by economists to measure living standards.
   D is based on the idea that we must constantly produce more per head than before.

3. Which is true? (ll. 25–36)
   A The financial centre of the UK is in the south.
   B Workers in the south are more productive than in the north.
   C Creating the Northern Powerhouse has helped to fix the problem.
   D Politicians have successfully rebalanced the UK economy away from London.

4. What is not explicitly mentioned in lines 37–61?
   A Despite new and more jobs, regional differences in the job market remain.
   B The employment situation in big cities has improved during the last decade.
   C Most of the million new jobs created are in Sheffield, Merseyside and London.
   D Finding a job in the big cities has often been more difficult than in the rest of the country.

5. Which is wrong? (ll. 62–77)
   A The minimum wage has increased in the last ten years.
   B There is a huge pay gap between London and the rest of the UK.
   C On average, jobs in the East Midlands are better paid than in the South East.
   D The minimum wage has increased to 59 % compared to 46 % of the average wage in 1999.

6. According to lines 78–103 …
   A a higher income automatically means a higher standard of living.
   B household incomes in Scotland are now 20 % higher than in the North East.
   C if you consider wages together with the cost of living, London is not the wealthiest part of the UK.
   D pay packets in the North are smaller because mortgages and rental payments are lower too.

7. In the end, the author thinks that … (ll. 104–117)
   A there should be fewer unemployment blackspots.
   B the North-South divide has been closed over the past decade.
   C the country is on the right track, but a lot of work still remains to be done in order to fully unite the UK.
   D some important measures have started to close the North-South divide once and for all.

A40 **5 Listening** → SB, S.152

b Listen to different people talking about the North-South divide. Put the words and phrases from the word bank in the right categories.

a thousand years of a dividing line | alive and kicking | cancer research, materials and high-performance computing | days of mining and shipbuilding have gone | disadvantages are very rarely mentioned | elsewhere in the world very different | engineering has been developed and evolved | great breakthroughs in world-leading science | grim myth needs busting | large-scale manufacturers have closed their mills | more mills of a smaller size with new technology | number one location for foreign direct investment by Japanese businesses | periods of decline | reasons have changed, but the line has remained fixed | revival of manufacturing | spectacular advances | talked down | talked up | universities, with good reputations | where all the opportunity lies | wonderful places, exciting opportunities for work | young people are attracting businesses from the Southeast to where the workforce is cheaper

1. history of the North-South divide	...
2. stereotypes about London and the North	London / the South: ... The North: ...
3. science in the Northwest	...
4. manufacturing and education	...
5. northshoring	...
6. perception of the Northeast outside the UK	...

TEXT C

3 Gapped summary → SB, S.155

Complete the summary with the most suitable words from the text (ll. 1–33) on pages 153–154. The first letter of the word is given to help you. Give the line numbers of the words that you used.

Roo lives in an England where the One Wage party is in control, which is the result of a revolution that happened 23 years before. The party introduced the so-called Fair State, which is based on the ideology of everybody earning one u-■ **1** wage. Rich and poor people don't exist any more; they had achieved a fair d-■ **2** of money among all the people in the country. Since then it has become absolutely i-■ **3** to hoard money. People offering resistance are taken away and often, like Roo's father, they are e-■ **4**. While all this has resulted in e-■ **5** crime and a-■ **6** to free healthcare, education and so forth, not everybody is totally happy. Thus, Roo wants to save money, even though she knows that the state m-■ 7 controls people, forcing them to spend all their money. Roo can't help her love of money. Yet, she also knows that if she is caught during an inspection, she will be sent away for r-■ **8**.

SKILLS FILES

S1 Communication skills

S1.1 Mastering communication situations

Language has a huge variety of functions to offer: you can use it to make small talk, to have heated discussions, to write personal or business correspondence, to give instructions, to express feelings etc. The following phrases will help you to master key communication situations like these:

EXPRESSING OPINIONS

Stating your opinion

The point is … | Wouldn't you say that …? | If you ask me … | As I see it … | It seems to me that … | As far as I understand … | As far as I'm concerned … | In my opinion … | I am of the opinion that … | I take the view that … | From my point of view … | To my mind … | I would like to emphasise that … | I would like to mention/say that … | I'd like to point out that … | I strongly believe that … | I'm sure/convinced/certain that … | It is obvious that … | Obviously/Without a doubt, it is wrong/right to say that … | I reject the idea that … | It is completely/absolutely/totally wrong to argue that …

Expressing probability/predicting

Definitely: Of course, it'll … | It's going to … | There's no question that … | It's sure to say … | It's bound to …
Probably: It'll probably … | I expect it to … | I wouldn't be surprised if … | I bet it'll …
Perhaps: I guess it might … | There's a chance it'll …
Probably not: I doubt (if) it'll … | I don't think it'll …
Definitely not: Of course it won't … | There's no chance of it …-ing. | I'm absolutely sure it won't …

Emphasising

definitely | extremely | indeed | absolutely | positively | obviously | naturally | always | never | without a doubt | certainly

DISCUSSING

Persuading/objecting

That's a good idea, but … | That might be OK, but … | I really don't think so because … | Why don't you …? | I see what you mean, but … | That's true, but …

Giving reasons

because | since | therefore | consequently | accordingly | As there are … | As a result of … Due to … | Because of …

Giving examples

for example | for instance | in another case | take the case of | to illustrate | as an illustration | to take another example | as shown by … | as illustrated by … | as expressed by …

Agreeing and disagreeing

Exactly. | I couldn't agree more. | That's just what I was thinking. | That's a good point. | I see where you're coming from, but … | I'm not sure if I agree … | Maybe, but don't you think that …?

Comparing and contrasting

Comparing: also | as well as | both | comparatively | in the same way | just as | like | similarly
Contrasting: although | besides | but | compared with | even though | however | in contrast to | instead | nevertheless | on the other hand | rather than | yet

Balancing pros and cons

On the one hand …, on the other hand … | although | however | We shouldn't forget that … | In contrast to … | On the contrary … | Weighing up the pros and cons …

STRUCTURING

Sequencing/structuring

I'm going to … | I would like to talk about … | I would like to point out/mention … | To begin with … | Now I want to describe … | There are three things to consider: Firstly … Secondly … Thirdly … | Finally …

Summarising/drawing a conclusion

All things considered … | Taking everything into account … | Briefly … | On the whole … | In short … | Finally … | That's why … | For this reason/these reasons … | Therefore … | As a result … | Consequently …

HANDLING CONVERSATIONS

Speaking politely
Could you please …?|Would you …?|May I …?|
Maybe you could …?|I was wondering if …? |
Excuse me, could you …?|Thank you.

Getting more information
Could you tell me some more about …?|
Would you mind telling me more about …?|
I'd like to know more about …|
Something else I was wondering about was …

Hesitating
Um …|Well …|Well, let's see now …|
You see …|You know …|The thing is …|
How can I put it?

Repeating
As I have (already) said …|As I have pointed out/ mentioned …

Checking understanding
OK so far?|Are you with me?|Is that clear?|Do you see what I mean?

Interrupting politely
If I could just come in here …|Sorry to interrupt, but …|
The way I see it …|Um … (repeat until the speaker lets you speak)

Preventing and handling interruptions
There are three points I'd like to make clear …|
Could I just finish my point? As I was saying …

MAKING SMALL TALK

Introducing oneself/introducing others
Hi, I'm …|Let me introduce myself …|
I don't think we've met. My name is …|
I'd like to introduce myself. My name's …|
Nice to meet you.|It's a pleasure to meet you.|
I'd like you to meet someone. This is …|
I'd like to introduce you to …|
There's someone I'd like you to meet …

Saying goodbye/closing
That's it for today.|That's all for now.|Bye for now!|
Thanks for …

Talking about likes and dislikes
What I like doing is …|I really/especially/particularly like …-ing|One of my biggest hobbies is …-ing.|
My favourite pastime is …-ing.|What I really dislike is …|
What I am really not a fan of is …-ing.|I just hate …-ing.

ASKING FOR UND GIVING HELP

Asking questions
I was wondering if you could help me. I'd like to know …|I wonder if you could tell me …|Excuse me, do you know …?|I'm sorry to bother you, but … |There's something you could help me with.

Asking for advice
What do you suggest/recommend?|What should I do?|What would you do if you were me?

Making suggestions/giving advice
I was wondering if you have ever thought of …|
I think it might be a good idea to …|Have you ever thought of …?|Don't you think it might be a good idea to …?|If I were you I'd perhaps …|Why don't you …?

Asking for a favour
Would/Could you do me a favour?|
Would you mind …-ing …?|May I …?|
Could you please …?

Asking for permission
May I …?|Can I …?|Could I perhaps …?|
Do you mind if I …?|Is it okay if …?

Refusing to help
I'm sorry, but …|I'd like to, but …|
I'd really like to help you, but …

EXPRESSING FEELINGS

Apologising
I'm sorry for …|I'm sorry that …|I would like to apologise for …|Please accept my apologies.|
It was my fault.

Thanking
Thanks a lot.|Thank you for …|That's very kind of you.|
You're welcome. / My pleasure. (when someone thanks you)

S 1.2 Giving a talk or presentation

The key to giving a good talk or presentation is to prepare well in advance. Think of a good structure for your talk or presentation and prepare prompt cards with keywords. Then you'll be ready to go!

A Preparing a talk or presentation

4 Prepare your introduction and conclusion
- Catch the listener's attention by starting with an interesting question or fact, a quote, a picture or a cartoon.
- Write a prompt card featuring your main points so you can give a brief outline of your talk or presentation at the beginning.
- Choose a final quote or example you'd like to use.
- Make a prompt card with the points you want to emphasise or summarise again.

3 Arrange your prompt cards in a logical order
Choose how you want to present your points:
- chronologically (presenting a person or historical events)
- contrasting (comparing different approaches or arguments)
- from least important to most important important or vice versa (arguing for or against something)

2 Choose the points you want to talk about and make prompt cards
- Choose three main points or arguments for the main part of your talk/presentation.
- Prepare a prompt card with keywords and useful phrases for each part of your talk or presentation.
- Note down any examples or quotations.

1 Gather material on your topic
- Brainstorm ideas and organise them in a word web.
- Do research and collect information from relevant sources (online, library, newspapers, ...).

1 Introduction
- *note down main points of talk*
- *keywords for initial joke / quote / example...*
- *note useful phrases*

4 Main point 3

3 Main point 2

2 Main point 1
- *one argument / point per card*
- *note keywords*
- *note useful phrases*

5 Conclusion
- *note down main points of talk*
- *keywords for final quote / example*
- *note useful phrases*

Before your talk
- Practise your talk or presentation out loud in front of a mirror.
- Ask a friend/relative to listen to you and give feedback.
- Prepare a handout for your audience which briefly lists your main points or arguments.
- Use keywords and make sure you include your sources on the handout.
- Test any equipment you need (laptop/tablet/ projector/speakers ...) as early as possible.

B Speaking in front of other people

Follow these Dos to make your talk or presentation as successful as possible for both you and your audience:

Dos for giving a talk or presentation

- Speak slowly and clearly.
- Use short, clear sentences.
- Use vocabulary that is known to your audience.
- Explain unknown terms or phrases.
- Vary your intonation so that you don't sound boring.
- For example, you could emphasise particularly important points by speaking a little more loudly.
- Look at your audience as often as possible and speak freely.
- Smile! (But don't laugh nervously!)
- Start by introducing yourself (if necessary) and your topic.
- Finish by thanking your audience for listening and asking if anyone has any questions.

USEFUL PHRASES

Introduction
Good morning/afternoon, (my name is ...).|
My topic today is .../The title of my talk today is: ...|
In my presentation today I want to talk about ...|
I will begin by explaining/describing ... and continue with ... Finally, I will ...

Main part/structuring ideas
Have you ever thought about ...|
Did you know that ...?|
I would like to cover three aspects in my talk: ...
First of all .../Secondly .../Finally ...|
Moving on to the next point, I would like to talk about ...|
For this reason/Therefore, we can assume that ...

Examples/quotes
In the words of ... (name of person) "..." (quote).|
This example proves that ...|
X once said that .../According to X ...

Commenting on visuals
As we can see from the cartoon/photo ...|
The statistics clearly show that a minority/a majority of ...

Conclusion
I think we can safely say that ...|
So in conclusion, I would like to sum up by ...|
Thank you for listening. Are there any questions?

S2 Group discussion

Preparing and having a discussion

The group discussion is the oral part of your exam. In small groups, you are going to discuss a given topic.

Preparation (exam – 20 minutes)	– Read the situation for the discussion and the tasks very carefully. – Look at the given material and make sure you understand it and are able to present and use it for your arguments. – Prepare arguments and aspects you would like to include in the discussion. – Note down single items only, no complete sentences. – Make a list of useful words and phrases. Use a dictionary. – Look up all the words you do not know. You can use a bilingual dictionary. – Sometimes you are asked to rank the provided material.
Introduction (exam – maximum one minute each)	Each student presents his/her point of view: – Do not interrupt each other or ask questions. – You may take notes while the others are talking. – Look at each other – not at your notes. – Use connecting words.
Discussion	– Defend your opinion, but stay polite and respectful towards the other participants. – Refer to the others' arguments when introducing a new argument. – Turn towards the others when referring to their argument or while they are talking. – Show that you are confident, but also interested in the others' arguments and their opinion. – Use the discussion phrases. – Help others, listen attentively to others. – Do not give up your idea/point of view too early. – Do not interrupt unless you feel it is really necessary. – Keep to the point. – Be open to compromise towards the end, especially if the task asks for a consensus. – Try to mediate between the others.
Conclusion (the end)	– Give a final statement. – Summarise./Come to a conclusion. – Try to find a compromise/solution everyone is happy with. – It is also OK not to agree with each other at the end. – Look into the future – which steps are to be taken next? – Say how satisfied you are with the whole discussion. – You can state which 1–2 arguments/ideas of the others impressed/convinced you the most.

USEFUL PHRASES

Introducing the topic
(As you know,) Our discussion today is about … | Who'd like to start? | I'm going to start.

Structuring a talk
I'm going to look at … | I'd like to talk about/point out/mention … | There are three things to consider. Firstly … Secondly … | Thirdly … | One point is … Another aspect is … | To begin with … | Now I want to describe … | Finally I'd like to …

Getting more information
Could you tell me more about …? | I'd like to know more about … | Something else I was wondering about was …

Agreeing and disagreeing
Exactly. I couldn't agree more. | That's just what I was thinking. | That's a good point. | I see what you mean, but isn't it also true that …? | I'm not sure if I agree with you about …

Asking questions
What I'd like to know is who/what …? | Why do you think that …? | Could you explain what you mean by …?

Checking that someone has understood you
Are you with me? | Do you see what I mean?

Hesitating
Well, let me see now … | How can I put it?

Interrupting / Being interrupted
I'm sorry to interrupt you, but … | Could I just finish my point? As I was saying …

S 3 Listening skills

Dealing with listening tasks

Listening tasks assess your listening comprehension, which is your ability to listen to and understand what someone is saying.
In everyday life, pure listening situations are limited to radio programmes, podcasts, radio plays and audiobooks.
Before you listen or watch, read through the assignments.
It is often possible to predict what the speakers are going to talk about.

While listening, follow these steps:

Listening for the 1st time
- focus on the general topic
- get the overall picture
- identify the main points

Listening for the 2nd time
- concentrate on specific details and relevant information

As with all comprehension situations, it is important to first look out for keywords (e.g. names, times, numbers, places) and try to find out about the context (speakers, their situation and the type of conversation they are having).

Listen to English-speaking people as often as possible:
- The internet is a great source of free audio and video materials in English. Listen to audio clips or watch videos a couple of times. For video clips, turn on the subtitles if they are available.
- If you find an interesting online article, use a text-to-speech reader. Copy the article into the reader and have it read out loud to you.
- Listen to audiobooks.

S 4 Reading skills

In order to improve your reading skills, read as much as possible.
Focus on aspects you find interesting, from football news to the latest film and fashion gossip – make reading a discovery.
While reading, be patient with yourself. Try not to read word for word, but instead focus on longer paragraphs. It is often enough just to get the basic idea of a paragraph.
In the long run, make a habit of reading English texts. Maybe checking an English news site every day/week might be a good start?

S 4.1 Mixed reading tasks

Reading tasks usually follow these three stages of the reading process:

pre-reading → while-reading → post-reading

Pre-reading	Before you start reading, ask yourself the following questions: – What will the text be about? – What does the title reveal? – Are there any subheadings or highlighted quotes? – What kind of text is it? – When was it published? – Are there any pictures/diagrams?
While-reading	– Read the assignments first. Find out what type of information you are looking for and then choose the appropriate reading technique. – Highlight the main ideas and make annotations. Marking and annotating a text helps you to focus while reading, as you are selecting and organising the most important information.
Post-reading	– Double-check your answers. – You might be asked to do further tasks related to the text you have just read to make sure you have understood it correctly, e.g. looking at vocabulary or analysing characters.

Marking a text
Underline or highlight keywords, key phrases, examples etc. Use different styles:

- main ideas of the text
- key phrases
- author's opinion
- examples
- characterisation

Annotating a text
Make notes next to the text to help you find information quickly, e.g.
- defining vocabulary
- summarising/paraphrasing passages
- defining and understanding examples, quotes …
- identifying important moments in the plot
- commenting on characters

1 Multiple matching

- Read the complete text and try to get an overview of what it is about.
- Read the task carefully and find out whether you have to match
  - questions and answers,
  - people and statements,
  - paragraphs and headings,
  - beginnings and endings of sentences,
  - a gapped text and missing sentences.
- There are usually two separate lists of items to be matched.
- Check with the help of your dictionary that you have thoroughly understood all the options.
- There are usually more options than needed.
- Match the correct options to the appropriate items.
- Mark the options you have already used to save time.
- Check your results thoroughly and make changes where necessary.

2 Short-answer questions / Sentence completion

This type of exercise contains ...
- either short comprehension questions, which should be answered with words or with a phrase from the text, or incomplete sentences, which should be completed with words taken from the text,
- or questions, which should be answered in note-form (sometimes in a table, mind map etc.). The key words or phrases should be taken from the text, but need not be given in complete sentences.
- Important!
  If not otherwise stated, you don't have to use your own words in these answers. You only have to find the correct passage in the text and take the appropriate word or words from there.

3 Multiple choice

Remember
- Only one answer is correct from the four answers given in the examination question.
- Look for the best possible answer from all four alternatives.
- The distractors (the wrong answers) are often partly true.

- Try to get an overview of the text and the questions.
- Don't panic if the text seems too difficult at first.
- Read the tasks carefully.
- Read the text a second time to find the answers to the individual tasks and mark the appropriate passages in the text.
- Only use your dictionary when necessary (especially when you cannot understand part of the multiple-choice questions).
- Do the tasks chronologically (normally the tasks refer to the text in a chronological order).

When sitting an exam:
- Don't spend too much time on "difficult" tasks.
- When in doubt, have a guess at the right answer (you won't be punished for a wrong answer).

4 Gapped summary

Remember
In this type of exercise you are presented with a summary of (a part of) the text. This summary is incomplete as certain key words are missing. It is your task to restore the missing words, and this can only be accomplished if you have both read and understood the main ideas of the original text. Make sure you write down the line number where you found the missing word.

- Mark the passage the summary is about.
- Important! Only use words from the text to fill the gaps. Don't change the words. In exams, you will not get any points for using your own words
- Lines (or numbers) in the gaps indicate how many words are needed.
- First check by looking at the context which type of word is expected (adjective, verb, noun).

5 Mediation: English – German

In this type of exercise you are asked to reproduce the contents of certain text passages in German.
- Often you have to find specific information from the text and list this information in key points.
- Sometimes you are asked to explain certain aspects of the text or explain idiomatic expressions.
- Important!
  Mediation does NOT mean translation! It usually refers to text passages where a literal ("word-by-word") translation does not make any sense.

Examples: (see text "A Harvest of Thorns", pages 58–59)

Mediation, type 1:

1. Bevor er ihm unverhohlen droht, wie versucht Foysol Jashel zunächst zu überzeugen, ihm seinen Ausweis auszuhändigen?
   Possible answer:
   Er erinnert ihn daran, dass er ein Gast Malaysias ist und auch Gast von Foysol. Er ist ihm also zu Dank verpflichtet und muss seinen Regeln folgen. (Z. 50–53)

Mediation, type 2:

2. Welche Konsequenzen spielt Jashel in seinem Kopf durch, falls sein Vertrag aufgelöst würde?
   Possible answer:
   - er würde die Chance verlieren, Geld nach Hause zu schicken
   - der Geldverleiher würde den Vertrag mit seiner Familie kündigen und Anspruch auf den Besitz der Familie geltend machen
   - seine Familie wäre mittellos (Z. 72–77)

Mediation, type 3:

3. Was ist mit dem Ausdruck „If he sang the agent's tune" (Z. 80) gemeint?
   Possible answer:
   „nach seiner Pfeife tanzen"

S 4.2 Reading techniques

Skimming	- Read the title, the introduction or the first paragraph, the first sentence of every paragraph and any headings and sub-headings. - Note any pictures, charts or graphs. - Pay attention to any words or phrases in italics or bold print. - The last paragraphs in non-fictional texts (e.g. scientific research, newspaper articles) often summarise the main ideas of the text.
Scanning	- Scanning is reading in order to find specific information. - Decide what specific information you are looking for. Ignore unrelated information. - Look out for relevant key words. Stop when you find one and read that part of the text carefully. Make notes if necessary. - How might the information be given in the text? For example, if you need a date, only look at the numbers in the text. - Headings can help you to identify sections which might contain the information. - The first sentence in a paragraph should indicate whether the information you need could be there, or not. Do not read the text in detail.
Close reading / reading for detail	- Sometimes it is necessary to understand a text in detail. Here, make sure you understand every word. - Look up unknown words in a dictionary and use the information you find on word category, register, collocation and usage to identify the word that best fits the context.

KWL: This technique is useful if you are reading a text to learn more about a certain topic.

Pre-reading	**K**	What I KNOW (What do I already know about the topic and the author?)
	W	What I WANT to know (Why am I reading the text? What exactly do I want to find out?)
While-reading	**L**	What I have LEARNED (What are my findings?)

SQ3R:
S SURVEY what you are asked to read. (What additional information about the text can I find if I survey the title, subheadings, images, charts …?)
Q Ask yourself QUESTIONS about the text. (What exactly am I looking for?)
3R READ the text and look for answers.
RECITE what you have found out in your own words.
REVIEW the text and your notes. (What am I going to do with my findings?)

S 5 Writing skills

S 5.1 Dealing with writing tasks

In order to improve the quality of your writing, consider following this step-by-step approach.

6 Proofread your text. Pay special attention to tenses, prepositions, word order and spelling.

5 Write a first draft of your text.

4 Your text should develop in a logical way. Use structuring devices and connectives. Pay attention to style and register.

3 Organise your ideas. Put your notes in a logical order and finalise them.

2 Brainstorm ideas and make notes on how to include the given material.

1 Make sure you understand the assignment.

S 5.2 Improve your writing

Use connectives to make your writing more logical. They are used to illustrate a connection between certain aspects or ideas.

Adding ideas	*moreover, besides, furthermore, in addition to that*
Sequencing	*first of all, to begin with, next, then, finally*
Emphasising	*above all, in particular, especially, significantly, indeed*
Similarity	*in the same way, similarly, likewise*
Cause and effect	*therefore, thus, however, although, unless*
Illustrating	*for example, for instance, as revealed by, in the case of, nevertheless, despite, in spite of, on the contrary*
Contrasting	*instead of, alternatively, otherwise, unlike, on the one hand …, on the other hand*
Conclusion	*In conclusion …, Therefore …, All in all …, To sum up …*

Proofreading
Before finalising your text, check it according to the following categories:
- spelling mistakes
- use of tenses
- sentence structure
- style and register

S 6 Writing specific text types

For each text type, you need to consider the typical structure, contents, purposes and writing style.

S 6.1 Material-based writing: Writing a composition

In a written exam, you will have to write a composition about a certain topic. You will usually have to deal with a controversial issue, including your own thoughts, your previous knowledge and information from up to three materials. At the end you draw a conclusion.

1 Preparation

- Define the topic clearly.
- Brainstorm ideas. Write down what you know about the topic in a mind map, table or list.
- If necessary, collect facts, arguments, statistics and other information from sources, e. g. your library or the Internet.
- Formulate your opinion on the topic.

2 Arranging your material

- Decide on the most important facts, arguments or pieces of information that you want to include in your composition (usually 3 items).
- Look at the given material and decide how they can help you with your arguments. Don't analyse, translate or quote the material, just consider their content.
- For each main argument try to think of two supporting arguments.
- Put your facts or arguments in a logical order. For example, you could:
  - start with general ideas and then go on to talk about details.
  - put things into chronological order.
  - start by giving all the arguments in favour and then give all the counter-arguments.
  - follow each argument in favour with a counter-argument.

3 Writing your composition

The introduction
- The introductory paragraph should introduce your topic and catch the reader's interest. You could:
  - give a relevant quotation.
  - make a provocative statement.
  - describe a relevant (humorous) personal experience.
- In your introductory paragraph you should also:
  - say clearly what your composition is going to be about in one or two sentences.
  - ask a question or questions which you will answer in your composition.
  - give a brief outline of the problem/topic at present and in the past.
- Don't forget the topic sentence at the end of the introduction.

The main part
- Start a new paragraph for each new idea.
- Begin each paragraph with a main idea or argument. Follow it up with your supporting or counterarguments (examples, statistics, personal experience etc.).
- Arrange sentences in a logical order. Don't forget to include the material.
- Join sentences using suitable connectives.
- Use adverbs to emphasise points.
- Use examples where possible.

The conclusion
- Do not introduce new ideas!
- Make a brief concluding statement summarising what you have written in your composition.
- You may:
  - give an outlook on further consequences / future developments / possible solutions.
  - state your own opinion / give a recommendation or appeal to the readers to reach their own conclusion.

4 Checking your composition

- Check that all your sentences are complete and that they make sense.
- Check your composition for grammar, spelling and punctuation mistakes. (Tip: Leave your composition overnight before checking it.)
- Write or print out the final version of your composition.

5 Writing a model composition

USEFUL PHRASES

Presenting aspects and examples
… consists of (two) aspects. | It is a … rather than a … problem/issue. | … should also be considered/mentioned. | … is relevant/completely irrelevant to … | There are various reasons why … | This also raises questions about … | Some researchers say … / Studies show … | Proponents/Opponents say / point out …

Referring to someone's statement/theory/opinion (in a text)
The author believes/states/suggests/claims that … | The author holds the view / is of the opinion that … | The author argues/suggests/demands that … | According to the text, the problem is that … | In recent years, there has been a debate on how to …

Expressing your criticism (in general)
Whereas the author thinks that … I feel very different about … | Unlike the author, I find it hard to believe that … | Contrary to the speaker, I am doubtful whether … | To be quite honest, I do not think that / I cannot (fully) agree with … / I am not convinced by … / I would like to question the view that … / I reject the idea that … | In my opinion/view this argument is wrong/weak/unconvincing because … | … the author ignores a fact/forgets to mention sth / is not aware of sth / focuses too much on sth / does not realise that …

Expressing your support (in general)
The author is absolutely right in saying that … | I do not think anyone would disagree with the author's statement that … | The speaker has my full support when he argues that … | In fact / As a matter of fact, I believe it is fully justified to say that … | I agree entirely with the speaker saying that … | I am of exactly the same opinion as … | I share the view that … | To my mind, … | this argument is very strong/powerful / convincing/plausible | the author presents convincing arguments / discusses the topic in detail / bases his case on facts and figures | the author's argumentation is thoroughly convincing/logical

Making concessions
To a certain extent, I can accept … | However, we shouldn't forget that … | Most of the arguments are hard to dismiss. | Yet there are experts who … | I agree in principle, but … |
Personally, I would not go so far as to say that … |
Although …, we should accept / must admit that … |
In spite of all this, … | Admittedly, …, but …

Giving arguments/reasons
One reason for my criticism/scepticism is that … | Another / A second / A further / An additional argument I would like to present is that … | I would also argue that … | Another point I would like to make is that … | The main reason, however, is that … | The most convincing argument is that … | That brings me neatly to my final and most important point: …

Your conclusion/summary
To sum up, … | In short, … | Considering all these arguments, … | I would conclude that … | I have come to the conclusion that … | It is safe to say that … | I would support the view that … | My suggestion is that … | My appeal to … is: … | In conclusion … | Having weighed up all the arguments, I would like to conclude with a quote: "…"

S 6.2 Writing a comment

In a comment you also deal with a controversial issue, a quote or a statement and give your personal opinion about it.

Structure your comment as follows:

Introduction
- Define the problem or topic.
- Get the reader's attention.
- Clearly state your opinion.

Main part
- Give reasons for your opinion.
- Support arguments with examples.
- Use connectives.

Conclusion
- Summarise the best argument.
- Restate your opinion.
- Give an outlook.

Before you start writing, read the quote or statement carefully and decide if you agree or disagree with it.
Start with the weakest argument and end with the strongest.
Write your comment in the simple present.
When writing a comment on a computer, run the spelling and grammar checker before you hand your text in.

USEFUL PHRASES

Giving examples
for example | for instance | in another case | take the case of | to illustrate | as shown/expressed by …

Referring to a point already made
as I have already said/noted | as suggested above …

Emphasising your statements
definitely | indeed | extremely | absolutely | positively …

Balancing pros and cons
On the one hand …, on the other hand … | although | however | We shouldn't forget that … | In contrast to … | On the contrary … | Weighing up the pros and cons …

Drawing a conclusion
That's why … | For this reason / these reasons | therefore | as a result | consequently | Taking everything into account … | The arguments seem to indicate that … | It is clear therefore that … | Thus it could be concluded that … | The evidence seems to be strong that …

S 6.3 Writing a blog post

A well-structured blog post will catch the readers' attention and make them want to read on.

BLOG

Choose an interesting, eye-catching headline

- Put the main point you are writing about in the first paragraph.
- All further details, explanations, examples etc. can go in the following paragraphs.
- It is always a good idea to end with a kind of conclusion, i.e. a final thought that summarises your main ideas.
- Try to write in a friendly and informal style.
- Always be polite and respectful of other cultures and opinions.
- Use the first person 'I' and try to include examples/anecdotes from your own experience.
- Think about your readers and what they might want to learn from what you are telling them.
- Use phrases and expressions that are suitable for expressing your opinion in a clear way.
- It might even be a good idea to directly invite your readers to join the discussion.
- In some blog posts it is common to add your username and the date of your post.

Never
- include links to commercial sites or resources.
- include links to inappropriate material.
- give specific names, places, addresses or contact details.

S 6.4 Writing an email

A great deal of today's communication is done via email. Formal emails are written in a polite and formal style. Therefore, use suitable forms of politeness and appropriate modal verbs.
Make sure that your salutation and complimentary close corresponds with your relationship with the person you are writing to. Depending on the topic you are writing about, you will need to use technical terms too.
Formal emails contain a salutation, a subject line, a complimentary close and the name of the person writing the email. The text itself should have clear structure and consist of short paragraphs only.

From: lhamilton@mail.uk   Sent: 04.06. ... 10:06
To: jwise@radiosouthwest.uk
CC:
Subject: Work placement at Radio SouthWest
Attachments: Louise_Hamilton_CV.docx

Dear Mr Wise,

With reference to the work experience advert on your website I would like to be considered for the position ...

...

Best regards,
Louise Hamilton

Sender

Recipient

Attachments: Be sure to name the attached files clearly.

Salutation: Start with "Dear ...," or just "Hello/Hi" if you know the adressee well.

Complimentary close: Close your email with "Kind/Best regards" or "Best wishes".

Date and time: These details will appear automatically.

CC = carbon copy (*Kopie an ...*): Add the email addresses of others who are also concerned by the subject.

Subject line: Always mention the precise subject matter to help the recipient best deal with your email.

Body: Start your email with a capital letter.

Signature block: If you are writing an email from one company to another, include your position and/or department below your name.

Email etiquette
- Limit your email to one subject only, be precise and clear.
- Make sure your email has a clear structure.
- Even though emails tend to be less formal than letters, remain polite.
- Do not use colloquial language or emoticons.
- Proofread your emails (grammar, spelling, punctuation, choice of words...).

In a personal email or letter, you directly and frequently address the person you are writing to.

EMAIL

Structure
- Use an appropriate salutation and a complimentary close.
- In personal letters also include the date.
- Very often, personal emails or letters start with stating the reason for writing.
- In the main part, go into more detail and focus on the purpose of your correspondence.
- You might want to end your email or letter by asking the person you are writing to a question, a favour etc.

Language and style
- Use the first-person perspective (1st person singular/1st person plural) in your text.
- The language you use very much depends on the topic you are writing about and on the relationship between you and the person reading your email or letter.
- Specific topics might require technical terms even in personal correspondence.

Before you send emails, always check for spelling and typing mistakes, and also for any sentences which could be misunderstood.

S 6.5 Creating an information sheet

In a brochure or flyer you inform an interested group of people about facts, issues, events or a problem.

Structure
- Give your text a very clear, concise heading so that the readers know at a glance what your brochure or flyer is about.
- Subheadings will provide a clear structure.

Language and style
- Depending on the situation or the topic you are writing about, you might consider addressing your readers directly.
- Use factual and objective language only; colloquial language is not suitable for a brochure or flyer.
- Listing points or facts one by one will make your text easier to understand.
- Depending on the topic you are writing about, you will also be expected to use technical terms.

S 6.6 Writing a story

When writing a story, you can either rely completely on your own imagination or you may choose to write on a given theme or topic.

1. Planning

Before beginning to write, you'll need to make a few decisions regarding the following elements:

The narrator
- The first-person narrator tells the story from his or her perspective.
- The third-person narrator takes on the perspective of one person telling other people's stories.

The characters
- Choose your protagonist and other characters. You may take inspiration from people around you (someone you notice who is always giggling / someone who speaks very fast/slowly etc.).

The setting
- Choose the place where you wish to set your story.

The time
- Decide on when your story will be set: this could, for example, be yesterday, last year or in the century to come.

The plot
- The beginning: You can either start by introducing the protagonist, or open in the midst of the action.
- The main part: Consider what could drive your plot. This might be some unresolved conflict or a problem, a funny or surprising incident.
- The ending: At the end of your story, the situation may be resolved; or you may choose to leave it unresolved (i.e. offer an open ending).

2. Writing

- Think about what your characters might say in specific situations.
- Look up any new words or expressions you would like to use.
- In writing your story, use either the past or present tense forms.
- Include adjectives and adverbs (e.g. for sensory perception, i.e. in order to describe sounds, colours, smells etc.) and describe details (e.g. of people und places).

The following example will give you an idea of how your story could begin:

It was evening and there were no cars or people on the street. I ran until I came to a big, old building, which looked dark and dirty. The sign said, 'Magic bought and sold here.' I pushed the door open.
"Good evening, young lady," said the old man behind the desk. He spoke very slowly and looked at me closely.
I knew he was thinking, 'What has she got for me?'
"Buying or selling?" he asked curiously.
"Er ... selling ... I think." My voice sounded less nervous than I was. My father would go crazy if he knew I was here, talking to a man who could take some of my magic skills, put them into a bottle and sell them to a stranger. But we needed money, and this was the only way to get some fast. I hated this place, hated this man, but he had what I needed, and I had what he wanted. "Show me what you've got for me then," he said. Although I was really scared, I took a deep breath and showed him my hands. His eyes suddenly looked round and shocked. "I can't believe it," he said. ...

S 7 Analysing language

S 7.1 Stylistic devices

Whenever you are asked to analyse the language of a text, you have to mention the stylistic devices used by the author. It is equally important to explain their function. What might be the desired effect on the reader?

Stylistic device	Definition	Example
Alliteration	A series of words beginning with the same letter or sound.	*bold, bright and beautiful*
Anaphora	The first part of the sentence is repeated to create a certain effect.	*I didn't like his hairstyle.* *I didn't want to tell him.*
Ambiguity	When something can be understood in more than one possible way and therefore be unclear or confusing.	*Kids Make Nutritious Snack (a headline meaning either "Kids make good food" or "Eating kids is good for you")*
Contrast	An obvious difference between two or more words.	*a fire-and-ice relationship*
Enumeration	Aspects are repeated step by step so as to create a list.	*old, grey, majestic*
Euphemism	Expressions that replace words that stand for something negative.	*"to pass away" instead of "to die"*
Exaggeration/Hyperbole	Ideas or opinions are made more important for the sake of effect.	*Her old mobile weighs a ton.*
Irony	Words are used in such a way that the actual meaning differs from the intended meaning.	*That was clever! Now it's broken.*
Metaphor	A word or phrase comparing something to something else which shows that they are similar.	*a heart of gold*
Metonymy	Referring to something by the name of something else that is closely connected with it.	*Number 10 (referring to the British Prime Minister or government)*
Oxymoron	Two words with opposite meanings are joined together to create a strong effect.	*a deafening silence*
Paradox	A statement that appears to contradict itself.	*"I'm nobody," he said to introduce himself.*
Pun	A play on words that produces an often comical effect.	*"All she ever wanted was a camouflaged blouse, but she couldn't find one."*
Rhetorical question	Does not expect a real answer. It is just asked to emphasise a certain point.	*You are enjoying the party, aren't you?*
Sarcasm	Like irony, the literal meaning differs from the intended meaning. Often used to criticise or mock somebody.	*"Wow, you're a genius!" (when someone made an obvious statement)*

S 7.2 Style, tone and register

When analysing a text, you might be asked to have a close look at the language used. Part of this is the analysis of style, tone and register:

Style is the typical way of writing or speaking used by a person; their choice of tone, grammar and narrative techniques.
Tone is the general mood, feeling or attitude being expressed; it is the emotional content of a text rather than the devices used.
Register is the choice of words, style and grammar used in a certain social context. It reflects status and situations often have rules for appropriate register.

Situation	Features	Examples
Formal: in a formal speech or letter; adressing someone unknown or higher in a hierarchy	- respectful, neutral, detached style - complete and complex sentences - formal expressions - foreign/specialist words	*After analysing the evidence, the hypothesis was concluded to be correct.* *I would be grateful for your advice on this.*
Informal: used in spoken rather than written language, when speakers know each other well	- more personal and familiar style - simple sentences, can be incomplete or ungrammatical, dialect or slang - vivid, colloquial or vulgar expression	*Morning all! How's things? Fancy a cuppa? Gotta go get a donut. Ain't you got brains? C'mon, stupid.*
Literary: used mainly in written literary texts	- eloquent/elevated style - complex sentences - rich vocabulary - use of stylistic devices - can combine registers for various effects	*"So we went on in the quiet, and the twilight deepened into night. The clear blue of the distance faded, and one star after another came out." (Wells,* The Time Machine*)*

- Style, tone and register are difficult to separate and are thus mainly considered together.
- It is useful to note the way a character speaks.
- Don't forget: Form follows function. Comment on the way these devices are used to convey an impression.

S 8 Analysing fictional texts

S 8.1 Fictional text types

Fictional texts are made up, which means that they are based on imagination.

Fictional texts	Novel	- a long, written, fictional prose narrative - has multiple characters, a plot and a narrator - is written in the past tense in most cases
	Short story	- same as novel but shorter - focuses on one major character
	Graphic novel	- comic strip format published as a book - written for adults - texts can be fictional or non-fictional
	Play	- written to be performed on stage - consists of dialogues and monologues
	Poem	- artful arrangement of words to create rhythm - words are used to create images in the readers' mind

S 8.2 Analysing novels and short stories

A Characteristics of the novel

Function	– tells a fictional story, which transports the reader into a fictional world (which can be close to real life or fantastical) – to entertain and sometimes educate the reader
Focus	– able to give large amounts of detail because length is unlimited – can focus on any number of characters/protagonists and show developments over time – different narrative perspectives possible → **S 8.4** – may cover several events or locations – can focus on a long period of time, sometimes over several generations – time settings could be historical, contemporary or futuristic
Structure	– long, informative introduction or direct start 'in the middle of things' (in medias res) – order of the plot can be chronological or written with narrative techniques such as frame story, flashbacks, back story or foreshadowing → **S 8.5** – mainly separated into chapters – cliffhangers (exciting endings to chapters, making the reader want to read more) – ending can be closed, open, predictable or unexpected – effect created by the relationship between style and content
Language and style	– always in the genre of prose (following the flow of natural speech) – can be written in many different styles – contains descriptive sections, reported speech and direct speech

B Characteristics of the short story

Function	– gives a short glimpse of a life-changing event or revelation – captures an important moment or an important feeling
Focus	– single event, single setting, short time span – only one or two characters
Structure	– direct beginning, little or no introduction – central turning point or surprising 'twist in the tale' near the end
Language and style	– often elliptical (details or sentence parts left out) – one distinctive language or style choice

S 8.3 Narrative perspectives

The effect of a story is strongly influenced by the point of view, or perspective, from which it is told. Narrative types can be mixed and the point of view can sometimes change over the course of the story.

Third-person omniscient narrator
This narrator does not play a part in the story. Although they are telling the story from the sidelines, they know everything about the characters' thoughts and feelings.
This style of narration is mainly neutral and more distanced than others.

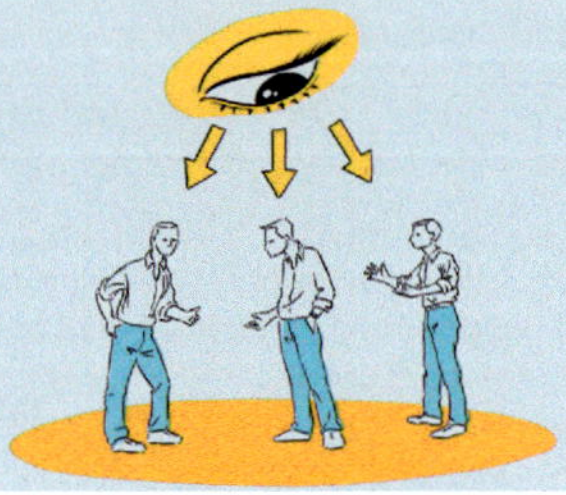

Third-person limited narrator
This narrator describes feelings and thoughts from the perspective of one particular character. It is often one of the main characters.
This point of view enables us to feel quite close to this character.

First-person narrator
This narrator is a character who tells the story from his/her own perspective ("I"). We understand and sympathise easily with this type of narrator. Keep in mind that the first-person narrator is not the author unless the text is autobiographical.

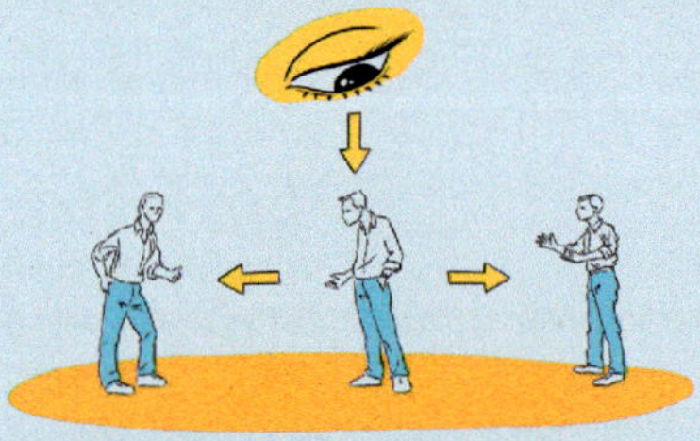

Objective narrator
The objective point of view does not reveal any of the characters' feelings or thoughts. It is as if the narrator is watching the action and describing it objectively. This perspective usually does not create a sense of proximity to the characters.

USEFUL PHRASES

Writing about narrative perspective
The story is told by a … narrator. | The narrator's views are very personal and subjective which can be seen … | The fact that the narrator is involved in the story leads to the effect that … | The narrator remains outside the plot. | The effect on the reader is … | The narrator describes the action and characters objectively.

S 8.4 Narrative techniques

When you analyse a fictional text, you should not only think about the story itself, but also about the ways in which it is told. These 'narrative techniques' influence the way the reader sees the story.

A Structure

The plot, i.e. the main events and the theme of a story, is usually structured in the following way:

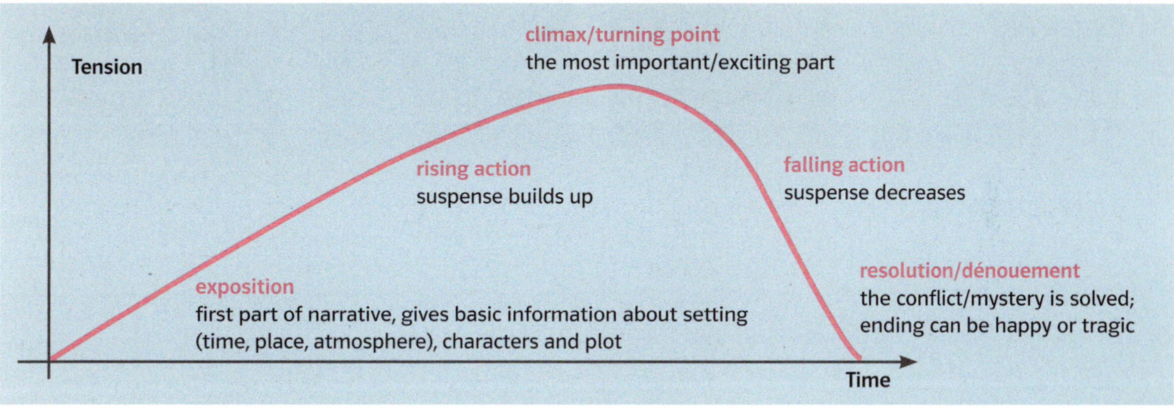

Tense as narrative technique
Tense influences the distance between readers and characters.
The use of **present tense** makes you feel closer to the action.
More distance is created when the narrator uses **indirect speech**.

B Chronology

Authors use different possibilities of relating the events in a story.

Back story	gives the history of characters, objects, places or events in the story
Flashback	the narrative is taken back in time
Flash-forward	future events are revealed
Foreshadowing	clues in the story that hint at a future development

C Narrative situation

Point of view	the narrator shows his/her attitude to the characters and can limit what the reader knows
Suspense	created by not giving away too much information; typical of crime or adventure stories
Tense	influences the distance between reader and characters (e.g. if the narrator uses present tense, you feel close to the action)
Irony	can be used as a distancing effect by the narrator
Narration	can vary between dialogues (direct speech), description and comments

S 8.5 Characterisation

When dealing with a novel, film or play, you will often be asked to analyse a certain character and his/her behaviour. In general there is a main character (protagonist, hero/heroine) and an antagonist (another important character who is in conflict with the protagonist).

Types of characters

Static / Flat character
- shows no development
- has no depth

Round character
- complex
- shows inner conflict
- is presented in detail

Dynamic character
- changes over time
- shows development

How to analyse a character:

Preparing
- Collect any relevant information from the text about the character (personal details, appearance, behaviour, what he/she says and what others say about him/her).
- Collect these facts as quotations and include line references.

Writing
1. Briefly present the character (personal details). Say what his/her function in the story is and how he/she relates to the other characters.
2. Describe the character's personality and behaviour.
3. Sum up their most important traits.

Direct characterisation
The narrator or a character tells the reader explicitly what a character is like.

Indirect characterisation
It is the reader's job to interpret a character through what the character thinks, does or says.

USEFUL PHRASES

Personal details
The protagonist is young/middle-aged/single/married …

Outward appearance
He/She is described as being tall/small/good-looking …

Positive character traits
He/She is/seems to be friendly/cheerful/good-natured/attentive/observant, intelligent/honest/trustworthy/sensitive/brave/generous/optimistic/polite …

Negative character traits
He/She seems to be bad-tempered/rude/violent/unreliable/pessimistic/dishonest/untrustworthy/mean/selfish/foolish/careless/ignorant …

Drawing conclusions about a character
The plot reveals that … |
His/Her statement "…" (line …) shows/proves that … |
He/She appears to be portrayed as … |
His/Her behaviour clearly indicates that … |
The character is described/presented/portrayed as …

Talking about relationships
to build up / to continue / to break off a relationship

S 9 Analysing non-fictional texts

S 9.1 Non-fictional text types

Non-fictional texts are based on facts and provide information and opinions about real-world issues. They can be categorised according to their **intention**, i.e. what effect they want to have on the reader:

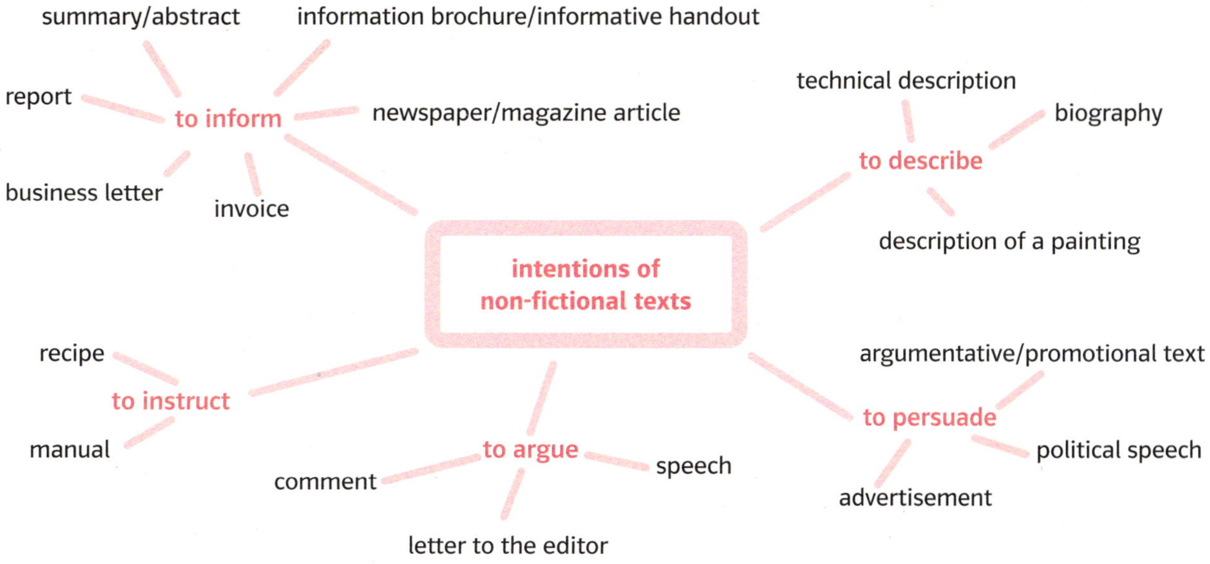

S 9.2 Structure of non-fictional texts

One of the key steps in dealing with non-fictional texts is to analyse the text structure. How is the information generally organised and presented?

Text structure	Explanation	Signal words and phrases
Chronological order / Sequence	Events are revealed in a sequence from beginning to end.	*first, then, next, finally*
Cause and effect	Cause and effect-relationships are described: – What causes a certain event? – What are the consequences?	*for, since, because, ... is caused by ... (cause), as a result, consequently, for this reason, therefore, ... leads to ... (effect)*
Problem and solution	A problem is described and possible solutions are presented.	*The problem is ..., The question is ..., A solution might be ..., One answer is ...*
Compare and contrast	Various comparisons are used to effectively describe and contrast ideas.	*Different from/to ..., Same as ..., Similar to ..., As opposed to ..., Instead of ..., Compared with/to ..., On the other hand ..., although, however, but*
Description	Ideas or concepts are described and illustrated. Visual details such as illustrations and diagrams are often added.	*for instance, for example, such as, to illustrate, to show*

S 9.3 Analysing argumentative texts

A Types of arguments

Argumentative texts offer a lot of claims and theses, each of which is or should be supported by logical arguments. In order to analyse an argumentative text, find out which types of arguments are used.

Practical argument	Refers to widely known facts and common experience in order to appear logical.	*Humans need oxygen to survive and plants produce oxygen – that's why it is important to protect the environment.*
Argument by illustration	Uses examples to support and illustrate a claim.	*The death penalty should be abolished because innocent people may be put to death. In 1990, for example, a man was executed in Florida for the murders of two police officers. Two years later he was found innocent.*
Argument by authority	Uses the opinion of experts and the results of statistics to prove a point.	*Recent studies show that very frequent use of social media affects mental health.*
Normative argument	Refers to accepted norms and values. Often based on common sense.	*To save our planet we will have to drastically reduce water and air pollution.*
Argument by analogy	The reader can easily draw parallels to other areas of life.	*In sports as well as in business, we can see globalisation, monopolies and illegal actions to "win at all costs" increasing.* *Sport is more and more heavily regulated to ensure that competition is fair and equal, thus business should be too.*

B Line of argumentation

Analysing the line of argumentation in a text includes describing and explaining how the argumentation is being developed throughout the text. How are the various parts of the text connected? What is the function of each individual paragraph?

S 9.4 Analysing newspaper articles

If you are asked to analyse a newspaper article, you need to identify the topic and the main points in the text. You will also have to identify and explain the type of article and its intention, as well as the article's structure.

A Types of articles

Reports / News articles	– discuss current or recent news of general interest or on a specific topic – are formal and objective – focus only on the facts – answer general questions like Who? What? When? Where? Why? How? – may contain photographs, personal accounts, statistics, graphs, polls etc. – are often written in the simple past tense
Feature articles	– deal in depth with a topic, person or event by providing a great deal of a background information – analyse a series of events or a development that is of human interest – have a storyline and are entertaining – may contain quotations, personal interviews and descriptions
Editorials	– are written by the editor of the paper or magazine – focus on current events – include the writer's opinion – are usually run all together on a specific page of the paper or magazine (editorial page)

Quality of news reports
News reports are supposed to inform the public about interesting and important events in an unbiased way. However, their quality and neutrality differ depending on the newspaper or magazine.

B Structure of articles

Newspaper articles are often structured like an inverted pyramid with the most important aspect at the top. More facts and additional details follow, with the least important ones at the end, so readers can stop reading when they feel they have enough information. The typical parts of a newspaper article are explained in the following example:

British backpacker Sam Woodhead missing in Australian outback

A British backpacker has disappeared after he set out on a run in the Australian outback.

The **headline** catches the reader's attention.

The last picture Sam Woodhead posted, two days before he went missing .

Pictures often have a **caption**.

The **lead paragraph** introduces the news story by telling the most important facts (who, what, when, where, why, how).

Sam Woodhead was reported missing from a cattle station after he failed to return from a jog two days ago.
Local authorities launched a hunt for him amid fears he may have lost his way in a hot, isolated region of central Queensland. His mother is understood to have urged police to widen the search on the grounds that her son, an experienced long-distance runner, could have travelled some way from his base, near the town of Longreach.

Sister uses social media to reach out

Subheadings are used to split articles into sections.

His sister, Rebecca, issued an anxious plea for news on her social media. "If anyone hears from my brother, please contact me ASAP" she posted. In another posting, she added: "Thanks so much for all your messages regarding Sam. Still no further news but we have the helicopter going out again in the morning, Aus time, and hundreds of people going on voluntary search party. Will keep you all posted."

Newspaper articles are usually written in **columns**.

S 10 Analysing and using visuals

Among the materials you get for writing a composition or for having a group discussion, there are often visuals like pictures, cartoons or diagrams. You should use the content or main idea of the material but you should not describe or quote it in any detail.

S 10.1 Analysing and using pictures and paintings

Introduction	– Give information about the type of picture and the artist/photographer. – Say when the painting/photo was most likely painted/taken. – Give a general description of what is in the picture and what you can see.
Analysis	– Describe the message conveyed by the picture and how this message is communicated. – Consider aspects like colour, contrast, tone, composition, focus, light and perspective. – Is the picture intended to have a certain effect on the viewer? Describe how this is achieved.
Evaluation	– Based on the results of your analysis, state whether the picture is effective and which elements are responsible for it being successful or unsuccessful. – Give your personal opinion (if asked) or your thoughts on what topic the picture represents.

USEFUL PHRASES

Introduction
The photo/sketch/portrait/still life/oil painting was taken/drawn/painted by … and published in (year) … | The main focus is … | The picture illustrates …

Evaluation
The overall effect of the picture is … because … | In my opinion, the painting/photo only shows one aspect of/ idealises/… | The picture reminds me of … because … | It is effective/moves me deeply because …

Analysis
The artist/photographer (probably) wants to express/show/criticise … | The artist presents … | The light/colours of … create an … atmosphere/give an impression of/contribute to … | The position of …

S 10.2 Analysing and using cartoons

A cartoon usually combines a drawing with a text and/or a caption. Cartoons often pick up on current events and criticise people, institutions or developments in society and politics. Some cartoons are just intended to be entertaining, e.g. making fun of a public figure. On the other hand, others can make a serious and important critical point, simply by using visual means. However, when analysing a cartoon, make sure you consider the emotional level of language it conveys.

Introduction	– Give information on the context (artist, date of publication and source). – Briefly say what the cartoon is about (a topic, an event, a person etc.).
Analysis	– Examine each important element (people, objects, text) and explain the message they convey. – Pay attention to the function of the characters (Do they represent well-known people or a particular group of people?) and typical techniques (see tip box).
Evaluation	– State whether you think the cartoon is effective and which elements are responsible for it being successful/ unsuccessful. – Give your personal opinion (if asked) or your thoughts on the topic presented in the cartoon.

Typical techniques used by cartoonists
- caricature (exaggerating certain striking characteristics)
- irony (depicting the opposite of what is really meant)
- exposing inconsistencies (e.g. contrasting a statement with a picture showing the exact opposite)
- emphasising stereotypes
- using wordplay and symbolism

USEFUL PHRASES

Introduction
The cartoon was drawn by … and was published / appeared in (source) on (date). | It was created in response to … | It shows / deals with / refers to / comments on … | The cartoonist makes fun of … / criticises … for (doing sth).

Analysis
The cartoon satirises/represents/is a caricature of … | This figure is a stereotype of … / is exaggerated / supposed to represent … / supports the message of … | The cartoonist is making fun of … | It is obvious that the artist wants to criticise/express/show …

Evaluation
The cartoon (only partly) achieves its aim of (doing sth). | I (do not) think the cartoon is funny / easy to understand because … | In my opinion, the cartoonist is (not) successful in presenting/criticising … because … | I (do not) like the cartoon because … | The cartoon appeals / does not appeal to me. | In my opinion, it is convincing/confusing/unfair/…

S 10.3 Analysing and using diagrams and statistics

Diagrams visualise statistics and make them much easier to understand.
Data can be graphically presented in different ways:

Bar chart

Bar charts present data in coloured bars so as to make it easier to compare figures directly.

Pie chart

A pie chart is usually used to illustrate percentages or proportions.
The entire circle represents 100%. Each segment shows a percentage of the whole.

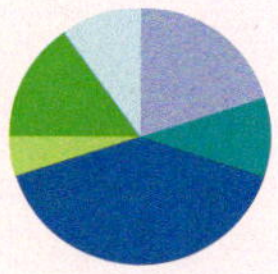

Line graph

A line graph shows a change/ development over a certain period of time.

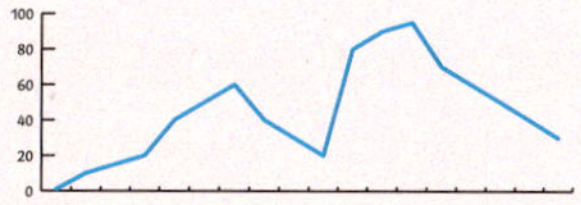

Flow chart

A flow chart shows the links between elements and their influence on each other.
It is best used to describe processes that contain decisions at certain points and where alternatives need to be shown.

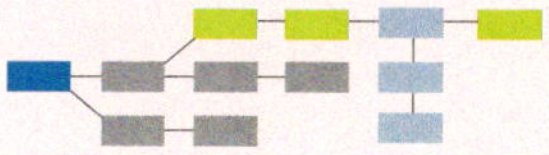

If you want to practise describing and analysing diagrams, you can search online for:
- Eurostat, the European Union statistical office
- ONS, the Office for National Statistics in the UK
- US data and statistics
- UNSD, the United Nations Statistics Division

USEFUL PHRASES

Bar chart
The vertical/horizontal axis shows/represents … | The chart indicates / makes clear that … | The number of … is far greater than / is significant in comparison to …

Line graph
The line graph of … shows the development of … from … to … | The vertical axis shows the number/ percentage/amount of … | The horizontal axis shows the time from … to … | The number of … increased/ rose/remained constant/decreased/fell (gradually/ steadily/rapidly/steeply/significantly) until … | This change was possibly caused by …

Pie chart
The chart is divided into … segments. | The pie chart shows/ represents … | The segments compare … | As you can see from the pie chart …

Flow chart
The process is divided into … stages/phases. | The first stage of the process is … | The process starts with/by … | In this phase … | First/Second/Third | Then | After that … | Before that … | Following … | This is followed by … | The next step is … | Alternatively … | There are then two possibilities … | Having completed … the … moves onto … | Finally … | The process concludes with …

S 11 Vocabulary skills

S 11.1 Expanding your vocabulary

In order to fill in the gaps in exam tasks correctly, you will need to be able to recognise *parts of speech* and know how to form them (e.g. *noun* ⟶ *verb*). To this end, it is helpful to learn words in their *word families* and to be aware of the basic rules regarding *word order* in sentences.

1. Recognising parts of speech

Parts of speech are the 'building blocks' of a language which are required for forming sentences.
The most important parts of speech are:

noun	Hauptwort/Nomen	book, Sam, girl, parents
verb	Tunwort/Verb	go, eat, feel, think
adjective	Wie-Wort/Adjektiv	small, intelligent, blue
adverb	Umstandswort/Adverb	slowly, yesterday, always
preposition	Verhältniswort/Präposition	next to, on, over , in, until
pronoun	Fürwort/Pronomen	he, them, yourselves, ones
article, determiner	Artikel, Begleiter	the, a, an, this, those
conjunction	Konjunktion	and, but, when, although
quantifier	Mengenbezeichnung	some, any, a couple of

2. Word order

When doing a 'fill in the gaps' task requiring various parts of speech, pay attention to the position of each gap in a sentence and to the words before and after it:

- Before a noun, there is most often an article or an adjective.
- An adjective always refers to a noun or pronoun.
- Every sentence has a verb in it.
- The basic word-order rule is **S-V-O**: *subject – verb – object*.
- In a sentence containing several adverbs, these parts of speech are often found in the following order: *manner – place – time*.

3. Mind maps

Mind maps are a great tool to cluster and organise new vocabulary which makes it easier to learn new words. You can either make a mind map for each new word you want to learn or you can collect vocabulary that relates to a specific topic.

A Learning new words

increase

- word class: noun
- sample sentence: There was an increase in the number of college students last year.
- meaning: a rise in the size or number of something
- word family: to increase, increasing
- synonyms: rise, growth
- antonyms: decrease, drop

antonym = a word with the opposite meaning
synonym = a word with a similar or the same meaning

B Collecting topic vocabulary

Young people's style

- self-expression
- self-comparison
- poor self-esteem
- to wear what you want
- social media influencers
- to blend in with the crowd
- a unique sense of style
- to compromise who you are
- personal style

S 11.2 Guessing unknown words

There is no need to be afraid of texts containing new words. You already know many different ways of guessing their meanings. After applying your guessing technique, it is likely that there are still some words you don't know the meaning of, but you will probably understand the most important points in the text.

Guessable words	Examples
Words that are also used in a German context	*bestseller, boycott, clown, laptop, track …*
Words that are similar to German words → watch out for false friends!	*individuality, install, parallel, to wander, …*
Words that are similar to words you know from another foreign language (e.g. French, Latin, Spanish, Italian) → watch out for false friends!	*academic, announcement, artificial, descendant, dignity, individuality, junior, minor, pasta, phase, …*
Compounds of words you already know	*handwriting, heartfelt, mixed ability, single-sex, washing machine, whole-heartedly, …*
Words from a word family you already know	*adventurous, announcement, to mirror, nationalism, relevance, …*
Words with prefixes or suffixes whose root you already know	*to dislike, impatient, to rewrite, profitable, paperless, …*
Words you already know, but with a different meaning – the new meaning may be guessed from the context	*to admit, light, plain, pretty, to report sb, …*
Words whose meaning you can guess from the context	*(he) dozed off (in his chair); (it's old-fashioned) out of date*

prefix = an element placed before a word that changes its meaning (*dis*like, *im*patient)
suffix = an element placed after a word that changes its meaning or word class (profit*able*, paper*less*)

S 11.3 Working with a dictionary

When you cannot guess a word from its context in the text, you can look it up in a dictionary. Using a dictionary takes time however, so decide if you really need to know the meaning of the word in order to understand the sentence or text.

A English-German, German-English (bilingual)
This type of dictionary is best used for translating or finding the meaning of new words quickly. You can use a bilingual dictionary to do mediation exercises.

Check the following information in your dictionary:

- Which word class does the word belong to?
- Which words does it often go together with?
- What topic or word field does it belong to?
- How is it pronounced?
- Are there irregular forms?
- What translations are given?
- Which of the translations can only be used in a limited context (AE, formal, slang etc.)?
- Which of the translations fits the context?

Example

fo·cus['fəʊkəs] <pl focuses, foci> [pl 'fəʊsaɪ] s ❶ (MATH OPT) Brennpunkt m ❷ (fig) Brennpunkt, Herd m, Zentrum nt; ~ (un)scharf eingestellt; ~ scharf einstellen vt ❶ (OPT PHOT) einstellen (on auf) ❷ (fig) konzentrieren (on auf); focus group s (in marketing) [ausgewählte]

B English-English (monolingual)

This type of dictionary is best used for writing an English text when you are not quite sure which is the best word to choose in a given context.

An English-English dictionary provides you with the following information:

- What part of speech is the word?
- Which words does it often go together with?
- What topic or word field does it belong to?
- How is it pronounced?
- Are there irregular forms?
- What synonyms and/or definitions are given?
- Which of the given meanings fits the context?
- Examples show how the word is typically used.

- Before looking up a word, identify whether it is a verb, noun, adjective, adverb etc.
- When you have found the entry for the word, make sure you look at the meaning for the correct word class.
- Read any additional information which the dictionary gives you about the word.
- Take your time to read the entry carefully.
- Make sure you find the entry which matches the use of the word in the given context.

Example

different uses of "air"

pronunciation in British and American English

intransitive or transitive verb

word class

noun without a plural form (uncountable)

other usages and where to find them

examples to show typical contexts

air [GAS] / eə^{r} / (US) /er/ *noun* [U] the mixture of gases which surrounds the earth and which we breathe: *I went outside to get some* **fresh** *air. ' You should put some air in your tyres – they look flat to me.*
➲ See also **airy** LIGHT; **airy** NOT SERIOUS; **airy** DELICATE.
• be walking/floating on air, to be very happy and excited because something very pleasant has happend to you: *Ever since she met Mark, she has been walking on air.*

air [MANNER] / eə^{r} / (US) / er / noun [S] manner or appearance: *She has* **an** *air* **of** *confidence about her.*

• airs and graces, false ways of behaving that are intended to make other people feel that you are important and belong to a high social class.
• put on airs (and graces) (ALSO give yourself airs (and graces)), DISAPPROVING to behave as if you are more important than you really are.

air [DRY] / eə^{r} / (US) / er / *verb* [*I or T*] to become dry and/or fresh, or to cause to become dry and/or fresh: *My mother always airs the sheets before she makes the beds. ' Leave the window open to let the room air a bit.*

S 12 Making a video

Preparing a video

Preparation
- find suitable actors, location(s) and setting
- decide on the use of light (bright, fading, …), colours (e.g. dark, warm, …), space (e.g. interior or exterior, wide or narrow) and cinematic devices
- produce a film script and a storyboard

Filming
- follow your storyboard
- repeat takes if necessary

Editing
- use suitable editing techniques (e.g. cut, fade in, fade out, slow motion, fast motion)
- add sound (e.g. music, dubbing, voiceover, effects)

Example of a script (adaptation of the first scene from *The White Tiger* by Aravind Adiga)

1 EXT. Beijing, Great Hall of the People -- DAY

Fade-in to time lapse of PEOPLE of all kinds walking across Tiananmen Square past the façade, including businessmen and street vendors. Chinese music.

2 INT. Beijing, Premier Wen Jiabao's office -- SAME TIME

Crosscut to Chinese PREMIER at desk, leaning back in chair, reading a printout letter (several pages). Secretary, nervous, stands waiting for reaction. Silence.

PREMIER

(annoyed, irritated; speaks in Chinese. Subtitle in English appears)

It's in English.

VOICEOVER BALRAM

(Balram, speaking in English with an Indian accent)

Mr Premier, Sir.

Neither you nor I can speak English, but there are some things that can be said only in English.

3 INT. Bangalore, India, huge and shabby room, nearly empty, one large 70's chandelier; fan above, splitting up the light; radio -- NIGHT

Fade-in to Balram cross-legged on floor with a silver laptop but talking, not typing. Dreamy look on his face.

BALRAM

… and at 11:32 p.m. today, which was about ten minutes ago, when the lady on All India Radio announced, "Premier Jiabao is coming to Bangalore next week", I said that thing at once.

Example of a storyboard (shot 3 from the film above)

Audio	Near silence, voice fades in	Radio background: Indian music	Fade out radio, Balram louder
Video			
Shot	Fade-in establishing shot: bird's eye view, chandelier to left, Balram small, centre	Move: slow crane zoom round back of Balram to front close-up at "announced"	Stop at: close-up frontal shot Balram, from "I said that thing at once."

S 13 Online research and checking sources

S 13.1 Checking sources

You will often have to research a topic before you can talk or write about it. There are many different ways of finding out information: by researching online, by going to a library and looking in books, newspapers or magazines or by talking to an expert. However, sources differ in quality and reliability, especially online. Therefore, it is absolutely vital that you check your sources before using them. Here is how you distinguish between reliable and unreliable sources:

Reliable	**Unreliable**
– written by respectable journalists, professors, experts or institutions	– without a named author – written by hobby "experts" – from the popular press
– up to date	– too old to be useful
– neutral and objective	– expressing a biased opinion
– covering both sides of a controversial topic	– offering one-sided information only
– with expert proof or personal experience	– just hearsay
– correct grammar and spelling	– many grammar and spelling mistakes

> Don't believe everything you read! Anyone can publish anything on the internet.
> Printed articles and books have normally been more carefully chosen and edited, but these can also be biased or too generalised and simple.

If you are unsure about certain news or facts, use a fact check website to validate your source.

S 13.2 Citing sources

You must document all the sources (texts, pictures, statistics, videos …) you have used in a presentation or written text. There are different citing styles, for example MLA, APA, Harvard or Chicago. The examples below are in MLA style since this is the most commonly used style.

A Citing in the text

Within your text, you can either cite your sources in a footnote or in brackets within the text. Add the footnote or brackets at the end of the sentence or paragraph in which you reference or use the source.

> Bill Smith analyses migration problems in Britain. He writes that real life is about integration.[1]
>
> [1] Smith, Bill. *Real Life in the UK*. London, Brown, 2014, p. 23.
>
> Bill Smith analyses migration problems in Britain. He writes that real life is about integration (Smith 23).

B Creating a list of references

For each of the sources that you have used and referenced in your text, include the following details in your list of references:

Author's name, Author's surname. *Title*. Place of publication, Publishing house, Year of publication.

References/Bibliography

Books:

Egger, Dave. *The Circle*. New York, Knopf, 2013.

Smith, Bill. *Real Life in the UK*. London, Brown, 2014.

Articles:

Jones, Owen. "London riots – one year on." *The Independent*, 24 July 2012.

Online sources:

Darzi, Ara. "Great communication in healthcare can save lives." *The Guardian* online, 18 November 2015, theguardian.com/healthcare-network/2015/nov/18/nhs-great-communication-healthcare-save-lives-behavioural-insight-nudge. Accessed 5 June 2019.

Copyrighted material

It is important to check whether the material you are including is copyrighted, i.e. it can only be used with the permission of the author. You can include copyrighted material in your presentation in class if you cite it correctly, but you are not allowed to publish or upload it online. Check the material for a copyright notice: the symbol "©" or the word "copyright" followed by the date of publication and the author's name. Pictures may have a watermark to show that they are copyrighted.

S 13.3 Quoting

Always make a clear difference between text you wrote yourself and text or facts written by others. You can cite a text in different ways:

Direct quotation: Copy the exact words of the source text and cite them with quotation marks. If you cite a whole sentence, add a colon (...: "...").

Indirect quotation: Paraphrase the source using your own words.

In her article "Great communication in healthcare can save lives", Ara Darzi states: "More than one in 15 hospital prescriptions contains some kind of error [...]". She argues that "the most frequent cause of avoidable harm to patients in hospital" is that prescriptions are not written clearly and do not contain all the necessary information (Darzi, *The Guardian.com*).

Symbols and abbreviations

[...]	to add to or leave words out of a direct quote
l./ll.	to indicate the line or lines you are quoting (e.g. in a poem or newspaper article)
p.	to indicate the page you are quoting from
ff.	to indicate the page on which the quote starts (ff. stands for "and the following pages")
'...'	to mark direct speech in a quote
/	to mark the beginning of a new line in a quoted poem

USEFUL PHRASES

Direct quotation (whole sentence)
In his/her book/article ..., X states: "..." (p.7ff.).

Direct quotation (built into your sentence)
X claims/argues/assumes/concludes that "..." (l.6). | X presents ... as "...", which ... (p.12).

Indirect quotation (paraphrasing)
X claims/reports/writes in ... that... | According to X, ... is/has/was/could ... (ll.7–9). | In X's article, he/she describes ..., which is based on/gives reasons for/explains why ... (l.4). | While X argues that ..., Y gives reasons for ... (l.23ff.; l.76ff.).

S14 Preparing for an exam

Dealing with exam tasks

Get hold of some mock (practice) exams and take the time to do them in a situation like the exam.

Step 1	**Working in the right setting** – Work in a quiet room and set yourself the exact time you will be given in the real exam. – Don't use any material to help you which is not allowed in the real exam.
Step 2	**Planning how to write** – Make sure you know what you are expected to do for each task. – Plan enough time to read the tasks very carefully, plan, write and check your answers. – Write a checklist of things to remember.
Step 3	**Writing your answers** – Use separate paper for notes and first drafts. – Write the task number/title above each answer. – Write clearly and neatly. It is important that the examiner can easily read what you write. – Check what you have written and write a clean copy if necessary.

S15 Methods

Milling around Marktplatz

1. Bearbeiten Sie die Aufgabe zunächst allein. Auf ein Signal der Lehrkraft stehen Sie auf und gehen durch den Raum. Nehmen Sie die Aufgabe und einen Stift mit.
2. Wenn erneut ein Signal ertönt, bleiben Sie stehen. Besprechen Sie die Aufgabe mit der Person, die Ihnen am nächsten steht.
3. Beim nächsten Signal trennen Sie sich und gehen weiter durch den Raum. Wiederholen Sie Schritt 2.

Think-pair-share Nachdenken-austauschen-teilen

Think: Schreiben Sie Ihre Ideen, Gedanken oder Lösungen zur Aufgabe alleine auf.

Pair: Tauschen Sie Ihre Notizen mit einem Partner / einer Partnerin aus und besprechen Sie diese.

Share: Präsentieren Sie Ihre Ergebnisse anderen Paaren oder der gesamten Klasse.

1-minute presentation Kurzpräsentation

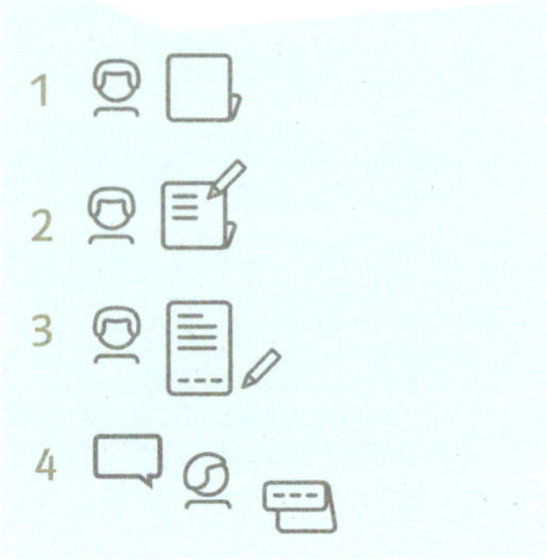

Nehmen Sie sich ein DIN A4-Blatt. Falten Sie es so, dass das untere Drittel nach hinten wegknickt.

Schreiben Sie den Text Ihrer Präsentation auf die oberen zwei Drittel.

Notieren Sie nun die wichtigsten Stichpunkte noch einmal auf dem unteren Drittel. Dies ist Ihr Spickzettel.

In Ihrer Präsentation verwenden Sie nur den Spickzettel. Wenn Sie nicht mehr weiter wissen, dürfen Sie kurz auf den Text oben schauen.

Placemat Platzdeckchen

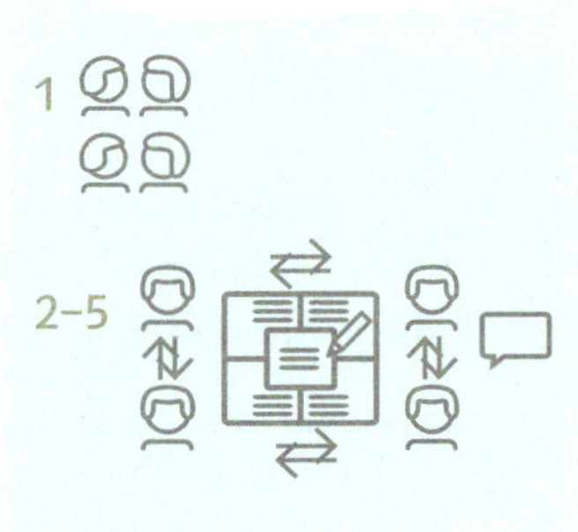

1. Bilden Sie Vierergruppen.
2. Teilen Sie ein großes Blatt Papier in fünf Bereiche ein.
3. Setzen Sie sich so hin, dass jeder in eine Ecke des Blattes schreiben kann.
4. Jedes Gruppenmitglied denkt allein über das Thema nach und schreibt Ideen auf seinen / ihren Teil des Blattes.
5. Tauschen Sie sich über die Ideen aus. Einigen Sie sich auf die besten Ideen und schreiben Sie diese in die Mitte des Blattes.

Round robin Blitzlicht

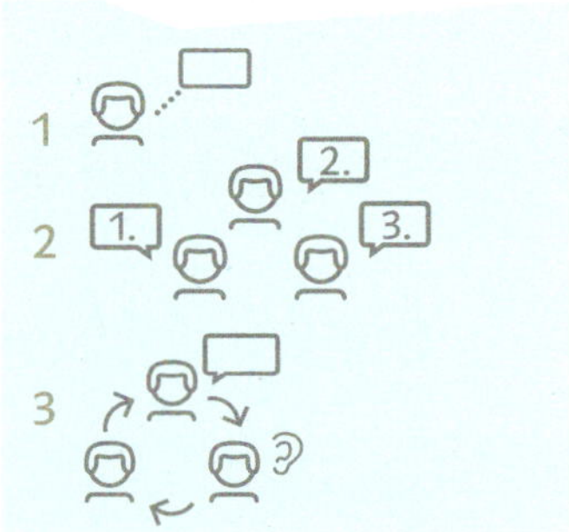

Überlegen Sie sich einen Satz zu der Aufgabe / der Frage / dem Thema.

Wenn alle bereit sind, tauschen Sie sich in der Klasse / in Gruppen aus, indem Sie nacheinander Ihren Satz sagen.

Alle anderen hören aufmerksam zu, kommentieren aber nicht.

Opinion line Meinungslinie

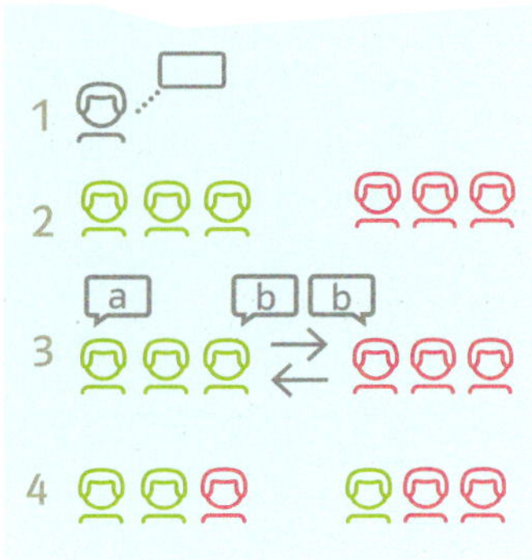

Überlegen Sie, welche Meinung Sie zum genannten Thema haben. Sind Sie dafür oder dagegen? Warum?

Stellen Sie sich auf einer gedachten Linie im Klassenzimmer auf. Auf der linken Seite stehen die Schüler/-innen, die DAFÜR sind. Auf der rechten Seite stehen die Schüler/-innen, die DAGEGEN sind.

Tauschen Sie sich zunächst innerhalb Ihrer Gruppe (a) und danach mit der anderen Gruppe (b) aus. Nennen Sie Ihre Argumente und Gründe.

Am Schluss positionieren Sie sich erneut. Haben Sie Ihre Meinung geändert?

Peer correction Partnerkontrolle

1. Bearbeiten Sie die Aufgabe zunächst selbstständig.
2. Tauschen Sie Ihre Lösungen mit einem Partner / einer Partnerin oder in Kleingruppen untereinander.
   Kontrollieren Sie die Lösungen.
3. Tauschen Sie sich danach zu der Aufgabe aus und korrigieren Sie den Text.

Tip-top Feedback

Sagen Sie zunächst, was Ihnen gut gefallen hat – also „top" war.

Sagen Sie nun, was noch nicht so gut war. Geben Sie einen Tipp, was man verbessern könnte.

Gallery walk Galerierundgang

Hängen Sie nach Ihrer Gruppenarbeit Ihr Produkt gut sichtbar im Klassenzimmer auf.

Einer von Ihnen, der „Experte", bleibt bei Ihrem Projekt stehen und erklärt es den anderen. Die anderen gehen herum. Nach jedem Durchgang wechselt der Experte.

Sehen Sie sich die Produkte der anderen an und geben Sie Feedback.

Werten Sie im Anschluss Ihre Ergebnisse in der Klasse aus.

G1 Tenses

G1.1 Simple present

Positive sentences	Negative sentences	Questions
I use social media. You use social media. He/she/it uses social media. We use social media. You use social media. They use social media.	I don't use social media. You don't use social media. He/she/it doesn't use social media. We don't use social media. You don't use social media. They don't use social media.	Do I use social media? Do you use social media? Does he/she/it use social media? Do we use social media? Do you use social media? Do they use social media? Questions with a question word: Why do I use social media? Why do you use social media? Why does he/she/it use social media? Why do we use social media? Why do you use social media? Why do they use social media?

! Be careful with these verbs: be, have.

Talking about the present V1 I1

Talking about the present V2 I2

Examples of typical use:
- Facts and general statements: The cartoon shows a family.
- Everyday activities or habits: Justin listens to podcasts on the bus.
  Tense markers: always, often, sometimes, never, usually, every day/week/month/year, on Mondays/Tuesdays…, at 7 o'clock/11 o'clock…
- A set sequence of events or actions: Young people spend too much time on their phones, get very little sleep and are tired the next day at school.
- For scheduled future events with an adverbial phrase of time: The programme finishes at ten o'clock.

G1.2 Present progressive

Positive sentences	Negative sentences	Questions
I am studying. You are studying. He/she/it is studying. We are studying. You are studying. They are studying.	I'm not studying. You aren't studying. He/she/it isn't studying. We aren't studying. You aren't studying. They aren't studying.	Am I studying? Are you studying? Is he/she/it studying? Are we studying? Are you studying? Are they studying? Questions with a question word: What am I studying? What are you studying? What is he/she/it studying? What are we studying? What are you studying? What are they studying?

! Some verbs are never used in the progressive form, especially those which express feelings or a belief: believe, love, hate, seem, have (in the sense of own), can, mean, want to, feel, notice, realise.

Talking about the present V1 I1

Talking about the present V2 I2

Examples of typical use:

- An activity that is going on right now and will continue for a limited period of time: Reese is giving an interview (now).
  Tense markers: now, just now, at the moment
- Planned future events with an adverbial phrase of time: Reese is flying to London next week.

Talking about the past
V 3 I 3

G1.3 Simple past

Positive sentences	Negative sentences	Questions
I played a video game. You played a video game. He/she/it played a video game. We played a video game. You played a video game. They played a video game.	I didn't play a video game. You didn't play a video game. He/she/it didn't play a video game. We didn't play a video game. You didn't play a video game. They didn't play a video game.	Did I play a video game? Did you play a video game? Did he/she/it play a video game? Did we play a video game? Did you play a video game? Did they play a video game? Questions with a question word: Why did I play a video game? Why did you play a video game? Why did he/she/it play a video game? Why did we play a video game? Why did you play a video game? Why did they play a video game?

! Be careful with irregular verbs.

Examples of typical use:

- For activities that began and ended at a specific time in the past: The technical team tested the device last week.
  Tense markers: yesterday, ago, last week/month/year, in 2017/…, on Tuesday/…
- For a series of events in the past, as in a story, often called the 'narrative past':
  As Kate didn't have a job, she went to Australia. Her aunt found her a job there and one thing led to another. After six months, Kate had a permanent job.

Talking about the past
V 3 I 3

G1.4 Past progressive

Positive sentences	Negative sentences	Questions
I was thinking. You were thinking. He/she/it was thinking. We were thinking. You were thinking. They were thinking.	I wasn't thinking. You weren't thinking. He/she/it wasn't thinking. We weren't thinking. You weren't thinking. They weren't thinking.	Was I thinking? Were you thinking? Was he/she/it thinking? Were we thinking? Were you thinking? Were they thinking? Questions with a question word: What was I thinking? What were you thinking? What was he/she/it thinking? What were we thinking? What were you thinking? What were they thinking?

Examples of typical use:

- An activity in the past that was already in progress when something else happened:
  Kate was working in a bar when she heard about the job in a bank.
- Several activities or events that were happening at the same time in the past:
  While Kate was living in England, she only had temporary jobs.

G1.5 Present perfect simple

Talking about the present perfect
V 4 I 4

Positive sentences	Negative sentences	Questions
I have finished. You have finished. He/she/it has finished. We have finished. You have finished. They have finished.	I haven't finished. You haven't finished. He/she/it hasn't finished. We haven't finished. You haven't finished. They haven't finished.	Have I finished? Have you finished? Has he/she/it finished? Have we finished? Have you finished? Have they finished? Questions with a question word: What have I finished? What have you finished? What has he/she/it finished? What have we finished? What have you finished? What have they finished?

! Be careful with irregular verbs.

! With the present perfect simple the result of the action is usually more important than the action itself. Never use the present perfect with adverbs of past time, e.g. yesterday, last week, three years ago, in 2017...

Examples of typical use:

- Activities that happened recently and whose effects are still being felt in the present: Kate has moved to Australia and she is still getting used to the different accent there.
- With certain adverbs: just, so far, ever, never, recently, lately, today, this week, already, (not) yet
  He has listed all his work experience so far. – Has he ever worked abroad?
- With for and since, for activities that started in the past and are continuing:
  Lisa hasn't checked her emails for two days. – She has received 20 emails since Tuesday.

G1.6 Present perfect progressive

Talking about the present perfect
V 4 I 4

Positive sentences	Negative sentences	Questions
I have been waiting. You have been waiting. He/she/it has been waiting. We have been waiting. You have been waiting. They have been waiting.	I haven't been waiting. You haven't been waiting. He/she/it hasn't been waiting. We haven't been waiting. You haven't been waiting. They haven't been waiting.	Have I been waiting? Have you been waiting? Has he/she/it been waiting? Have we been waiting? Have you been waiting? Have they been waiting? Questions with a question word: Why have I been waiting? Why have you been waiting? Why has he/she/it been waiting? Why have we been waiting? Why have you been waiting? Why have they been waiting?

Examples of typical use:
- Activities that have been going on either continuously or at intervals up to the present, often with adverbials of time such as all day, for a week, etc.: We have been looking at job adverts all evening.
- There is no mention of time but the activity has taken place very recently and the result is still visible: It has been raining.

G1.7 Past perfect simple

Positive sentences	Negative sentences	Questions
I had finished. You had finished. He/she/it had finished. We had finished. You had finished. They had finished.	I hadn't finished. You hadn't finished. He/she/it hadn't finished. We hadn't finished. You hadn't finished. They hadn't finished.	Had I finished? Had you finished? Had he/she/it finished? Had we finished? Had you finished? Had they finished? Questions with a question word: What had I finished? What had you finished? What had he/she/it finished? What had we finished? What had you finished? What had they finished?

! Be careful with irregular verbs.

Examples of typical use:
- An activity that happened before another activity in the past, showing the connection between the two activities:
  When I arrived at college, the lesson had already started.
  After I had finished my homework, I decided to go out.
- In reported speech, when the original statement is in the past or present perfect:
  Jane said that she had forgotten to do her homework.

G1.8 Past perfect progressive

Positive sentences	Negative sentences	Questions
I had been waiting. You had been waiting. He/she/it had been waiting. We had been waiting. You had been waiting. They had been waiting.	I hadn't been waiting. You hadn't been waiting. He/she/it hadn't been waiting. We hadn't been waiting. You hadn't been waiting. They hadn't been waiting.	Had I been waiting? Had you been waiting? Had he/she/it been waiting? Had we been waiting? Had you been waiting? Had they been waiting? Questions with a question word: Why had I been waiting? Why had you been waiting? Why had he/she/it been waiting? Why had we been waiting? Why had you been waiting? Why had they been waiting?

Examples of typical use:

- An activity that occurred over a period of time, and before another activity, in the past. The two activities are directly related: He was tired because he had been working so hard.
- In reported speech, when the original statement is in the present perfect progressive: He said that he had been working hard.

G1.9 Going to-future

Talking about the future
V 5 I 5

Positive sentences	Negative sentences	Questions
I am going to leave early. You are going to leave early. He/she/it is going to leave early. We are going to leave early You are going to leave early. They are going to leave early.	I'm not going to leave early. You're not going to leave early. He/she/it's not going to leave early. We're not going to leave early. You're not going to leave early. They're not going to leave early.	Am I going to leave early? Are you going to leave early? Is he/she/it going to leave early? Are we going to leave early? Are you going to leave early? Are they going to leave early?

Examples of typical use:

- For an action in the future that has already been planned or prepared: They're going to buy new tablets for the whole school.
- For a prediction about the future, when you can see that something is about to happen: Look at those clouds. It's going to rain soon.

G1.10 Future simple (will-future)

Talking about the future
V 5 I 5

Positive sentences	Negative sentences	Questions
I will finish college. You will finish college. He/she/it will finish college. We will finish college. You will finish college. They will finish college.	I won't finish college. You won't finish college. He/she/it won't finish college. We won't finish college. You won't finish college. They won't finish college.	Will I finish college? Will you finish college? Will he/she/it finish college? Will we finish college? Will you finish college? Will they finish college? Questions with a question word: When will I finish college? When will you finish college? When will he/she/it finish college? When will we finish college? When will you finish college? When will they finish college?

! English will = German werden
English want = German wollen

Examples of typical use:

- Things that are likely to happen at a defined or undefined time in the future: You'll be a great business person one day.
- For forecasts, such as the weather forecast: On Saturday, it will rain for most of the day.
- In if-clauses Type 1 – future situations that are probable/possible: If the weather is nice, I'll revise for my test in the park.

G1.11 Future progressive

Positive sentences	Negative sentences	Questions
I will be learning. You will be learning. He/she/it will be learning. We will be learning. You will be learning. They will be learning.	I won't be learning. You won't be learning. He/she/it won't be learning. We won't be learning. You won't be learning. They won't be learning.	Will I be learning? Will you be learning? Will he/she/it be learning? Will we be learning? Will you be learning? Will they be learning? Questions with a question word: What will I be learning? What will you be learning? What will he/she/it be learning? What will we be learning? What will you be learning? What will they be learning?

Example of typical use:

- Events – which are often planned – that will be going on at a certain time in the future when another event occurs: You will be sleeping by the time I get home.

G1.12 Future perfect simple

Positive sentences	Negative sentences	Questions
I will have finished. You will have finished. He/she/it will have finished. We will have finished. You will have finished. They will have finished.	I won't have finished. You won't have finished. He/she/it won't have finished. We won't have finished. You won't have finished. They won't have finished.	Will I have finished? Will you have finished? Will he/she/it have finished? Will we have finished? Will you have finished? Will they have finished? Questions with a question word: When will I have finished? When will you have finished? When will he/she/it have finished? When will we have finished? When will you have finished? When will they have finished?

! Be careful with irregular verbs.

Example of typical use:

- For an activity in the future that takes place before a second activity, to show the relation between them. The second activity is in the present tense:
  Joanna will have finished the college course by the time she is 20.

G1.13 Future perfect progressive

Positive sentences	Negative sentences	Questions
I will have been waiting. You will have been waiting. He/she/it will have been waiting. We will have been waiting. You will have been waiting. They will have been waiting.	I won't have been waiting. You won't have been waiting. He/she/it won't have been waiting. We won't have been waiting. You won't have been waiting. They won't have been waiting.	Will I have been waiting? Will you have been waiting? Will he/she/it have been waiting? Will we have been waiting? Will you have been waiting? Will they have been waiting?

Example of typical use:

- Used in the same way as the future perfect simple, but it places more emphasis on the length of time the activity is expected to take:
  They will have been studying English for eight years by the time they take the exam.

G1.14 Conditional I

Talking about conditions
V 6 I 6

Positive sentences	Negative sentences	Questions
I would take a gap year. You would take a gap year. He/she/it would take a gap year. We would take a gap year. You would take a gap year. They would take a gap year.	I wouldn't take a gap year. You wouldn't take a gap year. He/she/it wouldn't take a gap year. We wouldn't take a gap year. You wouldn't take a gap year. They wouldn't take a gap year.	Would I take a gap year? Would you take a gap year? Would he/she/it take a gap year? Would we take a gap year? Would you take a gap year? Would they take a gap year? Questions with a question word: Why would I take a gap year? Why would you take a gap year? Why would he/she/it take a gap year? Why would we take a gap year? Why would you take a gap year? Why would they take a gap year?

Examples of typical use:

- For suggestions, polite questions and requests:
  Which country would you visit? – Well, I would visit Australia.
  Would you like a drink?
  Would you help me, please?
- In if-clauses Type 2 – future situations that are improbable/unlikely:
  If I had enough money, I would start my own company.

Talking about conditions
V 6 16

G1.15 Conditional II

Positive sentences	Negative sentences	Questions
I would have applied for the job. You would have applied for the job. He/she/it would have applied for the job. We would have applied for the job. You would have applied for the job. They would have applied for the job.	I wouldn't have applied for the job. You wouldn't have applied for the job. He/she/it wouldn't have applied for the job. We wouldn't have applied for the job. You wouldn't have applied for the job. They wouldn't have applied for the job.	Would I have applied for the job? Would you have applied for the job? Would he/she/it have applied for the job? Would we have applied for the job? Would you have applied for the job? Would they have applied for the job? Questions with a question word: Why would I have applied for the job? Why would you have applied for the job? Why would he/she/it have applied for the job? Why would we have applied for the job? Why would you have applied for the job? Why would they have applied for the job?

! Be careful with irregular verbs.

Example of typical use:
- In if-clauses Type 3 – past situations that are unreal/impossible/hypothetical:
  If you had prepared before the interview, they would have given you the job.

Talking about conditions
V 6 16

G2 If-clauses

There are three main types of if-clauses (or conditional sentences) in English. They are basically used in the same way as conditional sentences in German. You can put the if-clause at the beginning or at the end of the sentence.

G2.1 Type 1 – Future situations (probable/possible)

a) if-clause: simple present – main clause: will-future
If you study hard, you will pass the exam.
Wenn du fleißig lernst, wirst du die Prüfung bestehen.

b) if-clause: present perfect – main clause: will-future
If you have studied hard, you will pass the exam.
Wenn du fleißig gelernt hast, wirst du die Prüfung bestehen.

c) if-clause: simple present – main clause: can + infinitive
If you study hard, you can pass the exam.
Wenn du fleißig lernst, kannst du die Prüfung bestehen.

d) if-clause: simple present – main clause: might + infinitive
If you study hard, you might pass the exam.
Wenn du fleißig lernst, wirst du eventuell die Prüfung bestehen.

G2.2 Type 2 – Future situations (improbable/unlikely)

a) if-clause: simple past – main clause: conditional I (would + infinitive)
If you studied hard, you would pass the exam.
Wenn du fleißig lernen würdest, würdest du die Prüfung bestehen.

b) if-clause: simple past – main clause: could + infinitive
If you studied hard, you could pass the exam.
Wenn du fleißig lernen würdest, könntest du die Prüfung bestehen.

G2.3 Type 3 – Past situations (unreal/impossible/hypothetical)

a) if-clause: past perfect – main clause: conditional II (would + have + past participle)
If you had studied hard, you would have passed the exam.
Wenn du fleißig gelernt hättest, hättest du die Prüfung bestanden.

b) if-clause: past perfect – main clause: could + have + past participle
If you had studied hard, you could have passed the exam.
Wenn du fleißig gelernt hättest, hättest du die Prüfung bestehen können.

c) if-clause: past perfect – main clause: might + have + past participle
If you had studied hard, you might have passed the exam.
Wenn du fleißig gelernt hättest, hättest du eventuell die Prüfung bestanden.

! Exceptions to the rules:

- The present tense is used in both clauses in general statements and for repeated activities or habits:
If plants don't get enough water, they die. – If she has time, she goes to the gym.
- For recommendations and advice use 'were' in the if-clause and conditional I in the main clause: If I were you, I would study a bit harder.
- 'If' can be left out when the order of the verb and subject are reversed:
Had I studied harder, I would have passed the exam.

! Be careful!

- If you start a sentence with an if-clause, use a comma. Don't use a comma if you start with the main clause:
If you study hard, you will pass the exam.
You will pass the exam if you study hard.
- Don't use 'will' in the if-clause, except to express willingness:
They can come to Britain if they'll work.
- Don't use 'would' in the if-clause except when you are making a polite request:
I would be grateful if you would hand in your homework on time in future.

Talking about processes
V7 I7

G3 The passive

The passive is often used when the action is more important than who or what performed it. The passive is frequently used in scientific and technical writing. The passive can be formed with or without an 'agent'. The 'agent' is the person or thing that causes an action to occur.

Form the passive using a form of 'to be' + past participle (+ by + agent)

The Youth Agency carries out research projects.

Research projects are carried out by the Youth Agency.

Simple present	Present progressive
I am invited for an interview. You are invited for an interview. He/she/it is invited for an interview. We are invited for an interview. You are invited for an interview. They are invited for an interview.	I am being interviewed for a survey. You are being interviewed for a survey. He/she/it is being interviewed for a survey. We are being interviewed for a survey. You are being interviewed for a survey. They are being interviewed for a survey.
Simple past	**Past progressive**
I was invited for an interview. You were invited for an interview. He/she/it was invited for an interview. We were invited for an interview. You were invited for an interview. They were invited for an interview.	I was being interviewed for a survey. You were being interviewed for a survey. He/she/it was being interviewed for a survey. We were being interviewed for a survey. You were being interviewed for a survey. They were being interviewed for a survey.
Present perfect	**Modal verbs**
I have been invited for an interview. You have been invited for an interview. He/she/it has been invited for an interview. We have been invited for an interview. You have been invited for an interview. They have been invited for an interview.	I can be contacted online. You must be contacted online. He/she/it mustn't be contacted online. We needn't be contacted online. You ought to be contacted online. They should be contacted online.
Future	**Future perfect**
I will be invited for an interview. You will be invited for an interview. He/she/it will be invited for an interview. We will be invited for an interview. You will be invited for an interview. They will be invited for an interview.	I will have been invited for an interview. You will have been invited for an interview. He/she/it will have been invited for an interview. We will have been invited for an interview. You will have been invited for an interview. They will have been invited for an interview.

! Be careful with irregular verbs.

G4 Relative clauses

Talking about describing people or things in more detail
V 8 I 8

Relative clauses are used to describe people or things. A relative clause usually begins with a relative pronoun.

Relative pronoun	refers to
who	people (subject or object)
whom	people (object), formal English
which	things
that	people or things (subject or object)
whose	possessions

G4.1 Defining relative clauses

- A defining relative clause is important for the meaning of the sentence. Without the relative clause the sentence would not make any sense. Defining relative clauses are not separated from the rest of the sentence by commas:
  The text message that/which you sent me didn't arrive.
  This is the woman who(m) I emailed yesterday.
  This is the boy whose smartphone was stolen.
- The pronouns 'that', 'which' and 'who(m)' can be left out if the pronoun is the object of the relative clause. This type of relative clause is known as a 'contact' clause:
  The apps we use are all free.
  This is the woman I emailed yesterday.

G4.2 Non-defining relative clauses

- The information in non-defining relative clauses is additional and descriptive. Even without the relative clause the sentence is clear. Non-defining relative clauses are separated from the rest of the sentence by commas:
  Aiden, who is still a teenager, runs a successful online business.

G5 Adjectives

Talking about qualities
V 9 I 9

Talking about qualities
V 10 I 10

Adjectives describe people and things: the tall man – bright lights

- The present participle (-ing form) and past participle of verbs can often be used as adjectives:
  an interesting book – the finished report
- Verbs are usually followed by adverbs, however some verbs are followed by adjectives:

to be	The laptop is heavy.
to become	Anne became nervous before the interview.
to feel	Thomas felt excited about his new job.
to get	Her smartphone got broken.
to look	The office block looks modern.
to seem	My new colleagues seem nice.

- Adjectives can be used as collective nouns. In such cases, the + adjective refers to a particular group of people as a whole:
  It is important to help the unemployed to find work.
  The very young and the very old are particularly at risk.

- The comparison of adjectives:

Positive form	Comparative form	Superlative form
cold	colder	the coldest
hot	hotter	the hottest
funny	funnier	the funniest
modern	more modern	the most modern

! Remember the irregular forms:
good – better – the best
much – more – the most
bad – worse – the worst
far – further – the furthest

Use more/-er than, as … as and not as … as to make comparisons:
An email is more modern than a letter.
My smartphone is newer than yours.
Tablets are just as popular as laptops.
The internet at school is not as fast as the internet at home.

Talking about qualities
V 9 I 9

Talking about qualities
V 10 I 10

G6 Adverbs

Adverbs are formed by adding -ly/-ily to an adjective:

Adjective	Adverb
safe	safely
happy	happily
real	really
reasonable	reasonably

! Remember the irregular forms:
good – well
fast – fast
hard – hard

- Adverbs describe actions (verbs): He walked quickly. She spoke slowly.
- Adverbs before other adjectives: This is an extremely good essay.
- Adverbs before other adverbs: He was driving incredibly fast.
- Adverbs before past participles: Credit cards are frequently accepted.
- Some useful adverbs: always, usually, often, frequently, sometimes, seldom, rarely, never, recently, soon, lately, in the past, in the future, largely, for the most part, partly, probably, possibly, hardly, definitely, obviously, clearly, basically, consequently, as a result
- The comparison of adverbs:

Positive form	Comparative form	Superlative form
fluently	more fluently	the most fluently

! Remember the irregular forms:
well – better – the best
badly – worse – the worst
fast – faster – the fastest

G7 Question tags

A question tag is added to the end of a sentence to turn it into a question. In German you use expressions like '*…, nicht wahr?*' and '*…, oder?*' in a similar way.

- If the statement is positive, the question tag is negative:
  He uses social media, doesn't he?
- If the statement is negative, the question tag is positive:
  He doesn't use social media, does he?
- The subject of the sentence is also the subject of the question tag:
  Lisa never turns off her smartphone, does she?
- If the statement is in the simple present, the question tag is formed with 'is/are' or 'isn't/aren't', 'do/does' or 'don't/doesn't':
  He likes video games, doesn't he?
- For statements in the simple past, the question tag is formed with 'was/were' or 'wasn't/weren't' or 'did/didn't':
  He took a gap year, didn't he?
- If the statement uses an auxiliary verb (to be, to have, will, etc.) or a modal (can, must, etc.), use the modal or auxiliary in the same tense in the tag:
  Tom is here, isn't he?
  Roger has bought a new laptop, hasn't he?
  Jill will be at the interview, won't she?
  You can contact me by email, can't you?

G8 Modal auxiliaries

Talking about ability, permission and necessity
V 11 I 11

- Will/would/can/could/may:

  Asking someone to do something:
  Will/Would/Can/Could you do me a favour?

  Asking for permission/giving permission:
  May I use your phone? – Yes, of course, you may.

  Talking about abilities:
  She can speak English.

- Must/mustn't/needn't:

  Instructing someone to do something or not to do something:
  You must prepare before an interview.
  You mustn't tell lies at an interview.

  Talking about a necessity or duty:
  I must send in my job application by Friday.
  You needn't be nervous before the interview.

- May/might/could/must/will:

  Expressing a possibility or probability:
  It may/might/could/will rain.
  You must be Mr Jones.

  Making a suggestion:
  We could look for typical interview questions online.

- Should/ought to/shouldn't/ought not to:

  Giving advice:
  You should/ought to use a dictionary.
  You shouldn't/ought not to arrive late for the interview.

- Modal auxiliaries only have a present and/or past tense form. Substitutes are used for other tenses:

Modal auxiliary	Substitutes	Examples
can/could	be able to	He won't be able to to work under pressure.
may/mustn't	be allowed to not be allowed to	We were allowed to use our smartphones in class. We weren't allowed to play music.
must/needn't	have to not have to	She will have to work this weekend. We didn't have to work late.

Talking about likes and dislikes
V 12 I 12

G9 -ing forms

An -ing form can be either a present participle or a gerund.

G9.1 The present participle

- The present participle is used in the progressive tenses (present progressive, past progressive, etc.):
  Mary is checking her emails. – The class was discussing the topic 'Take a gap year or find a job?'.
- The present participle can be used as an adjective: the winning party – a growing child
- The present participle can be used to shorten clauses, often after a conjunction, e.g: after, while, before, when
  I was riding my bike to work when I saw her. → While riding my bike to work, I saw her.
  The class listened to the entrepreneur who was talking about start-ups. → The class listened to the entrepreneur talking about start-ups.
  After we had collected ideas in a word web, we discussed them. → After collecting ideas in a word web we discussed them.
  Read the text before you answer the questions. → Read the text before answering the questions.

G9.2 The gerund

- The gerund is used after prepositions: You're very good at speaking English.
- The gerund is often used after certain verbs: like, hate, enjoy, love, mind, prefer
  I don't mind watching TV but I prefer reading and I also enjoy playing computer games.
- The gerund can be used as a noun: Laughing is good for you. – Studying is very important.
- Some verbs have the construction verb + preposition + gerund:
  to be afraid of, to look forward to, to feel like, to talk about, to insist on, to decide against, to think about/of, to succeed in, to apologise for
  I'm afraid of flying.
- When the following expressions are followed by a verb, use the gerund:
  There's no point in waiting any longer.
  It's not worth going to see the new James Bond film.
  A waste of money/time: It's a waste of time talking to you.
  To spend/to waste time/money: He spends all of his time sitting in front of a computer.

G10 Reported speech

Talking about passing on information
V 13 I 13

Reported speech (or indirect speech) is used to report what someone has said without quoting them.

- Start the reported speech with a reporting verb:
  a) Statements: say (that), tell sb. (that), answer, mention, explain, reply, etc.
     "I'm tired." → She says (that) she's tired.
  b) Questions: ask, want to know
     "Are you hungry?" → She asks me if I'm hungry.
     "Where do you go to school?" → She wants to know where I go to school.
  c) Commands: tell sb. to + infinitive
     "Leave me alone!" → She told me to leave her alone.

- If the reporting verb is in the present, present perfect or future tense, the tense stays the same:
  "Spending hours on social media is bad for you".
  → Mr Jones says spending hours on social media is bad for you.
  → Mr Jones has said spending hours on social media is bad for you.
  → Mr Jones will say spending hours on social media is bad for you.

- If the reporting verb is in the past tense, the tense of the reported speech changes:

simple present "I text my best friend every day."	→	simple past She said she texted her best friend every day.
present progressive "I am texting my best friend."	→	past progressive She said she was texting her best friend..
simple past "I texted my best friend last night."	→	past perfect She said she had texted her best friend the night before.
past progressive "I was texting my best friend."	→	past perfect progressive She said she had been texting her best friend.
present perfect "I have texted my best friend."	→	past perfect She said she had texted her best friend.
present perfect progressive "I have been texting my best friend."	→	past perfect progressive She said she had been texting her best friend.
past perfect "I had texted my best friend."	→	past perfect She said she had texted her best friend.
past perfect progressive "I had been texting my best friend."	→	past perfect progressive She said she had been texting her best friend.
will-future I will text my best friend every day."	→	conditional I She said she would text her best friend every day.

- Questions follow the same tense changes as statements:
  "How many jobs have you applied for?" → My friend asked me how many jobs I had applied for.

- Some adverbs of time also change in reported speech, for example:

now	→	then
yesterday	→	the day before/the previous day
here	→	there
last year	→	the year before/the previous year
today	→	that day
tomorrow	→	the next day

- Statements involving truths and facts do not have to change in reported speech:
  "The novel is by Zadie Smith." → The teacher said that the novel is by Zadie Smith.

G11 Word order

Generally, the word order in English sentences is subject – verb – object.
This is the case in main clauses and subordinate clauses:
We live in a world that is heavily influenced by the media.
I like Las Vegas because it has something for everyone.

G11.1 Statements

- Normally, place comes before time:
  I went to school yesterday.
  I've wanted to visit the UK for years.
- The adverbs in a sentence generally follow the sequence: adverb of manner – adverb of place – adverb of time:
  I was waiting patiently for tickets outside the stadium all morning.
  I will be working hard in London this summer.
- In English, adverbs of frequency (never, sometimes, often, always, etc.) are directly in front of the verb:
  I usually check my phone as soon as I wake up.
  I never leave home without my phone.

> ! But be careful – there is an exception when you use the verb to be:
> I'm always in the gym on Fridays.

G11.2 Questions

- Questions never begin with a main verb:
  Do you like British food?
  Did you get my message last night?

> ! But be careful – there is an exception when you use the verb to be:
> Are you thinking of taking a gap year?
> Am I the first person to arrive?

- Negative questions do not end with a main verb like they do in German:
  Aren't you going to miss German food?

G11.3 Negated statements

- The negation of don't/doesn't comes before the main verb, unlike in German:
  I don't have school on Friday afternoons.
  I don't use my mobile phone during lessons.

Erklärvideos und interaktive Übungen

Mit Hilfe von Erklärvideos und interaktiven Übungen können grammatische Phänomene wiederholt und gefestigt werden.
Die Videos sowie die Übungen finden Sie in den Medien zum Schülerbuch und im eBook.

Talking about the present	– simple present, present progressive – questions and negative sentences
Talking about the past	– simple past, past progressive
Talking about the present perfect	– present perfect simple, present perfect progressive
Talking about the future	– will-future, going to-future, present with future meaning
Talking about qualities	– adjectives, adverbs – comparison of adjectives and adverbs, exceptions
Talking about ability, permission and necessity	– modal auxiliaries and their substitutes
Talking about describing people or things in more detail	– relative clauses: who, which, that, whose
Talking about conditions	– if-clauses
Talking about likes and dislikes	– the gerund
Talking about processes	– the passive: present, past, future
Talking about passing on information	– reported speech

Das "Vocabulary" enthält die zu lernenden Vokabeln der Topics in chronologischer Reihenfolge.

Die blau gedruckten Vokabeln stammen aus den Audio- und Videotexten.

D1 Vokabellernliste

Symbole und Abkürzungen:
↔ ist das Gegenteil von
→ ist verwandt mit
= entspricht
sth something
sb somebody
(AE) Amerikanisches Englisch
(BE) Britisches Englisch
(sg) Einzahl (Singular)
(pl) Mehrzahl (Plural)
etw. etwas
jdn. jemanden
jdm. jemandem

D2 Topic 1 Being young

Getting started

vocational college [və,keɪʃnl 'kɒlɪdʒ]	Berufsschule	**vocational** = job-related
to **matter** ['mætə]	von Bedeutung sein; wichtig sein	**to matter** = to be important
long-term [,lɒŋ'tɜːm]	langfristig	**long-term** ↔ short-term
well-being [,wel'biːɪŋ]	Wohlbefinden	= the state of feeling healthy and happy
to **gain** [geɪn]	erwerben; sammeln; erreichen	Teresa **has gained** valuable experience during her internship.
to **volunteer** [,vɒlən'tɪə]	ehrenamtlich arbeiten	**to volunteer** → volunteer → voluntary
benefit ['benɪfɪt]	Vorteil; Nutzen	**benefit** → to benefit
issue ['ɪʃuː]	Frage; Problem	= an important topic that people are discussing
time frame ['taɪm ,freɪm]	Zeitrahmen	They set a **time frame** of four weeks for the project.
preconception [,priːkən'sepʃn]	vorgefasste Meinung	Not all **preconceptions** turn out to be true.
meaningful ['miːnɪŋfl]	sinnvoll; bedeutungsvoll	The words in the card were really **meaningful**. **meaningful** → meaning → to mean
to be aware of sth [,bi‿ə'weər‿əv]	sich einer Sache bewusst sein	I'**m aware of** the dangers of driving. **to be aware of sth** → awareness
to suppose [sə'pəʊz]	vermuten; annehmen	I **suppose** that this new digital teaching tool will be very useful.
to make sense [,meɪk 'sens]	Sinn ergeben; einleuchten	If something **makes sense**, you can understand it.
diet ['daɪət]	Ernährung	A healthy and well-balanced **diet** can improve your fitness.
wardrobe ['wɔːdrəʊb]	hier: Kleidung	His **wardrobe** consists of suits and ties.
racism ['reɪsɪzm]	Rassismus	**racism** → racist
gender equality [,dʒendər‿ɪ'kwɒləti]	Geschlechtergleichstellung	There's still a long way to go before we achieve complete **gender equality**.
to be concerned with sth [,bi kən'sɜːnd wɪð]	sich mit etw. beschäftigen; sich um etw. sorgen	**to be concerned with** = to be occupied with
particularly [pə'tɪkjələli]	besonders	**particularly** = especially
affordable [ə'fɔːdəbl]	bezahlbar	= not too expensive **affordable** → to afford
to **relate to** [rɪ'leɪt tə]	zu tun haben mit; zutreffen auf	1. This text **relates to** the effect of global warming. 2. The new laws mainly **relate to** families. **to relate to** → relation
achievement [ə'tʃiːvmənt]	Leistung; Erfolg	**achievement** → to achieve

Exam skills: Doing mixed reading tasks

relevant ['reləvənt]	wichtig; relevant	**relevant** = important, fitting
to **face** [feɪs]	gegenüber stehen; konfrontiert werden mit	1. They stood **facing** each other. 2. We **are faced** with a serious problem.
to **be the case** [ˌbi ðə 'keɪs]	zutreffen; der Fall sein	**to be the case** = to be true
to **take time off** [ˌteɪk taɪm‿'ɒf]	eine Auszeit nehmen	Lucy **took time off** to take care of her sick mother.
to **shape** [ʃeɪp]	formen; prägen	= to give sth or sb a definite form
internship ['ɪntɜ:nʃɪp]	Praktikum	I did an **internship** at my uncle's company last summer.
frequently [ˌfri:kwəntli]	häufig	**frequently** = often
disagreement [ˌdɪsə'gri:mnt]	Meinungsverschiedenheit; Streit	**disagreement** → to disagree
mental health [ˌmentl 'helθ]	psychische Gesundheit	= the medical condition of your mind
bullying ['bʊliɪŋ]	Mobbing	**Bullying** is a big problem on social media. **bullying** → to bully
advance [əd'va:ns]	Fortschritt; Vorstoß	It's difficult to keep up with the **advances** in technology.
concerning [kən'sɜ:nɪŋ]	bezüglich; hinsichtlich; betreffend	There are some problems **concerning** our new project.
to **be at the forefront** [ˌbi‿ət ðə 'fɔ:frʌnt]	im Vordergrund stehen	**forefront** = front line
degree [dɪ'gri:]	akademischer Grad; Hochschulabschluss	For this job you need a **degree** in biology.
savings plan ['seɪvɪŋz ˌplæn]	Sparplan	**savings** → to save

Text A – Youth culture in a digital age

wit [wɪt]	Scharfsinnigkeit; Verstand; Witz	= the ability to say or write things that are both clever and amusing
to **promote** [prə'məʊt]	werben für	The company **promoted** their new car. **to promote** → promotion
appreciation [əˌpri:ʃi'eɪʃn]	Wertschätzung; Würdigung	**appreciation** → to appreciate
currently ['kʌrəntli]	derzeit; zurzeit; momentan	We **currently** have three placements for EU students.
to **neglect** [nɪ'glekt]	vernachlässigen; außer Acht lassen	The building has become a ruin because its owners **neglected** it.
subscriber [səb'skraɪbə]	Abonnent/-in	I'm a **subscriber** of two really interesting magazines. **subscriber** → to subscribe
spare [speə]	Extra-; übrig	I left a **spare** house key with my neighbour.
appearance [ə'pɪərns]	Aussehen; Erscheinung; Auftritt	**Appearance** is important for actors and models.
to **take notice** [ˌteɪk 'nəʊtɪs]	beachten; zur Kenntnis nehmen; aufmerksam werden	I **took** no **notice** of the signs.
confidence ['kɒnfɪdns]	Vertrauen; Zuversicht	My success gave me **confidence** to write more songs. **confidence** → confident
to **chase** [tʃeɪs]	nachjagen; jagen	= to make an effort to get or win sb/sth
to **raise awareness** [ˌreɪz‿ə'weənəs]	das Bewusstsein schärfen; sensibilisieren für	This film is intended to **raise awareness** about the importance of good hygiene.
to **maintain** [meɪn'teɪn]	aufrechterhalten	The teacher has to **maintain** discipline in the classroom.
conscious ['kɒnʃəs]	bewusst	Becoming a vegetarian was a **conscious** decision.
fame [feɪm]	Ruhm	**fame** → famous

briefly ['bri:fli]	kurz	**briefly** = shortly
to be the centre of attention [ˌbi ðə ˌsentər͜ əv͜ ə'tenʃn]	im Mittelpunkt stehen; Beachtung finden	= to attract the attention of everyone around you
to terrify sb ['terəfaɪ]	jdm. Angst einjagen; jdn. erschrecken	Our neighbours' big black dog **terrifies** me.
escape [ɪ'skeɪp]	Flucht	**escape** → to escape
to be unsure (about) [ˌbi͜ ʌn'ʃɔ:r͜ əˌbaʊt]	sich einer Sache nicht sicher sein	Amy **was unsure about** what to do next.
to retreat [rɪ'tri:t]	sich zurückziehen	The actor **retreated** from public life last year.
to feel empowered [ˌfi:l͜ ɪm'paʊəd]	sich bestärkt fühlen	After completing the confidence training programme, I now **feel empowered** to take on new challenges.
to be supposed to [ˌbi sə'pəʊst tə]	sollen	Teachers **are supposed to** be role models, but this is not always easy.
to remain [rɪ'meɪn]	(übrig) bleiben	After the fire nothing **remained** of the house.
to transition (into) [træn'zɪʃn ˌɪntə]	übergehen; umwandeln	= to go through a process of change
to reveal [rɪ'vi:l]	offenbaren; zeigen	**to reveal** = to show
fault [fɔ:lt]	Fehler	Nobody is perfect, everyone has **faults**.
content ['kɒntent]	Inhalt	This website's **content** has been reviewed by experts.

Text B – Wish we could turn back time

fear [fɪə]	Angst; Furcht; Befürchtung	= The feeling you have when you are scared. **fear** → to fear
insecure [ˌɪnsɪ'kjʊə]	unsicher; verunsichert	**insecure** ↔ self-confident
loan [ləʊn]	Darlehen; Kredit	= amount of money given for a period of time, for example by a bank
the latter [ðə 'lætə]	letztere/-r/-s	= refers to the second of two things or people mentioned
to play pretend [ˌpleɪ prɪ'tend]	so tun als ob	Let's **play pretend** we were rich!
storyboard ['stɔ:ribɔ:d]	Storyboard (Szenenbuch)	A **storyboard** helped the actors film the scene.
frame [freɪm]	hier: Einzelbild eines Films; Rahmen	Each **frame** of the film was perfect.

Skills – Improving your vocabulary

command [kə'mɑ:nd]	Beherrschung; Kenntnis	I have a good **command** of French.
fluent ['flu:ənt]	fließend; flüssig	I'm German, but I can speak English **fluently**.
corresponding [ˌkɒrɪ'spɒndɪŋ]	entsprechend; dazugehörig	They sold fewer books in the **corresponding** period last year.
mutual ['mju:tʃuəl]	gemeinsam; gegenseitig	= sth shared by two or more people
to care (about sth) [keə]	(etw.) wichtig nehmen; sich interessieren (für); sich kümmern (um)	I **care** a lot about my friends. I meet them every weekend.
limited ['lɪmɪtɪd]	begrenzt; beschränkt; limitiert	Only a **limited** amount of tickets will be sold online.
trait [treɪt]	Eigenschaft; Merkmal	Generosity is one of my grandfather's good **traits**. **trait** = feature
profession [prə'feʃn]	Beruf	What **profession** are you in?
graduate ['grædʒuət]	Absolvent/-in	**graduate** → graduation → to graduate
to determine [dɪ'tɜ:mɪn]	bestimmen	In our meeting, we will **determine** the next steps of the project.

Text C – Going your own way

GCSE (General Certificate of Secondary Education) [ˌdʒiːsiːesˈiː]	*allgemeiner Abschluss der weiterführenden Schulen in GB*	Good **GCSEs** are an important qualification for future jobs.
apprenticeship [əˈprentɪsʃɪp]	Ausbildung; Lehre	**apprenticeship** → apprentice
to **set apart** [ˌset‿əˈpɑːt]	(sich) abheben	What **sets** her **apart** from her friends is her young age.
full-time [ˌfʊlˈtaɪm]	Vollzeit-; Ganztags-	**full-time** ↔ part-time
to **be willing to do sth** [ˌbi ˈwɪlɪŋ tə]	bereit sein, etw. zu tun	I'm more than **willing to** help you.
to **commit sth** [kəˈmɪt]	etw. einsetzen	= to invest sth into sth
distraction [dɪˈstrækʃn]	Ablenkung	**distraction** → to distract
engineering [ˌendʒɪˈnɪərɪŋ]	Maschinenbau; Technik	**engineering** → engine → engineer
surrounded by [səˈraʊndɪd baɪ]	umgeben von	He said he was **surrounded by** idiots at the meeting.
to **distribute** [dɪˈstrɪbjuːt]	ausschütten; verteilen	**to distribute** → distribution
entrepreneur [ˌɒntrəprəˈnɜː]	Unternehmer/-in	There are more and more female **entrepreneurs**.
to **launch** [lɔːnʃ]	starten; ins Leben rufen	We **launched** our first product in 2013. **to launch** = to start
approach [əˈprəʊtʃ]	Herangehensweise; Ansatz	= a method of dealing with a situation or a problem **approach** → to approach
leadership [ˈliːdəʃɪp]	Führung; Leitung	**leadership** → to lead → leader
to **recruit** [rɪˈkruːt]	anwerben; einstellen	We need to **recruit** workers to speed up the project. **to recruit** = to employ
expansion [ɪkˈspænʃn]	Erweiterung; Expansion	**expansion** → to expand
aspiring [əˈspaɪrɪŋ]	aufstrebend	= working hard to be successful
to **attend** [əˈtend]	besuchen; teilnehmen; anwesend sein	I cannot **attend**, but I will be with you in spirit.
to **decrease** [dɪˈkriːs]	sinken; zurückgehen	The United Nations is working to **decrease** hunger and poverty in the world. **to decrease** ↔ to increase

Exam skills – Material-based writing

to **quote** [kwəʊt]	zitieren	**to quote** → quotation
to **contain** [kənˈteɪn]	enthalten	Chocolate **contains** a lot of calories.
voter turnout [ˌvəʊtə ˈtɜːnaʊt]	Wahlbeteiligung	= the number of people that vote in an election
opponent [əˈpəʊnənt]	Gegner/-in	After the game, the chess player shook hands with his **opponent**.
mature [məˈtjʊə]	reif; erwachsen	Your behaviour isn't very **mature**. Sometimes you act like a baby!
to **argue** [ˈɑːgjuː]	behaupten; erörtern	I would **argue** that wealth is not as important as health.
to **form** [fɔːm]	formen; bilden	The two countries **formed** an alliance to protect their interests.
engagement [ɪnˈgeɪdʒmənt]	aktive Beteiligung	= the state of being actively interested in sth **engagement** → to engage in
to **harm** [hɑːm]	schädigen; schaden	**to harm** = to hurt; to damage
to **contradict** [ˌkɒntrəˈdɪkt]	widersprechen; widerlegen	**to contradict** ↔ to agree; to support
to **take into account** [teɪk ˌɪntʊ‿əˈkaʊnt]	berücksichtigen; in Betracht ziehen	A good project manager **takes** all factors **into account**. **to take into account** = to consider
to **state** [steɪt]	angeben; darstellen	**to state** → statement

D3 Topic 2 Attitude to life

Getting started

merely ['mɪəli]	nur; lediglich	These pills **merely** stop the pain. You still need to go to the doctor.
relation [rɪ'leɪʃn]	Verhältnis; Beziehung	I don't understand what this question is in **relation** to the topic.
revenue ['revnju:]	Ertrag; Einnahmen	Government **revenues** rose by 2% last year because of the higher tax rate.
nutrition [nju:'trɪʃn]	Ernährung	There are alternative sources of **nutrition** to meat from animals.
weight [weɪt]	Gewicht	The **weight** of 1 litre of water is 1 kilo.
anxiety [æŋ'zaɪəti]	Angst; Unruhe	**anxiety** = fear; worry **anxiety** → anxious
barely ['beəli]	kaum	She could **barely** breathe because she was so scared. **barely** = hardly
solitude ['sɒlɪtju:d]	Einsamkeit	= the state of being alone
to escape [ɪ'skeɪp]	entkommen; fliehen; flüchten	To **escape** her solitude, she started travelling with groups. = to run away from sth or sb
concern [kən'sɜ:n]	Sorge	Their major **concern** was the financing of the project. **concern** → to be concerned
cure [kjʊə]	Heilung	The doctor did her best but she didn't find a **cure** for my illness.
petrified ['petrɪfaɪd]	gelähmt; versteinert	When I got the bad news, I was **petrified**.
to feel at ease [ˌfi:l‿ət 'i:z]	sich wohl fühlen	It is important to **feel at ease** with your therapist.
stimulus, stimuli *(pl)* ['stɪmjələs, 'stɪmjəlaɪ]	Stimulus; Reiz	Foreign investment has been a **stimulus** to the industry.
to take the plunge [ˌteɪk ðə 'plʌndʒ]	den Sprung wagen	= to finally decide to do sth you've been thinking about for a long time
to prompt sb to do sth [prɒmpt]	jdn. veranlassen, etw. zu tun	That wasn't very polite! What **prompted you to** say that? = to make sb do sth
to subside [səb'saɪd]	nachlassen; abklingen	My headache began to **subside** after about 8 hours and was gone the next morning.
boundary ['baʊndri]	Grenze	The river Rhine is part of the **boundary** between Germany and France. **boundary** = border
reward [rɪ'wɔ:d]	Belohnung	Missing dog! £1,000 **reward**!

Text A – Diet and nutrition

to visualise ['vɪʒulaɪz]	veranschaulichen	**to visualise** → visual
plant-based [plɑ:nt'beɪst]	pflanzenbasiert	The restaurant offers meat and **plant-based** burgers.
previous ['pri:viəs]	früher; vorherig	the **previous** night = the night before
to reveal [rɪ'vi:l]	aufzeigen; preisgeben	Her facial expression **revealed** what she really felt.
dairy product ['deəri ˌprɒdʌkt]	Milchprodukt	= a product made from cow's milk

launch [lɔ:nʃ]	Markteinführung; Start	The **launch** of the new system is announced for next month. **launch** → to launch
all-time high [ˌɔ:ltaɪm 'haɪ]	Rekordhöhe	The price for petrol is at an **all-time high** because of the crisis in the Middle East.
credibility [ˌkredə'bɪləti]	Glaubwürdigkeit	After openly lying about his political motives, he lost all his **credibility**.
range [reɪndʒ]	Sortiment; Palette; Angebot	The car dealer has a huge **range** of models to choose from.
to **stock** [stɒk]	führen; vorrätig haben	The shop **stocks** men's and women's clothing.
counterpart ['kaʊntəpɑ:t]	Gegenstück; Entsprechung	An email is the digital **counterpart** of a letter.
collaboration [kəˌlæb'reɪʃn]	Zusammenarbeit	**collaboration** → to collaborate

Text B – Being mindful

mindful ['maɪndfl]	achtsam	We must be **mindful** of the consequences of our actions. **mindful** → mindfulness
to **target** ['tɑ:gɪt]	zielen auf; anpeilen	**to target** = to aim at
provision [prə'vɪʒn]	Bereitstellung	**provision** → to provide
curriculum, curricula *(pl)* [kə'rɪkjələm, kə'rɪkjələ]	Lehrplan	English and French are the two foreign languages on the school **curriculum**.
overwhelmed [ˌəʊvə'welmd]	überwältigt; hier: überfordert	We were **overwhelmed** by the response to our advert.
to **cope (with)** ['kəʊp wɪð]	zurechtkommen (mit); schaffen	= to be able to deal with sth difficult
to **perceive** [pə'si:v]	wahrnehmen	The discovery **was perceived** as a major breakthrough. **to perceive** → perception
to **be exposed to sth/sb** [ˌbi ɪk'spəʊzd tə]	jdm./etw. ausgesetzt sein	This part of the coast **is** very **exposed to** Atlantic winds.
to **spot** [spɒt]	erkennen; wahrnehmen	I **spotted** a mistake in his presentation.
to **intervene** [ˌɪntə'vi:n]	eingreifen	The teacher **intervened** in the students' argument. **to intervene** → intervention
to **equip sb with sth** [ɪ'kwɪp wɪð]	jdn. mit etw. ausstatten; jdn. mit etw. versehen	Each of our holiday apartments **is equipped** for four people. **to equip** → equipment
first aid kit [fɜ:st ˈeɪd kɪt]	Erstehilfekasten	= a box containing equipment needed to give medical help in an emergency
outburst ['aʊtbɜ:st]	Ausbruch; Anfall	**outburst** of anger/laughter
to **embrace sth** [ɪm'breɪs]	einschließen; aufgreifen	Couples usually learn to **embrace** their differences.
to **combat** ['kɒmbæt]	bekämpfen	**to combat** = to fight
self-perception [ˌselfpə'sepʃn]	Selbstbild; Selbstwahrnehmung	= the way you see yourself
authorities *(pl)* [ɔ:'θɒrətiz]	Behörden	local **authorities**, to report sb to the **authorities**
to **implement** ['ɪmplɪment]	einführen	**to implement** → implementation
emphasis ['emfəsɪs]	Betonung	= special or extra importance that is given to sth **emphasis** → to emphasise
adolescence [ˌædə'lesns]	Jugend	**Adolescence** is the period of your life in which you develop from being a child into being an adult.

Skills – Working with listening texts

challenging ['tʃælɪndʒɪŋ]	herausfordernd; schwierig	**challenging** → a challenge
to address [ə'dres]	angehen	**to address** a problem = to tackle a problem
to exercise ['eksəsaɪz]	trainieren; Sport treiben	**Excercise** regularly and you will feel a lot less stressed!
measure ['meʒə]	Maßnahme	The **measures** we have taken are designed to prevent bad accidents.
vending machine ['vendɪŋ mə,ʃi:n]	Verkaufsautomat	= an automat that sells food, drinks, cigarettes etc.
track and field [,træk‿ən 'fi:ld]	Leichtathletik	**Track and field** comprises the disciplines running, jumping and throwing.
to tackle (an issue) [,tækl‿ən‿'ɪʃu:]	(ein Problem) angehen	= to fight against (a problem)
device [dɪ'vaɪs]	Gerät	You find electronic **devices** in every household.
to bother ['bɒðə]	stören; belästigen	Sorry to **bother** you, but I need your help.
pattern ['pætn]	Muster	1. The way in which sth is done or repeated. 2. A design of lines, colours, shapes etc.
implication [,ɪmplɪ'keɪʃn]	Auswirkung; Folge	**implication** = consequence
sedentary ['sedntri]	sitzend	Most of my friends have **sedentary** jobs in offices.
potential [pə'tenʃl]	Potenzial; Möglichkeit	The **potential** of wind energy is still not fully exploited.
flip side ['flɪpsaɪd]	Kehrseite	You should take a look at the **flip side** of every decision.

Text C – The teachings of dark places

to associate with [ə'səʊʃieɪt wɪð]	in Verbindung bringen mit; verbinden mit	Many people **associate** Florida **with** sunshine.
essentially [ɪ'senʃli]	im Wesentlichen; im Großen und Ganzen	**Essentially**, I agree with you.
genocide ['dʒenəsaɪd]	Genozid; Völkermord	= the intentional murder of a whole community or ethnic group
to be bound to (do sth) [,bi 'baʊnd tə]	zwangsläufig (etw. tun)	If you don't work for school, you**'re bound to** fail.
to dedicate ['dedɪkeɪt]	widmen	The writer **has dedicated** her first book to her daughter.
memorial [mə'mɔ:riəl]	Denkmal; Gedenkstätte	The **memorial** commemorates all the soldiers who died in World War I.
to put sth on display [,pʊt‿ɒn dɪs'pleɪ]	etw. ausstellen; etw. zur Schau stellen	They **put on display** all the models of the new building. **to put on display** = to display
corpse [kɔ:ps]	Leiche	**corpse** = dead body
unbearable [ʌn'beərəbl]	unerträglich	The heat was **unbearable**.
to accompany [ə'kʌmpəni]	begleiten	If you **accompany** people, you go somewhere with them.
with regard to [,wɪð rɪ'gɑ:d‿tə]	in Bezug auf	**With regard to** the new contract, we have some questions. **with regard to** = concerning
to insist (on) [ɪn'sɪst‿ɒn]	bestehen auf; beharren auf	Are you sure it's OK for us to stay in your apartment in New York? – Absolutely. I **insist**!
to pursue [pə'sju:]	verwirklichen; verfolgen	to **pursue** a plan/a strategy = to try to make sth come true
stunning ['stʌnɪŋ]	atemberaubend; überwältigend	The view from the top of the mountain was simply **stunning**.

genuine ['dʒenjuɪn]	echt; ehrlich	If this offer is **genuine**, I will gladly accept it. **genuine** = real
misery ['mɪzri]	Elend; Armseligkeit	**misery** ↔ luck
ultimately ['ʌltɪmətli]	letztendlich	**ultimately** = finally
essential [ɪ'senʃl]	notwendig; wesentlich	**essential** ↔ unnecessary
skull [skʌl]	Schädel	= bones of the head that protect and surround the brain
confusion [kən'fju:ʒn]	Verwirrung	**confusion** → confused
grown-up [ˌgrəʊn‿'ʌp]	Erwachsene/-r	**grown-up** = adult **grown-up** → to grow up
to **bury** ['beri]	begraben	He has **buried** all his hopes for a position in management.
reassurance [ˌri:ə'ʃʊərns]	Beruhigung; Versicherung	**reassurance** → to reassure
remnant ['remnənt]	Überrest; Relikt	= sth that is left over (*here:* from another time)
supply [sə'plaɪ]	Versorgung; Vorrat	= food and equipment needed for a trip or (military) campaign **supply** → supplier → to supply
to **be under siege** [ˌbi‿ʌndə 'si:dʒ]	belagert werden	We must do everything possible to help the people **under siege**.
to **preserve** [prɪ'zɜ:v]	bewahren; erhalten	**to preserve** → preservation
possession *(no pl)* [pə'zeʃn]	Besitz	She was arrested for the **possession** of drugs. **possession** → to possess
desperate ['desprət]	verzweifelt; hoffnungslos	He was **desperate** when he lost his key and couldn't get back into the house.
to **dig** [dɪg]	graben	Grandpa **dug** in the sand to find the treasure. **to dig, dug, dug**
wreck [rek]	Wrack	Diving the **wreck** of the old ship was a fantastic experience.
naval mine [ˌneɪvl 'maɪn]	Seemine	**naval** = sea
to **attach** [ə'tætʃ]	anbringen; anhängen	**Attach** labels to things before you give them away.
descent [dɪ'sent]	Abstieg	**descent** ↔ rise **descent** → to descend
casualty ['kæʒjuəlti]	Todesopfer; Verletzte/-r	= a person who is killed or injured in an accident or war
shelter ['ʃeltə]	Schutz; Obdach	When the storm started, we found **shelter** in an old barn. **shelter** → to shelter
eerie ['ɪəri]	unheimlich	= strange and frightening
decay *(no pl)* [dɪ'keɪ]	Verfall	The abandoned house quickly fell into a state of **decay**.
random ['rændəm]	zufällig	The order of events in the film seemed totally **random**.
to **allocate** ['æləkeɪt]	zuteilen	Tickets will **be allocated** to those who apply first.
to **classify** ['klæsɪfaɪ]	klassifizieren; einordnen	= to put into or be in a particular class or group **to classify** → classification
relocation [ˌri:lə'keɪʃn]	Umsiedlung	**Relocation** means that people are moved from one place to another.
noose [nu:s]	Schlinge	to have a **noose** around one's neck = a circular loop at the end of a piece of rope
execution [ˌeksɪ'kju:ʃn]	Hinrichtung	= the carrying out or undergoing of a sentence of death **execution** → to execute

Writing – Benefits of volunteering

to **refer to sth** [rɪ'fɜː‿tə]	sich auf etw. beziehen	During her talk, she **referred to** a recent trip to Canada. **to refer to** → reference

Exam skills – Having a group discussion

shore [ʃɔː]	Ufer; Küste	Let's swim to the rock and then back to the **shore**.
to **defend** [dɪ'fend]	verteidigen	The members of the committee **defended** their decision. **to defend** → defence
to **persuade** [pə'sweɪd]	überreden; überzeugen	Jay wants to **persuade** his brother to come with them.
to **balance** ['bæləns]	ausgleichen; abwägen	We have to **balance** the costs of the project against the benefits.

D4
Topic 3 The world of work

Getting started

occupation [ˌɒkjə'peɪʃn]	Beruf; Beschäftigung; Tätigkeit	**occupation** = job; profession
leisure time ['leʒə taɪm]	Freizeit	**leisure time** = free time
automation *(no pl)* [ˌɔːtə'meɪʃn]	Automatisierung	There are fears that **automation** will produce a lot of unemployment.
gig economy ['gɪg‿ɪˌkɒnəmi]	auf Freiberuflern/ Freiberuflerinnen basierendes Wirtschaftsmodell	= a job market which consists of short-term or part-time work done by people who are self-employed or on temporary contracts
replacement [rɪ'pleɪsmənt]	Ersatz	When the music teacher left, the school had to find a **replacement** for her. **replacement** → to replace
remuneration [rɪˌmjuːnr'eɪʃn]	Bezahlung; Lohn	**remuneration** = payment; income; salary
invisible [ɪn'vɪzəbl]	unsichtbar	If something becomes **invisible**, you can't see it any more. **invisible** ↔ visible
barrier ['bæriə]	Barriere; Hindernis	Duties and taxes are the most obvious **barrier** to free trade.
to **prevent** [prɪ'vent]	verhindern; abhalten	A thunderstorm **prevented** me from sleeping last night.
beyond [bi'ɒnd]	über hinaus	What you have done goes above and **beyond** the task you were given.
hierarchy ['haɪrɑːki]	Rangordnung; Hierarchie	**hierarchy** → hierarchical
lecture ['lektʃə]	Vorlesung; Vortrag	The professor gave a very interesting **lecture**.
contradiction [ˌkɒntrə'dɪkʃn]	Widerspruch; Widersprüchlichkeit	= sth that is contrary or inconsistent to itself or its own logical basis
to **collaborate** [kə'læbreɪt]	zusammenarbeiten	**to collaborate** → collaboration
deduction [dɪ'dʌkʃn]	Abzug; Kürzung	**deduction** ↔ addition
retail *(no pl)* ['riːteɪl]	Einzelhandel	= the sale of goods to consumers
food bank ['fuːd ˌbæŋk]	Lebensmittelausgabe; Tafel	= a charity organisation that collects and distributes food
to **operate** ['ɒpreɪt]	bedienen; steuern	If you **operate** a machine, you make it do its work. **to operate** → operator

intervention [ˌɪntəˈvenʃn]	Eingriff; Intervention	military/political **intervention** **intervention** → to intervene
preference [ˈprefrns]	Vorliebe	**preference** → to prefer → preferable
to commit to sth [kəˈmɪt tə]	sich zu etw. verpflichten	Many people voluntarily **commit to** social projects. **to commit to** → commitment
to be outdated [ˌbi‿aʊtˈdeɪtɪd]	von gestern sein; altmodisch oder rückständig sein	**outdated** = old-fashioned **outdated** ↔ up-to-date
promotion [prəˈməʊʃn]	Beförderung	= being given a more important job or rank in the organisation that you work for **promotion** → to promote
to intimidate [ɪnˈtɪmɪdeɪt]	einschüchtern	Jim **was intimidated** by all the new technologies.
trade union [ˌtreɪd ˈjuːnjən]	Gewerkschaft	= an organisation that has been formed by workers in order to represent their rights and interests to their employers
to acquire [əˈkwaɪə]	aneignen; erwerben	He **has acquired** a reputation as this country's best violinist. **to acquire** = to purchase; to gain
gain [geɪn]	Gewinn; Zunahme	= an increase in size, amount etc. **gain** → to gain

Text A – Important job skills

to **graduate** [ˈgrædʒueɪt]	einen Abschluss erlangen; abschließen	= to finish one's education; to get a degree **to graduate** → a graduate
competency [ˈkɒmpɪtnsi]	Fähigkeit; Kompetenz	to have **competency** in a language/as a manager **competency** → competent
core skill [ˌkɔː ˈskɪl]	Kernkompetenz; grundlegende Fähigkeit	**core skill** = basic competence
to **compete (with/against)** [kəmˈpiːt]	konkurrieren (mit); sich messen (mit); hier: sich schlagen	**to compete (with/against)** → competition
concise [kənˈsaɪs]	präzise; kurz	= short, to the point
to **resolve issues** [rɪˌzɒlv‿ˈɪʃuːz]	Probleme lösen	Our friendly support staff helps you **to resolve** any technical **issues** that might occur.
to **assign** [əˈsaɪn]	zuweisen; zuordnen	When teachers **assign** homework, students usually feel an obligation to do it. **to assign** → assignment
to **set a deadline** [ˌset‿ə ˈdedlaɪn]	eine Frist setzen; einen Termin festlegen	= to set a time or date before which a particular task must be finished or a particular thing must be done
resilience [rɪˈzɪliəns]	Widerstandsfähigkeit	**resilience** → resilient
to **enable** [ɪˈneɪbl]	ermöglichen; befähigen	My job **enables** me to have enough free time for sport. **to enable** → ability
to **assess** [əˈses]	beurteilen	**to assess** = to evaluate
gap in the market [ˌgæp‿ɪn ðə ˈmɑːkɪt]	Marktlücke	to spot/fill a **gap in the market**
enterprise [ˈentəpraɪz]	unternehmerisch; Unternehmens-	**enterprise** skills/culture **enterprise** → entrepreneur
business acumen [ˌbɪznɪs‿ˈækjəmən]	Geschäftssinn; Geschäftstüchtigkeit	= the ability to make good judgments and quick decisions in business situations
perseverance [ˌpɜːsəˈvɪərns]	Ausdauer; Beharrlichkeit	= the quality of continuing with something even though it is difficult
to **suit** [suːt]	passen zu; stehen	Yellow clothes don't **suit** him.

to **adjust to** [ə'dʒʌst tə]	anpassen an; einstellen auf	This solution can be easily **adjusted to** our needs.
appointment [ə'pɔɪntmənt]	Termin; Verabredung	= arrangement to meet sb at a particular time and place

Text B – Modern slavery

harvest ['hɑ:vɪst]	Ernte	good/poor **harvest**, apple **harvest**
thorn [θɔ:n]	Dorn(e)	Roses usually have **thorns**.
garment ['gɑ:mənt]	Bekleidung; Kleidungsstück	Whenever my friend finds a **garment** that she doesn't wear any more, she gives it to a local charity. = a piece of clothing
outsourcing ['aʊtsɔ:sɪŋ]	Outsourcing (Ausgliederung von Produktions- oder Dienstleistungen an Externe)	The CEO decided that **outsourcing** was the only solution to avoid bankruptcy.
overseas [ˌəʊvə'si:z]	im Ausland; in Übersee	Lara left her home country to live **overseas** ten years ago.
construction [kən'strʌkʃn]	Bau; Baugewerbe	My parents both work in **construction**: my dad is an engineer, my mum is an architect.
apparel [ə'pærl]	Bekleidung	sports/women's/men's **apparel** **apparel** = clothing
to **survey** [sə'veɪ]	anschauen; überblicken	= to take a general or comprehensive view at sth
permit ['pɜ:mɪt]	Erlaubnis	work/hunting **permit** **permit** → to permit
legal status [ˌli:gl 'steɪtəs]	Aufenthaltstitel	The **legal status** shows if a person has the right to live in a certain place.
to **extend** [ɪk'stend]	ausstrecken	**to extend** → extension
palm [pɑ:m]	Handfläche	= the area of your hand between fingers and thumb
to **obey** [ə'beɪ]	gehorchen; befolgen	If you **obey** orders, you do what you've been told to do.
void [vɔɪd]	ungültig; nichtig	= to have no value **void** ↔ valid
to **deport** [dɪ'pɔ:t]	ausweisen	= to make sb leave the country against their will **to deport** → deportation
to **borrow** ['bɒrəʊ]	(sich) ausleihen	Can I **borrow** this T-shirt? – OK, but please remember to give it back.
fate [feɪt]	Schicksal	Hailey doesn't believe in **fate** because she thinks we have the power to make our own choices.
to **withdraw from** [wɪð'drɔ: frəm]	herausziehen aus	**to withdraw** = to remove; to pull out
tense [tens]	angespannt; verkrampft	**tense** ↔ relaxed **tense** → tension
mosque [mɒsk]	Moschee	**mosque** – church – synagogue = a house for worship and prayers
facility [fə'sɪlɪti]	Einrichtung	The outdoor **facilities** at the hotel were huge.
to **be at sb's mercy** [ˌbi‿ət sʌmbədiz 'mɜ:si]	jdm. ausgeliefert sein	The festival **was at the mercy of** the weather.
exploitation [ˌeksplɔɪ'teɪʃn]	Ausbeutung	**exploitation** → to exploit

Text C – Automating healthcare

nursing home ['nɜ:sɪŋ ˌhəʊm]	Pflegeheim	**nursing** → nurse
to **age** [eɪdʒ]	altern	He had always looked so young, but he seemed to **have aged** in the last few months. **to age** → age
to **shrink** [ʃrɪŋk]	schrumpfen	**to shrink** = to get smaller to **shrink**, **shrank**, **shrunk**
to **stroll** [strəʊl]	schlendern	= to walk slowly, in a relaxed manner
to **complement** ['kɒmplɪmənt]	ergänzen	Strawberries and cream **complement** each other perfectly. **to complement** → complementary
suburban [sə'bɜ:bn]	Vorstadt-	**Suburban** houses often have lots of space. **suburban** → a suburb
selling point ['selɪŋ pɔɪnt]	Verkaufsargument	Its great **selling point** among comparable products is its price.
dozen ['dʌzn]	Dutzend	= twelve of sth
waist [weɪst]	Bauch; Taille	These trousers are too small, or my **waist** is too big!
to **ease** [i:z]	erleichtern; vereinfachen	I gave him some pills to **ease** the pain. **to ease** → easy
severe [sɪ'vɪə]	stark; schlimm	**severe** = serious
lack of ['læk‿əv]	Mangel an	The children are suffering from a serious **lack of** vitamins.
deployment [dɪ'plɔɪmənt]	Verwendung; Einsatz	The **deployment** of these technologies is the way forward. **deployment** → to deploy
to **be in sb's favour** [ˌbi‿ɪn 'feɪvə]	jds. Vorteil sein	If something is **in your favour**, it helps you or gives you an advantage.
reluctant [rɪ'lʌktnt]	widerwillig; widerstrebend	I was **reluctant** to tell my parents what had happened, but they helped me.
pile [paɪl]	Stapel; Haufen	In my brother's room there's always a **pile** of clothes on the floor.
automotive engineer [ɔ:təˌməʊtɪv‿endʒɪ'nɪə]	Fahrzeugingenieur/-in	= sb who designs, tests and develops cars
social science [ˌsəʊʃl 'saɪəns]	Sozialwissenschaft	= the study of how humans interrelate in societies
to have an affinity [ˌhæv‿ən‿ə'fɪnəti]	eine Neigung haben; sich verbunden fühlen	She loves the city but **has an affinity** to country life as well.
to witness ['wɪtnəs]	beobachten; miterleben	They looked for a good place with a view to **witness** the fireworks later that night.
vehicle ['vɪəkl]	Fahrzeug	Cars, trains, bikes and tractors are **vehicles**.
inconceivable [ˌɪnkən'si:vəbl]	nicht vorstellbar	**inconceivable** = unbelievable
to occupy ['ɒkjəpaɪ]	füllen; einnehmen	*here:* **to fill**
to hamper ['hæmpə]	hindern; behindern	During the job interview he **was hampered** by a lack of self-confidence.
to elaborate on sth [ɪ'læbreɪt‿ɒn]	etw. näher ausführen	= to explain sth in detail
chore [tʃɔ:]	(lästige) Pflicht; Routinearbeit	You can go shopping when you've done your **chores**.
obsolete ['ɒbsli:t]	veraltet; überholt	**obsolete** ↔ modern; up-to-date

uncertainty [ʌn'sɜ:tnti]	Unsicherheit	There is always some **uncertainty** when you start a new job. **uncertainty** → uncertain
considerable [kən'sɪdrəbl]	beträchtlich	= great in amount or degree **considerable** → to consider
anonymous [ə'nɒnɪməs]	anonym	**anonymous** → anonymity
abusive [ə'bju:sɪv]	beleidigend; ausfällig	He's a nice guy, but sometimes his language is very **abusive**.

Writing – Working from home

thesis, theses *(pl)* ['θi:səs; 'θi:si:z]	These; Behauptung	= an idea or theory that is expressed as a statement and is discussed in a logical way
to **work remotely** [ˌwɜ:k rɪ'məʊtli]	aus der Ferne arbeiten	= to work from home or some other place that is not at the company

Discussion – Planning your career

paramedic [ˌpærə'medɪk]	Sanitäter/-in	**Paramedics** often help at accidents.
aspiration [ˌæspɪ'reɪʃn]	Bestrebung; Sehnsucht	I don't have any political **aspirations**.

D5
Topic 4 The digital age

Getting started

innocent ['ɪnəsnt]	unschuldig	**innocent** → innocence
guilty ['gɪlti]	schuldig	I didn't feel **guilty** because I hadn't done anything wrong.
issue ['ɪʃu:]	hier: Thema	**issue** = topic
to **surround** [sə'raʊnd]	umgeben	Our school **is surrounded** by a fence. = to be all around sth
to **depend (on)** [dɪ'pend‿ɒn]	abhängen (von)	I'm not sure what we'll do tomorrow. It will **depend on** the weather.
rapid ['ræpɪd]	schnell; rapide	**rapid** = quick
to **doubt** [daʊt]	zweifeln; bezweifeln	He says he loves me, but I **doubt** that. = if you are not sure whether sth is true or not
to **convey** [kən'veɪ]	vermitteln; wiedergeben; übertragen	The descriptions of nature in the text **convey** the atmosphere to the reader.
device [dɪ'vaɪs]	Gerät	You find electronic **devices** in every household.
to **provide** [prə'vaɪd]	geben; bereitstellen	**to provide** = to give
to **affect** [ə'fekt]	beeinflussen; betreffen	**to affect** = to influence
accessible [ək'sesəbl]	zugänglich	The museum is wheelchair **accessible**. **accessible** → accessibility → to access
with the advent of [ˌwɪð ði‿'ædvent‿əv]	mit dem Aufkommen der/des	**advent** = appearance; arrival
means *(pl only)* [mi:nz]	Mittel	The internet has become the most important **means** of mass communication very quickly.
within [wɪ'ðɪn]	innerhalb	**within** the country/a few years = inside the limits of sth
decade ['dekeɪd]	Jahrzehnt	= ten years

image ['ɪmɪdʒ]	Bild; Abbildung	Different jobs have different **images**, but the **image** isn't always the same thing as reality.
news item ['nju:z‿aɪtəm]	Nachrichtenmeldung	The next **news item** was a report on the presidential election.
to distribute [dɪ'strɪbju:t]	verteilen; ausschütten	**to distribute** → distribution

Text A – A different way of life

ordinary ['ɔ:dnri]	gewöhnlich; normal	= not unusual or different in any way
adolescence [ˌædə'lesns]	Jugend	**Adolescence** is the period of your life in which you develop from being a child into being an adult.
to **purchase** ['pɜ:tʃəs]	kaufen; erwerben	**to purchase** = to buy
name badge ['neɪm ˌbædʒ]	Namensschild	The nurse was wearing a **name badge**.
rocky ['rɒki]	steinig; hier: holprig	**rocky** → rock
to **offend** [ə'fend]	beleidigen; verletzen	It really **offends** me when you talk about me behind my back.
to **conduct research** [kənˌdʌkt rɪ'sɜ:tʃ]	eine Recherche durchführen	**to conduct** = to carry out; to execute
in stock [ɪn 'stɒk]	vorrätig	We have all the latest styles **in stock**.
to **recall** [rɪ'kɔ:l]	sich erinnern	**to recall** = to remember
to **expire** [ɪk'spaɪə]	ablaufen; auslaufen; enden	= to come to an end or to be no longer valid
to **assume** [ə'sju:m]	annehmen	You can't **assume** everybody shares your likes and dislikes.
to **remind sb of sb/sth** [rɪ'maɪnd‿əv]	jdn. an jdn./etw. erinnern	I almost forgot the meeting. Fortunately, Jane **reminded** me **of** it.
to **tip** [tɪp]	Trinkgeld geben	Before you leave a café, it's normal to **tip** the waiter or waitress. **to tip** → tip
incident ['ɪnsɪdnt]	Vorfall; Ereignis	There was a dangerous **incident** at work.

Text B – The power of images

to **shape** [ʃeɪp]	formen; prägen	**to shape** = to form **to shape** → shape
to **approach** [ə'prəʊtʃ]	(sich) nähern; annähern	Little children shouldn't **approach** strangers. **to approach** → approach
beyond [bi'ɒnd]	über hinaus	What you have done goes above and **beyond** the task you were given.
increasingly [ɪn'kri:sɪŋli]	zunehmend	Young people's lives are being **increasingly** shaped by social media.
to **derive from** [dɪ'raɪv frəm]	seinen Ursprung haben in	Where is this name **derived from**? **to derive from** = to come from
surveillance *(no pl)* [sɜ:'veɪləns]	Überwachung	**surveillance** = observation
suspect ['sʌspekt]	Verdächtige/-r	= a person who the police or authorities think may be guilty of a crime **suspect** → to suspect
target ['tɑ:gɪt]	Ziel	Who is the **target** group of this advertisement?
fundamentally [ˌfʌndə'mentli]	grundlegend	**fundamentally** = radically
crucial ['kru:ʃl]	entscheidend; äußerst wichtig	**crucial** = very important; essential
inevitable [ɪ'nevɪtəbl]	unvermeidlich	= sth that cannot be prevented or avoided

to **circulate** ['sɜ:kjəleɪt]	kursieren; in Umlauf sein	Anonymous leaflets **have been circulating** in town. **to circulate** = to spread
instantly ['ɪnstəntli]	sofort	**instantly** = immediately
key aspect ['ki: ˌæspekt]	Kernpunkt	A **key aspect** of her work is the development of intercultural projects.
to **range from ... to** ['reɪndʒ frəm ... tə]	reichen von ... bis	The students **range** in age **from** 16 **to** 19.
perception [pə'sepʃn]	Wahrnehmung	**perception** → to perceive
division [dɪ'vɪʒn]	Teilung; Aufteilung	There's a big **division** between rich and poor people in our country. **division** → to divide
to **deceive sb** [dɪ'si:v]	jdn. täuschen	He **has deceived** us all!
to **reveal** [rɪ'vi:l]	enthüllen; aufzeigen	**to reveal** = to show
assumption [ə'sʌmʃn]	Vermutung; Annahme	**assumption** → to assume
to **reinforce** [ˌri:ɪn'fɔ:s]	bekräftigen; verstärken	This latest film **reinforces** his status as a great actor. **to reinforce** → force
memorable ['memrəbl]	einprägsam; unvergesslich	**memorable** → memory

Text C – Welcome to a smarter world

GPS receiver [ˌdʒi:pi:'es rɪˌsi:və]	GPS-Empfänger	**GPS** = Global Positioning System
wifi ['waɪfaɪ]	WLAN	Many bars and restaurants try to attract guests with free **wifi**.
to **register** ['redʒɪstə]	registrieren	If you want to receive information from us please **register** here.
to **pour** [pɔ:]	gießen; einschenken	= to make a substance flow from a container into another container
record ['rekɔ:d]	Aufzeichnungen; Protokoll	**record** = document; file; register
meter ['mi:tə]	(Verbrauchs-)Zähler	= a device that measures and records information such as your electricity consumption
decrease ['di:kri:s]	Abnahme; Verminderung	**decrease** ↔ increase
electricity use [ˌelɪk'trɪsəti ˌju:s]	Energieverbrauch	Since we have had the new freezer, our **electricity use** has gone down significantly.
to **unplug** [ʌn'plʌg]	abstöpseln; ausstecken	**to unplug** ↔ to plug in
to **detect** [dɪ'tekt]	feststellen; entdecken	**to detect** = to discover
license plate *(AE)* ['laɪsns ˌpleɪt]	Nummernschild	= a plate showing a vehicle's registration number
to **notify** ['nəʊtɪfaɪ]	benachrichtigen; verständigen	= to officially tell sb about sth
pace [peɪs]	Geschwindigkeit; Tempo	The **pace** of life has increased.
insurance [ɪn'ʃʊərns]	Versicherung	My dad works at an **insurance** company.
in an instant [ˌɪn‿ən‿'ɪnstənt]	sofort	**in an instant** = immediately
commute [kə'mju:t]	Pendelstrecke	**commute** → commuter → to commute
mutual ['mju:tʃuəl]	gemeinsam	= sth shared by two or more people
to **debit** ['debɪt]	vom Konto abbuchen	When your bank **debits** your account, money is taken from it and paid to someone else.
to **trace** [treɪs]	verfolgen; nachverfolgen	Through online access he could **trace** all his credit card payments. **to trace** → trace

to **monitor** ['mɒnɪtə]	überwachen	= to check on a regular basis
to **bother** ['bɒðə]	sich die Mühe machen	He didn't even **bother** to help me.

Writing – Is TV necessary?

inappropriate [ˌɪnə'prəʊpriət]	unangemessen; unpassend	**inappropriate** = unsuitable **inappropriate** ↔ appropriate
habit ['hæbɪt]	Gewohnheit	People have good **habits** and bad **habits**.

Discussion – Doing without media

to **aim** [eɪm]	anstreben; abzielen auf	What do you **aim** to do in life? **to aim** → aim

D6 Topic 5 Diversity in society

Getting started

diversity [daɪ'vɜ:səti]	Unterschiedlichkeit; Vielfalt	**diversity** → diverse
aspiration [ˌæspɪ'reɪʃn]	Bestreben; Ehrgeiz	= a strong desire to achieve sth, such as success **aspiration** → to aspire
outlook ['aʊtlʊk]	Perspektive; Prognose	= a forecast of the future
to come to mind [ˌkʌm tə 'maɪnd]	in den Sinn kommen; einfallen	The idea of a common lingua franca **comes to mind** when one considers the many languages spoken in Europe.
to **deny** [dɪ'naɪ]	leugnen	If you **deny** something, you say it isn't true.
uncommon [ʌn'kɒmən]	ungewöhnlich	**uncommon** ↔ common
ethnic ['eθnɪk]	ethnisch; Volks-	What's your **ethnic** background? – I'm half German and half Spanish.
ethnicity [eθ'nɪsəti]	Ethnie; ethnische Zugehörigkeit	Unfortunately, many companies still discriminate based on **ethnicity**. **ethnicity** → ethnic
to reflect [rɪ'flekt]	widerspiegeln	= to give an image of sb/sth
Supreme Court [su:ˌpri:m 'kɔ:t]	Oberster Gerichtshof (der USA)	= highest federal court of law in the US
mutual ['mju:tuəl]	gegenseitig	The city wanted to fight discrimination and therefore promoted fairness, cooperation and **mutual** respect.
hate crime ['heɪt ˌkraɪm]	Verbrechen aus Hass; Hasskriminalität	= hostility towards members of certain groups
to embrace [ɪm'breɪs]	hier: akzeptieren; annehmen	*here:* to accept willingly
uncertain [ʌn'sɜ:tn]	unsicher; ungewiss	**uncertain** ↔ certain
prejudice ['predʒədɪs]	Vorurteil	There is widespread **prejudice** against workers over 50. **prejudice** → to be prejudiced against
to pass on [ˌpɑ:s‿'ɒn]	weitergeben	I've got a message for your brother. Could you **pass** it **on**, please?
layer ['leɪə]	Schicht; Lage	This cake has three **layers** of chocolate.
unified ['ju:nɪfaɪd]	verbunden; vereint	**unified** → to unify
gender ['dʒendə]	Geschlecht (sozial)	The **gender** of a girl is female. The **gender** of a boy is male.

chairperson ['tʃeəˌpɜ:sn]	Vorsitzende/-r; Vorsitz	The committee has ten members but only one **chairperson**.
outreach group ['aʊtri:tʃ ˌgru:p]	Kontaktgruppe	= a group bringing information and services to people who would not be able to obtain them in another way
encompassing [ɪn'kʌmpəsɪŋ]	umschließend	**encompassing** = including
inclusive [ɪn'klu:sɪv]	inklusiv; umfassend	My brother learns more slowly than me. He went to a special school, but now he is in an **inclusive** class at my school.
straight [streɪt]	gerade; hier: heterosexuell	**straight** = heterosexual
origin ['ɒrɪdʒɪn]	Ursprung; Herkunft; Abstammung	people of Asian/European/… **origin**
to put sth in perspective [ˌpʊt‿ɪn pə'spektɪv]	etw. relativieren; etw. ins rechte Licht rücken	Having a closer look at last year's figures **puts** the loss of the company **in perspective**.
to prevent [prɪ'vent]	vorbeugen; verhindern	We realised the danger and took steps to **prevent** it happening. **to prevent** → prevention
to cure [kjʊə]	heilen	Some types of cancer can now be **cured**.
expectation [ˌekspek'teɪʃn]	Erwartung	**expectation** → to expect

Text A – Gender: Changing perspectives

pronoun ['prəʊnaʊn]	Pronomen; Fürwort	'He', 'him' and 'which' are all **pronouns**.
non-binary ['nɒnbaɪnri]	nicht binär (hier: weder ganz weiblich, noch ganz männlich)	**non-binary** = not one of two possibilities
curriculum, curricula *(pl)* [kə'rɪkjələm, kə'rɪkjələ]	Lehrplan	Schools have to follow the national **curriculum** in England.
species *(sg or pl)* ['spi:ʃi:z]	Art; Spezies	There are over 200 **species** of birds in this country.
lack of ['læk‿əv]	Mangel an	The children are suffering from a serious **lack of** vitamins.
transgender [trænz'dʒendə]	transsexuell; transgender	= when the gender does not correspond with the birth sex
to **transition** [træn'zɪʃn]	eine Geschlechtsumwandlung haben	= to start living your life as a person of a different gender
to **estimate** ['estɪmeɪt]	schätzen	Can you **estimate** how long it will take?
immediate [ɪ'mi:diət]	direkt; unmittelbar; spontan	Her **immediate** reaction was happiness.
to **re-enter** [ri:'entə]	wieder einsteigen; zurückkehren	to **re-enter** = to return
to **transfer** [træns'fɜ:]	versetzen	They **transferred** to another school.
progressive [prə'gresɪv]	fortschrittlich	**progressive** = modern **progressive** → progress
sibling ['sɪblɪŋ]	Bruder/Schwester; Geschwisterkind	My brother and my sister are my **siblings**.
to **pick** [pɪk]	auswählen; aussuchen	**to pick** = to choose
upsetting [ʌp'setɪŋ]	verstörend	an **upsetting** experience **upsetting** → to be upset
counseling *(AE)* ['kaʊnslɪŋ]	Therapie	**counseling** = therapy
to **violate** ['vaɪəleɪt]	verstoßen gegen	= to break or act against a law or rule
to **repeal** [rɪ'pi:l]	aufheben	= to officially cancel a law
supportive [sə'pɔ:tɪv]	unterstützend	**supportive** → to support

shoutout ['ʃaʊtaʊt]	Gruß (im Radio, Fernsehen)	= a public greeting to a named person, especially on the radio or on television
to owe sb sth/owe sth to sb [əʊ]	jdm. etw. schulden	I think I **owe** you an explanation.
release [rɪ'li:s]	Erleichterung; Erlösung	= the state of being freed, as from imprisonment, duty, pain etc. **release** → to release
prevalent ['prevlənt]	weit verbreitet	**prevalent** = common; established
to **cause sb anguish** [ˌkɔ:z 'æŋgwɪʃ]	jdm. Leid zufügen	Prejudices can **cause anguish**.
legislation *(no pl)* [ˌledʒɪ'sleɪʃn]	Gesetze; Gesetzgebung	= process of making laws **legislation** = (a body of) laws

Text B – Celebrating diversity

obstacle ['ɒbstəkl]	Hürde; Hindernis	= sth that is in your way before you can reach your goal
to **imprint** [ɪm'prɪnt]	bedrucken	They also left a card, **imprinted** with their names. **to imprint** → to print
output ['aʊtpʊt]	Leistung; Ausstoß	= the amount of something that a person or thing produces
heritage ['herɪtɪdʒ]	Erbe; Herkunft	A country's **heritage** is all the qualities and traditions there that have continued over many years and have been passed on from one generation to another.
to **pursue** [pə'sju:]	verwirklichen; verfolgen	to **pursue** a plan/a strategy = to try to make sth come true
passion ['pæʃn]	Leidenschaft	**passion** → passionate
to **blend** [blend]	mischen; vermischen	**Blend** the ingredients until you have a smooth cream. **to blend** = to mix
contemporary [kən'tempərəri]	zeitgenössisch	Only the names are ancient in the story; the characters are modern and **contemporary**. **contemporary** ↔ old-fashioned; traditional
division [dɪ'vɪʒn]	Teilung; Aufteilung	**division** → to divide
admiration [ˌædmɪ'reɪʃn]	Bewunderung	**admiration** → to admire
tirelessly ['taɪələsli]	unermüdlich	**tirelessly** → tired
exposure *(no pl)* [ɪk'spəʊʒə]	Kontakt; Konfrontation; Ausgesetztsein	You should always limit your **exposure** to the sun. **exposure** → to expose to
to **acknowledge** [ək'nɒlɪdʒ]	anerkennen; einräumen	We were forced to **acknowledge** the fact that climate change is a huge problem. = to admit or accept that sth is true or that a situation exists

Text C – Inclusive workplaces

to **recruit** [rɪ'kru:t]	anwerben; einstellen	**to recruit** = to engage; to employ
open-plan office [ˌəʊpnplæn‿'ɒfɪs]	Großraumbüro	**Open-plan offices** were invented to improve teamwork.
eventually [ɪ'ventʃuəli]	letztendlich	**eventually** = finally
anxiety [æŋ'zaɪəti]	Angst; Unruhe	**anxiety** = fear; worry
consultant [kən'sʌltnt]	Berater/-in	= a person who gives expert advice on a specific subject
to **find comfort** [ˌfaɪnd 'kʌmfət]	sich wohl fühlen	**to find comfort** = to feel well
to be associated with [ˌbi‿ə'səʊʃieɪtɪd wɪð]	verbunden werden mit; stehen für	**to be associated with** = to be related to

sought after ['sɔ:t‿ɑ:ftə]	gesucht	= wanted by many people but not easy to get
to **reflect** [rɪ'flekt]	widerspiegeln	= to give an image of
disorder [dɪ'sɔ:də]	Störung	= a problem or illness which affects sb's mind or body
to **affect** [ə'fekt]	beeinflussen; betreffen; beeinträchtigen	**to affect** = to influence **to affect** → effect
sense [sens]	Sinn	Hearing and seeing are two of our five **senses.**
to **innovate** ['ɪnəveɪt]	Neuerungen einführen	**to innovate** → innovation
to **take the minutes** [ˌteɪk ðə 'mɪnɪts]	ein Protokoll führen	= to write down what was said and decided during a meeting
attendee [əten'di:]	Teilnehmer/-in	**attendee** → to attend
to **streamline** ['stri:mlaɪn]	optimieren	After they **streamlined** their production, they had half the costs.
to **cope (with)** ['kəʊp wɪð]	zurechtkommen (mit); schaffen	= to be able to deal with sth difficult

D7

Topic 6 Ecological issues

Getting started

wasteland ['weɪstlænd]	ungenutztes Grundstück	= area of land, not or no longer used for cultivation or building **wasteland** → waste → to waste
to **strengthen** ['streŋθn]	stärken	**to strengthen** = to improve; to make stronger/better **to strengthen** → strength
desirable [dɪ'zaɪərəbl]	wünschenswert; erstrebenswert	Good manners are **desirable** if you want to make a good impression on someone. **desirable** → desire
to **predict** [prɪ'dɪkt]	vorhersagen; voraussagen	It is hardly possible to **predict** the future.
to **attain** [ə'teɪn]	erreichen	This year I have finally **attained** my goal of studying abroad in Europe. **to attain** = to achieve

Text A – Ecology and economy

habit ['hæbɪt]	Gewohnheit	People have good **habits** and bad **habits.**
commerce *(no pl)* ['kɒmɜ:s]	Handel; Handels-	= the activity of buying and selling goods
to **release** [rɪ'li:s]	veröffentlichen	= to make sth available to the public
to **emit** [ɪ'mɪt]	ausstoßen; emittieren	**to emit** carbon dioxide/smoke/a cry **to emit** → emission
rapidly ['ræpɪdli]	schnell; rasch	Economies often grow very **rapidly** in emerging markets. **rapidly** = quickly
raw material [ˌrɔ: mə'tɪəriəl]	Rohstoff	= material still in its natural or original state, before processing or manufacture **raw material** ↔ manmade product
retailer ['re:teɪlə]	Einzelhändler/-in	**Retailers** need to respond to new consumer habits and changing markets with innovative store concepts and products. = a business that sells goods to customers
to **tend to** ['tend tə]	neigen zu; tendieren zu	The rents in cities **tend to** be more expensive than in suburbs.

vehicle ['vɪəkl]	Fahrzeug	**vehicle** = car, bus, tractor, truck, plane
in terms (of) [ɪn 'tɜ:mz‿(əv)]	bezüglich; hinsichtlich	This country is ruined not only due to our current economic crisis but also **in terms of** politics. **in terms of** = regarding; concerning
to **return** [rɪ'tɜ:n]	zurückgeben	to **return** a product/money/a favour **to return** = to give back
inefficiency *(no pl)* [ˌɪnɪ'fɪʃnsi]	Ineffizienz; Unwirksamkeit	**inefficiency** ↔ efficiency
to **expand** [ɪk'spænd]	(sich) ausdehnen; erweitern	The company **expanded** and hired more workers. = to become greater in size, number or importance
sustainable [sə'steɪnəbl]	nachhaltig	= causing little or no damage to the environment **sustainable** → sustainability
courier ['kʊriə]	Kurier/-in; Bote/Botin; Zusteller/-in	= sb who takes letters and parcels to different places/ people as a job
purchase ['pɜ:tʃəs]	Kauf	= sth you have bought **purchase** → to purchase
to **blame** [bleɪm]	verantwortlich machen; beschuldigen	Don't **blame** me! It's not my fault. *False friend:* **to blame** ≠ *blamieren*
convenient [kən'vi:niənt]	bequem; angenehm	= easy, or very useful or suitable for a particular purpose
landfill ['lænfɪl]	Mülldeponie	= a place where very large amounts of rubbish are buried **landfill** = dump
to **bury** ['beri]	begraben; vergraben	= to put sth into a hole in the ground and cover it up with earth
resources *(pl)* [rɪ'zɔ:sɪz]	Ressourcen; Rohstoffe	= the things that a country has and can use to increase its wealth, such as coal, oil or land
to **release** [rɪ'li:s]	freisetzen; freigeben	**to release** carbon dioxide/gas into the atmosphere

Text B – Facing climate change

mosque [mɒsk]	Moschee	**mosque** – church – synagogue = a house for worship and prayers
guardian ['gɑ:diən]	Hüter/-in; Wächter/-in	**guardian** → guard → to guard
notion ['nəʊʃn]	Vorstellung; Auffassung	Do you have a **notion** of how much the car costs? **notion** = idea
domestic [də'mestɪk]	Inlands-; inländisch	**domestic** ↔ foreign
interdependent [ˌɪntədɪ'pendənt]	voneinander abhängig	**interdependent** → to depend
barely ['beəli]	kaum	**barely** = hardly
to **couple** ['kʌpl]	verbinden; koppeln	**to couple** = to combine; to link
objective [əb'dʒektɪv]	Ziel	The main **objective** of today's meeting is to elect a new chairperson.
permit ['pɜ:mɪt]	Erlaubnis; Genehmigung	**permit** → to permit → permission
to **collaborate** [kə'læbreɪt]	zusammenarbeiten	**to collaborate** = to work together **to collaborate** → collaboration
to **tackle (an issue)** [ˌtækl‿ən‿'ɪʃu:]	(ein Problem) angehen; anpacken	= to fight against (a problem)
fossil fuel ['fɒsl ˌfju:əl]	fossiler Brennstoff	= non-renewable fuel made from coal, oil or natural gas
subsidies *(pl)* ['sʌbsɪdiz]	Subventionen	There are government **subsidies** available for farmers. **subsidies** → to subsidise

to **transition** (to/into) [træn'zɪʃn (tə/ɪntə)]	in etw. anderes übergehen; sich umwandeln	**to transition** = to transform
to **phase out** [ˌfeɪz‿'aʊt]	allmählich abschaffen	Our business is going digital and will **phase out** paper by next year.
self-interest [ˌself'ɪntrest]	Egoismus; Eigeninteresse	**self-interest** = selfishness
sense [sens]	Sinn	Hearing and seeing are two of our five **senses**.
to **concern** [kən'sɜːn]	betreffen	This is my problem, it doesn't **concern** you at all. **to concern** = to be relevant to; to affect
obstacle ['ɒbstəkl]	Hürde; Hindernis	= sth that is in your way before you can reach your goal
rhetorical device [rɪˌtɒrɪkl dɪ'vaɪs]	rhetorisches Stilmittel	Repetition and parallelism are **rhetorical devices**.

Text C – Green cities

to **boast** [bəʊst]	prahlen; angeben	He **has boasted** of being involved in the bank robbery. **to boast** = to show off
to **rise** [raɪz]	steigen; sich erheben	He watched the smoke **rise** from the chimney.
civilized *(AE)* ['sɪvlaɪzd]	zivilisiert	**civilized** → civilization *(AE)*
to **set out to do sth** [set‿'aʊt tə]	sich daranmachen, etw. zu tun	My friend and I **set out to** discover this futuristic city.
to **shrink** [ʃrɪŋk]	schrumpfen	**to shrink** = to get smaller **to shrink, shrank, shrunk**
to **occupy** ['ɒkjəpaɪ]	füllen; einnehmen	This bed is huge, it **occupies** the whole room. *here:* **to fill**
to **resemble** [rɪ'zembl]	ähneln	She so **resembles** her mother. **to resemble** = to be/look like
to **be fond of sb/sth** [bi 'fɒnd‿əv]	jdn./etw. gern haben; jdn./etw. mögen	= to like sb/sth very much
gadget ['gædʒɪt]	Gerät; technische Spielerei	Smartphones and play stations are **gadgets**.
to **fail to do sth** ['feɪl tə]	versäumen, etw. zu tun; es nicht schaffen, etw. zu tun	A lot of actors **fail to** find success.
to **charge** [tʃɑːdʒ]	berechnen; verlangen	The majority of sellers **charged** a fair price. = to ask for a certain amount to be paid for goods or services
unoccupied [ʌn'ɒkjəpaɪd]	unbeschäftigt	**unoccupied** ↔ occupied
to **lack** [læk]	mangeln; fehlen	Our government **lacks** the money to provide sustainable public transport.
precaution [prɪ'kɔːʃn]	Vorsichtsmaßnahme	**precaution** = safety measure
sturdy ['stɜːdi]	fest; stabil	**sturdy** shoes, a **sturdy** box **sturdy** = robust
inevitable [ɪ'nevɪtəbl]	unvermeidlich; zwangsläufig	= sth that is certain to happen and cannot be prevented or avoided
horrified ['hɒrɪfaɪd]	entsetzt	I'm **horrified** by the amount of traffic in this city. **horrified** → horror
abolition *(no pl)* [ˌæbə'lɪʃn]	Abschaffung	= to officially cancel or end sth **abolition** → to abolish
patience ['peɪʃns]	Geduld	**patience** ↔ impatience **patience** → patient
astonishing [ə'stɒnɪʃɪŋ]	erstaunlich	**astonishing** = surprising
inquiry [ɪn'kwaɪəri]	Nachforschung; Anfrage	He made some **inquiries** and discovered she had left the country.

appeal [ə'pi:l]	Reiz	= the quality in sb/sth that makes them attractive or interesting
urban planner [ˌɜ:bn 'plænə]	Stadtplaner/-in	= a person who plans infrastructure and housing in cities and towns
to lecture ['lektʃə]	Vorlesung halten	She worked as a marketing specialist but also **lectured** at university.
to be concerned with sth [ˌbi kən'sɜ:nd wɪð]	sich mit etw. beschäftigen	**to be concerned with** = to be occupied with
housing ['haʊzɪŋ]	Wohnbau; Wohnungen	Poor **housing** and family stress can affect both physical and mental health.
cycle lane ['saɪkl ˌleɪn]	Fahrradspur; Radfahrstreifen	= a lane of the road that is reserved for bikes
congestion [kən'dʒestʃn]	Verkehrsstau; Verstopfung	A smaller number of trucks and cars would lead to less traffic **congestion**.
forward-thinking [ˌfɔ:wəd'θɪnkɪŋ]	innovativ; vorausschauend	**forward** ↔ backward
urban sprawl [ˌɜ:bn 'sprɔ:l]	Zersiedelung (einer Stadt)	= the spread of settled areas from cities into the countryside
factor ['fæktə]	Faktor; Umstand	Your opinion was not a **factor** in my decision.
basic needs *(pl)* [ˌbeɪsɪk 'ni:dz]	Grundbedürfnisse	Food and drink, shelter and sleep are the most important **basic needs**.
sanitation *(no pl)* [ˌsænɪ'teɪʃn]	sanitäre Anlagen	Not all houses in the poor areas have **sanitation**.
facility [fə'sɪlɪti]	Einrichtung	The outdoor **facilities** at the hotel were huge.
to make use of [meɪk 'ju:z ˌəv]	benutzen; verwenden	What tricks do they **make use of**?
to perform [pə'fɔ:m]	funktionieren	The tires **perform** well on uneven terrain. **to perform** = to work
to depict [dɪ'pɪkt]	darstellen	**to depict** = to illustrate

Discussion – 'Save the planet' exhibition

depth [depθ]	Tiefe	The pool has a **depth** of two metres. **depth** → deep
nuanced ['nju:ɑ:nst]	nuanciert; nuancenreich	a **nuanced** text/view

D8 Topic 7 Social issues

Getting started

buck *(AE) (coll)* [bʌk]	Dollar	**buck** = dollar
sobriety *(no pl)* [sə'braɪəti]	Nüchternheit; Abstinenz	**sobriety** → sober
historical [hɪ'stɒrɪkl]	historisch; geschichtlich	**historical** → history
context ['kɒntekst]	Kontext; Zusammenhang	It depends on the **context** if this is good or bad.
sociology [ˌsəʊsi'ɒlədʒi]	Soziologie	= the study of society or of the way society is organised
to make ends meet [ˌmeɪk ˌendz 'mi:t]	über die Runden kommen	They work but they do not earn enough money to **make ends meet**. = to have just enough money to pay for the things you need
tension ['tenʃn]	Spannung	You could feel the **tension** in the air at the meeting.
distribution [ˌdɪstrɪ'bju:ʃn]	Verteilung	**distribution** → to distribute

funding ['fʌndɪŋ]	Finanzierung; finanzielle Unterstützung	= money provided for a particular purpose
incarceration [ɪnˌkɑːsr'eɪʃn]	Inhaftierung	= the act of putting sb in prison **incarceration** → to incarcerate
to favour ['feɪvə]	bevorzugen	**to favour** = to prefer
to measure ['meʒə]	messen	He **measured** the speed of the plane.
to be on the rise [ˌbi‿ɒn ðə 'raɪz]	steigen; ansteigen	The number of people living in poverty **is on the rise.** **rise** → to rise
vulnerable ['vʌlnrəbl]	verletzlich; verwundbar	= weak and easily hurt
affluent ['æfluənt]	wohlhabend	**affluent** = rich
to drop out (of school) [ˌdrɒp 'aʊt]	(die Schule) abbrechen	She **dropped out of school** at the age of 14.
disproportionately [ˌdɪsprə'pɔːʃnətli]	unverhältnismäßig	**disproportionately** ↔ proportionately **disproportionately** → proportion
mandatory ['mændətri]	verpflichtend	Attending school is **mandatory.** = sth you have to do
sentence ['sentəns]	Urteil; Strafe; Strafmaß	The gang's **sentence** was five years in prison.
privilege ['prɪvlɪdʒ]	Privileg; Recht; Vorrecht	**privilege** → privileged
universal healthcare [ˌjuːnɪvɜːsl 'helθkeə]	allgemeine Gesundheitsversorgung; Krankenversicherung für alle	**health care** = health insurance
to obtain [əb'teɪn]	erhalten; sich verschaffen	**to obtain** = to acquire; to get
self-employed [ˌselfɪm'plɔɪd]	selbstständig	I work for myself now, I'm **self-employed.**
burden ['bɜːdn]	Last; Belastung	= sth that causes a lot of difficulty, worry or hard work
to **participate** [pɑː'tɪsɪpeɪt]	teilnehmen	**to participate** = to take part
pressing ['presɪŋ]	dringend; akut	This is a very **pressing** problem. We must deal with it quickly.

Text A – Living in a modern world

urban ['ɜːbn]	städtisch; Stadt-	Towns and cities are **urban** areas. **urban** ↔ rural
corporate ['kɔːprət]	Firmen-; Unternehmens-	**corporate** → corporation
amenities *(pl)* [ə'miːnətiz]	Ausstattung; Annehmlichkeiten	= useful or pleasant facilities or services
vast [vɑːst]	riesig; enorm	**vast** = huge
attempt [ə'tempt]	Versuch	first/second/brave **attempt** = an effort to do sth
to **benefit from sth/sb** ['benɪfɪt]	von etw./jdm. profitieren	Both sides **have benefited from** the talks. = to be in a better position because of sth **to benefit from** → benefit
ambassador [æm'bæsədə]	Botschafter/-in	It was an honour to meet the Japanese **ambassador.**
decade ['dekeɪd]	Jahrzehnt	I've known him for **decades.** = ten years
to **be locked** [ˌbi‿'lɒkt]	gebunden sein; festgelegt sein	**to be locked** in a contract **locked** = bound
to **extend** [ɪk'stend]	erweitern; ausdehnen; verlängern	**to extend** → extension
indeed [ɪn'diːd]	in der Tat; tatsächlich; allerdings	The last task in the exam was very difficult **indeed.**
furnished ['fɜːnɪʃt]	möbliert	**furnished** → furniture

accommodation [əˌkɒmə'deɪʃn]	Unterkunft; Unterbringung	= buildings or rooms where people can stay (e.g. for a holiday) or live
to **foster** ['fɒstə]	fördern; pflegen	= to help to develop sth
angle ['æŋgl]	Winkel; Blickwinkel	The **angle** from which you look at something influences your perspective.
proposition [ˌprɒpə'zɪʃn]	Aussage; These	= a statement or an idea which people can consider or discuss to decide whether it is true **proposition** → to propose
to **squeeze** [skwi:z]	drücken; pressen; quetschen	He **squeezed** her arm reassuringly. **to squeeze** = to press
downside ['daʊnsaɪd]	Kehrseite; Nachteil	**downside** ↔ upside
offence [ə'fens]	Vergehen; Straftat	= a crime that breaks a particular law and requires a particular punishment
to **lack** [læk]	mangeln; fehlen	Naomi **lacks** patience. She's not very good with kids. = to have not enough of sth
intent [ɪn'tent]	Absicht; Vorsatz	**intent** = intention; aim
to **range from ... to** ['reɪndʒ frəm ... tə]	reichen von ... bis	Participants of the festival **range from** artists **to** tourists who happened to come by.
laundry ['lɔ:ndri]	Wäscherei; Waschküche; Wäsche	He had put his dirty **laundry** in the clothes basket.
property ['prɒpəti]	Eigentum	After you buy a house, it is your **property**.
vacant ['veɪknt]	frei	I'm sorry, but we don't have any **vacant** rooms. **vacant** = free

Text B – Divides and gaps

divide [dɪ'vaɪd]	Spaltung; Kluft	= a significant distinction between two groups, often one that causes conflict **divide** → to divide
to **evolve** [ɪ'vɒlv]	(sich) entwickeln	Popular music **evolved** from folk songs. **to evolve** = to develop
output ['aʊtpʊt]	Leistung; Ausstoß	The factory's **output** increased by 5 per cent.
average ['ævrɪdʒ]	Durchschnitt	to be above/below **average**
metro ['metrəʊ]	Stadt-	= short for 'metropolitan' **metro** = urban
mayor [meə]	Bürgermeister/-in	The **mayor** is the head of the town council.
hourly pay [ˌaʊəli 'peɪ]	Stundenlohn	The average **hourly pay** is £18 in London.
minimum wage [ˌmɪnɪməm 'weɪdʒ]	Mindestlohn	In many jobs people do not earn more than the **minimum wage**.
to **emerge** [ɪ'mɜ:dʒ]	sich abzeichnen; entstehen	**to emerge** = to appear
to **factor in sth** ['fæktər‿ɪn]	etw. berücksichtigen; mit etw. rechnen	Once you **factor in** all the extra costs, low-budget airlines aren't always the cheapest option.
to **shrink** [ʃrɪŋk]	schrumpfen	**to shrink** = to get smaller **to shrink, shrank, shrunk**
stubborn ['stʌbən]	eigensinnig; störrisch	Jack doesn't accept advice or help from his cousins. He's really **stubborn**.
to **need busting** [ˌni:d 'bʌstɪŋ]	beseitigt werden müssen	The myth of some people being better than others **needs busting**.

heyday ['heɪdeɪ]	Höhepunkt; Blütezeit	the **heyday** of one's career = the time when sth is most powerful, successful or popular
decline [dɪ'klaɪn]	Niedergang	Rome's **decline** in the fifth century **decline** ↔ rise
manufacturing [ˌmænjə'fæktʃrɪŋ]	Produktion; Produktionsbetrieb	**manufacturing** → to manufacture
mill [mɪl]	Fabrik	**mill** = factory
coffin ['kɒfɪn]	Sarg	= a box in which a dead body is buried or cremated
alive and kicking [əˌlaɪv‿ənd 'kɪkɪŋ]	gesund und munter	= emphasising not only that sth continues to survive, but also that it is very active **alive** ↔ dead
to **persuade** [pə'sweɪd]	überreden; überzeugen	Jay wants to **persuade** his brother to come with them.
perception [pə'sepʃn]	Wahrnehmung	**perception** → to perceive
authorities *(pl)* [ɔ:'θɒrətiz]	Behörden	local **authorities**, to report sb to the **authorities**

Text C – The future of money

urge [ɜ:dʒ]	Drang	Sometimes I get **urges** to just stay in bed. **urge** → urgent
to **gather** ['gæðə]	sammeln; zusammentragen	**to gather** = to collect
shameful ['ʃeɪmfl]	beschämend	Being bullied is very **shameful**. **shameful** → shame
to **eliminate** [ɪ'lɪmɪneɪt]	beseitigen; eliminieren	The priority should be to **eliminate** child poverty. **to eliminate** → elimination
parental leave [pəˌrentl 'li:v]	Elternzeit	These days it is not uncommon for fathers to take **parental leave**.
to **demolish** [dɪ'mɒlɪʃ]	vernichten	**to demolish** = to destroy
figure ['fɪgə]	Zahl; Betrag	We need a true **figure** of how many people in this country haven't got a job. **figure** = number
to **restore** [rɪ'stɔ:]	wiederherstellen; restaurieren	If you **restore** something to its original state, you make it like it used to be.
to **chew** [tʃu:]	kauen	Be certain to eat slowly and **chew** your food extremely well. **to chew** → chewing gum
heritage ['herɪtɪdʒ]	Erbe; Herkunft	*here:* a person's origins
barely ['beəli]	kaum	She could **barely** breathe because she was so scared.
to **inherit** [ɪn'herɪt]	erben	If you **inherit** money or a house, you get it from a person who has died and left it to you. **to inherit** → heritage
smoothly ['smu:ðli]	glatt; reibungslos	**smooth** ↔ rough
shelter ['ʃeltə]	Schutz; Obdach	During the earthquake we found **shelter** under a table. **shelter** → to shelter
to **choke** [tʃəʊk]	sich verschlucken	to **choke** on a noodle
sip [sɪp]	Schluck	Try our new smoothie! Take a **sip**! **sip** → to sip
to **frown** [fraʊn]	die Stirn runzeln	His parents **frowned** when he told them about his plans.
laziness ['leɪzɪnəs]	Faulheit	She treats her son's **laziness** with patience. **laziness** → lazy

desire [dɪ'zaɪə]	Wunsch; Verlangen	**desire** = wish
legacy ['legəsi]	Vermächtnis; Erbe	= sth handed down from the past
universal basic income (UBI) [ˌjuːnɪ'vɜːsl ˌbeɪsɪk‿'ɪnkʌm]	allgemeines Grundeinkommen	One of the ideas to get rid of poverty is a **universal basic income**.
to prevent [prɪ'vent]	vorbeugen; verhindern	We realised the danger and took steps to **prevent** it happening. **to prevent** → prevention
to get by [ˌget‿'baɪ]	zurechtkommen; über die Runden kommen	= to manage to live or do things in a satisfactory way
to oversimplify [ˌəʊvə'sɪmplɪfaɪ]	zu stark vereinfachen	**to oversimplify** → to simplify → simple
altogether [ˌɔːltə'geðə]	insgesamt; ganz und gar	There are **altogether** 15 students in my group.
misconception [ˌmɪskən'sepʃn]	Irrglaube; Fehlvorstellung	The idea that birds can eat bread is a common **misconception.**
the less fortunate [ðə ˌles 'fɔːtʃnət]	die Bedürftigen	= people who have less wealth and comfort
to make sense [ˌmeɪk 'sens]	Sinn ergeben; einleuchten	If something **makes sense**, you can understand it.
to be work in progress [bi ˌwɜːk‿ɪn 'prəʊgres]	in Arbeit sein	**to be work in progress** ↔ to be finished
domestic abuse [dəˌmestɪk‿ə'bjuːs]	häusliche Gewalt	= physical or psychological abuse towards a member of one's own household
exploitation [ˌeksplɔɪ'teɪʃn]	Ausbeutung	**exploitation** → to exploit
to subsidise ['sʌbsɪdaɪz]	subventionieren; bezuschussen	The school **subsidised** the students' bus tickets.

Writing – Social and antisocial behaviour

to fulfil [fʊl'fɪl]	erfüllen	All the necessary conditions for peace **were fulfilled**.
to commit a crime [kəˌmɪt‿ə 'kraɪm]	ein Verbrechen begehen; eine Straftat begehen	**to commit a crime** = to break the law
weapon ['wepən]	Waffe	Part of the military budget gets set aside to purchase better **weapons** every year.
innocent ['ɪnəsnt]	unschuldig	**innocent** ↔ guilty **innocent** → innocence
crucial ['kruːʃl]	entscheidend; äußerst wichtig	**crucial** = very important; essential
to divert [daɪ'vɜːt]	ablenken	= to direct sb's attention to sth else

Discussion – 'Love the world' project

discourse ['dɪskɔːs]	Rede; Unterhaltung; Diskussion	What's the **discourse** about? – They are talking about social issues. **discourse** = discussion; talk
to launch [lɔːnʃ]	starten; ins Leben rufen	We **launched** a new website. **to launch** = to start

IRREGULAR VERBS

be, was/were, been	sein
beat, beat, beaten	schlagen
become, became, become	werden
begin, began, begun	anfangen
break, broke, broken	(zer)brechen
breed, bred, bred	züchten, erzeugen
bring, brought, brought	(mit)bringen
build, built, built	bauen
buy, bought, bought	kaufen
cast, cast, cast	(ab)stimmen
catch, caught, caught	fangen
choose, chose, chosen	wählen
come, came, come	kommen
cost, cost, cost	kosten
cut, cut, cut	schneiden
do, did, done	tun, machen
draw, drew, drawn	zeichnen
drink, drank, drunk	trinken
drive, drove, driven	fahren
eat, ate, eaten	essen
fall, fell, fallen	fallen
feel, felt, felt	(sich) fühlen
fight, fought, fought	(be)kämpfen
find, found, found	finden
flee, fled, fled	fliehen, flüchten
fly, flew, flown	fliegen
forbid, forbade, forbidden	verbieten
forget, forgot, forgotten	vergessen
freeze, froze, frozen	frieren
get, got, got	bekommen
give, gave, given	geben
go, went, gone	gehen, fahren
grow, grew, grown	wachsen
hang, hung, hung	hängen
have, had, had	haben
hear, heard, heard	hören
hide, hid, hidden	(sich) verstecken
hit, hit, hit	schlagen
hold, held, held	(fest)halten
hurt, hurt, hurt	(sich) wehtun
keep, kept, kept	aufbewahren
know, knew, known	wissen; kennen
lead, led, led	führen
leave, left, left	(ver)lassen
lend, lent, lent	(ver)leihen
let, let, let	lassen
lie, lay, lain	liegen
lose, lost, lost	verlieren
make, made, made	machen
mean, meant, meant	meinen, bedeuten
meet, met, met	treffen
pay, paid, paid	bezahlen
quit, quit, quit	aufgeben; aufhören
read, read, read	lesen
ride, rode, ridden	reiten, fahren
ring, rang, rung	klingeln
rise, rose, risen	steigen
run, ran, run	laufen
say, said, said	sagen
see, saw, seen	sehen
seek, sought, sought	suchen
sell, sold, sold	verkaufen
send, sent, sent	senden
set, set, set	setzen; aufstellen
shoot, shot, shot	(er)schießen
show, showed, shown	zeigen
shrink, shrank, shrunk	schrumpfen
shut, shut, shut	schließen
sing, sang, sung	singen
sink, sank, sunk	sinken
sit, sat, sat	sitzen
sleep, slept, slept	schlafen
speak, spoke, spoken	sprechen
spend, spent, spent	ausgeben; verbringen
spread, spread, spread	ausbreiten
stand, stood, stood	stehen
steal, stole, stolen	stehlen
stick, stuck, stuck	kleben, feststecken
strike, struck, struck	schlagen; betreffen
strive, strove, striven	anstreben, sich bemühen
swim, swam, swum	schwimmen
take, took, taken	nehmen
teach, taught, taught	unterrichten
tear, tore, torn	zerreißen
tell, told, told	sagen; erzählen
think, thought, thought	denken
throw, threw, thrown	werfen
understand, understood, understood	verstehen
wake, woke, woken	aufwachen
wear, wore, worn	tragen
win, won, won	gewinnen
write, wrote, written	schreiben

Asking about words and meanings	
What does (the word) … mean?	Was bedeutet (das Wort) …?
I don't understand the word …/the expression …/ this sentence.	Ich verstehe das Wort … nicht/den Ausdruck … nicht/diesen Satz nicht.
How do you say … in English?	Wie sagt man … auf Englisch?
Could you repeat that/say that again?	Würden Sie das wiederholen/nochmal sagen?
Giving your opinion	
I think (that) …	Ich denke/meine, dass …
In my opinion …	Meiner Meinung nach …
I find … (really) good/interesting/boring.	Ich finde … (echt) gut/interessant/langweilig.
Agreeing and disagreeing	
I agree (with Martina).	Ich stimme (Martina) zu.
I disagree/don't agree (with Bernd).	Ich stimme (Bernd) nicht zu.
Yes, I think the same/I think that, too.	Ja, ich denke das Gleiche/das meine ich auch.
I think you are wrong.	Ich finde, dass du Unrecht hast.
Talking about texts	
In the text the reader learns that …	Im Text erfährt der Leser/die Leserin, dass …
The first paragraph tells us that …	Der erste Absatz sagt uns, dass …
In the second paragraph we read/learn that …	Im zweiten Absatz liest/erfährt man, dass …
The last paragraph is about …	Im letzten Absatz geht es um …
In the text it (also) says that …	Im Text steht (auch), dass …
Finally, we learn/read that …	Zuletzt erfährt/liest man, dass …
Working in class	
Would you write that on the board, please?	Würden Sie das bitte an die Tafel schreiben?
Could you play the recording again, please?	Würden Sie die Aufnahme bitte nochmal vorspielen?
I'm not sure what we have to do.	Ich bin nicht sicher, was wir tun müssen.
I haven't got a partner.	Ich habe keinen Partner/keine Partnerin.
We need another person in our group.	Unserer Gruppe fehlt eine Person.
Our group's finished.	Unsere Gruppe ist fertig.
We need a bit more time.	Wir brauchen noch ein bisschen Zeit.
Could I borrow a/your dictionary?	Darf ich ein/Ihr Wörterbuch leihen?

Bildquellennachweis

8 plainpicture GmbH & Co. KG, Hamburg (Cavan Images/Cavan Social); **10.1** Getty Images, München (Tetra images/Roberto Westbrook); **10.2** ShutterStock.com RF, New York (Grand Warszawski); **10.3** ShutterStock.com RF, New York (LStockStudio); **10.4** ShutterStock.com RF, New York (Jacob Lund); **12** ShutterStock.com RF, New York (Jacob Lund); **15** ShutterStock.com RF, New York (Roman Samborskyi); **16** stock.adobe.com, Dublin (Monkey Business); **18.1** ShutterStock.com RF, New York (ESB Professional); **19** ShutterStock.com RF, New York (Tutatamafilm); **20** ShutterStock.com RF, New York (Rawpixel.com); **21** ShutterStock.com RF, New York (Pavel L Photo and Video); **25** ShutterStock.com RF, New York (Peshkova); **26** ShutterStock.com RF, New York (Halfpoint); **27** CartoonStock Ltd, Bath (Paul Fell); **30** ShutterStock.com RF, New York (Monkey Business Images); **31** ShutterStock.com RF, New York (MoreVector); **32.1** ShutterStock.com RF, New York (CrispyPork); **32.2** ShutterStock.com RF, New York (Rawpixel.com); **32.3** ShutterStock.com RF, New York (My Good Images); **32.4** ShutterStock.com RF, New York (Dan POTOR); **S.33** graphitecture book & edition, Bernau am Chiemsee, Source: Global Wellness Institute, 2020; **36.1** ShutterStock.com RF, New York (elenabsl); **38.1** ShutterStock.com RF, New York (Drazen Zigic); **38.2** ShutterStock.com RF, New York (Drazen Zigic); **39** Aspen Institute: Project Play. https://www.aspenprojectplay.org/; **41.1** ShutterStock.com RF, New York (Alex Guevara); **43** ShutterStock.com RF, New York (Dina Julayeva); **44.3** Oser, Liliane, Hamburg; **45.1** ShutterStock.com RF, New York (Zurijeta); **51.1** ShutterStock.com RF, New York (Juan Carlos L. Ruiz); **52.1** ShutterStock.com RF, New York (kung_tom); **52.2** ShutterStock.com RF, New York (Matt Gibson); **52.3** ShutterStock.com RF, New York (ian johnston); **52.4** ShutterStock.com RF, New York (ESB Professional); S. **52.5** graphitecture book & edition, Bernau am Chiemsee, Source: Understanding Society, 2016; **56** ShutterStock.com RF, New York (eamesBot); **57.1** stock.adobe.com, Dublin (s_l); **57.2** Getty Images Plus, München (scyther5); **57.3** ShutterStock.com RF, New York (New Africa); **57.4** Getty Images Plus, München (iStock/Miroslav Krupan); **58.1** Getty Images, München (Tetra images/Roberto Westbrook); **58.2** Getty Images, München (Desiree Navarro/Getty Images North America); **61.1** Getty Images Plus, München (iStock/miriam-doerr); **63** Getty Images Plus, München (iStock/miriam-doerr); **64.2** ShutterStock.com RF, New York (Foxy burrow); **65.1** ShutterStock.com RF, New York (Joshua Resnick); **65.2** ShutterStock.com RF, New York (Gorodenkoff); **65.3** ShutterStock.com RF, New York (REDPIXEL.PL); **65.4** ShutterStock.com RF, New York (LightField Studios); **65.5** ShutterStock.com RF, New York (Gorodenkoff); **65.6** ShutterStock.com RF, New York (gualtiero boffi); **S.66** graphitecture book & edition, Bernau am Chiemsee, Source: Your Voice, 2019; **67.1** laif, Köln (Davide Lanzilao/Contrasto); **69.1** Alamy stock photo, Abingdon (MediaPunch Inc); **69.3** Getty Images Plus, München (Christopher Robbins); **72.3** CartoonStock Ltd, Bath (Mark Lynch); **74.1** Picture-Alliance, Frankfurt/M. (Aaron Favila/AP Photo); **74.2** ShutterStock.com RF, New York (Dilok Klaisataporn); **74.3** ShutterStock.com RF, New York (Chatchai.wa); **74.4** ShutterStock.com RF, New York (Fit Ztudio); **75** Oser, Liliane, Hamburg; **76.1** ShutterStock.com RF, New York (DenPhotos); **76.2** ShutterStock.com RF, New York (Stephen Barnes); **76.3** Getty Images, München (Westend61); **76.4** Getty Images Plus, München (iStock/humonia); **76.5** Mauritius Images, Mittenwald (Jonathan Goldberg/Alamy); **78** Ernst Klett Verlag GmbH, Stuttgart; **79.1** Picture-Alliance, Frankfurt/M. (REUTERS/Stringer .); **82.1** Mauritius Images, Mittenwald (TopFoto); **82.2** akg-images, Berlin (AP); **82.3** NASA, Washington , D.C.; **82.4** Getty Images, München (Getty Images North America/Michael Zagaris); **82.5** ullstein bild, Berlin (Gerhard); **82.6** Mauritius Images, Mittenwald (Jeremy sutton-hibbert/Alamy/Alamy Stock Photos); **83.1** Getty Images, München (Vittorio Zunino Celotto/Getty Images Europe); **86.3** www.CartoonStock.com, Bath (Harley Schwadron); **87** www.CartoonStock.com, Bath (Silvano Mello); **91** ShutterStock.com RF, New York (fotogestoeber); **92.1** IMAGO, Berlin (Christian Thiel/imago stock&people); **94.1** https://creativecommons.org/licenses/by-sa/4.0/deed.de, Mountain View ; CC-BY-SA-4.0 Lizenzbestimmungen: https://creativecommons.org/licenses/by-sa/4.0/legalcode, Statista, https://www.statista.com/chart/18538/issues-considered-major-problems-by-americans/ Source: Institute for Public Relations, Morning Consult. Based on a survey of 2,200 American conducted in March 2019., siehe *3; **94.2** CartoonStock Ltd, Bath (Trevor White); **95.2** ShutterStock.com RF, New York (13_Phunkod); **96.1** Getty Images Plus, München (DigitalVision/Stephen Zeigler); **96.2** ShutterStock.com RF, New York (AlessandroBiascioli); **96.3** Getty Images Plus, München (E+/SolStock); **96.4** Getty Images Plus, München (E+/SrdjanPav); **96.5** graphitecture book & edition, Bernau am Chiemsee, Source: Deutschland; Fittkau & Maaß Consulting; Oktober/November 2019; ElitePartner ©2021 Statista 2021; S.**96.6** graphitecture book & edition, Bernau am Chiemsee, Source: Data: Statistisches Bundesamt, 2023; **96.7** graphitecture book & edition, Bernau am Chiemsee, Source: Statistisches Bundesamt © Statista 2022; **98.2** laif, Köln (Cassidy Araiza/The Guardian); **101.1** ShutterStock.com RF, New York (Denis Makarenko); **101.2** Getty Images, München (Lee Parker/CameraSport); **104** Getty Images, München (LEON NEAL/AFP); **107** ShutterStock.com RF, New York (BGStock72); **108.2** graphitecture book & edition, Bernau am Chiemsee, Data from: CDC National Centre for Health Statistics, National Health Interview Survey, 2009-2012; **108.3** ShutterStock.com RF, New York (Daisy Daisy); **109** ShutterStock.com RF, New York (Thinglass); **111** ShutterStock.com RF, New York (Salim Hanzaz); **112.1** Getty Images, München (Portland Press Herald); **117.2** ddp media GmbH, Hamburg (Steffens); **117.3** ShutterStock.com RF, New York (Rawpixel.com); **117.4** ShutterStock.com RF, New York (Lightspring); **117.5** ShutterStock.com RF, New York (Tasha Art); **118.1** ShutterStock.com RF, New York (Liv Oeian); **118.2** ShutterStock.com RF, New York (Chat Karen Studio); **118.3** ShutterStock.com RF, New York (franco lucato); **118.4** ShutterStock.com RF, New York (majicphotos); **118.5** United Nations Sustainable Development Goals, https://www.un.org/sustainabledevelopment/ The content of this publication has not been approved by the United Nations and does not reflect the views of the United Nations or its officials or Member States.; **120.1** ShutterStock.com RF, New York (Natee Photo); **122** stock.adobe.com, Dublin (Marco Birn); **122** graphitecture book & edition, Bernau am Chiemsee, Source data: data.footprintnetwork.org, https://creativecommons.org/licenses/by-sa/4.0/deed.de, Mountain View ; CC-BY-SA-4.0 Lizenzbestimmungen: https://creativecommons.org/licenses/by-sa/4.0/legalcode, siehe *3; **123.1** ShutterStock.com RF, New York (Nicole Glass Photography); **123.2** Getty Images, München (Getty Images News/Stephanie Keith); **126** ShutterStock.com RF, New York (alfotokunst); **127.1** ShutterStock.com RF, New York (Pavel Chagochkin); **127.2** laif, Köln (NOAH BERGER/The New York Times/Redux/laif); **129** Getty Images Plus, München (iStock Editorial/Getty Images Plus/MNStudio); **130** Getty Images, München (Corbis Historical/Forrest J. Ackerman Collection/Cristina Monaro Artist: Anton Brzezinski); **131.1** ShutterStock.com RF, New York (R. de Bruijn_Photography); **131.2** CartoonStock Ltd, Bath (Chris Madden); **132.2** graphitecture book & edition, Bernau am Chiemsee, Source: Transport Scotland, 2018; **133** ShutterStock.com RF, New York (helgascandinavus); **136**

ShutterStock.com RF, New York (Great Divide Photography); **139** ASOMOVE; **140.1** Alamy stock photo, Abingdon (WENN Rights Ltd); **143.2** ShutterStock.com RF, New York; **144.1** ShutterStock.com RF, New York (Wei Huang); **144.2** ShutterStock.com RF, New York (Nomad_Soul); **143.1** graphitecture book & edition, Bernau am Chiemsee, Source: https://creativecommons.org/licenses/by-sa/4.0/deed.de, Mountain View ; CC-BY-SA-4.0 Lizenzbestimmungen: https://creativecommons.org/licenses/by-sa/4.0/legalcode ©Statista, https://www.statista.com/chart/24350/total-annual-household-waste-produced-in-selected-countries/, Quelle: UNEP Food Waste Index Report, 2021; **144.3** ShutterStock.com RF, New York (Jacob Lund); **144.4** ShutterStock.com RF, New York (wavebreakmedia); **148** Getty Images, München (DANIEL LEAL/AFP); **150.1** ShutterStock.com RF, New York (Janaka Dharmasena); **152** ShutterStock.com RF, New York (JustAnotherPhotographer); **157.1** ShutterStock.com RF, New York (Leremy); **157.2** ShutterStock.com RF, New York (Leremy); **157.3** ShutterStock.com RF, New York (Leremy); **157.4** ShutterStock.com RF, New York (Leremy); **157.5** ShutterStock.com RF, New York (Leremy); **157.6** ShutterStock.com RF, New York (Leremy); **157.10** ShutterStock.com RF, New York (Ground Picture); **158.2** ShutterStock.com RF, New York (Ivan Kruk); **161.2** Getty Images, München (HGL/Getty Images Europe); **161.3** Getty Images, München (WireImage/Mike Marsland); **162.1** ShutterStock.com RF, New York (Terry Murden); **162.2** ShutterStock.com RF, New York (David Burrows); **164.1** Getty Images, München (Jonathan Leibson/Getty Images Entertainment); **166.2** CartoonStock Ltd, Bath (Kjell Nilsson-Maki); **182** Getty Images, München (Corbis Historical/Forrest J. Ackerman Collection/Cristina Monaro Artist: Anton Brzezinski); **189** iStockphoto, Calgary, Alberta (clu); **190** Alamy stock photo, Abingdon; **192.1** stock.adobe.com, Dublin (Igor Mojzes); **192.2** Thinkstock, München (iStock/gpointstudio); **196** iStockphoto, Calgary, Alberta (R-J-Seymour); **197** ShutterStock.com RF, New York (Jacob Lund); **200** ShutterStock.com RF, New York (Rawpixel.com); **201** ShutterStock.com RF, New York (Diego Cervo); **204** stock.adobe.com, Dublin (kaipong); **206.1–3** Romo, Virginia, Stuttgart; **208.1** Bananastock, Watlington/Oxon; **208.2** MEV Verlag GmbH, Augsburg; **208.3** Thinkstock, München (iStockphoto); **208.4** Avenue Images GmbH, Hamburg (Stockbyte RF, George Doyle); **211** Getty Images Plus, München (swissmediavision/E+); **213.1–3** Ernst Klett Verlag GmbH, Stuttgart; **215** www.panthermedia.net, München (keerati); **216** plainpicture GmbH & Co. KG, Hamburg (plainpicture); **218** Romo, Virginia, Stuttgart; **Umschlag** stock.adobe.com, Dublin (FS-Stock)

*3 Lizenzbestimmungen zu CC-BY-SA-4.0 siehe: http://creativecommons.org/licenses/by-sa/4.0/legalcode

Textquellennachweis

18.2 Song: Stressed Out, Texter: Tyler R Joseph, Verlag/Subverlag: Neue Welt Musikverlag GmbH, Hamburg; **22** © Hazel Sheffield/The Independent; **29** From: Half Sleep © 2011, Matt Krampitz; **32.5** Attributed to Hippocrates of Kos (c. 460 – c. 370 BC); **32.6** Constitution of the World Health Organisation, 1948; **32.7** attributed to Cameron Trammell; **32.8** Attributed to Jaime Lyn Beatty; **34** Rebecca Smithers © 2019 Guardian News & Media Ltd.; **36.2** Liz Lightfoot, © 2019, Guardian News & Media Ltd.; **41.2** © Kashmira Gander/The Independent; **44.1** Helen Keller. Qoted in: Helen and Teacher: The Story of Helen Keller and Anne Sullivan Macy by Joseph P. Lash, 1980; **44.2** anonymous; **45.2** André Paul Guillaume Gide †1951; **45.3** Chief Seattle †1866; **45.4** From: Medium Raw: A Bloody Valentine to the World of Food and the People Who Cook, © 2010 Anthony Bourdain; **47** Stefan Nestler, Deutsche Welle, 2019; **49** © 2011 R.S.Thomas; **50** Emilio Rappold, spiegel.de, 02.08.2017; **51.2** From: Into the Wild, Jon Krakauer, 2007; **54** © Copyright 2019 GTI Media Ltd.; **58.3** by Corban Addison, Thomas Nelson Pub, 2017; **61.2** 2020, Bryan Lufkin, British Broadcasting Corporation; **64.1** Frithjof Harold Bergmann, Neue Arbeit, Neue Kultur. Aus dem Amerikanischen übersetzt von Stephan Schuhmacher, Arbor Verlag, 2004; **67.2** Excerpt(s) from THE CIRCLE by Dave Eggers, copyright © 2013 by Dave Eggers.; **69.2** Serenitie Wang, Daniel Shane, https://edition.cnn.com, CNN Business, 16 April 2019; **70** Nadi Albino, Robert E. Moritz, weforum.org, 29th July 2021; **72.1** Sonia Sotomayor Q&A session at quarterly meeting of the Philadelphia Bar Association (11 March 2011), as reported in "Sotomayor receives Philadelphia Bar's Diversity Award" by Jeff Blumenthal http://www.bizjournals.com.; **72.2** https://www.duden.de/rechtschreibung/Quotenregelung; **73.1** Tiffany Shlain, https://www.pewresearch.org/internet/2017/05/03/the-future-of-jobs-and-jobs-training/; **73.2** Devin Fidler, https://www.pewresearch.org/internet/2017/05/03/the-future-of-jobs-and-jobs-training/; **73.3** Orsola de Castro, https://earth.org/fast-fashion-quotes/; **73.4** Michelle Obama in Vogue, 2016; **74.5** attributed to Malcolm X; **74.6** Charlie Brooker in Black Mirror, 2011-2013; **74.7** From: So you've been publicly shamed © 2015 Jon Ronson; **74.8** Quotation from "We Think: The Power Of Mass Creativity" by C. W. Leadbeater, Profile Books (GB); **76.6** From: Eleanor Oliphant is completely fine © Gail Honeyman 2017, Harper Collins Publishers UK; **79.2** Roland Bleicker, 2018 E-International Relations, www.e-ir.info; **83.2** Andreas Weigend, Data for the people: How to make our post-privacy economy work for you; Publisher: Basic Books, New York, 2017; **86.1** Hugh Mackay, The Age, 11.12.2004; **86.2** „Neue Studie zur TV-Nutzung Lineares Fernsehen verliert mehr und mehr Zuschauer" von Joachim Huber, Der Tagesspiegel, 25.09.2019; **88** https://www.plannthat.com/9-positive-effects-of-social-media-you-might-not-know-about/; **90** Dietmar Schantin; Institute for Media Strategies, London, 2018; **92.2** From: Little Brother © 2008 Cory Doctorow; **95.1** Charta der Meinungsfreiheit, Börsenverein des Deutschen Buchhandels e.V.; **98.1** Amy Silverman © 2019 Guardian News & Media Ltd.; **102** Akram Khan © 2019 Guardian News & Media Ltd.; **105** Hazel Davis © 2017, Guardian News & Media Ltd.; **108.1** Andrew Parsons, tokio.sportschau.de, 2021; **110** Georgina Quach © 2021 Guardian News & Media Ltd.; **112.2** Abdi Nor Iftin, Call Me American; Alfred A. Knopf, Random House, 2018, S. 274-276; **114** Bianca Nogrady © 2017 Guardian News & Media Ltd.; **116** 2022, Charta der Vielfalt e. V.; **117.1** Attributed to Winston Churchill; **120.2** Emine Saner, 2020 Guardian News & Media Ltd.; **123.3** Jacinda Ardern, Prime Minister of New Zealand at the United Nations, September 2019; **127.3** Ecotopia © 1975 Ernest Callenbach; **132.1** Statistisches Bundesamt, https://www.tagesschau.de/ 15.09.2021; **132.3** Alexandra Paul; **134** William Park, https://www.bbc.com/future/bespoke/follow-the-food/how-to-feed-the-world-in-the-next-crisis.html; **137** Reena Shah, www.bbc.com, 29.09.2021; **140.2** Dry by Neal Shusterman and Jarrod Shusterman, Simon & Schuster Inc., 2018, p. 3-8; **142.1** Robert Swan in Recipe for Survival © 2022 Dana Ellis Hunnes; **142.2** Christoph Link, Stuttgarter Zeitung, 23. April 2019; **144.5** The good life Texter: Hume, Jon Cobbe/Thistlethwayte, Rai Paul, Verlag/Subverlag: Sony ATV Music Publishing Australia P/L Sony/ATV Music Publishing (Germany) GmbH, Berlin; **144.6** Imagine Texter: LENNON, JOHN WINSTON, Verlag/Subverlag: 1971 Ono Music/Lenono Music/Budde Music Publishing GmbH; **144.7** Born this way Texter: Blair, Paul/Garibay, Fernando/Germanotta, Stefani/

Laursen, Jeppe, Verlag/Subverlag: Gariby Music Publishing/Warner-Tamerlane Publishing Co./Neue Welt Musikverlag GmbH, Hamburg Glostream Music Publishing/Universal Music Corporation/Universal/MCA Music Publishing GmbH, Berlin House of Gaga Publishing LLC/Sony ATV Songs LLC/Sony/ATV Music Publishing (Germany) GmbH, Berlin; **146** Will Coldwell, © 2019 Guardian News and Media Ltd.; **150.2** 04. December 2019, Charlie McCurdy, www.bbc.com; **153** Rosalyn Kelly, One wage; from Momaya Short Story Review 2017 Utopia Dystopia, Momaya Press, S. 103-112; **157.7** Jens Reichenbach, Neue Westfälische, www.nw.de, 23.06.2022; **157.8** Kölner Stadt-Anzeiger, 19.06.2022; **157.9** Ruşen Tayfur, Westdeutsche Allgemeine Zeitung, www.waz.de, 23.06.2022; **159** Stephanie Miskin, BBC, 04.05.2021; **161.1** © 2018 Guardian News & Media Ltd.; **164.2** From: Wild. A Journey from Lost to Found © 2013 Cheryl Strayed; **166.1** From, Dom Helder Camara: Essential Writings, Dom Helder Camara, 2009; **167** https://www.oxfam.de/unsere-arbeit/themen/soziale-ungleichheit; **175.1** attributed to Malcolm X; **175.2** Charlie Brooker in Black Mirror, 2011-2013; **175.3** From: So you've been publicly shamed © 2015 Jon Ronson; **175.4** Quotation from "We Think: The Power Of Mass Creativity" by C. W. Leadbeater, Profile Books (GB)